one gets something pretty
that one must break
into it. This is a brutal
world — my masters!
How _are_ you? And
how's Johnny?
We exist with difficulty
here. Jess wants to be
remembered to You
and Your Wife. The
Sat. Review notices my
story in the _Cosmo_ with
great discrimination.
          Ever Yours
                Jph Conrad.

CONRAD'S WESTERN WORLD

And what is a novel if not a conviction of our fellow-men's existence strong enough to take upon itself a form of imagined life clearer than reality and whose accumulated verisimilitude of selected episodes puts to shame the pride of documentary history?

JOSEPH CONRAD

CONRAD'S
WESTERN WORLD

NORMAN SHERRY

Professor of English, University of Lancaster

CAMBRIDGE
AT THE UNIVERSITY PRESS
1971

Published by the Syndics of the Cambridge University Press
Bentley House, 200 Euston Road, London N.W.1
American Branch: 32 East 57th Street, New York, N.Y.10022

© Cambridge University Press 1971

Library of Congress Catalogue Card Number: 70-130910

ISBN: 0 521 07972 1

Printed in Great Britain
at the University Printing House, Cambridge
(Brooke Crutchley, University Printer)

CONTENTS

Contents

ILLUSTRATIONS

vii

Illustrations

In memory of Peter Ure

ACKNOWLEDGEMENTS

The following study could not have been carried out without the help of many scholars, descendants of men who knew Conrad, and certain institutions. Research into the background of *Heart of Darkness* was made possible by the help of John Carrington of the Université Libre du Congo, to whom I was introduced by Professor Robert Steel of the University of Liverpool; the Reverend Angus MacNeil of the Baptist Mission Station at Bolobo, to whom I was introduced by Professor Roger Anstey of the University of Kent; the Reverend B. W. O. Amey of the Baptist Missionary Society headquarters in London who gave me permission to read the diaries of the Reverend George Grenfell which are lodged there; Roland G. Metzger of the American Baptist Foreign Mission Society of Valley Forge, Pennsylvania; Dr R. E. Ockenden of the British Council, London, who put me in touch with Miss Kathryn Dexter and Robin Stubbs in Brussels; Captain H. Robdrup of the Monstrings- & Forhyringsvaesenet in Copenhagen who was untiring in helping me to track down Danish seamen who had worked in the Congo during Conrad's stay there, and who put me in touch with Miss Duhst, only living daughter of Captain Duhst, who knew Conrad for a short time in the Congo; Captain Krüger of the East Asiatic Company who assisted me with information about Captain Koch, master of the *Roi des Belges*; M. Vereecke, Chairman of the Associated Central West Africa Lines; Dr P. Davies of the Department of Economics and Commerce, the University of Liverpool; Mr H. F. C. Hussey of the Board of Trade, Cardiff; Mr K. R. Mason, shipping editor of *Lloyd's Records*; Mr Lugard of the Dutch House, Nieuwe Afrikaansche Handels-Vennootschap; the British Ambassador

x

Acknowledgements

in Kinchassa; the Captain Superintendent of H.M.S. *Conway* for information about G. F. W. Hope; David Garnett for answering my questions about his father, Edward Garnett, and Conrad; Mrs Jean Hope, widow of Herford Hope, G. F. W. Hope's son, and her son Mr Roger Hope of Liverton, Newton Abbot, who provided me with Hope's typescript dealing with Conrad and with a photograph of the *Nellie*; Donald Wilson and Michael Freyne of the Department of French, the University of Liverpool; Miss Marjorie G. Wynne of Yale University Library for unfailing courtesy and assistance, and the John Quinn Memorial Collection Manuscript Division, the New York Public Library, Astor, Lenox and Tilden Foundations.

My research into the sources of *Nostromo* principally involved a study of the literature on South America and in this area I am primarily in debt to librarians: to Miss Gillian Hepworth of the Cohen Library, University of Liverpool for her vast patience in handling my various requests for books; Mr Ingham of the Picton Reference Library, Liverpool; Bernard Naylor, Librarian of the Institute of Latin American Studies, who sent me the galley proofs of his recent checklist of travellers' accounts of the area in the nineteenth century; Tony Newell of the Cohen Library. In addition I am indebted to J. R. Fisher of the Department of Modern History, University of Liverpool; Mrs Dorothea Smith of Liverpool, who helped me to contact the Mayor of Luri and Cesar Cervoni's son in Marseilles, and to whom I was introduced by Professor C. A. Mayer of the University of Liverpool.

For information on the sources of *The Secret Agent* my thanks are due to Mr Dodds, Public Relations Officer of New Scotland Yard who, if he was not able to provide much information, treated my many queries with patience and good manners; to M. Carlo Laroche, Le Conservateur en chef de la Section Outre-Mer, Archives de France; Stephen

Acknowledgements

Clissold, of the Foreign Office Research Department; Professor Hugh Seton Watson; R. C. H. Briggs, secretary of the William Morris Society; John Bebbington of Sheffield City Library who allowed me to browse through the Edward Carpenter Collection there; Mr C. G. Allen of the British Library of Political and Economic Science; Mr Clive E. Driver of the Rosenbach Foundation for assistance over the manuscript of 'The Informer'; Mr Darlington, Archivist of the Greater London Record Office; the Superintendent of the Hampstead Cemetery; various Chief Constables who helped me with reference to the anarchist outrages of the nineteenth century—Chief Constable Muir of Durham Constabulary, Chief Constable Hood of Manchester Constabulary, Chief Constable Goodchild of the West Midlands Constabulary, Chief Constable Barker of Sheffield and Rotherham Constabulary; Mr Henchy of the National Library of Ireland; Miss D. M. Moss of the Radio Times Hulton Picture Library; the editors of The Illustrated London News & Sketch Ltd.; the Town Clerk of Poole; the Third Secretary of the British Embassy in Buenos Aires who traced a descendant of Krieger for me; the Town Clerk of Colchester, Mr Catchpole; the Borough Librarian of Colchester, P. R. Gifford; Mrs Helen Rossetti Angeli, who at ninety years of age was of wonderful assistance; Mrs Dennis, her daughter; Leonard Gribble, authority on the British police, who suggested books that might be of use to me; Professor David Quinn of the University of Liverpool, Owen Dudley Edwards of the University of Aberdeen, Professor R. Dudley Edwards of University College, Dublin, Professor Pender of University College, Cork, for their assistance in Fenian matters; Allan Smith, David Goodway, Miss Ella Twynam, another nonagenarian who knew the London Anarchists, Rudolf de Jong of the Internationaal Instituut voor Sociale Geschiedenis, for assistance in anarchist matters; Edward Thompson, the School

Acknowledgements

of History, University of Warwick, Professor Lyons of the University of Kent at Canterbury who provided me with a list of useful books on Fenian matters; the descendant of A. P. Krieger, Mrs Beatrice Ogilvie, for two letters from Conrad to her grandfather and information about her grandfather; Mr Mann of Poole, a centenarian who helped me to trace the Krieger family, and Mr John G. Hillier who discovered Mr Mann for me; Mrs Hinnell; the Reverend Charles B. Dobree, Incumbent of St Mary's, Brent Eleigh, who sought out an unknown Conrad manuscript for me.

My gratitude is also due to A. van Marle of Amsterdam with whom I have been in contact now since 1966 and who has given his help so unstintingly that it is not possible to detail it here; the late Richard Curle, Conrad's great friend, and John Conrad, Conrad's younger son, for their assistance and interest; Professor Edward Shils who has not swerved in his interest in and support for my research; to Professor Kenneth Muir of the University of Liverpool, J. I. M. Stewart of Christ Church, Oxford, J. C. Maxwell of Balliol College, Oxford, and Jocelyn Baines, author of the definitive biography of Conrad, Brian Nellist of the University of Liverpool, and A. van Marle, all of whom gave me help in terms of reading the manuscript at various stages, of discussing the study with me, and of making useful suggestions. Mention must be made of the late J. D. Gordan, whose study of sources inevitably provides inspiration for anyone entering this field and of Jocelyn Baines whose biography of Conrad has been my daily companion.

I should like to thank Mrs M. Thompson for her industry and patience in the typing of the manuscript and Miss Margaret Burton for her support in this.

Finally, my gratitude is due to the late Professor Peter Ure whose death occurred as I was finishing the manuscript and to whom the book is dedicated in memory of a fine scholar

Acknowledgements

and man who fifteen years ago mapped out for me the direction these studies should take.

Some parts of this study have appeared in the *Review of English Studies* (vol. 18, 1967), *Modern Language Review* (vol. 64, 1969) and the *Philological Quarterly* (vol. 48, 1969), and I am grateful to the editors and publishers of these journals for permission to reprint. I am indebted to Yale University Library for permission to quote from Conrad's manuscripts and to J. M. Dent and Sons, the publishers and trustees of the Joseph Conrad estate for permission to publish the newly found Conrad letters and to use quotations from their Collected Edition of the Works of Joseph Conrad (London, 1947) to which reference is made throughout.

N.S.

December, 1970

NOTE

The superior figures in the text relate to the
references starting on p. 396

xiv

I

INTRODUCTION

In *Conrad's Eastern World* I tried to recreate the world
Conrad knew during his years as a sailor in far eastern waters
between 1883 and 1888. I was concerned there on the
one hand to make a contribution to Conrad biography,
since those significant years had remained relatively un-
documented, and on the other to seek out those suggestions
in the life of the east, in the gossip of the ports, which
became Conrad's heritage as a seaman and which were used
by Conrad the novelist. Conrad himself suggested the possibility of his inspiration having derived from actual events
and people when he stated: 'One's literary life must turn
frequently for sustenance to memories and seek discourse
with the shades...'[1] Events of which he retained 'memories'
might have been noted in official records or newspapers of
the area; 'shades' might be those of once-living men whose
descendants might be traced. Biography and source material
were, therefore, intimately linked in the case of those stories
which returned to his experiences in the far east for their
inspiration.

In this sequel to *Conrad's Eastern World* the direction
could not be the same. The works selected for study ranged
over the period 1896 to 1906 in terms of dates of composition,
and only one major work, *Heart of Darkness* (1899), and one
short story, 'An Outpost of Progress' (1896), looked back to
Conrad's personal experience, in this instance his Congo
visit of 1890–1. Thus, the biographical element must of
necessity be smaller, since Conrad's life *as a writer* is well
documented and that life, except in certain specific circum-

stances, did not provide source material for the works being dealt with. The world of a South American republic or of the London anarchists was not in any substantial way part of Conrad's experience either at the time of writing *Nostromo* (1904) and *The Secret Agent* (1906) or at any period earlier in his life.

I have, however, been able to make certain contributions to Conrad biography where it is important to the works studied. Conrad's period in the Congo has been further illuminated by the addition of new material, and an unusual but interesting influence upon Conrad revealed by the study is that of certain friendships he formed in the course of his life, particularly those with G. F. W. Hope, A. P. Krieger, R. B. Cunninghame Graham, and Ford Madox Ford. All of these friendships in some way affected his creative life. Graham and Ford not only guided Conrad towards particular subjects for novels, but each contributed further in supplying Conrad with necessary background material and to a slight degree with the inspiration for particular characters based upon themselves. It would seem likely, for example, that Charles Gould in *Nostromo* owes something in history and appearance to Graham, and that Ford makes an appearance in 'The Informer'. G. F. W. Hope, Conrad's sailor friend, made his contribution to *Heart of Darkness* and I have been fortunate in discovering a formerly unknown account of Conrad written by Hope. A. P. Krieger, until now a shadowy and insubstantial figure in Conrad's life, can be seen to have been involved, if my account of him is acceptable, in an unexpected but substantial way in *The Secret Agent*.

In the course of my search certain unhoped-for bonuses came my way: one was an early and previously unknown manuscript by Conrad taking the form of notes for a novel, the other was an unexpected contact with the son of one of Conrad's friends of his Mediterranean days—Cesar Cervoni.

Introduction

So far as Conrad's source material was concerned, it became possible to detect a strong movement away from inspired analyses of personal experience or the related experiences of others (which is in some ways the mark of an amateur) to the contemplation of material entirely outside the bounds of his own experience (which in some ways is the mark of a professional). Such a movement, for some of his works at least, was inevitable. Conrad drew a great deal upon his past experience, but this was bound to be worked out in time. To Cunninghame Graham he wrote on 7 October 1907, 'Living with memories is a cruel business. I—who have a double life one of them peopled only by shadows growing more precious as the years pass—know what that is.'[2] And so an extension of possible subjects by means of reading was a natural development. More and more, as he progressed as a novelist, Conrad turned to reading, not simply as in his early days in order to buttress his limited knowledge of the far east, but in order to find the plot itself, the characters in all their variety, and the themes. In writing to his aunt, Madame Poradowska, after the French translation of *The Secret Agent* had appeared, Conrad said: 'for you well know that anarchy and anarchists are outside my experience... I created this out of whole cloth',[3] and I hope to show how far Conrad went in order to create *The Secret Agent* 'out of whole cloth'. A vast literature must have been 'consumed' by Conrad in his study prior to the beginning of a novel. That it was precisely in those subjects where he was farthest from his own basic experience that he succeeded most, is a measure of this remarkable novelist's extraordinary achievement.

For Conrad, writing was a 'cruel business': 'I sit down religiously every morning, I sit down for eight hours every day—and the sitting down is all. In the course of that working day of 8 hours, I write 3 sentences which I erase...sometimes it takes all my resolution and power of self control to refrain from butting my head against the wall.'[4] It became no less cruel, no less arduous when it was a matter of breathing life into material derived primarily from reading than it had been when he was mainly resuscitating memories of the past.

Finally, the change in source material reveals a change of interest. The exploration of the nature of such qualities as 'courage' and 'fidelity' within an isolated, dangerous, but morally neutral area of sea or river has given way to an interest in more public concerns, and as the settings have moved from the far east to the 'western world' of South America, the Congo, and London, so the interest now lies partly in the examination of the nature of specifically 'western' movements—colonial exploitation, material progress, left-wing revolutions. The individual is now seen in relation to such backgrounds, and thus the three major works studied are related as explorations of 'man in society'. In *Heart of Darkness*, Conrad deals with a primitive society but one which is both explored and exploited by the colonists from a more evolved society; here his concern is with the extent to which, once he is in a situation of isolation and primitive-ness, the disciplined white man is sustained by a code of behaviour evolved in his civilised society. In *Nostromo*, Conrad moved from a primitive society to a young emerging one, where the struggle is for social power and wealth; the forces here—the greed, power-hungriness and awful cruelty —blindly promote or impede or are stimulated by the actual building-up of the economic substructure, the 'material interests'. In his 'darkest' novel, *The Secret Agent*, Conrad turns to the fully evolved society which in contrast is liberal, relatively humane and protected, yet which has its underside of cruelty and savage force, where even love kills people. It is Conrad's ability to see through the public claims being made in certain fields of activity such as these that accounts for the increasingly ironic—even desperate and cynical—tone.

I shall consider first *Heart of Darkness* in relation both to Conrad's own connection with Africa and to the sources he found there for the novel and for his short story 'An Outpost of Progress'; and secondly the sources of *Nostromo* and 'Gaspar Ruiz', both having a South American setting; and finally *The Secret Agent* and the short stories, 'The Informer' and 'An Anarchist', the last two representing Conrad's preliminary attempts to deal with the then popular subject of anarchy and anarchists.

In the conclusion I have tried to reveal the movement of Conrad's mind over his material, to present the evolution of Conrad's fiction, and at each stage to monitor the intricate changes which Conrad made to his sources so that the processes of his art can be seen whole.

HEART OF DARKNESS

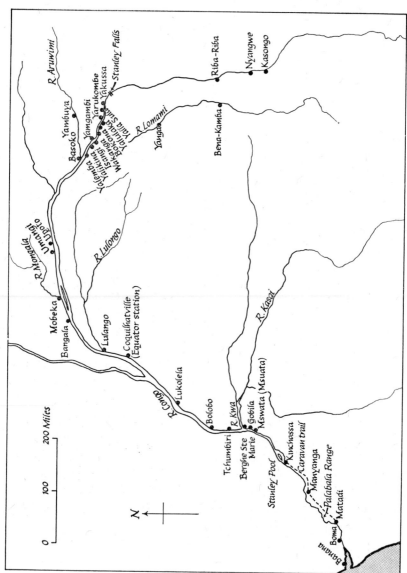

The river Congo

2

THE FASCINATION OF AFRICA

'*Heart of Darkness* is...experience pushed a little (and only very little) beyond the actual facts of the case',[1] Conrad claimed of this short novel, and, as a result, the natural inclination has been to take Marlow's experience in the story as that of Conrad. His first biographer, G. Jean-Aubry, stated that 'the adventures which the author lends to Marlow, his mouthpiece, are no other than those of which he himself was at the same time witness and victim'.[2] This would lead, naturally, to the further identification between the commercial agent Kurtz of *Heart of Darkness* and the particular commercial agent in the Congo at the time of Conrad's visit who was called Klein, whose name appears in the manuscript of *Heart of Darkness*, and who, like Kurtz, died on the down-river trip. And this also is stressed by Jean-Aubry: 'it is beyond a doubt...that between these two persons, one real and the other imaginary, there was more than a simple resemblance of name'.[3]

The artistic finish of the story, however, and Conrad's own confessed aim of wishing, as he states in his Author's Note, to give 'that sombre theme...a sinister resonance',[4] suggest a quite significant process of transmutation between experience and the completed fiction. '"Youth"', he records, 'in its facts, in its inwardness and in its outward colouring, begins and ends in myself', but in *Heart of Darkness* it was 'no longer a matter of sincere colouring. It was like another art altogether'.[5] But not enough has been known about Conrad's Congo experience outside the story, in spite of his Congo diary, to allow for any but the most tenuous of speculations about the relation between fact and fiction.

9

Heart of Darkness

If we were able to extend our knowledge of this period of Conrad's life we *should* discover to what extent personal experience formed Marlow's journey; but we should also be able to demonstrate what Conrad meant by experience 'pushed a little beyond the actual facts'; and we should be able to decide whether that 'sombre theme' of the tale was part of his actual experience or whether it derived from Conrad's imaginative working over that experience. We should then be in a position to consider the nature of Conrad's literary skill in developing the 'sinister resonance'.

It has been possible to add to our knowledge of the Congo Conrad knew, and of his experiences there, and to recreate also the particular influences and ideas surrounding the colonisation of that part of Africa at that time which had some bearing on Conrad's story. I have pieced this information together from contemporary newspaper accounts, particularly from the *Mouvement Géographique*,* and from private and official documents. This new information suggests that Conrad did not have the limited but moral success of Marlow; on the contrary, the experience was for him singularly unproductive and distressing and, worse perhaps, frustrating. It shows that Mr Klein, reputed source for Kurtz, had as little of the devil in him as could be possible, and that even the more probable source for Kurtz, whom I have discovered, was not corrupted in quite the same way by the Congo as Kurtz was. And, as one might expect in a story that has such metaphysical overtones, even in terms of geographical fact Marlow's journey moves away from Conrad's. But the basis of the journey, its rhythm of movement from station to station on the river and its motivations, is certainly retained by Conrad, and experience and story can most usefully be studied in terms of this pattern.

* A small weekly review, published in Brussels, and the official organ of the Independent State and the commercial companies of the Belgian Congo.

10

I shall deal, therefore, with the obtaining of the command of the river-steamer on the Congo which involves the death of the previous captain; the sea journey from Europe to Boma ('the seat of government') at the mouth of the Congo; the first stage of the up-river journey by steamer from Boma to Matadi (the 'Company Station'); the overland journey from Matadi to Kinchassa (the 'Central Station'); the final stage of the up-river journey by steamer from Kinchassa to Stanley Falls (the 'Inner Station'); and the descent of the river.

*

'...to understand the effect of it [the experience] on me', says Marlow at the beginning of his tale, 'you ought to know how I got out there, what I saw, how I went up that river' (p. 51). As to how he got out there, Conrad's experience was very much that of Marlow. Marlow had returned to London after 'six years or so' sailing in the east, and Conrad in 1889 had just returned to London after intermittently sailing in the east since 1883, ending with fourteen months as master of the *Otago*. Marlow finds difficulty in getting another berth, and so at that time did Conrad when, in his Bessborough Gardens lodgings, he began writing *Almayer's Folly*. Determining to try for a job in the Congo with a trading company, Marlow makes use of his relatives on the continent to get him a job, and Conrad obtained his post as skipper of a steamer on the Congo with the Société Anonyme Belge pour le Commerce du Haut-Congo (SAB) through the influence of his aunt in Brussels, Marguerite Poradowska.

Marlow quickly got his appointment, but it took several months before a vacancy came up for Conrad, and when it came it was a more significant appointment than Marlow's. Marlow is appointed simply as skipper of a steamboat on the river, but Conrad wrote to his cousin, Karol Zagórski: 'As far as I can make out from my "lettre d'instruction"

I am destined to the command of a steamboat, *belonging to M. Delcommune's exploring party*, which is being got ready. I like this prospect very much, but I know nothing for certain as everything is...to be kept secret' [my italics].⁶ This exploring party was the Katanga expedition which, under Alexandre Delcommune, brother of the SAB manager at Kinchassa, was to explore the river Lomami, a tributary of the Congo, in the following year.

Marlow, having obtained his command, 'flew round like mad to get ready, and before forty-eight hours [he] was crossing the Channel to show [himself] to [his] employers and sign the contract' (p. 55). Conrad did, indeed, 'fly around like mad to get ready', though in rather different circumstances. He did not cross the Channel to show himself to the director of the SAB, Captain Albert Thys, by whom he had already been interviewed in November 1889, but saw him again in Brussels on his return from a visit to his uncle in Poland about 26 April 1890. But certainly Conrad after receiving his appointment went back and forward between the Continent and England making the arrangements for his journey, and his own record of this time suggests his excitement. To Zagórski he wrote: 'If you only knew the devilish haste I had to make! From London to Brussels and back again to London! And then again I dashed full tilt to Brussels...If you knew...in what a universal cataclysm, in what a fantastic atmosphere of mixed shopping, business, and affecting scenes, I passed two whole weeks.'⁷

Conrad's three visits to Brussels over the business and his two interviews with Thys are, therefore, compressed into Marlow's first impression of the sepulchral city. Given this fact and Conrad's own excitement and eagerness for the position, it is unlikely that his impressions at this time coincide exactly with Marlow's. His description of the managing director in his office tallies closely with the actual

SAB director, Captain Thys, 'an impression of pale plumpness in a frock coat', as a photograph of Thys (Plate 2*a*), which was taken about this time, shows, but whether the ominous impression given by the attitudes of the two women concierges, the words of the clerk and of the doctor in the story are based on what Conrad experienced I have not been able to discover.* It would seem more likely that Conrad is here deliberately re-writing his experience to fit Marlow's story.

The vessel he was to travel in, the *Ville de Maceio*, had left Antwerp on 30 April 1890, but Conrad and an agent called Harou caught the vessel before it departed from Bordeaux on 10 May. The *Mouvement Géographique*, 4 May 1890, reports as follows:

la *Ville de Maceio*, de la Compagnie française des Chargeurs Réunis du Havre, a quitté Anvers le 30 avril...pour Boma et Matadi. ...La *Ville de Maceio* fera, le 10 mai, escale à Bordeaux, où ira s'embarquer M. Harou, ancien agent de la force publique de l'Etat, et M. Korzeniowski, capitaine de steamer, qui partent pour l'Afrique pour le compte de la Société du Haut-Congo.

Although some of the actual excitement surrounding these events in Conrad's life appears in the story it is tempered by a growing uneasiness in Marlow's mind, as well as by the fact that he is speaking after the full experience of dis-illusionment:

I had been represented...as an exceptional and gifted creature...a man you don't get hold of every day. Good Heavens! and I was going to take charge of a two-penny-half-penny river-steamboat with a penny whistle attached! It appeared, however, I was also one of the Workers, with a capital—you know. Something like an emissary of light, something like a lower sort of apostle (p. 59).

* The old doctor measures Marlow's head with calipers: 'I always ask leave, in the interests of science, to measure the crania of those going out there.' As early as August 1881, Conrad's uncle wrote to him on behalf of a Mr Kopernicki: 'He is engaged on a great work which has already brought him European fame: "Comparative studies of human races based on types of skulls." This particular branch of science is called "Craniology". He earnestly requests you to collect during your voyages skulls of natives, writing on each one whose skull it is and the place of origin' (Najder, p. 74).

When he left for the Congo, it is unlikely that Conrad saw his position in such an ironic light, already viewing his future command in this way. Apart from his own enthusiasms and sense of adventure was the expectation he also had of taking part in the exploration of this land, as master of the steamer of the planned Katanga expedition. Conrad would surely have seen his own situation against the background of recent events which must have played their part in turning his attention to Africa, for Africa at that time was closely connected in the public mind with the amazing and audacious exploits of Henry Morton Stanley. It was in January of the year 1889 that Stanley's message that he had found Emin Pasha, the man he had gone to Africa to look for in 1887, reached London, and throughout the summer further news of his expedition continued to be published in the press. It was Stanley who had established trading posts on the Congo for King Leopold of the Belgians, and it was only in the previous year (1888) that the Belgian concern for trading in the Congo—the Société Anonyme Belge pour le Commerce du Haut-Congo—had been formed.

Conrad could not, at that time, have held the opinion he arrived at later that the whole of the Congo affair was a 'prosaic newspaper "stunt"' and 'the vilest scramble for loot that ever disfigured the history of human conscience and geographical exploration'.[8] Nor, presumably, was he fully aware of the dangers and difficulties he was likely to encounter on a journey that was to take him by ship from Bordeaux to Matadi, overland from Matadi to Kinchassa (two hundred miles of very difficult country), and by river-steamer from Kinchassa to Stanley Falls—the heart of darkness.

3

THE DEATH OF FREIESLEBEN

Before following Conrad further on his journey, it would be as well to consider the incident of the death of the previous steamer captain, Fresleven, as Marlow calls him. Marlow's story about this man, into whose shoes he stepped, is of some significance given its placing in the story and its tone, and since it is in part effective in bringing out the 'sinister resonance'. Our knowledge of the actual circumstances of the death of this captain has been meagre, but it seems quite certain that in spite of the influence Conrad had through his aunt with the director of the SAB, his obtaining of a post with the company depended directly upon this tragic incident. Jean-Aubry has claimed—and others have naturally followed him—that Captain Marlow's story of the death of his predecessor gives 'an authentic account of the circumstances' as they relate to Conrad.[1] But this is to ignore Conrad's given principles of composition. Although the actual event was as fraught with ironic implications as Conrad could wish, just as the events surrounding his obtaining the command were telescoped and dramatised for Marlow's narrative, so Conrad makes suitable changes to the story of the death of the river-steamer captain. Marlow records:

It appears the Company had received news that one of their captains had been killed in a scuffle with the natives. This was my chance, and it made me more anxious to go. It was only months and months afterwards, when I made the attempt to recover what was left of the body, that I heard the original quarrel arose from a misunderstanding about some hens. Yes, two black hens. Fresleven—that was the fellow's name, a Dane—thought himself wronged somehow in the bargain, so he went ashore and started to hammer the chief of the village with a stick...he whacked the old nigger mercilessly, while a big crowd of his people watched him, thunderstruck, till some man—I was told the chief's son—in desperation at hearing the old chap yell, made a tentative jab with a spear at the white man—and of course it went quite easy between the shoulder-blades. Then the whole population cleared into the forest, expecting all kinds of calamities to happen, while, on the other hand, the steamer Fresleven commanded left also in a bad panic, in charge of the engineer, I believe (pp. 53-4).

Marlow's story is one of hearsay, as the phrases 'I heard', 'I was told', 'I believe' emphasise, and we can be reasonably certain that when Conrad accepted the command he knew only the bare fact of Freiesleben's death, as did Marlow of Fresleven's, and that he learnt the rest of the story, as it is implied that Marlow did, from people he met in the Congo. That the source was a verbal one is suggested by the spelling of the captain's name and certain other aspects of Marlow's narrative which also help us to determine Conrad's sources.

But Marlow made a closer contact with the incident when he attempted to reclaim and bury the captain's remains: 'Afterwards nobody seemed to trouble much about Fresleven's remains, till I got out and stepped into his shoes. I couldn't let it rest, though; but when an opportunity offered at last to meet my predecessor, the grass growing through his ribs was tall enough to hide his bones. They were all there' (p. 54). This might very well be an account of the death of Conrad's predecessor and of Conrad's action in trying to get his remains buried. Jean-Aubry certainly accepted the fact of the murder: 'It is equally exact—as Marlow says—that Captain Korzeniowski obtained his command because one of the captains of the Company had just been killed in the Congo by natives.'[2] But the quotation he gives from the *Bulletin Officiel de l'Etat Indépendant du Congo* (July 1891), suggests that the murder was part of a much more significant and much nastier affair, ultimately, than Conrad allows in his story:

The Death of Freiesleben

Latterly, the only really troubled situation was in the region of Tchumbiri, at Bolobo. In face of the persistent ill-will and acts of aggression culminating in the assassination of the captain of one of the steamers of the Société du Haut-Congo, over a year ago, it has been necessary to make an example. The security of the white man demands that outrages of this kind be vigorously repressed.[3]

If Conrad omitted the aftermath of the vigorous repression, if he failed to show that the incident was regarded as an 'act of aggression'—aspects that might, after all, have fitted into his scheme of things—what reason had he for doing so, and how many other aspects did he alter? The calamity of the 'repression' is hinted at in *Heart of Darkness* but not specified. '...the village was deserted, the huts gaped black, rotting, all askew within the fallen enclosures. A calamity had come to it, sure enough' (p. 54).

Reconstructing the events of the assassination has not been easy, but it has been worthwhile in that it allows us to study an example of Conrad's technique in this story.

The Société Anonyme Belge pour le Commerce du Haut-Congo, Conrad's employer, is no longer in existence, though its successor, the Entreprises Agricoles et Industrielles de la Busira au Lomami is, and occupies the same premises— 13 rue Bréderode, Bruxelles—as the SAB did when Conrad was interviewed there in April 1890 by Albert Thys. They, when I approached them, had no information about the dead captain, except for a copy of his death certificate.[4] (See Appendix A, p. 375 below, for a copy of the death certificate of Freiesleben.) According to this, Johannes Freiesleben was twenty-nine years old when he was assassinated on 29 January 1890 at Tchumbiri. What is unusual about the death certificate is that it was not made out until May 1890, and this would account for the fact that Conrad, after a long delay, was given his appointment suddenly at the end of April, the news presumably having just then reached Thys.

I have been able to discover other accounts of Freiesleben's death which vary in details but which probably, taken together, reflect the versions of the tale which must have circulated in the area at that time. One of the most interesting I found in a diary kept by the famous pioneer missionary in the Congo, George Grenfell, which is housed in the Baptist Missionary Society Headquarters in London. There are a number of relevant entries in his diary which show us how the news of the assassination spread locally, giving us a contemporary account of the event and of the Belgian response to it. Though the death certificate shows that Captain Freiesleben died on 29 January 1890, the first reference in the Reverend Mr George Grenfell's diary does not appear until 19 February 1890:

Just as we were leaving [Bangala] the *Florida* came in with the news that on the 29th Captain Friesleden [*sic*] had been shot by the natives about five miles between Bwemba [the next two words were indecipherable] ...It is said that he was not dead when the engineer pushed off with full steam—being himself wounded, he would not go back with the crew and bring off the captain's body, or to retaliate—One prisoner was secured in the flight to the beach. The *Florida* left her cargo and passed down to [Stanley] Pool for new Capt. and Engineer and to report the matter to the authorities.

The next entry in the diary referring to the case does not appear until 4 March 1890:

La Ballay came in yesterday...with Lingenji on board & comes in from Chumbiri—he tells me that the Lisangi people fired on the *Ballay* two days ago—apparently they are taking up the palaver of the Bankanya people who killed Capt. Freerleban [*sic*] at the close of Jan. last. Lingenji says the murdered man is still unburied—his hands and feet have been cut off—his clothes taken away and his body covered in a native cloth— He has seen trousers, coat, slippers, watch etc. in the town. The hair is cut off and made into a fringe and tied round his face. The account Lingenji gives is after this wise—'the capt. went on shore & seeing a woman on the beach bathing a child & being an interesting little thing gave it two brass rods [this was the currency in use then, as *Heart of*

Darkness suggests]—the woman, the chief's wife, took the rods to her husband and said 'see what the white man has given the child'. The old man could see nothing but bad in the gift and got angry and sent the woman back, but the captain would not take the rods and said he would go with her and talk to her husband about it. The Chief however was very angry and would not listen in fact he took up his big knife and made as though he would cut the Capt. Whereupon the Captain said alright cut away and turned sideways offering his back for a blow—The Chief not daring to cut but still vociferating and turning the Captain away then got a slap on the side of his face. This he returned and a scuffle ensued in which the Chief was knocked down. The Bangalas [the crew of the river-steamer] who were on the beach seeing this said to the Capt. Lets go for the guns, but 'no' said the Capt., we don't want to fight—The old man lay groaning and said I'm very bad, I'm very bad, and his son, hearing this and having heard the white man say don't bring the guns, was bold enough to fetch his and shot the Captain in the stomach...The foregoing is substantially and as near as I can translate to Lingenji's version—consequently must be somewhere on the lines of the native account of the sad affair...From other white men we heard that Capt. was not yet dead when the engineer pushed off with full steam the eng. himself being wounded in the arm.

Though this does not square with Conrad's account in all particulars, quite clearly it is very close. The quarrel here seems to have been over the giving of a present (and all that might have meant, perhaps, in terms of physical intimacy between the chief's wife and the young captain). There is a difference in the way in which the captain is killed, not by a spear—'it went quite easy between the shoulder-blades'— but by a gunshot wound. As in Conrad's version, the chief is knocked to the ground and in each case it is the chief's son who comes to his father's rescue and we have the flight of the steamer's crew, the failure of the engineer to take off the body of his captain, and the evidence that the captain's body was left in the jungle unburied for over a month.

Grenfell's account indicates, however, that there was some danger of the incident sparking off a major rebellion in the area—'the Lisangi people...are taking up the palaver of the

Bankanya people'—which could of course have disrupted trade. Conrad gives no suggestion of this. A punitive expedition was sent out to repress the possible rebellion, and to recover and bury the remains of Captain Freiesleben. On 23 March 1890, over seven weeks after the assassination, Grenfell records in his diary: '*Stanley* and *Ville de Gand* passed down to Chumbiri to punish them for the murder of Capt. of *Florida*. They have had a fight at Jebu—24 women prisoners on board. Town all burned.' And on 28 March the final entry: '*Ville de Gand* returned—having lost a Bangalan and had one wounded in the fight at Chumbiri...The body of Captain Freesben [*sic*] recovered and buried.' A more detailed account of the incident, and particularly of the punitive expedition, appears in a book on Scandinavians in the Congo by H. Jenssen-Tusch:

On 16 March a punitory expedition was sent out from this station, consisting of the *Stanley*, Captain Madsen, and the *Ville de Gand*, Captain Duhst, with all in all six white officers and 370 soldiers on board under the command of district commissioner Baert and Lieutenant Lothaire, who later became so well known. Captain Duhst reports the following on this expedition: We arrived at the mission station near Tschumbiri on 24 March at 10 a.m. There we learnt that Captain Freiesleben's corpse was still lying on the earth at the spot where he was killed, but that the natives had evacuated part of the town...Since Tschumbiri is a very large town with many thousands of natives, our people had to put up a hard fight before they succeeded in forcing their way down (westwards) to where the corpse was found. We could see the town burning in several places, a number of canoes with dead and wounded came paddling towards us along the riverside. A woman taken prisoner informed us where Freiesleben's corpse was lying. He was found in the same position in which he had fallen; the remnants of his clothes proved his identity. His remains were collected and taken to the mission station in Berghe Sainte Marie, where they were buried with military honours.[5]

Freiesleben had been buried, therefore, in March, over a month before Conrad had obtained his position as master of the *Florida* on 7 May. Conrad must have seen the effects of the punitive expedition on the town of Tchumbiri since it was here that Klein was buried, and hence Marlow's description of the ruined town must be based on Conrad's own observation. But he could not, like Marlow, have searched out Freiesleben's remains. Marlow's vivid recounting of this whole incident would seem to derive from equally vivid detail obtained by Conrad from his verbal sources for the event.

One possible such source was the commercial agent Alphonse Keyaerts who, according to the *Mouvement Géographique* of 2 November 1890, travelled with Conrad from Stanley Pool to Stanley Falls in the *Roi des Belges*, and was a witness to the issuing of Freiesleben's death certificate at Leopoldville in May 1890. Keyaerts was the original, moreover, though we do not know to what extent, of the character Kayerts, chief of the ill-fated trading station in 'An Outpost of Progress'.

Conrad's second source might well have been Captain Koch, who must have known Freiesleben well, and who was master of the *Roi des Belges* on this same trip up-river. The *Mouvement Géographique* records that Koch and Freiesleben left for the Congo together from Liverpool on the *Nubia* on 12 September 1889.

But most certainly Conrad heard the story from a man with whom, as I shall show, he made part of his return journey on the caravan trail to Matadi prior to his departure from the Congo. This was a Danish captain, Duhst, skipper of the *Ville de Gand* which was involved in the punitive expedition, whose diary was the basis of a hitherto unnoticed account of Conrad in the Congo by a Captain Lütken, published in the now defunct *London Mercury*, May 1930. Two specific details—the dispute over provisions and the 'grass growing through' Freiesleben's ribs—seem traceable to Captain Duhst. Captain Lütken writes:

Freiesleben, a Danish captain...was killed by the natives at Tchumbei *in some dispute over firewood or fresh provisions*; but his bones were recovered on the 24th March, 1890...The steamers had soldiers on board and some Belgian officers...and there was a good deal of shooting and burning of native huts...Duhst, who *was* there, tells of *the grass growing through the bones of the skeleton which lay where it had fallen* [my italics].[6]

4

BORDEAUX TO BOMA

'I left in a French steamer, and she called in every blamed port they have out there...It was upward of thirty days before I saw the mouth of the big river' (pp. 60–2). The basic details of Conrad's sea journey have here been transferred accurately to Marlow's. Conrad was at sea in the *Ville de Maceio* for just over a month (10 May to 12 June) before he disembarked at Boma.[1] The names of the 'blamed' ports which Conrad gives that 'seemed to belong to some sordid farce acted in front of a sinister back-cloth' (p. 61) are near enough the names of the actual ports at which the ship would call. In the manuscript, after 'blamed port they have out there', Conrad had inserted 'beginning with Dakar', and he gives 'Gran Bassam, Little Popo' in the text. Actually, the ship called at Teneriffe in the Canaries first, then at Dakar, Conakry, Freetown (where Conrad posted a letter to his cousin, Karol Zagórski, on 22 May), Grand Bassam, Grand Popo, Libreville (where he sent off a letter to his aunt on 10 June), and finally Banana at the mouth of the Congo, after which she moved up Banana Creek to Boma (see map facing p. 9, above).

Already during this sea voyage, which is preparatory to the journey up-river, Marlow is increasingly uneasy about the nature of the colonising activity of which he has become a part. His journey is presented in an essentially emotive fashion as giving him 'the general sense of vague and oppressive wonder'; the feeling that he is being kept away 'from the truth of things, within the toil of a mournful and senseless delusion' grows upon him. The activity he witnesses, based presumably upon what Conrad saw as the ship moved down the coast of Africa towards the mouth of the river Congo, makes the journey 'a weary pilgrimage among hints for nightmares'. In the descriptions of the settlements—'a God-forsaken wilderness with what looked like a tin shed and a flagpole in it', the activities—'landed more soldiers— to take care of the custom-house clerks, presumably', and the shelling of the coastline, the emphasis is on the futility of such empty pretension in face of the wilderness.

While we cannot be certain that this was Conrad's reaction to his experiences at the time, the technique employed—that of underlining the futility by removing the point and purpose of the actions—is to be observed throughout the story, and it can be shown that often Conrad is deliberately distorting his experience to obtain such an effect. This seems to suggest that Marlow's journey is already in part 'fictional' in its events, mood, and purpose. On the other hand, it was not a happy journey for Conrad, though his uneasiness appears to have stemmed from a growing concern about his health and a sense of isolation from the other passengers. After five days on board, he was writing to his aunt: 'Suppose I tell you at the beginning that I have escaped the fever thus far! If I could only assure you that all my letters would start with this good news... We left Bordeaux on a rainy day. A dreary day, a not very merry sailing: haunting memories; vague regrets; still vaguer hopes. One is sceptical of the future.'[2] And his next letter to her also refers to fears for his health: 'While awaiting the inevitable fever, I am very well.'[3] In a letter written to Karol Zagórski while at Freetown, twelve days after having left Bordeaux, he writes:

What makes me rather uneasy is the information that 60 per cent. of our Company's employés return to Europe before they have completed even six months' service. Fever and dysentery! There are others who are sent home in a hurry at the end of a year, so that they shouldn't die in the Congo. God forbid! It would spoil the statistics which are excellent, you see![4]

Conrad's sense of isolation would seem to have been partly due to his unfamiliar role as passenger, and partly because he was on a French ship with French passengers. This may seem strange, given that he spoke French, yet he transfers this feeling to Marlow who feels isolated 'amongst all these men with whom I had no point of contact' (p. 61), and there is a further suggestion in the manuscript: 'Of all my life this passage is the part most unreal. My idleness of a passenger, my isolation amongst all these frenchmen' (MS, p. 37).

What seems likely is that Conrad established an acquaintance with the trader, Harou, who was to be his troublesome companion for some time and was to earn a mention in *Heart of Darkness*. This agent was Prosper Harou and not, as Jean-Aubry suggests, his elder brother Victor Harou, collaborator with Stanley in the establishment of Vivi, the first important post on the river Congo.[5] But from Prosper Harou Conrad must have heard a great deal of Stanley and his explorations, and also of the Congo of which Harou already had some personal experience.[6] It may well have been Harou's conversation that first aroused Conrad's fears for his own health in the Congo.

Conrad left the *Ville de Maceio* on 12 June, disembarking at Boma, the seat of government for the Congo. This was the beginning of his up-river journey. Marlow also disembarks at the seat of government, but Marlow's journey is remarkable at this point, when compared with Conrad's, for the suppression of any indication of conditions at Boma, and for the emphasis given to a piece of gossip Conrad obviously obtained from another captain.

Boma receives little notice in *Heart of Darkness*: 'We anchored off the seat of the government. But my work would not begin till some two hundred miles further on. So as soon as I could I made a start for a place thirty miles higher up' (p. 62). The phrase 'as soon as I could' conceals Conrad's stay of one night at Boma, as the manuscript of *Heart of Darkness* shows: 'Next day [cancelled] I was glad to think my work only began two hundred miles from there. I could not be too far away from that comedy of light at the door of darkness. I left early next day [again 'next day' is scored out] As soon as I could I left for a place thirty miles higher up.' The only description we are given of Boma in the story is a reference to a 'primitive little wharf' and the 'government chaps', but in the manuscript Conrad had given a detailed account of the seat of government at the mouth of the Congo, a place which he obviously disliked:

We went up some twenty miles and anchored off the seat of the government. I had heard enough in Europe about its advanced state of civilization; the papers, nay the very paper vendors in the sepulchral city were boasting about the steam tramway and the hotel—especially the hotel. I beheld that wonder. It was like a symbol at the gate. It stood alone, a grey high cube of iron with two tiers of galleries outside, towering above one of those ruinous-looking foreshores you come upon at home in out-of-the-way places where refuse is thrown out...I had one dinner in the hotel and found out the tramway ran only twice a day, at mealtimes. It brought I believe the whole government with the exception of the governor general down from the hill to be fed by contract. They filled the dining room, uniforms and civil clothes sallow faces, purposeless expressions. I was astonished at their number. [This last sentence is written in above the line] An air of weary bewilderment at finding themselves where they were sat upon all the faces, and in their demeanour they pretended to take themselves seriously just as the greasy and dingy place that was like one of those infamous eating shops you find near the slums of cities, where everything is suspicious, the linen, the crockery, the food, the owner, the patrons, pretended to be a sign of progress; as the enormous baobab on the barren top of the hill amongst the government buildings, soldiers' huts, wooden shanties, corrugated iron hovels, soared, spread out a maze of denuded boughs as though it had been a shade giving tree, as ghastly as a skeleton that posturing in showy attitudes would pretend to be man (MS, pp. 41–3).[7]

Bordeaux to Boma

This may be a jaundiced account of Boma but it is not inaccurate in its detail. The Belgians were proud that both steam tramway and hotel were opened on the same day, 4 March 1890, three months before Conrad arrived. The *Mouvement Géographique*, 4 May 1890, reported:

L'hôtel et le tram de Boma. — Ainsi que nous l'avons annoncé, le restaurant et l'hôtel des Magasins généraux de Boma ont été inaugurés le 4 mars, et le même jour le tram à vapeur a commencé son service régulier entre Boma-rive et Boma-plateau.

Les divers trams pour le transport des agents à l'hotel et le retour chez eux après les repas partent aux heures suivantes:

De Boma-plateau: 6 heures, 11 h. 45 m. et 6 h. 30 m.;
De l'hôtel: 6 h. 30 m., 1 heure et 7 h. 45 m.

Le premier déjeuner a lieu de 5 h. 45 m. à 7 h. 15 m.; le deuxième à midi et le dîner à 6 h. 45 m.

La Compagnie des magasins généraux est chargée des transports de l'Etat par tram entre Boma-rive et Boma-plateau.

Le passage des voitures remplies de voyageurs a rempli, les premiers jours, les noirs de Boma du plus vif étonnement. Ils les suivaient en courant, en riant et en applaudissant. Le service est fait par deux locomotives.

Chaque jour, la table d'hôte de l'hôtel réunit environ 75 Européens.

The hotel used to stand next to the Post Office, two 'symbols of civilisation' together. Boma then, far from being 'primitive', was a well-established, well-organised seat of government.

Conrad's journey on 13 June from Boma to Matadi was like Marlow's by a small steamer: 'I had my passage on a little sea-going steamer. Her captain was a Swede, and knowing me for a seaman, invited me on the bridge. He was a young man, lean, fair, and morose, with lanky hair and a shuffling gait' (p. 62). There is an immediate bond between Marlow and this Swede—both being sailors and both sharing a contempt for the 'government chaps'. But it is the Swede's story of the man who committed suicide that is of real significance: '"The other day I took up a man who hanged himself on the road. He was a Swede, too." "Hanged himself!

27

Why, in God's name?" I cried. He kept on looking out watchfully. "Who knows? The sun too much for him, or the country perhaps"' (p. 63). Thus the menace of the country is brought out again—a menace not so much to health as to the mind, and so the tale falls into place in this theme of the *Heart of Darkness*. Yet it seems likely, surprisingly enough, that Conrad is drawing here upon an actual event of which he must have heard in the Congo.

I have found no instance of a Swede committing suicide under these circumstances but there was a case of a Dane, a Captain Wass, who arrived in the Congo the year before Conrad. The story is recorded by H. Jenssen-Tusch. Writing of Captain Duhst's overland journey from Matadi to Stanley Pool in 1889 he says: 'On the caravan trail [Duhst] contracted fever after a few days and had to keep to his tent...Captain Wass went with Duhst on the caravan trail, but turned back after two days marching "because he did not want to relinquish his life", but shortly afterwards committed suicide at Boma on 30 June 1889, thus barely two months after his arrival in Africa. He had surely become insane because of the climate.' Wass was the only Scandinavian to commit suicide on the caravan trail before 1891 and there can be little doubt that Conrad had Wass in mind.[8]

In removing from the manuscript the description of Boma and in giving a resonant emphasis to the suicide of Wass, Conrad can be seen shaping his material to fit the increasing isolation and sense of foreboding of Marlow's journey.

5

THE COMPANY STATION—MATADI

Marlow's account of the Company Station, based presumably on Matadi where Conrad left the steamer for the long journey overland to Kinchassa, is made up of a series of extraordinarily powerful confrontations, confirming examples of the pointless and brutal activity of the colonists. Marlow's first view of the station extends the earlier suggestions of meaningless and sinister activity:

At last we opened a reach. A rocky cliff appeared, mounds of turned-up earth by the shore, houses on a hill, others with iron roofs, amongst a waste of excavations, or hanging to the declivity. A continuous noise of the rapids above hovered over this scene of inhabited devastation. A lot of people, mostly black and naked, moved about like ants. A jetty projected into the river. A blinding sunlight drowned all this at times in a sudden recrudescence of glare. 'There's your Company's station', said the Swede, pointing to three wooden barrack-like structures on the rocky slope. 'I will send your things up. Four boxes did you say? So. Farewell.'

I came upon a boiler wallowing in the grass, then found a path leading up the hill. It turned aside for the boulders, and also for an undersized railway-truck lying there on its back with its wheels in the air. One was off. The thing looked as dead as the carcass of some animal. I came upon more pieces of decaying machinery, a stack of rusty rails. To the left a clump of trees made a shady spot, where dark things seemed to stir feebly. I blinked, the path was steep. A horn tooted to the right, and I saw the black people run. A heavy and dull detonation shook the ground, a puff of smoke came out of the cliff, and that was all. No change appeared on the face of the rock. They were building a railway. The cliff was not in the way or anything; but this objectless blasting was all the work going on (pp. 63–4).

But Marlow now is given a view of the effect of this pointless activity in terms of human cruelty and tragedy—he sees the file of 'criminals' chained together: 'All their meagre breasts panted together, the violently dilated nostrils quivered, the eyes stared stonily uphill' (p. 64), and he comes upon the grove of death: 'They were dying slowly—it was very clear. They were not enemies, they were not criminals, they were nothing earthly now,—nothing but black shadows of disease and starvation' (p. 66). It is Marlow's first confrontation with the 'flabby, pretending, weak-eyed devil of a rapacious and pitiless folly', and it is a confrontation made first of all in terms of the human suffering such a devil brings about. Attempting to avoid the chain-gang, he encounters the grove of death, and in escaping from this he meets the company's chief accountant, the miracle of self-preservation and callousness, oblivious to everything but his accounts and his starched shirts.

It is not surprising that this powerful passage has been taken to reflect Conrad's actual experience of Matadi—a particularly damning description of the place and of the Europeans and their activities. Jean-Aubry comments: '...his impression could hardly have been favourable' and 'His stay at Matadi hardly offered Conrad any enjoyment.'[1] These statements may be true, but they do not prove that Marlow's Company Station is based exactly on Conrad's Matadi. The greater part of the episode is made up of Marlow's impressions immediately on arrival. The rest of his stay there—ten days in all—is briefly passed over. There is no questioning the literary skill of the episode, but this in itself suggests that it does not reflect entirely Conrad's actual experience.

Matadi was, at this time, an important post with 170 Europeans living there, four factories established, and the SAB station. And a railway was, of course, being built. Part of Marlow's description of this would be accurately enough a visitor's first impression: 'A horn tooted to the right, and

I saw the black people run. A heavy and dull detonation shook the ground, a puff of smoke came out of the cliff.' It is Marlow's commentary—'The cliff was not in the way,' etc. —which transforms the necessary blasting into a futile activity. Similarly, Conrad, like Marlow, would have had opportunity to observe a railway truck, machinery and rails, but whether they were actually abandoned and rusting is doubtful. The work on the railway was in its initial stages, and the first rails and sleepers had been brought out from Belgium on the vessel Conrad travelled in. The *Mouvement Géographique*, 4 May 1890, records: 'La *Ville de Maceio*... a quitté Anvers le 30 avril après avoir embarqué 715 tonnes de marchandises pour Boma et Matadi, parmi lesquelles le premier envoi de rails et traverses pour le chemin de fer du Congo.' And Conrad would hardly have thought the activity involved in the building as pointless in view of the next stage of his journey, for the railway was to do away with the exhausting and dangerous caravan journey from Matadi to Kinchassa.

It is very likely that Conrad observed and disapproved of the treatment of native workers on the railway. Criticism had already appeared in the British Press—*The Times* and the *Morning Post*—of the methods used in recruiting native labour as this passage from the *Mouvement Géographique*, 26 January 1890, shows:

Le Personnel Noir

Dès aujourd'hui, on a acquis la conviction que le recrutement des ouvriers noirs pour le travail de construction se fera sans difficulté. Déjà le directeur a à sa disposition, sur le terrain, plus de 250 ouvriers engagés les uns au Congo, les autres à Sierra-Leone et à Monrovia.

Un important contingent de 1,200 Zanzibarites ne tardera pas à arriver à Matadi. S'il faut en croire une dépêche du *Times*, c'est celui de ces prétendus esclaves qui, au dire du correspondant du *Morning Post*, auraient été enrôlés de force à Zanzibar par l'Etat du Congo. Le journal anglais a été induit en erreur. Ces 1,200 hommes libres ont été régulièrement engagés devant les autorités et d'après les lois du pays, non par l'Etat, mais par la Compagnie du chemin de fer. Leur engagement a été fait par les soins de Sewa-Hadji, le trafiquant zanzibarite, qui a fait au mois de juillet dernier le voyage de Bruxelles pour s'entendre avec la Compagnie du chemin de fer.

D'autres contingents sont encore attendus le mois prochain et le suivant, de telle sorte que pour la bonne saison et le moment de l'ouverture des travaux de construction, environ 2,000 ouvriers sous la direction de 40 à 60 blancs seront réunis à Matadi et dans les environs.

And there was a great loss of life of native workers on the railway, particularly in 1892. Louis Goffin, a Belgian engineer and author of *Le Chemin de fer du Congo* (1907), writes:

We found ourselves, as everybody knows, face to face with great natural obstacles. Moreover, our black personnel, quite as much as the staff of white men, was decimated by sickness. Out of two thousand negroes employed on the construction in 1892, *one hundred and fifty* a month died from illness principally in that valley of the Mpozo...

All along the track one would see corpses of negroes dead of smallpox, dysentery, beri-beri. At times in the morning we might find before the door of our cabin the corpse of some negro dead during the night, placed there by his exasperated comrades as a protest...The men who still remained untouched by sickness were demoralized by fear, and had to be compelled to work by dint of sheer force, the force used being the negative one of depriving them of all salary or even rations...It was, in fact, forced labour. But what were we to do? It was vitally necessary to construct this line of railway, to suppress for ever the far more awful tax of human porterage along this route of the caravans between the Upper and Lower Congo, 'un sentier sinistre, jalonné de cadavres'.[2]

Goffin's account does appear to provide evidence for Conrad's grove of death, but Goffin is writing of events which took place two years after Conrad's visit, events which occurred in the Mpozo valley beyond Matadi. Moreover it does not seem likely—from the hygienic point of view alone—that a 'grove of death' would have been allowed to exist within the bounds of a community such as Matadi then was.*

* It is certainly very probable that Conrad met the accountant of the company. In fact he was likely to have met two of them. The *Mouvement Géographique*, 26 January 1890, refers to the departure for the Congo to work for the railway of two accountants:

The Company Station—Matadi

We have, of course, Conrad's own record of his stay at Matadi in 'The Congo Diary'.[3] The entries, although they indicate dissatisfaction with the Europeans (apart from Casement, Gosse and Underwood) and note a provincial cattiness ('Prominent characteristic of the social life here; people speaking ill of each other'), do not indicate significant condemnation of Matadi or of the activities there:

Arrived at Matadi on 13th of June, 1890.
Mr. Gosse, chief of the station (O.K.) retaining us for some reason of his own.
Made the acquaintance of Mr. Roger Casement, which I should consider as a great pleasure under any circumstances and now it becomes a positive piece of luck. Thinks, speaks well, most intelligent and very sympathetic.
Feel considerably in doubt about the future. Think just now that my life amongst the people (white) around here cannot be very comfortable. Intend avoid acquaintances as much as possible.
Through Mr. R.C. have made the acquaince of Mr. Underwood, the Manager of the English Factory (Hatton & Cookson) in Kalla Kalla. Avge comal—hearty and kind. Lunched there on the 21st.

24th. Gosse and R.C. gone with a large lot of ivory down to Boma. On G.['s] return intend to start up the river. Have been myself busy packing ivory in casks. Idiotic employment. Health good up to now.
Wrote to Simpson, to Gov. B., to Purd., to Hope, to Capt. Froud, and to Mar. Prominent characteristic of the social life here; people speaking ill of each other.

Saturday, 28th June.
Left Matadi with Mr. Harou and a caravan of 31 men. Parted with Casement in a very friendly manner. Mr. Gosse saw us off as far as the State station.

Conrad's experience of Matadi would seem to have been boring rather than shocking. Apart from his dislike of most

'Pour la Compagnie du chemin de fer:...Maka et Beunck, comptables.' Indeed, the manuscript strengthens the view that he met such a person and indicates that it was an accountant who introduced Conrad, on his arrival at Matadi, to the European community. The following line is heavily scored out by Conrad and I am not entirely certain that my reading is correct: 'He introduced me to the station...with the English captain' (p. 54). What I think Conrad is saying here is that he was introduced *as* the *English* captain.

33

of the whites, he found some he could associate with pleasantly, and his health was good. He found employment (though not congenial employment) in packing ivory, and he must have been preparing for the next and most difficult stage of his journey. It would seem also that at times he went out with Casement to find porters for the company. A letter in the Maloney Collection states:

For some three weeks he (Casement) lived in the same room in the Matadi Station of the Belgian Société du haut-Congo...He knew the coast languages well. I went with him several times on short expeditions to hold 'palavers' with neighbouring village-chiefs. The object of them was procuring porters for the company's caravans from Matadi to Leopoldville or rather to Kinchassa (on Stanley Pool) (letter from Conrad to Quinn, 24 May 1916).

To equate Marlow's experience with Conrad's at this point, then, is to ignore the facts of the settlement at Matadi, and the evidence which Conrad provides in his diary. Particularly striking is the fact that the diary contains no mention of a grove of death or of the ill-treatment of the natives (up to this point), which surely would have been recorded had they formed part of his experience.

It is interesting that Casement does not appear in Marlow's story, and yet he might have provided a contrast to the other Europeans. Conrad's account of him in 'The Congo Diary' is enlarged by his comments in a letter to Cunninghame Graham (26 December 1903):

a limpid personality. There is a touch of the Conquistador in him too; for I've seen him start off into an unspeakable wilderness swinging a crookhandled stick for all weapons, with two bull-dogs...at his heels, and a Loanda boy carrying a bundle for all company. A few months afterwards it so happened that I saw him come out again, a little leaner a little browner, with his stick, dogs and Loanda boy, and quietly serene as though he had been for a stroll in a park.[4]

It is difficult to know whether Conrad is keeping to fact here, and whether he could 'a few months afterwards' have witnessed

34

Casement strolling from the jungle—or disappearing into it
for that matter. Conrad had been only ten days at Matadi
when he records that Casement had gone with some ivory
down to Boma, and on the 28th he left the station, having
said good-bye to Casement at Matadi. It seems possible that
Conrad is using the basic impression he received of Casement
as a starting point for an elaboration in the direction of his
ideal adventurer and explorer—the special kind of men, such
as Mungo Park, Doctor Barth, and Livingstone.[5] And this
ideal is reflected later in *Heart of Darkness* in the figure of
the Harlequin who wanders through the jungle in Casement's
casual fashion: 'If the absolutely pure, uncalculating, un-
practical spirit of adventure had ever ruled a human being,
it ruled this be-patched youth' (p. 126).

Whoever was the original of the Harlequin, he, like Casement, would be artistically wrong at Marlow's first station,
and right from every point of view at the heart of darkness.

6

MATADI TO KINCHASSA—THE CENTRAL STATION

The next stage of Conrad's journey was the overland route of 230 miles from Matadi to Kinchassa. He kept a record of this in his Congo diary, giving his personal experiences and impressions, but I have found an unpublished account of the route overland written in 1888 by a missionary, G. W. Brourke, as a report for his head office in London, which sets out the general difficulties Conrad, and anyone else making this journey, had to face then.

...there is only one means of transport. All must go on men's heads for about 230 miles...[From Matadi] a road leaves the river, or rather a narrow footpath, and runs across the hills, along rocky ridges, down into deep gorges, through rushing streams, up steep slopes, over sandy plateaux away to Stanley Pool—about 17 days continuous marching for a white man...and the finding of...porters keeps all the energies of the Europeans on the stretch from year's end to year's end, for the country here is but sparsely populated and the villages few and far between, a great contrast to the swarming populations of the Upper river.

Two more circumstances increase the difficulty for the road is only available for half the year—during the dry season, when the streams are shrunk in their beds, and paths can be made anywhere over the short burnt stalks of the withered grass, but the first weeks of rain soon transform the parched brown hills to a bright green, and soon the high strong tangled grass is nearly as real an obstacle as the swollen streams, now thundering down the rocky beds after each heavy shower and carrying all before them. The available time is thus divided by half, the next difficulty doubles the difficulty of recruiting—for the carriers that leave the lower river will only go a little more than half way, a mere bit of native prejudice inherited from the recent times of intertribal war, but not to be got over anyway. This involves a fresh set of recruiting and receiving depots half way. The government and the missions are at Lukunga, the Dutch House at Ndunga a few miles off. At these places the loads are deposited by the caravans of native carriers until fresh men can be got to take them on to the [Stanley] Pool. So completely do the carriers feel the situation in their own hands that having received their loads they return to their own villages taking their loads with [them] and after some days, weeks, or often *months* of repose, they re-assemble under their headmen, and complete the journey.[1]

This was written two years before Conrad made the journey but the only difference in the situation for him was that the halfway recruiting depot for the Belgians had been moved on to Manyanga. Conrad's diary shows him encountering the exhausting nature of the terrain and the difficulties with porters which Brourke deals with, but a comparison of the diary with Marlow's account of his journey in *Heart of Darkness* from the Company Station to the Central Station also reveals how Conrad treated his own experience in writing Marlow's story.

For Conrad it must have been the most gruelling part of his Congo journey, lasting as it did from 28 June to 2 August 1890, with a rest at Manyanga from 8 July to 25 July, yet the experience as passed on to Marlow is dealt with in a paragraph and is one of the least significant aspects of *his* experience. 'Next day I left that station at last, with a caravan of sixty men, for a two-hundred-mile tramp. No use telling you much about that' (p. 70), Marlow begins, and ends with: 'On the fifteenth day I came in sight of the big river again, and hobbled into the Central Station' (p. 72). 'The Congo Diary' begins: 'Saturday 28th June. Left Matadi with Mr. Harou and a caravan of 31 men' and ends some 36 days later with the halt at Nselemba on Friday the 1st of August,[2] Nselemba being about fifteen miles from Kinchassa, which Conrad presumably reached on 2 August. Conrad crams into one paragraph of *Heart of Darkness* all the unpleasant and macabre aspects of his own journey in order to enhance the nightmare quality of the story and account for Marlow's feeling that he was becoming, ironically speaking, 'scientifically interesting'. The pleasanter aspects of Conrad's journey are left out. Thus Conrad's difficulties in coping single-handed with the sick Prosper Harou and the troublesome carriers are part also of Marlow's journey. On the third day's march Conrad records in his diary, 'Harou giving up. Bother', and later, 'H. lame and not in very good form...Harou arrived very ill with billious [*sic*] attack and fever...[Harou] vomiting bile in enormous quantities...put him in hammock ...Harou suffering much through jerks of the hammock.'[3] Harou becomes Marlow's 'white companion' with the exasperating habit of fainting on the hot hillsides who 'got fever, and had to be carried in a hammock' (p. 71). On 30 July Conrad records in his diary: 'Row with carriers all the way...Expect lots of bother with carriers tomorrow. Had them all called and made a speech, which they did not understand.'[4] And Marlow 'had no end of rows with the carriers. They jibbed, ran away, sneaked off...quite a mutiny. So, one evening, I made a speech in English with gestures...' (p. 71). The contempt for human life and the unexplained and unexpected meeting with a corpse—'Met an off[er]. of the State inspecting. A few minutes afterwards saw at a campg place the dead body of a Backongo. Shot? Horrid smell' (3 July)[5]—is recorded in *Heart of Darkness* as 'the body of a middle-aged negro, with a bullet-hole in the forehead, upon which I absolutely stumbled three miles farther on' (p. 71). And the diary entry for the following day, 4 July: 'Saw another dead body lying by the path in an attitude of meditative repose'[6] is echoed in the novel by: 'Now and then a carrier dead in harness, at rest in the long grass near the path, with an empty water-gourd and his long staff lying by his side' (p. 71).

But Conrad does not pass on to Marlow his bout of fever

on the journey and he makes Marlow's a journey through an 'empty land' dotted with abandoned and ruined villages. Again, this is part of the technique for developing the 'resonance', for Conrad's journey took him to many market places, to various stations, and he passed *en route* other caravans: 'Great market at 9.30. Bought eggs and chickens', he records on 2 July; 'Good many caravans and travellers' (3 July); 'At 11 arrived on the m^{ket}. place. About 200 people' (7 July); 'Most comfortable and pleasant halt' (Manyanga, 8 July); '...Mission of Sutili. Hospitable reception by Mrs. Comber...The looks of the whole establishment eminently civilized' (27 July).[7] To make this point is not to lessen the arduousness and unpleasantness of Conrad's journey—he does comment: 'Getting jolly well sick of this fun' on 5 July, and 'Glad to see the end of this stupid tramp' on 1 August[8]—but it should be observed that Marlow's journey is not Conrad's and most significantly the two journeys differ in the length of time they take.

*

It is at this point in Marlow's narrative that Conrad begins to move increasingly from the facts of his own journey, though hints of the actual circumstances continue to show through.

On his arrival at the important Central Station, where he expects to take over command of his river-steamer, Marlow is greeted with the news that his ship has sunk:

On the fifteenth day I came in sight of the big river again, and hobbled into the Central Station...White men with long staves in their hands appeared languidly from amongst the buildings, strolling up to take a look at me, and then retired out of sight somewhere. One of them, a stout excitable chap with black moustaches, informed me with great volubility and many digressions, as soon as I told him who I was, that my steamer was at the bottom of the river. I was thunderstruck. What, how, why? Oh, it was 'all right.' The 'manager himself' was there. All quite correct. 'Everybody had behaved splendidly! splendidly!'—'you must,' he said in agitation, 'go and see the general manager at once. He is waiting!' (p. 72).

It is known that while Conrad reached Kinchassa (Marlow's Central Station) to find that his steamer, the *Florida*, was wrecked,[9] he was not, like Marlow, delayed there three months, nor was he involved in salvage work. In fact, Conrad spent only twenty-four to forty-eight hours at Kinchassa, leaving again in the *Roi des Belges* for Stanley Falls. His second Congo notebook, the Up-river book, which charts the navigation of the upper Congo, has on its title page the note: 'commenced 3 August 1890 S.S. *Roi des Belges*'.[10] The *Mouvement Géographique* records, however, on 2 November 1890: 'La flottille du haut Congo.—Le steamer *Roi des Belges*, de la Société du haut Congo, a quitté le Pool *le 4 août*' [my italics].

Conrad does seem to have been hurried off up-river the day after his arrival at Kinchassa and allowed no time to recuperate from his journey overland. That he resented this is suggested by a letter from his uncle: 'Three days ago I received a letter from you forwarded by good old Krieger. It was dated the 3rd August from Stanley-Pool...I see from your last letter that you feel a deep resentment towards the Belgians for exploiting you so mercilessly.'[11] So far as I have been able to discover, the only action that could be interpreted by Conrad as exploitation up to 3 August was this hurrying him off after his long caravan journey. But it was necessary that Conrad should do this journey to Stanley Falls as soon as possible under the guidance of a captain experienced in the navigation of the river. Until Conrad also had this experience he could not be expected to take command of a steamer.* A letter to his aunt explains the position he

* Jenssen-Tusch writes of Captain Madsen's original journey on the river: 'Captain Madsen...went directly to Upper Congo and on expedition on board the *Stanley* under Shagerström to establish the station at Basoko, from there in the new *Ville de Bruxelles* to the Falls, all in order to get acquainted with the sailing routes' (p. 193).

held on the journey up-river in the *Roi des Belges*: 'I received your three letters all at once on my return from Stanley Falls, where I went as supernumerary in the vessel *Roi des Belges*.'[12] And if Conrad had not taken this opportunity, he would have had to wait for the next journey of the *Roi des Belges* or for the repair of *Florida*.

But the incident of the wrecking of the *Florida* can be traced further in the novel. In *Heart of Darkness* the steamer had 'started two days before [Marlow's arrival] in a sudden hurry up the river with the manager on board, in charge of some volunteer skipper, and before they had been out three hours they tore the bottom out of [the steamer] on stones, and she sank near the south bank' (p. 73). As in the story, the manager of the station at Kinchassa, Camille Delcommune, had started up-river in the *Florida* some time before Conrad's arrival, and the steamer had been wrecked—though not sunk as was Marlow's command. The *Mouvement Géographique* records: 'la *Florida*...ayant à bord M. Camille Delcommune, directeur adjoint, s'est échouée à la sortie du Pool. Le steamer *Roi des Belges* s'est immédiatement porté à son secours, l'a renflouée et a ramené le bateau à Kinchassa pour y subir les réparations nécessaires' (21 September 1890). On 2 November, a further report gives more details: 'La *Florida* a donné le 18 juillet dernier sur un rocher non loin de Msouata. Trois jours après, le steamer *Roi des Belges* se portait à son secours, la renflouait et la ramenait le 23 juillet à Kinchassa, d'où, après avoir été mise sur le slip pour réparations, elle a dû repartir ces jours pour les Stanley-Falls' (2 November 1890). The *Florida* had been wrecked, salvaged and brought back to Kinchassa by 23 July, at which date Conrad was still at Manyanga *having his seventeen days' rest*.

The wrecking of the *Florida* was not due to the lack of experience of 'some volunteer skipper'. After the assassination of Freiesleben, the former master of the *Florida*, the Government of the Congo lent the Société du Haut-Congo one of their best skippers to take over until Conrad's arrival. This was a Captain Shagerström. The missionary George Grenfell reports in his diary for 19 February 1890, after recording the news of Captain Freiesleben's death: 'Capt. Shagerström bringing the *Florida* up river, being loaned by the state to the SAB.' But that loan could not be extended too long and the company was clearly in need of Conrad's services.

Conrad's extremely brief stay at Kinchassa calls into question the likelihood of Marlow's experiences at the Central Station being a reflection of Conrad's experiences at Kinchassa. Certainly there was no work on a wrecked ship for Conrad, but was he, like Marlow, witness to the arrival of an exploring expedition; did he, again like Marlow, make the acquaintance of a mechanic and a brick-maker; and was there a fire at Kinchassa at that time as there was at the Central Station during Marlow's stay there? We have to remember first that Conrad stayed at Kinchassa for a longer period on his down-river trip and that he is most probably making use of this also. The exploring expedition, for example, arrived during his second visit[13] and artistic requirements led him to include it in Marlow's one stay at the Central Station. The fire and the brick-maker would also seem to be aspects of Conrad's dual experience of Kinchassa.

Marlow meets the brick-maker as a result of a fire at the Central Station during which a hut 'full of calico, cotton prints, beads' was destroyed. There was most certainly a fire at the Kinchassa station. The Société Belge du Haut-Congo records in its annual report for the period 1 January to 31 December 1890: 'Au débit du compte *Profits et Pertes* figure une somme de 49,615 fr. 29 c., perte sèche subie par un incendie à Kinchassa, qui a détruit 74,615 fr. 29 c. de marchandises, alors que nous n'étions assurés que pour 25,000 francs' (*Mouvement Géographique*, 1 November 1891).

Matadi to Kinchassa—the Central Station

The brick-maker, 'this papier-maché Mephistopheles', the man with eyes like 'mica discs', the manager's sycophant and spy, is disliked and mistrusted by Marlow:

He was a first-class agent, young, gentlemanly, a bit reserved, with a forked little beard and a hooked nose. He was stand-offish with the other agents, and they on their side said he was the manager's spy upon them...The business intrusted to this fellow was the making of bricks—so I had been informed; but there wasn't a fragment of a brick anywhere in the station, and he had been there more than a year—waiting. It seems he could not make bricks without something, I don't know what—straw maybe. Anyways, it could not be found there, and as it was not likely to be sent from Europe, it did not appear clear to me what he was waiting for (p. 77).

But Conrad is deliberately heightening the absurdity of the situation by distorting what were the facts. There *was* a brick-maker at Kinchassa, and he would appear to have succeeded in making bricks. His name was Deligne, and he had been at Kinchassa less than a year. The *Mouvement Géographique* for 9 March 1890 reports the imminent departure for the Congo of Deligne, on 25 March, only 16 days before Conrad himself left Bordeaux and five days earlier than the departure of the *Ville de Maceio* from Antwerp: 'Le prochain départ pour le Congo aura lieu par le steamer *Lualaba*, qui quittera Anvers le 25 courant...Carlier, capitaine de steamer ...Deligne, briquetier.' Far from the brick-maker being idle, he seems to have been singularly active:

La briqueterie de Kinchassa. — La Société du haut Congo a pris les dispositions et mesures nécessaires pour que l'établissement à Kinchassa, qui est son quartier général sur le Pool, possède bientôt des installations convenables pour loger son personnel et pour emmagasiner ses marchandises.

Un spécialiste, M. De Ligne, y a été envoyé il y a quelques mois avec l'outillage nécessaire et dès aujourd'hui une briqueterie, rapidement installée, est en plein rapport.

Elle se composait, à la date du 20 août, de 140 mètres de hangar, de 245 × 6 mètres de séchoirs en plein air, sol sablé; d'un atelier de moulage de cinq tables complètes où travaillent 5 briquetiers noirs et 25 gamins porteurs; d'un grand atelier contenant trois grandes caves à épurer les argiles d'après le procédé suisse et d'un broyeur; enfin de deux fours accolés pouvant cuire chacun 30,000 briques en 42 heures (*Mouvement Géographique*, 22 November 1890).

*

We are still left with certain aspects of this episode which may or may not reflect Conrad's experience. What the incident in the novel reveals most strongly is Marlow's dislike of the manager there, a dislike which appears immediately and without specific reason on his first meeting the man:

My first interview with the manager was curious. He did not ask me to sit down after my twenty-mile walk that morning. He was commonplace in complexion, in feature, in manners, and in voice. He was of middle size and of ordinary build. His eyes, of the usual blue, were perhaps remarkably cold, and he certainly could make his glance fall on one as trenchant and heavy as an axe. But even at these times the rest of his person seemed to disclaim the intention. Otherwise there was only an indefinable, faint expression of his lips, something stealthy—a smile —not a smile—I remember it, but I can't explain.* It was unconscious, this smile was, though just after he had said something it got intensified for an instant. It came at the end of his speeches like a seal applied on the words to make the meaning of the commonest phrase appear absolutely inscrutable. He was a common trader, from his youth up employed in these parts—nothing more. He was obeyed, yet he inspired neither love nor fear, nor even respect. He inspired uneasiness. That was it! Uneasiness. Not a definite mistrust—just uneasiness—nothing more. You have no idea how effective such a...a...faculty can be. He had no genius for organizing, for initiative, or for order even. That was evident in such things as the deplorable state of the station. He had no learning, and no intelligence. His position had come to him—why? Perhaps because he was never ill [14] (pp. 73–4).

* Conrad's physical description of the manager does not entirely match Delcommune, but the description of the eyes shows a distinct resemblance: 'His eyes, of the usual blue, were perhaps remarkably cold, and he certainly could make his glance fall on one as trenchant and heavy as an axe' are in evidence in the photograph of Delcommune (Plate 2*b*) as also is 'an indefinable, faint expression of his lips, something stealthy— a smile—not a smile—I remember it, but I can't explain.'

This immediate and unexplained antipathy on Marlow's part reflects Conrad's dislike of the acting manager of the station at Kinchassa, Camille Delcommune.

There is little doubt of Conrad's enduring distaste for him. Jean-Aubry recalls that Conrad

despised this man heartily. He often talked to me about the Congo...
but what remains most vividly in my mind is, first, the landscape with
the river wide as a sea...and second, the hostile and disagreeable figure
of Camille Delcommune...During the last period of his life, when he
used to take pleasure in recalling with a sort of tenderness the memories
of his wandering life, he never showed any feeling of tenderness for the
'pilgrims' (as he called them ironically in 'Heart of Darkness'), whom
he came across in the Congo, least of all for this one.[15]

But what could there have been in their first encounter on 2 August to inspire that immediate dislike which Marlow records? A portion of the interview between Marlow and the manager which is passed over without too much notice reflects, I think, the reason for the antagonism between Conrad and Delcommune on their first meeting:

He began to speak as soon as he saw me. I had been very long on the
road. He could not wait. Had to start without me. The up-river stations
had to be relieved. There had been so many delays already that he did
not know who was dead and who was alive, and how they got on—and
so on, and so on. He paid no attention to my explanations...(pp. 74-5).

The slight differences in word and tone in a passage scored out in the manuscript, and the use of direct speech there, probably reflect more closely the actual interview: 'He said directly "you have been a very long time coming up". I explained why, and he went on as though I had not spoken. "So long that I had to start without you. The stations must be provisioned and the agent's [*sic*] relieved"' (MS, p. 64). Something of Delcommune's brusqueness in ignoring Conrad's explanations of his delay seem to come over here, and suggests that the main source of disagreement was not the delay over the wrecked steamer, which Marlow experienced, but the time taken by Conrad to make the journey from Matadi to Kinchassa, which caused Delcommune some embarrassment. It was a journey which was never expected to take longer than twenty days, and which could be done in seventeen days, but which had taken Conrad *thirty-five days*.

Oddly enough, Conrad makes no reference elsewhere to the time he took over the journey. In a letter to Madame Poradowska, he refers to it as a 'twenty day caravan',[16] and he allows Marlow only fifteen days: 'On the fifteenth day I came in sight of the big river again, and hobbled into the Central Station.'* But Conrad took thirty-five days, because of his stay at Manyanga, and, moreover, according to 'The Congo Diary', he had already been delayed some time at Matadi for no apparent reason: 'Mr. Gosse, chief of the station (O.K.) retaining us for some reason of his own.'[17] Conrad and Harou were 'retained' there from 13 June to 28 June, and spent altogether *fifty days* in getting from Matadi to Kinchassa.

Delay then characterises this first part of Conrad's journey from Boma to Kinchassa and forms an odd contrast with the haste he had shown in Europe in preparing for his trip. The delays he experienced seem attributable only in part to sickness, and the lack of reference in his letters to the unusually long time he took over the journey from Matadi to Kinchassa seems to suggest that this is something he did not wish to admit to. Camille Delcommune probably had, in his view, something to complain about. He was only thirty-one, two years Conrad's junior, and had only recently been appointed deputy director. The fire at Kinchassa, more extensive than the one Conrad refers to in *Heart of Darkness*, quite clearly

---

* Marlow says of the Central Station: 'It was on a back water surrounded by scrub and forest, with a pretty border of smelly mud on one side, and on the three others enclosed by a crazy fence of rushes. A neglected gap was all the gate it had, and the first glance at the place was enough to let you see the flabby devil was running that show' (p. 72). For a sketch of the Kinchassa station at this time see Plate 4*a*.

would leave the manager in a very nervous state, whilst the wrecking of the *Florida* must have seemed a major disaster. I imagine it only needed Conrad's delayed arrival to predispose him to take deep offence. Conrad, mortified by such a reception, never forgave Delcommune and when he came to write *Heart of Darkness* took his revenge in an extraordinary fashion. Conrad's reasons for disliking Delcommune, which must have accumulated as they travelled to and from Stanley Falls together, were of too personal a nature to be significant in the story, but he *could* make Delcommune the source for the unpleasant manager who is intriguing against Kurtz. The delays in the story centre round the wrecked river-steamer which Marlow is to command and there are definite suggestions that the manager is deliberately delaying the salvaging of the vessel, for though *delay* is central to Marlow's story, Conrad removes the blame for it from Marlow to the manager. With extreme nicety he calculates that the repair work on the steamer will take three months— 'that ought to do the affair'—the implication being that this delay will ensure that Kurtz does not receive help in time to enable him to recover from his illness. Thus the death of Kurtz is laid at the manager's door.

7

KINCHASSA TO STANLEY FALLS

Jean-Aubry said of the journey to Stanley Falls, 'Everything that Marlow describes there is evidently the direct reflection of scenes, apprehensions, worries, impressions, recollections of Captain Korzeniowski.'[1] We have no record which gives us Conrad's experiences of this journey as we have in his Congo diary of his caravan journey. His Up-river book, begun on leaving Kinchassa for Stanley Falls, is a seaman's technical record of the navigation of the river. But information that I have been able to discover about conditions on the river Congo at that time suggests that there are striking differences between Marlow's journey and Conrad's.

The purpose of the up-river journey in *Heart of Darkness* is to relieve the trading-posts, particularly that of Kurtz: 'There were rumours that a very important station was in jeopardy, and its chief, Mr. Kurtz, was ill' (p. 75). The journey is slow and seemingly interminable. It takes the river-steamer two months to travel from the Central Station to Kurtz's Inner Station. It is a pioneer journey into an unknown and uncharted world, and the stealthy danger of such a journey is constantly stressed:

The reaches opened before us and closed behind, as if the forest had stepped leisurely across the water to bar the way for our return. We penetrated deeper and deeper into the heart of darkness. It was very quiet there. At night sometimes the roll of drums behind the curtain of trees would run up the river and remain sustained faintly, as if hovering in the air high over our heads, till the first break of day (p. 95).

The journey up-river is a return to the primeval in geographical and ethical time:

Kinchassa to Stanley Falls

Going up that river was like travelling back to the earliest beginnings of the world, when vegetation rioted on the earth and the big trees were kings...We were wanderers on prehistoric earth, on an earth that wore the aspect of an unknown planet...We could not understand because we were too far and could not remember, because we were travelling in the night of first ages (pp. 92–6).

Marlow, in charge of the steamer, is engrossed in the difficulties of navigation on this unknown waterway; and this takes his mind off the brooding jungle and the idle, bickering manager and 'three or four' agents who are also on board:

I had to keep guessing at the channel; I had to discern, mostly by inspiration, the signs of hidden banks; I watched for sunken stones; I was learning to clap my teeth smartly before my heart flew out, when I shaved by a fluke some infernal sly old snag...And I didn't do badly either, since I managed not to sink that steamboat on my first trip (pp. 93–4).

The isolation of the Inner Station is a necessary condition for Kurtz's fall from grace—he has been isolated for a whole year and for nine months there has been 'no news—strange rumours'. There is no mention of any other steamer on the river, and the only sign of human habitation is the occasional native village or the small and uncertainly established white settlement: 'Sometimes we came upon a station close by the bank, clinging to the skirts of the unknown, and the white men rushing out of a tumble-down hovel, with great gestures of joy and surprise and welcome, seemed very strange' (pp. 94–5).

But the journey made by the *Roi des Belges* was very different. It was to begin with remarkable for its speed. The steamer covered the thousand miles from Kinchassa to Stanley Falls in little less than one month, a feat which the *Mouvement Géographique* found it worthwhile to comment upon:

M. Camille Delcommune, directeur adjoint de la Société du haut Congo, vient d'exécuter un voyage aux Stanley-Falls dans des conditions de rapidité qui méritent d'être mentionées. Il a quitté Kinchassa le 4 août, à bord du steamer *Roi des Belges*, remorquant deux allèges et deux canots indigènes. Le premier septembre il arrivait aux Falls, soit vingt-huit jours après son départ du Stanley-Pool (21 December 1890).

It has been suggested that, as in the story, the purpose of the *Roi des Belges*'s journey was to reach the SAB agent at Stanley Falls, Georges Antoine Klein, presumed original of Kurtz.[2] However, a report in *Mouvement Géographique* suggests that the steamer's journey had another purpose and one which equally accounted for her haste. It appears that the *Roi des Belges* was going to the aid of a second disabled steamer, the *Ville de Bruxelles*, which had come to grief two days before the *Florida*: 'La *Ville de Bruxelles* a donné le 16 juillet dernier sur un *snag* (tronc d'arbre écroulé dans le lit du fleuve), dans le voisinage d'Oupoto. Pendant deux semaines, le bateau est resté dans une position critique...' (*Mouvement Géographique*, 2 November 1890).[3] Grenfell recorded in his diary:

10 August 1890. *Roi des Belges* passed up with help for *Ville de Bruxelles* —she had just finished towing the *Florida* down to the Pool after having nearly broken in two near [indecipherable].

30 August 1890. *Ville de Bruxelles* comes down happily, little the worse for her accident—got under steam an hour or so before *King of Belgium* arrived with help—great credit to the captain.

The *Ville de Bruxelles* was a large troop-carrier belonging to the State and her disablement might have created a dangerous situation on the river.[4]

The journey of the *Roi des Belges* would, then, appear to have been a routine business trip for Delcommune, hastened by the delay already occasioned by the wrecking of the *Florida* and by the desire to help the troop-carrier *Ville de Bruxelles*, but not because of the urgent need to reach Klein.

Although some reaches of the river must have given a sense

of oppressiveness and isolation, this could not have been the overall impression of the journey. Conrad would have seen several other steamers on the river between Kinchassa and Stanley Falls, as the tables giving the movement of shipping through the port of Bangala from July to October 1890 show (see Appendix B, p. 377 below, for copy of tables).[5] Bangala is halfway between Kinchassa and Stanley Falls[6] and the *Roi des Belges* arrived there on 19 August. Apart from passing the *Ville de Bruxelles*, the steamer would pass the *Holland* which went south from Bangala on 24 July arriving at Kinchassa approximately on 8 August; the missionary vessel *Peace* which left Bangala for Bolobo on 14 August; and the *Holland* again on her return journey to the Falls (she reached Stanley Falls two days after the *Roi des Belges*' departure from there). And the fact that there was traffic on the great river— there were eleven vessels at that time on the upper reaches, including three belonging to the SAB—leads to another conclusion. Had there been such a need to relieve up-river stations or to bring down from Stanley Falls the SAB agent Klein, as is suggested in the story, help could have been given by many other steamers.

Apart from the activity of the various steamers on the river, there were a number of well-established settlements of one kind and another. For example, there were trading and missionary stations at Tchumbiri, Bolobo, Coquilhatville (Equator station), and Bangala (see map facing p. 9, above), the latter being a very important station indeed. And after steady steaming up to Upoto (the point where the *Ville de Bruxelles* was wrecked), the *Roi des Belges* would run into a rash of stations, European and Arab. At the village of Mwangi alone there were Belgian, Dutch and French factories. Journals kept by a Belgian missionary and by Alexander Delcommune (brother of Camille) during expeditions on the Congo in 1890 and 1888 respectively[7] dispel the idea of the Congo as a deserted stretch of water with an occasional station 'clinging to the skirts of the unknown'. The Belgian missionary, from Bangala onwards, recorded passing villages constantly, as well as factories and stations. Alexander Delcommune reported 'que nulle part sur le haut Congo, il n'a vu, pendant les cinq jours que dure la navigation entre l'Arouhouimi et les Falls, une pareille densité de population' and he frequently records passing two or three villages or Arab posts in a day. Particularly impressive was the camp at Basoko.* The Belgian missionary commented:

Le lundi 3 mars, nous arrivons à la station, ou plutôt au camp de l'Etat, placé au confluent de l'Arouhouimi. Ce camp, étant données les forces dont peuvent disposer les Arabes voleurs de nègres, est une véritable forteresse. L'enceinte, d'un mètre d'épaisseur et de quatre mètres de hauteur, se compose de deux rangées de pieux entre lesquels on a tassé de la terre glaise. Cette enceinte grimpe aux abords de la rivière, sur une hauteur assez considérable. Cette hauteur a été convertie en une espèce de donjon où brillent les gueules de quatre canons. Le donjon domine tellement le fleuve que nulle flotte de ravisseurs d'esclaves ne pourrait passer ici impunément. Nuit et jour, une sentinelle fait la garde.

One danger that Marlow had to face during his journey was the attack on the steamer by natives about a mile-and-a-half below Kurtz's station:

Arrows, by Jove! We were being shot at! I stepped in quickly to close the shutter on the land-side...I had to lean right out to swing the heavy shutter, and I saw a face amongst the leaves on the level with my own, looking at me very fierce and steady; and then suddenly, as though a veil had been removed from my eyes, I made out, deep in the tangled gloom, naked breasts, arms, legs, glaring eyes—the bush was swarming with human limbs in movement, glistening, of bronze colour. The twigs shook, swayed, and rustled, the arrows flew out of them, and then the shutter came to. 'Steer her straight', I said to the helmsman... A fusillade burst out under my feet. The pilgrims had opened with their Winchesters, and were simply squirting lead into that bush...

* See Plate 3 *b* for a photograph of this fortress at Basoko, which Conrad must have seen.

...Looking past that mad helmsman, who was shaking the empty rifle and yelling at the shore, I saw vague forms of men running bent double, leaping, gliding, distinct, incomplete, evanescent. Something big appeared in the air before the shutter, the rifle went overboard, and the man stepped back swiftly, looked at me over his shoulder in an extraordinary, profound, familiar manner, and fell upon my feet. The side of his head hit the wheel twice, and the end of what appeared a long cane clattered round and knocked over a little camp-stool...my feet felt so very warm and wet that I had to look down. The man had rolled on his back and stared straight up at me; both his hands clutched that cane. It was the shaft of a spear that, either thrown or lunged through the opening, had caught him in the side just below the ribs; the blade had gone in out of sight, after making a frightful gash; my shoes were full; a pool of blood lay very still, gleaming dark-red under the wheel; his eyes shone with an amazing lustre (pp. 110–12).

When the vessel is attacked we are made strongly aware that Marlow is the moral superior of his companions. He does not panic; he does not fire wildly into the bush; he does not allow the crew to eat the dead helmsman; and, perhaps most important of all, Marlow saves the day at this point and later, when the vessel leaves the Inner Station, by dispersing the native warriors with a blast of the vessel's steam whistle.

None of these incidents, I am reasonably certain, formed part of Conrad's experience on the river. The attack, for one thing, is very much part of the plot, centring round Kurtz and his native followers. But the Congo from Isangi, at the confluence with the Lomami, to Stanley Falls, a distance of sixty miles, was under the strong influence of the Congo Arabs and, at least during this part of the journey, an attack, if it came, would not come because of the influence of a Kurtz (Klein) but as the direct result of orders from the Arab leaders themselves. And this kind of attack, possible two years later, was not likely to occur at the time of Conrad's journey. And had the *Roi des Belges* been subject to an attack of this seriousness a report would most certainly have appeared in the *Mouvement Géographique* and some action would have been taken by the State.

Marlow's method of dispersing the natives—by the use of the steam whistle—is given some emphasis in the story:

With one hand I felt above my head for the line of the steam whistle, and jerked out screech after screech hurriedly. The tumult of angry and warlike yells was checked instantly (p. 112).

The retreat, I maintained—and I was right—was caused by the screeching of the steam-whistle. Upon this they forgot Kurtz and began to howl at me with indignant protests (p. 121).

The Harlequin, when we meet that gentleman at the Inner Station, tells Marlow, 'One good screech will do more for you than all your rifles. They are simple people.' And finally, on leaving the Inner Station with the sick agent Kurtz on board, and with the 'pilgrims' ready to fire on the assembled natives who do not wish to see Kurtz leave, Marlow again uses the steam whistle with interesting effect:

I pulled the string of the whistle, and I did this because I saw the pilgrims on deck getting out their rifles with an air of anticipating a jolly lark. At the sudden screech there was a movement of abject terror through that wedged mass of bodies. 'Don't! don't you frighten them away', cried someone on deck disconsolately. I pulled the string time after time. They broke and ran, they leaped, they crouched, they swerved, they dodged the flying terror of the sound (p. 146).

There is plenty of evidence that such use of the steam whistle to disperse crowds of armed natives had been employed effectively on the Congo. Both H. M. Stanley and the missionary George Grenfell record using it. In 1887, Stanley took over the settlement at Yambuya on the Aruwimi (see map facing p. 9, above) without a fight simply by the use of the steam whistle:

It was now nine o'clock, my throat was dry, the sun was getting hot, and I signalled to the steamer *Stanley* to come across and join us, and when near enough, according to agreement, a second signal caused the steam whistles to sound, and under cover of the deafening sounds, pent up as they were by the lofty walls of the forest, both steamers were steered to the shore, and the Zanzibaris and Soudanese scrambled up the steep sides of the bluff like monkeys, and when the summit was gained not a villager was in sight.[8]

George Grenfell wrote in his diary on 15 October 1886 how, during a journey up the river Kasai, his steamer *Peace* met with 'a hostile reception at the hands of the people who assembled to the no. of some 500, some 20 or 30 of whom waded into the water up to their waists, threatening us with their spears, and bows and arrows'. The famous German explorer, Wissman, who was present, recorded the conclusion of this incident:

Mr. Grenfell, who had once seen the effect of the powerful voice of his *Peace* when investigating the Mubangi, now sounded the steam-whistle. The impression was again so overpowering that all the natives took to their heels in wild fear, disappearing in the thickets and rushing towards the village. Only one old white-haired Herculean chief, who was standing close to the river, felt ashamed to run, but was terrified to such a degree that he staggered backward, and only kept his footing by catching hold of a tree.[9]

The Yambuya settlement on the Aruwimi river to which Stanley refers was almost a hundred miles above the confluence of the Congo and the Aruwimi, and the steamers of the white man—in that area and at that time—were an entirely new phenomenon to the natives. This applies also to Grenfell's explorations of the river Kasai which in 1886 was relatively unexplored. But the same could not be said of the natives situated some two miles below the Stanley Falls station in Conrad's time, who must have regarded both steamers and whistles as commonplace occurrences and are unlikely to have been affected by them.

The agents made their own contribution to Marlow's difficulties, and, while there is no evidence that the passengers on the *Roi des Belges* behaved in a like manner, the *Mouvement Géographique* at least gives us the names of those men who accompanied Conrad on this up-river journey. They were 'MM. le directeur adjoint Camille Delcommune, les capitaines de steamer Koch et Conrad, les agents Keyaerts, Rollin et Vander Heyden, le mécanicien Gossens' (2 November 1890).* These were Conrad's companions on the voyage whom he named ironically 'pilgrims'. We can see that this term is derived from the fact that in the Congo all the agents (and no doubt Conrad himself) walked around with staves. In the text we have the phrase: 'They wandered here and there with their absurd long staves in their hands, like a lot of faithless pilgrims bewitched inside a rotten fence' (p. 76). J. R. Werner writes: 'I had to walk up to him and remonstrate by means of the long staff which every white man in this country carries.'[10]

*

One can usually rely upon Conrad, as befits a seaman, to give an exact description of the vessels he sailed in, and the account of the river-steamer Marlow commanded is as accurate an account of the *Roi des Belges* in which Conrad travelled on the upper Congo as his descriptions of the *Judea* and the ship in *The Shadow-Line* proved to be of their respective real-life models, the *Palestine* and *Otago*:

* Captain Ludwig Rasmus Koch was a Dane and only twenty-five at this time—eight years Conrad's junior.[11] He had sailed for the Congo in the *Nubia* from Liverpool on 12 September 1889, in the company of the ill-fated Johannes Freiesleben. Of the three agents on board—Rollin, Vander Heyden and Keyaerts—the two former were newcomers to the Congo. They had sailed together in May from Europe: 'Le steamer *Lulu Bohlen*, de la ligne Woermann, de Hambourg, fera, le 3 mai, escale à Flessingue pour embarquer...Rollin et Vander Heyden, agents commerciaux, pour la Société du Haut Congo' (*Mouvement Géographique*, 4 May 1890), and arrived in the same month as Conrad: 'Le steamer *Lulu Bohlen* est arrivé à Boma le 2 Juin...Le *Ville de Maceio* [le 13] à 5 heures' (*Mouvement Géographique*, 20 July 1890).[12] Only one of the agents on the *Roi des Belges* seems to have earned Conrad's dislike so as to become individualised in the story as 'the pilgrim in pink pyjamas'—'a little fat man, with sandy hair and red whiskers, who wore side-spring boots, and pink pyjamas tucked into his socks' (p. 102). This is most likely to be Alphonse Keyaerts. He was thirty-eight, and had left Antwerp on 1 July 1889 for the Congo (*Mouvement Géographique*, 30 June 1889). The mechanic Gossens' departure for the Congo was reported in the *Mouvement Géographique* for 26 January 1890.

This steamboat was exactly like a decked scow. On the deck, there were two little teak-wood houses, with doors and windows. The boiler was in the fore-end, and the machinery right astern. Over the whole there was a light roof, supported on stanchions. The funnel projected through that roof, and in front of the funnel a small cabin built of light planks served for a pilot-house...I spent my days perched up there on the extreme fore-end of that roof, before the door. At night I slept, or tried to, on the couch (pp. 108–9).

The *Roi des Belges* (see Plate 5) was also for Marlow, however, a 'tin-pot steamer' 'like an empty Huntley and Palmer biscuit tin', 'a two-penny-halfpenny river steamboat with a penny whistle attached', and nothing in his attitude reflects the affection Conrad revealed through his fiction for other ships. A number of photographs of the *Roi des Belges* are in existence, and these show unmistakably the 'two little teak-wood houses', 'the boiler...in the fore-end', 'the machinery right astern', and the funnel projecting through the roof. Though this wood-burning stern-wheeler was very small— she was only 15 tons—she was not old. J. R. Werner recalls returning to Leopoldville in 1887 and seeing it on the slipway waiting to be assembled.[13]

Marlow describes how he spent his days perched 'on the extreme fore-end of that roof, before the door [of the cabin]'. Apart from the couch, the cabin contained 'two camp-stools, a loaded Martini-Henry leaning in one corner, a tiny table, and the steering-wheel. It had a wide door in front and a broad shutter at each side. All these were always thrown open, of course' (p. 109). In the manuscript this passage is followed by a sentence which has been scored out: 'I stood outside or sat on a stool outside the door' (MS, p. 130). No doubt Conrad spent his days in this way also, but with the important difference that Conrad was not, like Marlow, in charge of the steamer: none of the responsibilities and none of the heroic actions of Marlow were his. Conrad would share the bridge with Captain Koch who would, like Marlow, be engrossed in the navigation of this extremely difficult and dangerous river.[14] John Rose Troup[15] gives an indication of the life of the steamer's captain in describing his own journey in the *Roi des Belges*:

Shagerström,[16] the captain, would be at his post on the bridge, shouting his orders, and we would soon be again on our way...Shagerström used to take up his quarters [on the upper deck] from the time we started till we pulled up for the night, *some ten hours*, and would have his breakfast and *lunch sent up to him while he was engaged in piloting us through the intricate channels of the mighty Congo!* There was no one to share this task with him, to relieve him of his anxieties [my italics].

It is this kind of responsibility that Conrad transfers to Marlow: Conrad himself, as supernumerary, was occupied in making notes on the navigation of the river, as his Up-river book shows:

11.N(A) Long reach to a curved point. Great quantity of dangerous snags along the star^d shore. Follow the slight bend of the shore with caution. The Middle of the Channel is a S-B- [sandbank] always covered. The more northerly of the two islands has its lower end bare of trees covered with grass and light green low bushes, then a low flat, and the upper end is timbered with light trees of a darker green tint.[17]

Although Conrad does not make too much of it in the story, it must not be forgotten that the *Roi des Belges* was a wood-burning vessel and that the finding of wood was an essential part of each day. The steamer had in tow two lighters for carrying the wood-supply and two native canoes. One of these would be used to transport some of the native crew. The narrator's comment in the *Heart of Darkness*, 'the woodcutters slept, their fires burned low' is a reference to the fact that no native was allowed to sleep in the steamers at night,[18] but had, after cutting up the wood for the boilers, to sleep ashore. John Rose Troup gives a description of this nightly event:

Then under the general supervision of the white men they began wood cutting. Trees that were dry enough for firewood were selected, and the task of cutting down and drawing them to the water's edge was entered upon. At dusk huge fires were lit, and by the blaze of these the men cut up the logs into small chunks, three or four feet in length; thus they would be occupied all night in preparing fuel for the next morning... It was a picturesque enough sight, attended with its noise and bustle, the thud, thud of the axes, the crash of the falling trees, then the firelight scene, with the scraping of the saw, and chop, chop, followed always by a dull thud as the blocks were thrown on the piles, and were then tossed from hand to hand till they were all loaded on to the steamer; added to all this were the weird cries and monotonous songs of the men at their work...[19]

The crew of the steamer in the story provide an aspect of the primitive and the bizarre suited to a journey to the heart of darkness. They are, to begin with, cannibals: 'Fine fellows—cannibals—in their place. They were men one could work with...And, after all, they did not eat each other before my face':

'Catch 'im' he snapped, with a bloodshot widening of his eyes and a flash of sharp teeth—'catch 'im. Give 'im to us.' 'To you, eh?' I asked; 'what would you do with them?' 'Eat 'im!' he said, curtly, and, leaning his elbow on the rail, looked out into the fog in a dignified and profoundly pensive attitude. I would no doubt have been properly horrified, had it not occurred to me that he and his chaps must be very hungry...Why in the name of all the gnawing devils of hunger they didn't go for us— they were thirty to five—and have a good tuck in for once, amazes me now when I think of it (pp. 103-4).

The crews of steamers were from the upper Congo, mostly from Bangala. S. P. Verner writes:

A crew of them [Bangalas] consists of about twenty-five, including a number of their wives, who are permitted aboard with them. Their work is the cutting and loading of wood, the discharge and loading of cargo, acting as firemen, cooks and stewards, and very often they are needed to get the steamer off a sandbank. A few of them make excellent pilots, and upon the skill of the Bangala 'at the wheel' has the fortune of the Congo Free State's navy not infrequently depended.[20]

Like Marlow's cannibal crew, the Bangalas were joyfully cannibalistic. The brother of Bapulula (popular pilot on the mission steamer *Peace* on the river at this time), when asked if he ate human flesh, answered, 'Ah! I wish I could eat everybody on earth'.[21] Dr Bentley, the missionary, recalls talking to an old man at Bangala, three years before Conrad went up the river, who was reported to have killed and eaten seven of his wives.[22]

The food which the crew, according to Marlow, live on in the story (apart from rotten hippo meat) certainly seems unpalatable:

the only thing to eat—though it didn't look eatable in the least—I saw in their possession was a few lumps of some stuff like half-cooked dough, of a dirty lavender colour, they kept wrapped in leaves, and now and then swallowed a piece of, but so small that it seemed done more for the looks of the thing than for any serious purpose of sustenance (p. 104).

Conrad is describing accurately here the Bangala crew's diet of cassava. Grenfell[23] reports: 'Manioc...known to us under the name of tapioca...The root, after being well washed to get rid of its inherent prussic acid was ground into a white flour and then mixed with water till it formed a stiff dough. This was made into rolls of sausage shape (or large round balls) wrapped in banana leaves.'

Conrad brings out strongly the incongruous touch that the crew are paid with brass wire:

Besides that, they had given them every week three pieces of brass wire, each about nine inches long; and the theory was they were to buy their provisions with that currency in river-side villages. You can see how *that* worked. There were either no villages, or the people were hostile, or the director, who like the rest of us fed out of tins, with an occasional old he-goat thrown in, didn't want to stop the steamer for some more or less recondite reason. So, unless they swallowed the wire itself, or made loops of it to snare the fishes with, I don't see what good their extravagant salary could be to them. I must say it was paid with a regularity worthy of a large and honourable trading company (p. 104).

However ludicrous this appears, the truth is that brass wire *was* the staple currency in the Congo. J. Rose Troup writes:

The mitako, or brass rod, is the currency among the natives at Leopoldville and most of the regions of the Upper Congo. It is in general imported
to the Congo by the State in large rolls or coils of 60 lbs. in weight. After
its arrival at Leopoldville it is cut up into the regulation lengths (about
2 feet), making it resemble in size and appearance an ordinary stair-rod;
the value of each of these pieces at Leopoldville is reckoned at $1\frac{1}{2}$d.[24]

Although crews made up of cannibals who ate peculiar food
and were paid in a peculiar currency were commonplaces
on the Congo, to Conrad they must have appeared bizarre
and incongruous and he makes use of these details and his
reaction to them to further his aim of describing a mysterious
and macabre journey.

Disentangling fact from fiction in the actual journey up-
river, we are left not with a mysterious and dangerous journey
into the unknown and the primitive during which the passengers
are beset by an ignorant greed for ivory, and the captain,
Marlow, is the isolated and dedicated workman intent on
the immediate difficulties of his job,[25] but with a routine,
highly organised venture along a fairly frequented riverway
linking quite numerous settlements of trading posts and
factories, and with a number of competent and busy men on
board, and with Conrad there to learn the route under the
guidance of a skilled captain.

8

STANLEY FALLS—THE HEART
OF DARKNESS

The famous Inner Station, desolate and decaying, is the true physical site of the heart of darkness, where Kurtz in isolation from civilisation, in his proximity to the primitive jungle, had his 'unlawful soul' beguiled 'beyond the bounds of permitted aspirations'. It was here that he was, according to the Harlequin, 'shamefully abandoned', 'There hadn't been a drop of medicine or a mouthful of invalid food for months here.' Marlow views the station first through glasses:

Through my glasses I saw the slope of a hill interspersed with rare trees and perfectly free from undergrowth. A long decaying building on the summit was half buried in the high grass; the large holes in the peaked roof gaped black from afar; the jungle and the woods made a background. There was no enclosure or fence of any kind; but there had been one apparently, for near the house half-a-dozen slim posts remained in a row, roughly trimmed, and with their upper ends ornamented with round carved balls. The rails, or whatever there had been between, had disappeared. Of course the forest surrounded all that. The river-bank was clear...Examining the edge of the forest above and below, I was almost certain I could see movements—human forms gliding here and there (p. 121).

The round carved balls on posts are discovered to be human heads—'with the shrunken dry lips showing a narrow white line of the teeth' (p. 131). The Harlequin tells Marlow that 'The camps of these people [the natives] surrounded the place, and the chiefs came every day to see him [Kurtz]. They would crawl...' (p. 131). Kurtz is carried out of his house on a stretcher and he is immediately surrounded by 'streams of human beings...with spears in their hands, with bows, with shields, with wild glances and savage movements' and only Kurtz can persuade them to remain peaceful. During the night, Kurtz crawls away on all fours through the undergrowth to try to reach his followers' camp in the nearby jungle.

Although Conrad gives here an extreme and macabre example of degeneration, biographers and commentators generally have passed over the question as to how closely the Inner Station was modelled upon Conrad's knowledge of Stanley Falls and how far the SAB agent there, Klein, was a source for Kurtz. Jean-Aubry, failing, as he says, 'a more precise description of Conrad's...stay at Stanley Falls',[1] takes as evidence of Conrad's impressions and feeling of solitude while he was there the passage in his 'Geography and Some Explorers':

The subdued thundering mutter of the Stanley Falls hung in the heavy night air of the last navigable reach of the Upper Congo, while no more than ten miles away, in Reshid's camp, just above the Falls, the yet unbroken power of the Congo Arabs slumbered uneasily. Their day was over...

A great melancholy descended on me...there was no shadowy friend to stand by my side in the night of the enormous wilderness, no great haunting memory, but only the unholy recollection of a prosaic newspaper 'stunt' and the distasteful knowledge of the vilest scramble for loot that ever disfigured the history of human conscience...[2]

There can be little doubt that the solitude and disillusionment Conrad refers to here were his most outstanding feelings at this point in his journey but these do not give us any impression of Stanley Falls station. The particularised references to that place in the passage quoted above—the Arab station and the Arab power—are much more useful in helping us to picture the station, and they are accurate. They do, moreover, suggest immediately that the Falls station differed considerably from the Inner Station where the nearest military post was three hundred miles away. And more precise descriptions which I have found confirm that Stanley Falls was quite another matter. It would, for instance, have been impossible for an agent to have been abandoned there. The *Mouvement Géographique*, 16 July 1890, lists the number of *State* officials at the station at that time:

Districts des Stanley Falls

Tobback	Résident aux Falls.
Lippens	Résident à Kassongo.
Tamine	Sous-commissaire de district.
Rynwalt	Sous-lieutenant.
Michiels	Sergent.
Van Hoeck	—
Gérain	— (Kassongo).

This does not include those who, like Klein, were attached to commercial houses.

And far from consisting of a decayed hut on a hill, the Falls station was, as might be expected, a built up and well-organised settlement, a large and important station which was very busy and where the trade in ivory was thriving. In 1893, three years after Conrad's visit there, Albert Chapaux gave a detailed account and a plan of the station in his book:

Stanley-Falls (25° 10′ 42″ long. E. et 0° 30′ 18″ lat. N.), cheflieu du district des Stanley-Falls. — La station des Falls, qui avait été établie primitivement par Stanley dans l'île Usana (les événements ont démontré que c'était une faute grave), fut reconstruite en 1888 sur la rive droite du fleuve, un peu en aval de l'ancienne station. C'est le capitaine Van Gèle qui fit choix de l'emplacement et qui y installa MM. Bodson et Hinck; ces deux officiers firent les premiers travaux en attendant l'arrivée du résident officiel, le capitaine Haneuse. Celui-ci occupa tous ses instants, avec une activité et une initiative dignes des plus grands éloges, à la construction et à l'embellissement de sa station; il fit de réels prodiges et fut admirablement secondé par Bodson et Hinck. Après eux, le capitaine Bia, puis le lieutenant Tobback s'occupèrent plus spécialement du développement des cultures et des plantations.

La station proprement dite s'étend le long de la rive droite, tandis que la résidence, habitée par le résident des Falls, est située sur la rive gauche, à proximité des établissements arabes, aujourd'hui occupés par l'Etat.

Stanley Falls—the Heart of Darkness

Les bâtiments qui composent la station sont très nombreux; en voici la nomenclature, dont les chiffres correspondent à ceux indiqués sur le croquis: 1° maison en pierres des chutes, construite par Haneuse, servant au résident ou chef de la station; 2° maison en pierres des chutes, construite par Hinck, servant de salle à manger et contenant des chambres;

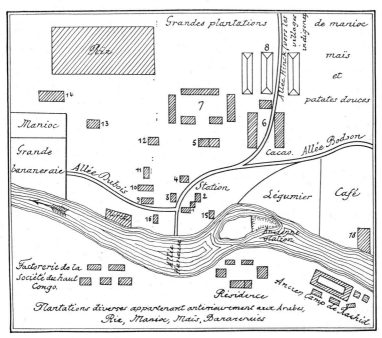

Stanley-Falls, d'après des croquis de MM. Hincke et Daenen.

3° magasin en pisé; 4° maison en pierres, construite par Bodson, servant de logement aux agents; 5° prison en pierres; 6° habitations de la force publique; 7° habitations des esclaves libérés; 8° grands hangars pour les ouvriers; 9° magasin de transit; 10° magasin et cuisine; 11° poulailler; 12° maison des boys; 13° magasin à poudre; 14° grand hôpital; 15° et 16° tonnelles de maracoujas.

Les plantations et les cultures ont pris aux Falls une extension plus considérable que dans les autres stations; en aval de la station, les bananeraies occupent plusieurs centaines d'hectares; le riz, le maïs et le manioc y sont cultivés avec soin et produisent une forte et abondante nourriture. En amont de la station, les résidents ont apporté des soins particuliers à la récolte du café et du cacao; en 1893, on pouvait y compter plus de 2,000 pieds de ces précieuses denrées. Le potager des Falls est très riche et les arbres fruitiers y croissent en grand nombre. L'abandon définitif des Falls par les Arabes à la suite de la victoire de M. Chaltin a acquis à l'Etat toutes leurs installations et leurs cultures qui enrichiront considérablement cette station déjà si favorisée.[3]

I have two photographs of the Stanley Falls station which give some impression of what Conrad saw on his arrival at that station on 1 September 1890. The first is a photograph taken in March 1896 from the other side of the river giving a view of the whole length of the station. What strikes one here is not so much the hill on which the station is built— that is very small—as the number of the outbuildings. Of course, many of these *may* have been built during the six years that elapsed between Conrad's visit and that of the missionary who took this photograph. And certainly a war between the Arabs and the Belgians had taken place which might have led to an increase in the buildings at the station afterwards. Yet in terms of trade, the station had not expanded nor at this time increased its export of ivory.

The second photograph (Plate 3*a*) is most important. It is entitled 'Le Gouverneur passant l'inspection de la station de Stanley-Falls' and is a view of a military inspection at the Falls. At least ten Europeans, along with a detachment of native personnel, are gathered on the parade ground during a Governor's inspection of the station. Apparent are the many buildings that made up this important station, and the main road (called Allée Bodson) which also appears in my first photograph of the Falls station. Unfortunately the photograph is undated and the Governor-General unidentified, but I think that it is possible to date it accurately. Prior to the campaign against the Arab power in the upper Congo by the Belgians (1892–5), only one Governor-General had officially visited the Stanley Falls station and this was

Governor-General Janssen in 1889. Albert Chapaux writes: 'Le 15 septembre, [1889] le gouverneur, à bord de la *Ville de Bruxelles*, partit pour le Haut-Congo...il arriva aux Falls, où il trouva Tippo-Tip,* qui avait retardé son départ pour Nyangué afin d'avoir sa première entrevue avec le gouverneur général.'[4] I believe the photograph shows this inspection and therefore gives a very accurate impression of the station Conrad saw. The number of buildings reinforces my view that Kurtz's Inner Station was not based on Stanley Falls.

Without determining at this stage whether Klein's character approximates to Kurtz's in terms of egomania, we can at least, from the external evidence available to us, determine that certain details which appear in the story would be unlikely to be based on fact. We know that Klein was *not* alone and he could not, like Kurtz, have presided 'at certain midnight dances ending with unspeakable rites' or 'taken a high seat amongst the devils of the land—I mean literally'.

*

In *Heart of Darkness*, Kurtz's activities close the area to trading because, presumably, he has aroused disturbances among the natives. The greatest danger at Stanley Falls was, and always had been since its establishment by Stanley himself in 1883, from the Arabs and not from any hostility among the natives. In August 1886 the Arabs had besieged and taken the station.[5] Indeed, Belgian influence had been re-established only two years before Conrad's visit, but to build up good relations with the Arabs was another matter and there continued to be in the area from Basoko to Stanley Falls increasing tension between Arabs and Belgians. This was inevitable, given their common interest in the collecting of ivory, and the Belgians' disapproval of Arab methods of doing this—by raiding, killing, and collecting slaves whom

* Important Arab chief in the area, sometimes called Tippo-Tib.

they then sometimes sold for ivory. The Belgians attempted reconciliation—an expedition under Jerome Becker arrived in the early months of 1889 with the task of establishing good relations.[6] But peaceful diplomacy was impossible as M. Mahute, an officer at the camp of Basoko, shows: 'Ce qui cependant donne le plus de travers est cette f...[*sic*] politique arabe. Devant nous on vous fait des salamaleks sans nombre, pendant que derrière on fait des misères à vos gens. Il faut conduire cela sans brusquer, car les ordres du Gouvernement exigent de la diplomatie pacifique.'[7] This statement was made five days before Conrad arrived in the Congo!

The Belgians also used other methods. In 1889 a fortified post was established at Basoko, evidence that the Arabs would not be allowed to carry out slave raids any lower down the river Congo. George Grenfell, on reaching Bangala at 1 p.m. on 23 May 1890, records in his diary: 'Saw one of the wonderful machine guns under the verandah—it is destined for Basoko to exert a little moral "suasion" on the arabs.' So hostility between the Arabs and the Belgians was growing in spite of the public ceremonial when visits were made and received.

But the profitable collection of ivory went on. Becker, leader of the conciliatory expedition, bought large amounts from Tippo Tib and was bringing them down-river right into 1890. Grenfell reports in his diary for 3 and 4 April 1890: '*Florida* laden heavily with ivory...5 tons ivory on board... passed 5 p.m. Becker on board.' R. P. P. Ceulemans tells us, taking the information from the diary of Nicholas Tobback, the Resident of the Falls at the time of Conrad's visit, that Tobback established himself in the home of Tippo Tib and 'se disait un négociant de premier ordre'.[8] Ceulemans also quotes Tippo Tib as saying: 'chaque mois deux ou trois vapeurs de l'Etat ou des maisons de commerce emportaient tout l'ivoire'.[9]

Stanley Falls—the Heart of Darkness

Perhaps the greatest competitor of the Belgian commercial firm, the SAB, was the Dutch trading house, the Nieuwe Afrikaansche Handels-Vennootschap. The manager of this company, Antoine Greshoff, was a great friend of the missionary George Grenfell and often Grenfell records in his diary Greshoff arriving in his little steamer *Holland* at the mission station at Bolobo during his journey up the river Congo from Stanley Pool to Stanley Falls. On 23 July 1888, Grenfell refers to such a visit and makes a special mention of the large amount of ivory Greshoff had collected from the upper Congo: 'The *Holland* came in this mg.—6 tons or so of ivory on board.' And a letter from Grenfell to Greshoff then on leave in Rotterdam dated 28 June 1890 (the day Conrad left Matadi on the caravan trail for Kinchassa) gives some indication of the fierce rivalry that existed between the Belgians and the Dutch:

The *Holland* passed up a [indecipherable] ago. She was [making] haste so as to keep ahead of the *Ville de Bruxelles* but as that craft is not in sight so there is no need for the *Holland* to fear being overtaken. Unfortunately I was not able to send word by telegraph and I suppose he is still going at it full tilt, thinking the V. de B. is close astern.

And a close watch was kept by the Belgian authorities on the activities of the Dutch house. The following account appeared in *Mouvement Géographique* on 31 May 1889:

Les Hollandais déploient une grande activité dans l'exploration commerciale du haut fleuve et de ses affluents et ne cessent d'augmenter le nombre de leurs établissements et de renforcer le personnel. Ils ont en ce moment 5 stations sur le haut fleuve: 2 au Stanley-Pool, 1 à Loulonga, 1 à Ngomba et 1 aux Falls. Ces stations comptent 14 agents blancs et 3 nouveaux Européens sont en route pour Léopoldville. Ils n'ont encore qu'un steamer sur le haut, mais il est probable qu'ils n'en resteront pas là.

The result of Kurtz's behaviour is, as the manager tells Marlow, that 'The district is closed to us for a time. Deplorable! Upon the whole, the trade will suffer.' But there is no evidence that the Stanley Falls station was closed to trade immediately after Conrad's visit there or in the immediate future. Alexandre Delcommune's expedition of 1890 arrived at the Stanley Falls station before beginning the exploration of the river Lomami. Delcommune's account of his arrival at the Falls station on 16 December 1890 (three months after Conrad's departure from that station) presents a picture of a settled community:

Le 16, à huit heures du matin, sous une pluie battante, nous arrivons aux Stanley-Falls, où nous sommes cordialement reçus par le résident, M. Lherman, le lieutenant Reginald et M. Langeld, non moins que par toute la smala arabe. Mais Raschid, pro-vali des Falls, qui remplace son oncle Tippo-Tip, est parti pour Kassongo. Son absence me contrarie. C'est sur lui que je comptais pour l'acquisition de canots. Nos relations antérieures ayant toujours été des plus amicales, je ne doutais pas qu'il ne fît, cette fois encore, tout ce qui lui était possible pour me rendre service.[10]

It is noticeable from this passage that Delcommune is met by representatives of all the various interests at the Falls station, which again does not indicate any interruption of the general running of the station. M. Lherman was Resident at that time through the absence of M. Tobback; M. Langeld was manager of the Dutch trading house; and the Arabs are also represented, though not by the then Chief Arab, Raschid. It would seem from this account also, that Klein, the SAB agent, had not yet been replaced.

This then was the situation both before and after Conrad's visit to the Stanley Falls station. It was a thriving station bedevilled only by political difficulties in the relations with Arab slavers, and by strong competition at this great centre for ivory between the Dutch and Belgian houses.

There would seem to be nothing in the situation at the Falls station, therefore, to give Conrad the inspiration for

Stanley Falls—the Heart of Darkness

Kurtz's desolate and isolated Inner Station with the conditions necessary for his temptation and fall. Nothing brings out more clearly Conrad's imaginative leap between his experience and his story than a comparison of the climaxes of the two journeys—Marlow's and Conrad's—the one at the Inner Station, and the other at Stanley Falls.

9

KLEIN

Jean-Aubry considered that 'the principal character of this story...was not merely an imagined creation and a kind of symbol, but rather, if not a literal copy, at least a sketch of a real person...substantially true to reality'.[1] And finding the agent Georges Antoine Klein at Stanley Falls, he goes on: 'One could not presume, without explicit proof, the complete resemblance between Kurtz and Klein, but it is beyond a doubt...that between these two persons, one real and the other imaginary, there was more than a simple resemblance of name.'[2] The fact that Conrad used the name Klein in the manuscript of *Heart of Darkness* and then crossed it out and substituted Kurtz lends support to this conclusion, but apart from this 'simple resemblance of name' there would seem to be little else of similarity between Klein and Kurtz. We know, from the evidence given by Jean-Aubry, that Klein was a commercial agent at the Falls, that he was sick with dysentery, and that he did die on the *Roi des Belges* in the course of Conrad's down-river trip on that steamer. Thus, in certain essentials, he resembles Kurtz, though not in fundamentals of character, action and reputation—so far as I have been able to discover. Before attempting to discover more about Klein, we can conclude that he was not involved in activities like those of Kurtz, since it would have been impossible for an agent at the Falls to have obtained the necessary isolation and privacy. We would not expect then to find any startling reports about Georges Antoine Klein, but I have been able to uncover some new information about him.

Klein

According to his birth certificate, Georges Antoine Klein was born in Paris on 9 April 1863 and was therefore twenty-seven in 1890 (see Appendix C for copy of Klein's death certificate).[3] He had arrived in the Congo not much earlier than Conrad himself, and the *Mouvement Géographique* provides evidence of his having followed the same route as Conrad up to Kinchassa beginning late December 1888:

MM. Klein et Vandendorpe, au service de la Société belge du haut Congo, s'embarquent à Liverpool sur le bateau qui quitte ce port directement pour le Congo, le 26 courant (*Mouvement Géographique*, 23 December 1888).

Le *Cameroon*, venant de Liverpool, a jeté l'ancre le 15 février devant Boma, amenant un certain nombre d'agents de l'Etat et MM. Klein et Vanden Borre, agents de la Société du Haut-Congo (*Mouvement Géographique*, 31 March 1889).

MM. Klein et Vandenborre sont arrivés en bonne santé à Kinchassa. Le 25 mai, les six agents partis d'Europe à bord de l'*Ambrez* sont arrivés à Matadi (*Mouvement Géographique*, 2 June 1889).

Klein must have reached Kinchassa some time in March, presuming that he was not held up between Boma and Kinchassa. He remained there in all probability for some months, since Grenfell records on 19 May 1889 while he was at Kinchassa: 'Saw Klein of SAB also Mr. Morrison and another of the family of 6 recently arrived of whom one died of sunstroke on the way up.' Later, Klein was transferred higher up-river, perhaps to Stanley Falls itself or to Bangala, for on 17 February 1890 Grenfell records: 'Left Umangi with Klein in SAB canoe in tow en route for Isangi.' Definite information of Klein's area as a commercial agent is found in the *Mouvement Géographique* of 20 July 1890: 'M. Cloetens a pris la direction de l'établissement de Kinchassa; M. Heyn, celle de Manyanga; M. Gosse, celle de Matadi; M. Engeringh, celle de Louébo; M. Michiels, celle de l'Équateur, et M. Klein, celle des Falls. M. Hodister

conserve la direction du district commercial de Bangala.'
No date is given for these appointments, though they could
have been made as early as May 1890. We can tell from
Conrad's Congo diary that Gosse was at Matadi and Heyn
at Manyanga in June of that year: '[13 June] Mr. Gosse,
chief of the station [at Matadi]'; '8 July...Arrived at
Manyanga at 9 a.m. Received most kindly by Messrs. Heyn
and Jaeger.'[4] Klein had, therefore, taken up his post as agent
at the Falls station only a month or so before Conrad arrived
in the Congo.

The fact of his being agent at the important Stanley Falls
station perhaps gives the impression that he was a more
important and influential person than was actually the case,
for Klein worked under the orders of the famous agent,
Hodister. On 17 August 1890 the *Mouvement Géographique*
records Hodister's exploration of the Mongala river and the
report ends with this statement: 'M. Hodister a actuellement
sous ses ordres sept agents européens, ainsi répartis: à
Bangala, M. Noblesse; à Mobeka, M. Beckers; à Gongo,
MM. Vandenborre et Rombouts; à Oupoto, M. Morrison;
aux Falls, M. Klein à bord du steamer *Général Sanford*,
M. Olufsen.'[5]

Klein probably was sick with dysentery when Conrad
arrived at Stanley Falls in the *Roi des Belges*. His sickness
was not in itself remarkable since fever and dysentery were
endemic in the Congo, and, it so happens, dysentery was
especially rife at this time in the Basoko and Stanley Falls
area. George Grenfell reports in his diary for 24 May 1890:
'Dysentery reported very prevalent at Basoko and Falls—
is also the reported reason for leaving Yambuya.'

The picture of Klein that has emerged so far is of a young
man with a year-and-a-half's experience in the Congo, and
probably no more than four months as agent at Stanley
Falls. There is no suggestion of his being outstanding or

eccentric in any way, and he merits only the conventional, passing mention in contemporary accounts. Nothing suggests Conrad's conception of Kurtz.

Marlow's steamer leaves the Inner Station under impressive circumstances:

When next day we left at noon, the crowd...flowed out of the woods again, filled the clearing, covered the slope with a mass of naked, breathing, quivering bronze bodies...three men plastered with bright red earth from head to foot, strutted to and fro restlessly...they... stamped their feet, nodded their horned heads, swayed their scarlet bodies... and the woman with helmeted head and tawny cheeks rushed out to the very brink of the stream...I pulled the string of the whistle...(pp. 145–6).

But it is unlikely that such a barbaric crowd saw the *Roi des Belges* off at Stanley Falls. An extremely impressive demonstration was staged on the departure of the Resident on 7 April 1889, he, of course, being much more important than the manager of the commercial house. Jenssen-Tusch writes:

On 7 April 1889, the Belgian commander at the Falls was to go home to Europe. For the occasion the natives came in their big canoes, equipped as if for war, all painted white, yellow, or red, with huge tufts of feathers on their heads, and performed a whole series of fighting scenes on the river...Finally an attack was performed as a force that had occupied the beach at the station. When the performance was over, they were treated to boiled rice and meat, after which diverse exchange goods were tossed to the warriors a few at a time, while the headmen themselves were given sizeable gifts.[6]

The departure of the Belgian agent at the Falls and the manager from Kinchassa would hardly merit this, though it is possible that the event was marked in a lesser way and that Conrad is drawing in part upon this experience.

On the journey down-river a partnership develops between Marlow and the dying Kurtz, which Marlow accepts as he watches Kurtz's spiritual struggles: 'both the diabolic love and the unearthly hate of the mysteries it had penetrated fought for the possession of that soul'; 'It is strange how

I accepted this unforeseen partnership, this choice of night-mares forced upon me in the tenebrous land invaded by these mean and greedy phantoms [the manager and the pilgrims]' (p. 147). But the strong feeling Marlow had for Kurtz could not have been based upon any similar feeling Conrad might have had for the sick Klein, a man he had only recently met. And there was no pressure of a 'choice of nightmares' to force Conrad to sympathise with Klein, no devilish struggle going on for Klein's soul. Conrad's journey may indeed have been unpleasant. He may very well have felt isolated as a result of the antagonism of Delcommune but, so far as I know, he did not share this antagonism with Klein. He would most certainly have been aware of the sufferings of any sick men, on board that small steamer. J. R. Werner writes of a similar occurrence in 1888, giving us some idea of Conrad's experience here:

I leave my readers to imagine the discomfort of this run, especially for the two sick men, whose pain, in spite of all we could do for them, must have been considerably increased by the throbbing and shaking of the little steamer, which, owing to her heavy-laden condition, was more violent than usual...Next morning, one of them, who was down with dysentery, and whose sufferings had been so much intensified by the shaking of the steamer that we thought he could never reach Equator [station] alive, seemed to have rallied so far that we again hoped to bring him safely to Leopoldville; all the more so, as he told us that the agonising pain of the day before had nearly ceased. We started as early as possible in order to reach the Baptist Mission Station at Lukolela before night; but our patient soon began to sink rapidly, and at 10 a.m. Mr. Dhanis came to me to ask if I could not go any faster, as he did not think the sick man could live many hours. But the little *A.I.A.* was doing all she knew; and there was nothing for it but to await the end, which came a little after mid-day, when, slowly and silently, death entered the boat, and we could do no more. The Zanzibaris, who had been attending on him since we left Bangala, washed the corpse, and covering it with blankets, laid it out on a kind of hurdle astern—as we had decided to try and reach Lukolela sooner than dig a nameless grave in the forest.[7]

76

Klein

Kurtz was buried 'in a muddy hole' by the 'pilgrims' but my research has shown that Klein was given proper burial and that as late as 1960 someone in Europe was sufficiently concerned to do something about the upkeep of his grave. Jean-Aubry, who corresponded with the Société du Haut-Congo about the death of Klein, received the following terse account from them: 'Klein, Georges Antoine: French, engaged as commercial agent...Died September 21st, 1890, on board the steamer *Roi des Belges* during a voyage. Death due to the results of dysentery. Interred at Chumbiri [Tchumbiri] (Bolobo).'[8] At that time there was an American Baptist mission at Tchumbiri which was transferred to the British Baptist Missionary Society in the 1930s. This is no longer in existence, the nearest mission being now at Bolobo, Grenfell's original establishment. With the help of the missionary there, Angus MacNeil, whom I contacted through Professor Roger Anstey of the University of Canterbury, I was able to discover the site of Klein's grave at Tchumbiri. On 25 March 1968 Angus MacNeil sent me the following letter:

Klein was apparently buried at Tchumbiri, but his grave was left unmarked. Around the 1940's the Belgian Authorities contacted the Mission at Tchumbiri requesting them to locate the grave, if possible, and promising a small sum of money for its regular upkeep. An old woman was found who remembered seeing Klein's burial and she was able to point out the place where the grave is. This is marked by a few stones today, just to the side of some other European graves. My informant for all this is a man called Djamba Louis, who worked for some time as a Pastor at Tchumbiri and who was given the job of identifying and organising the upkeep of Klein's grave...The only thing some other old men could remember hearing about Klein's death, was that he died somewhere up-river from Tchumbiri and was brought back down-river to be buried.

I received further and final details in a letter dated 6 June 1968:

It was the Belgian Colonial Administration who contacted Djamba Louis, through the Commissaire de District at Inongo...The first contact was made with Rev. J. N. Clarke, a BMS missionary at Tchumbiri who died there in the late forties. According to Djamba Louis, this contact was in the early 1940's. Nothing was done about it apparently. Then Djamba himself was contacted as late as 1957 and for three years, until Independence in 1960, received the sum of 400 Congolese Francs every six months, for the upkeep of Klein's grave. The grave had been identified earlier, I gather. Since 1960, there has been no grant made.

The grave where Klein is buried, is the one nearer to the river in Billington's sketch[9]...The whole of the area in Billington's sketch is now vacant land, since all the buildings on the Station were gradually moved further up hill, away from the river.

If Klein had been buried in the European grave, then I judged from Billington's sketch that he was buried some 150 yards from the river and that Conrad, therefore, looking from the deck of the *Roi des Belges* or from the pilot's cabin, could have witnessed the burial. In reply to a request for verification of this, Angus MacNeil wrote: 'The graveyard for Europeans is, as you have imagined, something like 150 yards back from the river. It would have been quite possible to have watched a burial from the vantage point of a boat tied up at the landing beach, provided the grass was cut.' Klein, then, was buried in the old mission graveyard at the Tchumbiri Station and for some reason buried slightly outside the Christian graveyard. Two photographs of the grave were taken by Angus MacNeil at my request. The first (Plate 4*b*) is a close-up of the stones marking Klein's grave; the second, with the grave of the founder's wife Jessie Billington, in the forefront, shows Klein's grave just beyond in a partially cleared space.

In his job, his illness, his death and place of burial Klein is the obvious source for those same aspects of Kurtz, but only in the bare facts of those aspects. A great deal has been added to what Conrad knew of Klein to transform him into Kurtz, and it was not simply, as Jean-Aubry suggests, that the facts about Klein were 'modified, enlarged to the needs of artistic effect'.

THE JOURNEY DOWN-RIVER

The *Roi des Belges* had arrived at the Falls on 1 September, and she appears to have been delayed there for five or six days, the cause of this delay being presumably not the collecting and loading of ivory, as in *Heart of Darkness*, though this would be done, but the sickness of many of the party. In a letter to his aunt from Kinchassa dated 26 September, after his journey down-river, Conrad wrote: 'at the Falls (its native country) I had an attack of dysentery lasting five days'.[1] Garnett records something of Conrad's experience of this illness at the Falls station. Speaking of the scenes which Conrad omitted from the text of *Heart of Darkness* but which he had earlier related to his friend, he writes: 'I regretted the omission of various scenes, one of which described the hero lying sick to death in a native hut, tended by an old negress who brought him water from day to day, when he had been abandoned by all the Belgians. "She saved my life", Conrad said, "the white men never came near me."'[2]

Although there is some doubt about the authenticity of this particular incident[3] there is no doubt that Conrad was sick and that Captain Koch, master of the *Roi des Belges*, was also sick. And as a result of Koch's illness, Conrad was at last given the opportunity to do what he had come to the Congo for—that is, take command of a river-steamer. A letter written by Camille Delcommune to Conrad at Stanley Falls and dated 6 September reads:

Société Anonyme Belge pour le   Stanley Falls,
Commerce du Haut-Congo.   September 6th 1890

Monsieur Conrad Korzeniowski,
Captain.

I beg herewith to ask you to take command of the s.s. 'Roi des Belges'
from this date until the recovery of Captain Koch.

Believe me, etc.,
(Signed) Camille Delcommune[4]

And so it would seem that Conrad had just recovered from
his illness when he took the steamer away from Stanley Falls
with Klein and Koch both sick on board.

'The brown current ran swiftly out of the heart of darkness,
bearing us down towards the sea with twice the speed of
our upward progress' (p. 147). Marlow's words form an
accurate comment upon the return journey of the *Roi des
Belges*. The steamer left Stanley Falls presumably on 6
September 1890 and was in Kinchassa once more on 24
September 1890, a journey of eighteen days compared with
the up-river journey of twenty-seven days. She left under
Conrad's command, and it has been concluded that he brought
her down to her port of registry, Kinchassa: 'it is certainly
in the capacity of Captain that he brought the steamer back
from Stanley Falls to the [Stanley] Pool', Jean-Aubry states.
But I believe that Conrad's ambition was fulfilled for an
even shorter period of time than this, and if his journey
up the Congo had been a frustrating and disappointing one
for him, his journey down-river was to prove even more
disillusioning.

Conrad's instructions were that he was to take command
'until the recovery of Captain Koch' and it would seem that
Captain Koch had recovered by 17 September when the
steamer reached Bangala, approximately halfway on the
journey. Evidence of this can be found in Otto Lütken's
article in the *London Mercury* where an entry is quoted from

Captain Duhst's diary, Duhst being then sick with dysentery at Bangala. The entry records that Captain Koch of 'the steamship *Roi des Belges*' had visited him but 'made no mention of having Conrad on board as second-in-command'. (Lütken argues from this that Conrad did not even make the journey to Stanley Falls.)[5] And the possibility of such a visit being made is confirmed by the stay of the *Roi des Belges* at Bangala for one night. The *Mouvement Géographique* lists her as arriving on the 15th and departing on 16 September 1890 (*Mouvement Géographique*, 28 December 1890. See Appendix B for tables showing movement of shipping through Bangala). If Captain Koch was well enough to visit Duhst at Bangala, it would seem likely that he was well enough to resume command, at least from this point.

After Kurtz's death, Marlow is struck down by fever and comes near to death himself—'they very nearly buried me... I have wrestled with death' (p. 150). We are given no further details of Marlow's journey. There is a sudden leap from the river back to the sepulchral city: 'I found myself back in the sepulchral city resenting the sight of people hurrying through the streets' (p. 152). After filling in the details of Conrad's journey subsequent to the burial of Klein, we can conclude that, apart from a period of severe illness, Conrad does not transfer these details to Marlow, though the particular *quality* of his experiences and the feelings they roused in him have been present in Marlow's story from the beginning of his tale.

Conrad does not appear to have been ill on the down-river journey to Kinchassa. His letter to his aunt, written on his return to Kinchassa, refers to his having had the fever 'four times in two months' 'in *going up* the river' [my italics] and an 'attack of dysentery lasting five days' at the Falls.[6] But if not actually ill, he must have been in a weakened state after so much illness.

Conrad would seem to have reached Kinchassa once more on 24 September, and to have found waiting for him there a letter from his cousin, Maria Tyszkowa, and three letters from his aunt, Madame Poradowska. He replied to the first on the day of his arrival, 24 September, and to the second on 26 September. These two letters are of great interest because they show that between these two dates the final blow was delivered to Conrad's hopes of still salvaging something of his expectations in coming to the Congo, and that this blow was delivered by Camille Delcommune, Conrad's determined opposer. To his cousin Conrad wrote: 'I am very busy with all the preparations for a new expedition to the River Kassai. In a few days I shall probably be leaving Kinchassa again for a few months, possibly even for a year or longer.'[7] This takes us back to Conrad's hope, expressed in that letter to Zagórski of 22 May, that he would command the steamboat for Alexandre Delcommune's exploring party. Conrad must still at this date have been reasonably certain of this if he could, on the very day of his arrival from the Falls, set about preparing for the expedition. But two days later he wrote to his aunt: 'I can hope for neither promotion nor increase of salary while he [Delcommune] remains here. Moreover, he has said that he is but little bound here by promises made in Europe, so long as they are not in the contract. Those made me by M. Wauters are not.'[8] The possibility of joining the expedition having gone, there appears to have been no hope even of the command of a river-steamer: 'Likewise I can look forward to nothing, as I have no vessel to command. The new boat will be finished in June of next year, perhaps.'[9] With accuracy Conrad adds, 'my status here is vague' and later gives the news of his leaving 'in an hour by canoe for Bamou, to select wood and have it cut to build the station here. I shall remain encamped in the forest two or three weeks.' The tone of depression in this letter to his aunt was surely justified. Since his arrival in the Congo he had suffered from fever and dysentery, had been allowed to command a steamer, in all probability, for a mere ten days, had also been employed in packing ivory and now was to collect wood. There could not have been a more depressing and degrading situation for a man of Conrad's experience and qualifications, who had already commanded the *Otago* in Australian waters.

His troubles would appear to have arisen directly from Camille Delcommune's dislike of him, which seems to have amounted to some kind of persecution. Conrad wrote to his aunt:

Everything is repellent to me here. Men and things, but especially men. And I am repellent to them, too. From the manager in Africa—who has taken the trouble of telling a good many people that I displease him intensely—down to the lowest mechanic, all have a gift for getting on my nerves; and consequently I am perhaps not as pleasant to them as I might be. The manager is a common ivory-dealer with sordid instincts who considers himself a merchant though he is only a kind of African shopkeeper. His name is Delcommune.[10]

If the sycophancy towards the manager which Marlow describes in *Heart of Darkness* existed in fact, then Conrad would find no sympathisers among the Europeans once Delcommune's dislike of him had been made known (cf. Marlow's 'The pilgrims looked upon me with disfavour').

That it was Camille Delcommune rather than his brother Alexandre who was decisive in wrecking Conrad's hopes is proved by the fact that Alexandre, as leader of the exploring expedition, had not arrived at Kinchassa by the time Conrad wrote this letter to his aunt on 26 September. The Eldorado Exploring Expedition which Conrad deals with in a bitterly ironic manner in the *Heart of Darkness* arrived in the story 'during the next three weeks':

Instead of rivets there came an invasion, an infliction, a visitation. It came in sections during the next three weeks, each section headed by a donkey carrying a white man in new clothes and tan shoes, bowing from that elevation right and left to the impressed pilgrims. A quarrelsome band of footsore sulky niggers trod on the heels of the donkey; a lot of tents, camp-stools, tin boxes, white cases, brown bales would be shot down in the courtyard, and the air of mystery would deepen a little over the muddle of the station. Five such instalments came, with their absurd air of disorderly flight with the loot of innumerable outfit shops and provision stores, that, one would think, they were lugging, after a raid, into the wilderness for equitable division. It was an inextricable mess of things decent in themselves but that human folly made look like spoils of thieving.

This devoted band called itself the Eldorado Exploring Expedition, and I believe they were sworn to secrecy. Their talk, however, was the talk of sordid buccaneers: it was reckless without hardihood, greedy without audacity, and cruel without courage; there was not an atom of foresight or of serious intention in the whole batch of them, and they did not seem aware these things are wanted for the work of the world. To tear treasure out of the bowels of the land was their desire, with no more moral purpose at the back of it than there is in burglars breaking into a safe. Who paid the expenses of the noble enterprise I don't know; but the uncle of our manager was leader of that lot (p. 87).

Delcommune's expedition arrived at Kinchassa in much the same way, but in three instalments, not five, and over a period of two, not three, weeks. The *Mouvement Géographique*, 2 November 1890, reports:

L'expédition du Katanga sous le commandement de M. Alex. Delcommune, avec tout son matériel et ses charges, devait être au Stanley-Pool, dans les premiers jours d'octobre. Voici, en effet, ce que nous écrit un des membres de l'expédition:

Matadi, 14 septembre 1890.

Le 23 août, le steamer *Biafra* est arrivé à Boma ayant à bord MM. Hakansson, docteur Briart, de Roest, de Soutschoff et 334 nouveaux enrôlés, soldats et artisans.

Le lendemain 24, le bateau continua la navigation jusqu'à Matadi, d'où il repartit le 25 après avoir débarqué tous ses passagers. 1 sergent-major, 5 sergents et 150 soldats ont été choisis pour l'expédition; les autres ont été remis à M. Charmanne, directeur du chemin de fer. M. Coquilhat, inspecteur d'Etat, a obligeamment mis à la disposition de M. Delcommune un sous-officier de la force publique pour l'instruction militaire de sa troupe.

The Journey Down-River

Le 1er septembre, un premier détachement d'avant-garde composé de 50 soldats et des porteurs nécessaires quittait Matadi sous le commandement de MM. Hakansson et de Roest. Le 3 le deuxième détachement suivit avec MM. Protsche et Didderich. Quant au troisième, il partira le 15 ou le 16 avec MM. Delcommune, Briart, de Soutschoff et le sous-officier de la force publique.

L'embarcation démontable et toutes les charges de l'expédition—il y en a environ 900! — sont déjà arrivées à Léopoldville.

A Léopoldville, l'expédition s'embarquera pour le Lomami à bord du steamer *Florida*, de la Société du haut Congo. Si rien ne vient entraver sa navigation et si la bonne fortune qui a favorisé ses débuts continue, on estime qu'elle sera au poste de Bena-Kamba, point extrême de la navigation sur le Lomami, dans le courant du mois de décembre.

Assuming that each detachment took twenty days to cover the caravan route from Matadi to Kinchassa—and this was the average time taken—then the first detachment would have arrived on 20 September, four days before the *Roi des Belges* returned to Kinchassa from up-river; the second would have arrived on 23 September and the third, with the commander of the expedition, Alexandre Delcommune, on 5 October.

It is possible that Conrad waited for the arrival of Alexandre Delcommune before giving up hope entirely of doing something useful in the Congo. Perhaps he hoped that Alexandre might rescind his brother's decision. If Conrad had these hopes, he was disappointed. Delcommune's expedition left Kinchassa on 17 October (not 13 October as stated by Jean-Aubry) without Conrad:

L'expédition Delcommune — L'expédition placée sous le commandement de M. Alexandre Delcommune avait quitté Kinchassa, le 17 octobre dernier, à bord des deux steamers *Ville de Bruxelles*, à l'Etat, et *Florida*, à la Société du haut Congo. La *Ville de Bruxelles* arriva à Bena-Kamba le 30 novembre. Elle y fut rejointe par la *Florida*. Les deux steamers viennent de revenir au Pool, rapportant des nouvelles de l'expédition, dont l'état sanitaire était excellent (*Mouvement Géographique*, 3 May 1891).

It is difficult to know whether Conrad had any particular contact with Alexandre Delcommune. Marlow says of the manager's uncle who is based on Alexandre Delcommune that he 'spoke to no one but his nephew', and it might have been the case that Alexandre avoided Conrad, thus confirming for Conrad the hostility of the Delcommune brothers towards him. Conrad's description of the manager's uncle could be based upon Alexandre's physical appearance, though with a malicious exaggeration of certain characteristics: 'he resembled a butcher in a poor neighbourhood, and his eyes had a look of sleepy cunning. He carried his fat paunch with ostentation on his short legs' (p. 87). (See Plate 6: Alexandre Delcommune is in the centre of the photograph.)

Jean-Aubry writes: 'On October 19th he [Conrad] decided to abandon everything, and return to Europe',[11] presumably basing this on what was said in a letter from Tadeusz Bobrowski to Conrad: 'On the 24th inst., I received your letter of the 19th October from Kinchassa informing me of the unfortunate outcome of your expedition to the Congo, and also of your return to Europe.'[12] This does not necessarily mean that Conrad made his decision on the 19th and/or returned to Europe on that day, but only that he communicated his intentions to his uncle on that day. The departure of the Katanga expedition without him was no doubt decisive, since he could write of his intentions so firmly two days after its departure.

There were some difficulties in leaving the Congo, as Conrad was aware. 'But what I regret most of all is having bound myself for three years', he wrote to his aunt,[13] and his uncle had reminded him that 'by breaking your agreement you would expose yourself to considerable financial loss, and you certainly lay yourself open to an accusation of irresponsibility which may be harmful to your future career'.[14] These were weighty considerations, and no doubt Conrad was fully aware of how they increased the disagreeableness of his position. Writing to his aunt, he puts forward the two possible ways in which he might leave the Congo without being forced to break the contract himself: 'Either those in authority will pick a German quarrel with me to ship me home...or another attack of dysentery will send me back to Europe.'[15] It would seem that the latter possibility came to pass and Conrad suffered another attack of dysentery between 26 September and 19 October which provided a legal way out of his contract. The *Biographie Coloniale Belge* records of him: 'Peu après son retour à Kinshasa, une violente atteinte de dysenterie devait justifier son rapatriement sur certificat médical.'[16]

Of Conrad's down-river journey, then, only the death of Klein and the arrival of the Delcommune exploring expedition found their way as recognisable incidents into *Heart of Darkness*, and then the second incident was transferred to Marlow's up-river journey.

Little has been known of Conrad's return journey from Kinchassa to Boma. It does appear that the short journey from Kinchassa to Leopoldville was made by native canoe. Conrad recalls this part of the journey in *A Personal Record*:

I call to mind, for instance, a specially awkward turn of the Congo between Kinchassa and Leopoldville—more particularly when one had to take it at night in a big canoe with only half the proper number of paddlers. I failed in being the second white man on record drowned at that interesting spot through the upsetting of a canoe. The first was a young Belgian officer, but the accident happened some months before my time, and he, too, I believe, was going home; not perhaps quite so ill as myself—but still he was going home. I got round the turn more or less alive, though I was too sick to care whether I did or not (p. 14).

The awkward turn of the Congo Conrad is referring to was Kallina Point, named after the man who drowned there.[17]

Apart from this we have little information except that Conrad was ill and that he 'was at Matadi on December 4'.[18] If Conrad left Kinchassa on 19 October, then it took him six weeks to reach the Atlantic coast, a much longer time than he took on the upward journey which lasted thirty-five days. But I have found confirmation in extracts from Duhst's diary, quoted by Lütken, that Conrad *was* extremely ill on the caravan trail, and this must have delayed him. Duhst first mentions Conrad on 23 October at Fumemba, the town called Mfumu Mbe in Conrad's Congo diary: 'Camped in a negro town, which is called Fumemba. I am in company with an English captain Conrad from the Kinchassa Company: he is continually sick with dysentery and fever.'[19] Four days later on 27 October, Duhst records: 'Marched from 6 morning until 9, when we ate breakfast. We are just on the spot where Lieutenant Puttervelle died and I was ill with fever. Here the ways part, and I took leave of Captain Conrad, who is going to Manyanga and Isangila, and from there to Vivi. Went on alone; camped by a river (Mpjucka).'[20] Duhst arrived at Boma on 10 November, and he wrote: 'Have not seen Captain Conrad since I left him in Manyanga.' Duhst sailed for Europe on 17 November, and this is his last reference to Conrad. It is possible that Conrad stayed at Manyanga to recuperate, as he did on the upward journey. There can be no doubt at all that Conrad's illness was at its most severe during this last journey over the caravan trail. Mrs Conrad recalls early in her account of Conrad: 'I had heard from several of his friends how nearly he had died from dysentery while being carried to the coast when he left the Congo.'[21] It must be this period of sickness that Conrad is reflecting in Marlow's 'And...they very nearly buried me...I have wrestled with death.'

It is not known on which vessel Conrad left Matadi for Europe, but if he took the first available vessel after arriving at Matadi on 4 December, then it is likely he travelled either on the *Adolph Woerman* or in the *Lualaba*. The *Mouvement Géographique* 1891 reports the arrival of both of these vessels at Boma in December: 'Le steamer allemand *Adolph Woerman*, parti de Flessingue le 3 novembre, est arrivé à Boma le 8 décembre, et le steamer anglais *Lualaba* parti d'Anvers le 18 novembre, est arrivé à Boma le 14 décembre' (p. 8). Since no passenger lists have survived, there is no way of ascertaining which of these Conrad sailed in.

Marlow returns to the 'sepulchral city' (Brussels) sick, resentful, and bitter. He is nursed by his aunt, is visited by a representative of the trading company, by Kurtz's cousin, and by a journalist, all anxious to obtain some of the papers Marlow brought from Kurtz in the heart of darkness. Eventually, he visits Kurtz's Intended, to return to her her portrait and letters and tell her of Kurtz's last words. Such activities on the part of Marlow are a fitting conclusion to his experience. Conrad's were, so far as one can discover, not the same.

Certainly Conrad spent two days in Brussels. His aunt refers in a letter of 4 February to 'Les deux journées que je vous ai vu ont été bonnes; depuis, je broie du noir.'[22] And it is very possible that Marlow's feelings as to the sepulchral city were those of the sick Conrad in Brussels. But Conrad could not have been nursed for any significant period by his aunt, and he certainly did not visit Klein's Intended in Brussels since Klein was born and had lived in Paris. Marlow's reference to the death of Kurtz's mother: 'His mother had died lately, watched over, as I was told, by his Intended' (p. 152) is not based on the true facts. Klein's mother was very much alive and in a recent letter from Busira-Lomami (successors to the original employers of Conrad in the Congo) the director writes: 'Au sujet de Mr. Georges A. Klein, nos archives sont encore plus pauvres. Nous retrouvons simplement une lettre dans laquelle est annoncé l'envoi, par Madame Klein mère, d'une couronne destinée à la tombe de son fils et expédiée à l'adresse du

Révérend Georges Grenfeld [*sic*], missionaire à Bolobo' (letter dated 20 November 1967).

Conrad returned to London on leaving Brussels, and wrote to his aunt from there on, so far as can be ascertained, Sunday 1 February, saying that his doctor 'to commence with put me to bed—on account of my legs...I am a bit anemic but organically sound.'[23] We learn more of his condition at this time from a letter from his uncle, who refers to a letter of Conrad's written during his first fortnight in England (4–16 February) in which Conrad obviously complains of his swollen legs and the thinness of his hair. Conrad's friend G. F. W. Hope comments in an unpublished manuscript:

when he [Conrad] arrived he looked half dead with fever, so Krieger, who knew the Doctor at the German Hospital at Dalston, got him in there, and he and I used to go to see him frequently. The Nurse said she thought he would die, but he pulled round, and in a few weeks was able to go to his rooms, Gillingham Street, near Victoria Station.[24]

If by 'arrived' here, Hope means arrived in London from the Congo, he cannot be recalling events accurately, for on 8 February Conrad wrote to his aunt that he felt stronger and went out a little, and was hoping to go to Antwerp the following week. And in a letter of 17 February he tells her he has been in Scotland. It is not until 27 February that he writes to her from hospital telling her he has 'Rheumatism in left leg and neuralgia in right arm'. Jean-Aubry tells us that Conrad spent 'the greater part of February and the whole of March [1891] in the German Hospital in London',[25] but the effects of the Congo upon Conrad were life-long. The influence of the experience, particularly the severe sickness and the sense of failure and frustration which his Congo trip must have engendered, are surely accurately reflected in Marlow's feelings of estrangement from the human race when, on his return, he 'tottered about the streets...grinning bitterly at perfectly respectable persons'.

The Journey Down-River

And so Conrad's disastrous journey to the Congo ended with, in its personal details, nothing of a sombre resonance, and apparently without any magnificently malevolent Kurtz-like figure having been encountered. Kurtz can, of course, be viewed as a symbolic representation of the evil of that particular exploitation and its effects on man's soul. I think, however, that there was another person in the Congo at that time who did not impinge upon Conrad personally and who was certainly not a Kurtz in his ending, but from whom Conrad took many characteristics.

II

KURTZ

In *Heart of Darkness* the meeting with Kurtz is the central point of tension and meaning: 'I went up that river to...where I met the poor chap. It was the farthest point of navigation and the culminating point of my experience.' Gradually, Marlow's purpose of taking a steamboat up-river is transmuted into a search for the man he has heard so much about. Since Georges Antoine Klein was certainly not the inspiration for Kurtz's more sensational qualities, it can be concluded that Marlow's growing interest in Kurtz, to the point where to meet him becomes Marlow's primary aim, cannot reflect an aspect of Conrad's journey. Yet there is a strong sense in the story that, given its autobiographical basis, someone like Kurtz probably existed and somehow was part of the design Conrad saw being woven in the area.

In support of this thesis is the method by which Kurtz is introduced—by means of the gossip of the various characters Marlow encounters. This is, of course, an excellent literary technique which engages and raises the reader's interest, at once creating suspense, plot and a basic irony, but it is also a process of acquaintanceship existing in real life. It is possible, then, that Conrad found the inspiration for Kurtz while he was in the Congo, and therefore that someone approximating to Kurtz was in the area then, someone who was sufficiently noticeable to be talked of in such a way.

If we ignore for the moment Kurtz's final involvement with the powers of darkness, the attributes and characteristics he is allotted are not at all improbable ones in that situation, although it might be felt that, taken together, such qualities add up to an unusual being. For Kurtz is outstanding on many levels—as a commercial agent, as a man of artistic and creative merit, and as a man of lofty moral principles which lift him above the level of the common trader.

Marlow hears of him first as a trader from the company's chief accountant:

One day he remarked, without lifting his head, 'In the interior you will no doubt meet Mr. Kurtz.' On my asking who Mr. Kurtz was, he said he was a first-class agent; and seeing my disappointment at this information, he added slowly, laying down his pen, 'He is a very remarkable person.' Further questions elicited from him that Mr. Kurtz was at present in charge of a trading post, a very important one, in the true ivory-country, at 'the bottom of there. Sends in as much ivory as all the others put together' (p. 69).

The manager at the Central Station assures Marlow that 'Mr. Kurtz was the best agent they had, an exceptional man, of the greatest importance to the Company'.

It is while Marlow is travelling up-river towards Kurtz and his station that he thinks over his knowledge of Kurtz: 'Hadn't I been told in all the tones of jealousy and admiration that he had collected, bartered, swindled, or stolen more ivory than all the other agents together?' (p. 113). And at the Inner Station there is the huge collection of ivory:

Ivory? I should think so. Heaps of it, stacks of it. The old mud shanty was bursting with it. You would think there was not a single tusk left either above or below the ground in the whole country. 'Mostly fossil', the manager had remarked, disparagingly. It was no more fossil than I am; but they call it fossil when it is dug up. It appears these niggers do bury the tusks sometimes—but evidently they couldn't bury this parcel deep enough to save the gifted Mr. Kurtz from his fate. We filled the steamboat with it, and had to pile a lot on the deck (pp. 115–16).

Kurtz, moreover, who is 'remarkable' and 'exceptional', is talked of by everyone, is expected to go far—'Oh, he will go far, very far...He will be a somebody in the Administration before long. They, above—the Council in Europe, you know—mean him to be' (p. 70)—and has unusual influence with the Council in Europe: 'He has asked the Administration to be sent there [the Inner Station] with the idea of showing what he could do; and I was instructed accordingly. Look at the influence that man must have. Is it not frightful?' (p. 89)

He is also a man of wide gifts. A painting of his hangs in the brick-maker's hut, and of 'all his gifts the one that stood out pre-eminently, that carried with it a sense of real presence, was his ability to talk, his words—the gift of expression'. Proof of this lies in his report for 'the International Society for the Suppression of Savage Customs': 'It was eloquent, vibrating with eloquence, but too high-strung I think. Seventeen pages of close writing he had found time for' (p. 117). And when he talked all night to the Harlequin, 'The night did not seem to last an hour' (p. 127). Moreover, he is an explorer: 'he had discovered lots of villages, a lake too' (p. 128).

And as if this were not enough, Kurtz is 'an emissary of pity, and science, and progress' (p. 79), 'a gifted creature', a man of high beliefs and principles, as his report shows:

But it was a beautiful piece of writing. The opening paragraph, however, in the light of later information, strikes me now as ominous. He began with the argument that we whites, from the point of development we had arrived at, 'must necessarily appear to them [savages] in the nature of supernatural beings—we approach them with the might as of a deity', and so on, and so on. 'By the simple exercise of our will we can exert a power for good practically unbounded', etc. etc. From that point he soared and took me with him. The peroration was magnificent, though difficult to remember, you know. It gave me the notion of an exotic Immensity ruled by an august Benevolence. It made me tingle with enthusiasm (p. 118).

Kurtz is of 'the new gang—the gang of virtue', as opposed to the common run of agents. He has 'higher intelligence, wider sympathies, a singleness of purpose' which are needed 'for the guidance of the cause intrusted to us by Europe' (p. 79).

If a man even approximating to Kurtz in these attributes existed in the Congo during 1890, Conrad must surely have heard of him. And there was such a man. Klein was, as we know, working under the orders of a much more important agent. This man was Arthur Eugene Constant Hodister, and his character, charisma and success, as I have been able to re-discover them, suggest that he was at least in part the inspiration for Kurtz (See photograph of Hodister, Plate 1 *b*). Hodister was a highly successful commercial agent and explorer, a man of wide abilities, and a man of principles who was definitely on the side of virtue. He had, moreover, influential friends in Europe, and he did go far in terms of his career.

I do not think that Conrad ever met Hodister, but I believe that he heard of him, through gossip and hearsay, in much the way he records Marlow's hearing of Kurtz and, just as Kurtz became a topic of conversation at the Company Station and then especially at the Central Station, it is very likely that Conrad heard Hodister talked of at Matadi, but that such references to him increased enormously once he reached Kinchassa.

*

Hodister had joined the Société du Haut-Congo in 1889, though he had been engaged by the Comité d'Études du Haut-Congo in 1883, and was a member of the Sanford exploring expedition in 1886. When Conrad was in the Congo, Hodister was an important agent 'in the interior', 'the true ivory-country'. According to the *Biographie Coloniale Belge*, Hodister 'fut nommé chef de district des Bangalas le 1er mai 1889'.[1] And we know from the *Mouvement Géographique* that he had seven agents under his orders—at the Falls station and at Bangala, at Mobeka, Gongo and Oupoto in the Mongala area,[2] and on the small steamer, the *General Sanford*.

References to Hodister during the 1890–1 period show that he was indeed an energetic collector of ivory, and the comments about him in Grenfell's letters and diary suggest that his activities were a source of interest to people in the area. On 16 February Hodister's steamer, the *General Sanford*, was reported to have arrived in Bangala from Mobeka on the Mongala with a cargo of ivory,[3] and Grenfell noted in his diary: 'Hodister was at Bangala—He came down 2 days ago with 5 tons of ivory in the *General Sanford*. Spent nearly 2 days in digging his way across the bar of the Mongala river, himself often working up to his waist in water. He reports fine country and people in the upper Mongala' (19 February 1890).

On 5 April the *General Sanford* returned again from Mobeka, with a cargo of ivory. According to the *Mouvement Géographique*, Hodister was off again to Mongala on 8 April returning on 10 June. Grenfell records:

At Bangala on our return there on the 11th [June 1890] we found Mr. Hodister had come down the Mongala on previous day—He had had a hard rough time of it [if] one may judge from his worn appearance, so different from that of February last. He made an interesting journey of 45 hrs in canoe after 92 hours in str. Baert [Captain] furthest being 52 hours by str.[4] It thus appears that H. has been more than twice as far...He brought down a good piece of ivory say 5 tons—says people fought him taking him to be an Arab, and he will wear an old fez, and a wrapper he allowed he did not look very much better (14 June 1890).

This meeting with Hodister was of such interest that Grenfell referred to it not only in his diary, but also in two letters written on the same day, 23rd June 1890—one to his friend Antoine Greshoff, manager of the Dutch house, then on leave, and the other to the important American official and great friend of Leopold II, General Sanford himself. The slight difference of attitude to Hodister's achievement that exists in the two letters is interesting, reflecting, no doubt, the divided opinion of Hodister that existed on the Congo according to whom it was one supported in terms of trading interests. To Greshoff he wrote: 'Just as we were coming back (we did not get further than halfway up the Itumbiri, no chop)[5] we met Mr. Hodister on his return from the Mongala—he had evidently had a hard time of it for he looked very different from what he was when I saw him Feb. last. *He seemed satisfied with the ivory tho' much of it appeared to me to be very old'* [my italics] (—cf. the manager in *Heart of Darkness*: 'I don't deny there is a remarkable quantity of ivory—mostly fossil'). But on the same day, Grenfell wrote to General Sanford:

We arrived at Bangala a few hours after Mr. Hodister after his Mongala trip. He reports having made a journey of 92 hours by steamer and 45 by canoe. He has had great obstacles to surmount and his success speaks well both of his pluck and endurance. One may judge from appearances, he has suffered very considerably and is very different from what he was when I saw him February. The loss of nearly all his personal belongings, the scarcity of [indecipherable but probably 'food'] absolute want at times, made the latter portion [of his] journey especially trying. *He reports having been mistaken for an arab, and as he says seeing that he was reduced to an native [dress?] the mistake was not very surprising. He brought down a splendid load of ivory,* and seems abundantly [paid?] thereby for all the hardships of the journey [my italics].

These exploits of Hodister, which Grenfell finds interesting enough to write about, were obviously being discussed in the area at the time when Conrad arrived there, and they show that he was a well-known and successful collector of ivory, who yet aroused a dichotomy of response among others in the area.

But his expeditions are interesting for another reason than his successful collecting of ivory. Reporting on Hodister's expedition in April, the *Mouvement Géographique*, 17 August 1890, refers to it as 'une nouvelle exploration de la Mongalla et de son principal affluent l'Eloba'.[6] And Grenfell's statements: 'He reports fine country and people on the upper Mongala', 'It thus appears that H[odister] has been more than twice as far [up the Mongala as Captain Baert, the first explorer of the area]', point to the fact that Hodister was not simply collecting ivory, but was carrying out exploring expeditions of a difficult and hazardous kind up the Mongala in a territory that was little known. Albert Chapaux writes:

Le cours de la Mongalla, qui avait déjà été exploré par le lieutenant Baert en 1886, fut l'objet de deux voyages de M. Hodister, agent de la Compagnie du Haut-Congo. Dans le second de ces voyages, M. Hodister remonta cette rivière jusqu'au point où ses branches supérieures se réunissent, puis il reconnut la rivière Monai, la plus importante de ces branches.[7]

And he shows also that Hodister in the course of his explorations discovered a lake: 'Hodister découvrit une large expansion de la rivière, de deux kilomètres de long sur six de large, et à quelques heures de navigation en amont, un second pool de moindre étendue: il remarqua pour la première fois des observatoires aériens, que les indigènes de ces parages établissent sur les arbres à proximité de la rivière.'[8] It will be remembered that Kurtz also went on exploring expeditions and had discovered a lake: '"Very often coming to this station, I had to wait days and days before he would turn up", he said...."What was he doing? exploring or what?" I asked. "Oh, yes, of course"; he had discovered lots of villages, a lake too...but mostly his expeditions had been for ivory' (pp. 127-8). And like Kurtz, Hodister was on terms of friendship and trust with the natives. Chapaux reports: 'il fit ce voyage en compagnie d'un chef de la Haute-Mongalla, qui se montra fort dévoué et lui rendit de grands services',[9]

Au village du N'guma, tous les indigènes s'enfuient à son approche; il réussit à les ramener, grâce à Itiaka, le chef, qui, 'très connu et très respecté, parvient à faire venir une petite pirogue montée par un homme, pour le prendre et le conduire, non pas à terre, puisqu'il n'y en a pas, toutes les berges étant inondées, mais sur une plate-forme, où va se tenir le palabre. Sur cette plate-forme il est bientôt entouré; je vois des gens qui glissent du plancher de leur case dans leur minuscule batelet et vont le rejoindre. Itiaka parle; il raconte mon premier voyage, mes achats, mes présents; il explique que, contrairement à ce que fait Mobeka, je n'ai rien pris sans payer, que je n'ai emmené ni enlevé personne; puis il explique, avec force gestes, le bateau, la machine, son mouvement, il en imite le bruit et tout cela avec de telles gesticulations et un tel brio que, quoique me trouvant à 200 mètres de là, je comprends tout ce qu'il veut dire.'

Cette harangue eut le meilleur effet: plus loin, 'ils fuient dans leur petit canot léger, puis, après notre passage, nous suivent de loin, en coupant au plus court entre les îles d'herbes. Ils nous jettent généralement une poule au vol, dans chaque village; à cet effet, un canot, monté par les plus hardis ou le plus agile, s'avance à une quinzaine de mètres, nous lance la poule, qui, plutôt que de s'abattre dans l'eau, vient au bateau; aussitôt le donateur fuit à toute vitesse, sans que je puisse rien lui rendre en retour de sa largesse.'[10]

Herbert Ward, himself a Congo explorer, wrote: 'Such confidence had Hodister inspired among these people that they entrusted their women to his care during their absence on the war expedition against Oupoto; and I found numbers of the female relatives of the departed warriors congregated around his station, implicitly believing in his powers to defend them.'[11] From these examples of Hodister's relationship with the natives it is possible to draw the conclusion that Kurtz's similar relationship was very probably based by Conrad on what he had heard of Hodister. 'His ascendancy was extraordinary. The camps of these people surrounded the place, and the chiefs came every day to see him'[12] (p. 131).

Hodister was a man of great energy, enterprise and courage, perhaps a kind of 'universal genius'. Apart from his expeditions, his reports, his ivory collection, and his charts of the shipping at Bangala, 'il se livra à des observations météorologiques très précises, les premières qui aient été faites dans le Haut-Congo'.[13]

Finally, Hodister was undoubtedly a man of high principle

—one of the 'gang of virtue', who saw himself as having a mission above that of mere commercial enterprise, with a suggestion of the important influence of the benevolent white man over the natives, 'an august Benevolence' ruling 'an exotic Immensity'. This 'virtue' of Kurtz is revealed to Marlow through Kurtz's report for the future guidance of the International Society for the Suppression of Savage Customs. His interest in such suppression derives from his intimate knowledge of the savage customs, which in his case had led to actual involvement. Hodister was also in favour of suppressing savage customs and although there was no International Society for the Suppression of Savage Customs there was the Société Antiesclavagiste de Belgique, with which Hodister was associated and which published this about him in its journal, *Mouvement Antiesclavagiste*, August 1892:

Le coup était d'autant plus facile à faire contre Hodister que ses habitudes étaient connues de tous. Il s'en remettait surtout, en bon chrétien qu'il est, à la volonté de Dieu; il n'avait guère d'autres armes avec lui que des fusils de chasse. C'est avec ce même bagage qu'en 1890 il avait fait sa remarquable exploration de la Mongalla; il n'en avait pas davantage quand, la même année, il explora, le premier, les contrées qui séparent le Lomami du Congo, allant par terre de Bena-Kamba à Riba-Riba et Nyangwé, au travers d'un pays encore inconnu à cette époque et tristement célèbre aujourd'hui (p. 238).

Hodister was against slavery and barbaric customs, his hatred coming from a knowledge of them which approximates to Kurtz's. And he appears to have been present 'at certain midnight dances ending with unspeakable rites'. The event which first turned Hodister against such customs was as follows:

Le roi de Massabé était Tyabo, un Noir qui savait lire et écrire, parlait le portugais et l'anglais, s'habillait et se nourrissait à l'européenne et depuis douze ou treize ans était employé par le gérant d'une factorerie hollandaise établie en cet endroit. Cependant, Tyabo était un potentat cruel envers ses sujets, faisant brûler vifs ses esclaves s'ils tentaient de s'enfuir, faisant mettre à mort pour une vétille ses épouses. Hodister assista aux noces de Tyabo avec sa quinzième femme, une toute jeune fille. De même, il fut témoin de sacrifices humains ordonnés par le chef dans des cérémonies funéraires. Tout cela l'impressionna beaucoup et tout son séjour en Afrique il essaya de mettre fin à ces coutumes sauvages, par son action directe et sa force de persuasion.[14]

And though he did not write a report on this subject, he did produce a paper for the Société Belge des Ingénieurs et Industriels on the evening of the opening of the Congrès Antiesclavagiste and this paper, originally entitled 'A propos d'esclavage', was published in the *Mouvement Géographique*, 4 October 1891, with the title 'Laissez les Nègres Tranquilles'. In it, Hodister describes in detail a slaving raid made by one tribe on another. The following extract will give an indication of its subject matter and style:

Il est quatre heures du matin; un grand calme règne; on n'entend que le cri doux et mélancolique de la chouette d'Afrique; les sentinelles se sont retirées ou sommeillent, accroupies; les cases sont fermées, tout dort, tout repose, dans une sécurité absolue. Tout à coup un coup de feu, puis des cris terrifiants éclatent, déchirant ce grand silence, suivis par une fusillade qui semble partir de tous côtés, trouant les cases de paille; les canotiers ont fait feu; ils se sont élancés, laissant les pirogues à la garde des femmes, attaquant les villages par devant, les N'Gombés par derrière, les indigènes, brusquement arrachés au sommeil, terrifiés, se jettent hors des cases; ils sont affolés; oubliant tout, femmes, enfants, la première pensée est de fuir, de se précipiter vers le bois. L'épouvante est au comble: des coups de feu, des cris horribles retentissent, se mêlant aux cris d'épouvante des femmes et des enfants, puis le bruit étouffé d'une lutte corps à corps, un corps qui tombe, une plainte sourde, des cris aigus, déchirants; la terre tremble, piétinée par des sentinelles, des combattants et des fuyards. Bientôt une étincelle dans la nuit noire, un bruit sec, pétillant: c'est une case isolée que l'on a allumée pour mieux voir, sans cependant incendier le village; il faut d'abord piller. Cependant, quelques hommes ont sauté sur leurs armes, et la résistance s'organise sur quelques points. Dix villages composés d'une rue, bâtis à la suite les uns des autres, sont ainsi attaqués à la fois; mais bientôt, accablés par le nombre, les habitants succombent. Au bruit de la fusillade succèdent les cris de désespoir des prisonnières, les cris des blessés et des mourants. L'horizon blanchit, le soleil paraît brusquement et vient éclairer ce champ de carnage et de désolation; alors on achève les blessés, on ligotte solidement les prisonniers, et le pillage commence; chaque case est visitée: utensiles, outils, provisions, ivoire, tout est enlevé et soigneusement transporté dans les canots des vaincus, qui ainsi serviront à transporter leurs propres dépouilles; les cases ont été vidées; l'incendie fait son œuvre; une ligne de feu s'allume; toutes les constructions légères flambent, et là où la veille on voyait de jolis villages, entourés de la plantation comme d'un cadre de verdure, une population gaie et heureuse, il n'y a plus qu'une grande tache noire vide; des hommes, des femmes, des enfants attachés pêle-mêle, des cadavres jonchant la terre, des flaques de sang, dégageant une odeur âcre, épouvantable, et les assassins, horribles sous leur peinture de guerre qui a coulé dans la lutte, sous la sueur et le sang.

Ah! quel tableau, qui donc pourra en dire l'horreur? Combien de fois mon cœur n'a-t-il pas saigné en arrivant sur des lieux saccagés, brûlés, que j'avais vus quelques semaines auparavant si florissants. La haine, la mort, la dévastation, les plus mauvais sentiments humains déchaînés ont comme contraste une nature splendide, un soleil éblouissant, versant indifférent sa lumière et sa chaleur au milieu d'un pays éternellement souriant.

The flamboyance of the style here reminds us of the eloquence of Kurtz, but there is a further connection. Hodister admits in this paper to a close knowledge of these customs, an intimacy almost amounting to involvement: 'J'ai assisté — impuissant, hélas! à l'empêcher — au départ de l'expédition d'une tribu importante', and his exclamation: 'Ah! quel tableau, qui donc pourra en dire l'horreur?' is perhaps reflected in Kurtz's 'The horror!'[15]

Hodister's eloquence reveals itself also in his constant writing of reports, and he had an outlet where these were concerned which brought him and his achievements to the attention of others. His great admirer was A. J. Wauters who, as chief editor of the *Mouvement Géographique*, published many of Hodister's reports. Hodister sent him a detailed account of the wreck of the *Ville de Bruxelles* with the results of his own examination of the steamer, though he could not have had any official connection with it. Hodister's account of his Mongala exploration was published in full detail, and his long report of his Lomami and Lualaba exploration was published on the front page with an introduction by Wauters, while accounts of other important journeys were published without comment.[16]

*

Conrad must have heard through the gossip of the people he encountered something of these exploits of Hodister, and it is possible also that he found himself, quite unexpectedly, linked with Hodister. In *Heart of Darkness* jealousy and dislike of the agent Kurtz is common to the manager of the Central Station and his uncle, the leader of the Eldorado Exploring Expedition. And the uncle suggests that he has done his best to weaken the influence this dangerous man has in Europe: 'The danger is in Europe; but there before I left I took care to...' It is possible that Conrad is here reflecting the actual state of feeling that existed between Camille Delcommune, manager at Kinchassa, and his elder brother, Alexandre, leader of the Katanga exploring expedition and Hodister.

Rivalry between Camille Delcommune and Hodister was very likely since Hodister had been so successful as an agent, got his exploits into print so often, and had great influence in Europe. Apart from Wauters, Hodister must have known General Sanford well, and Thys also thought highly of him: 'Hodister était très apprécié par ses chefs et ses compagnons. Thys le jugeait un homme d'une grande compétence et d'un jugement sûr. Wauters, Directeur du *Mouvement Géographique*, écrit qu'il était adoré de ses hommes.'[17] Alexandre Delcommune had, at this point particularly, an even stronger reason for objecting to Hodister. His exploring expedition had been in the process of being organised for a long time, and its stated aim was to explore the Lomami. But Hodister had just stolen Delcommune's thunder by his own exploration of this area, an exploration which had been given the maximum publicity in the *Mouvement Géographique*. At that particular time, Hodister might well have appeared as a rival to each of the Delcommune brothers—as a trader to one, and as an explorer to the other.

Conrad's final frustrating contact with the Delcommunes and society generally at Kinchassa, just before he took his decision to return to Europe, must have been one in which the exploits and reputation of Hodister were intimately entangled. For the brick-maker at the Central Station specifically links Kurtz with Marlow: 'You are of the new gang—the gang of virtue. The same people who sent him specially also recommended you...Light dawned upon me. My aunt's influential acquaintances were producing an unexpected effect upon that young man.' And this sharing of influential acquaintances was in fact true of Conrad and Hodister. A. J. Wauters, one of Hodister's patrons in Europe, was also a good friend of Madame Poradowska, Conrad's aunt, and no doubt, as a result of the influence of his aunt, Wauters could be considered Conrad's patron also. While still at sea *en route* for the Congo, Conrad was writing to his aunt: 'When you get back to Brussels I should like you to let me know whether any ships are being built, so that I can put in my request. You will be able to learn about this through M. Wauters.'[18]

I think it is very likely that Camille Delcommune, already jealous of Hodister's success and his influential friends in Europe, would be determined from the beginning to dislike Conrad, as a protégé of the same men, to give him as little encouragement as possible, and certainly to frustrate any hopes Conrad might have been entertaining especially since they depended on promises made by men in Europe who were supporting Hodister. News of Hodister's explorations of the Lualaba and Lomami must have intensified his attitude.

If Conrad did not actually meet Hodister, he came close to it, and if he did not go up river to rescue Hodister, as Marlow did Kurtz, he was on the river at the same time. Moreover, this knowledge of Hodister and his reputation came just prior to Hodister's moment of greatest fame and when his exploits must have been the talk of the river. Hodister's activities during the few months Conrad was in the Congo demonstrate his amazing energy and courage and also show him preparing for his greatest triumph.

After his exploring and ivory-collecting expeditions in the Mongala area, Hodister took the *General Sanford* down-river to Kinchassa, presumably bringing down the large amount of ivory he had collected. The shipping movements for Bangala show that he arrived back there from Leopoldville on 11 July 1890, so that he must have been in the Leopoldville/Kinchassa area at the end of June, beginning of July. Conrad arrived at Kinchassa on 2 August, and may have seen Hodister's collection of ivory there and must certainly have heard of his visit. Something of this activity of Hodister would appear to be reflected in the conversation Marlow overhears between the manager and his uncle:

'Anything since then?' asked the other [the manager's uncle] hoarsely. 'Ivory', jerked the nephew; 'lots of it—prime sort–lots—most annoying, from him'...'How did that ivory come all this way?'...The other explained that it had come with a fleet of canoes...Kurtz had apparently intended to return himself...but after coming three hundred miles, had suddenly decided to go back, which he started to do alone in a small dugout with four paddlers, leaving the half-caste to continue down the river with the ivory. The two fellows there seemed astounded at anybody attempting such a thing. They were at a loss for an adequate motive. As to me, I seemed to see Kurtz for the first time. It was a distinct glimpse: the dugout, four paddling savages, and the lone white man turning his back suddenly on the headquarters...setting his face towards the depths of the wilderness, towards his empty and desolate station. I did not know the motive (pp. 89–90).

Conrad may very well have heard Hodister's latest consignment of ivory discussed in such terms at Kinchassa.

Hodister, on his up-river journey, went on to Bangala where he stayed six days, leaving again on 17 July for Stanley Falls. In this part of the journey he passed the wrecked *Ville de Bruxelles*, which he examined and reported on. Conrad, in the *Roi des Belges*, followed Hodister up-river from Kinchassa on 4 August, reaching Bangala on 19 August and Stanley Falls on 1 September. But he would not have found Hodister there, though it is possible that people had told him on the journey that Hodister would be at the Falls station, for Hodister went on a further expedition, his exploration of the Lomami and the Lualaba rivers. He reached Bena-Kamba on 16 August and spent from then until 24 September exploring the region between Bena-Kamba and Riba-Riba (see map facing p. 9, above). He then returned down-river reaching Bangala again on 13 October where he wrote the detailed account of his explorations, dated 16 October, which appeared in *Mouvement Géographique*, 1890, p. 119. He was at this time following Conrad down-river, Conrad having left Stanley Falls on 6 September and reaching Kinchassa on 24 September. The *Mouvement Géographique*, 22 March 1891, shows that Hodister left Bangala on 2 December, reaching Boma on 2 January—'[il] a fait son voyage...d'une façon particulièrement rapide' as the *Mouvement Géographique* comments, arriving at Kinchassa on 17 December. He was then, like Conrad, on his way to Europe.

In contrast to Conrad's journey from Leopoldville to Matadi from 19 October to 4 December, Hodister did the distance from the Pool to Vivi in 12 days, passing through Manyanga and Isanghila. It would seem likely that Conrad just missed meeting him at the exit port of Boma. And so, although Conrad did not go up-river to rescue Hodister, and almost certainly never met him, he must have known a good deal about him and the effect his exploits were having on other agents, and he possibly found himself tenuously associated with him. It is likely therefore that when he came to write *Heart of Darkness*, he recalled Hodister, his later successes, and his tragic end, and saw him as an appropriate source for Kurtz.

What I have outlined to this point about Hodister was all Conrad could have known about him at that time, but his later exploits went even further, proving him to be indeed one of 'the gang of virtue', and fulfilling the brick-maker's prophecy regarding Kurtz, 'To-day he is chief of the best station, next year he will be assistant-manager, two years more and...but I daresay you know what he will be in two years' time.' The implication is that Kurtz will then be manager, but Hodister's promotion took him beyond this.

*

On his return to Europe, Hodister was appointed director of the Syndicat Commercial du Katanga which was again to put him firmly on the side of virtue. The Syndicat was planning an expedition the purpose of which was to establish trading posts on the Lomami and Lualaba, right in the Arab country where Tippo Tib and other Arab leaders held sway. This had been the object of his earlier exploration of the area while Conrad was at Stanley Falls. But he was also to try to rid the area of slavery by his trading methods, and by helping to establish posts of the Société Antiesclavagiste de Belgique. The *Biographie Coloniale Belge* entry on Hodister describes the next stage of his success:

Reçu à Bruxelles par le Conseil d'administration de la SAB, il lui exposa son projet de fonder une société destinée à exploiter commerciale-ment la région comprise entre le Lualaba et le Lomami. Son but était d'amener les Arabes à vendre leurs produits à cette société, plutôt que d'organiser des caravanes vers la côte. On servirait ainsi, disait-il, à la fois le commerce et la cause antiesclavagiste, en supprimant les razzias d'esclaves destinés à transporter les produits à la côte. Le Conseil, se ralliant à ses vues, nomma Hodister directeur de la nouvelle société formée sous le nom de 'Syndicat commercial du Katanga'.[19]

On his departure from Antwerp on this new and very important mission, he received the special distinction in the *Congo Illustré*—edited by A. J. Wauters who was also secretary of the new commercial syndicate—of having his profile presented. The account is interesting as revealing Conrad's major source for 'Mistah' Kurtz:

Nul mieux que le voyageur dont nous publions ci-contre la grave physionomie, n'était à même de prendre la direction d'une telle affaire, qui exige à la fois de l'expérience et du tact, du calme et des relations d'amitié...

L'année dernière, quelques mois avant son départ d'Europe, il annonça aux Arabes du Lualaba sa prochaine arrivée, et M. Ectors, un agent de la Société antiesclavagiste, revenu hier de la province arabe, nous disait que partout Hodister était attendu, que des approvisionnements d'ivoire avaient été préparés en vue d'affaires importantes à conclure avec lui, qu'en bien des endroits des maisons avaient été bâties à son intention, que partout la plus cordiale, la plus hospitalière des réceptions l'attendait.

On peut être certain que rien ne sera négligé par l'explorateur pour rendre son labeur également utile aux intérêts du commerce, à ceux de la civilisation et à ceux de l'Etat. Un séjour d'un tel homme, sérieux, habile, actif, compétent, et prudent, dans les centres arabes du haut Congo fera plus, nous en sommes certains, pour introduire l'influence bienfaisante de l'Europe dans ces milieux lointains, que toutes les expéditions militaires et que toutes les missions administratives que l'on pourra y envoyer.

Ceux qui redoutent pour la tranquillité publique les effets de l'arrivée d'un tel missionnaire chez les trafiquants arabes de Nyangwe, disent combien ils ont peu la saine notion des choses d'Afrique. C'est par les efforts du commerce que celle-ci sera surtout régénérée, par ceux du commerce privé, protégé, secondé, et aussi contrôlé par les représentants du pouvoir politique.

Les journaux belges et étrangers ont bien souvent, cette semaine, imprimé le nom de l'ami auquel nous consacrons cette page. Les dernières lettres reçues de lui sont datées du Lomami, au commencement du mois d'avril dernier. Le directeur du syndicat commercial du Katanga y exprimait sa foi en l'œuvre qu'il avait entreprise.

Il racontait l'accueil amical que lui avaient fait les Arabes et celui des indigènes, parfois hostiles, du Lomami. Il écrivait que lorsque ceux-ci lui tiraient des coups de flèches il se rendait à terre, seul, sans arme, agitant des brasses d'étoffes en signe de paix et d'amitié. Il réussissait par cet acte de confiance et de bravoure à se concilier la bienveillance de ces féroces enfants des forêts, subjugués par cette preuve de courage simple, calme et héroïque.

Cet acte seul prouve que l'homme auquel nous consacrons cette notice, tout d'actualité, n'est pas un voyageur ordinaire, et dans la galerie des portraits que nous publions ici à chacune de nos éditions, celui d'Hodister devra être placé parmi ceux qui seront à la cimaise (I, 129).

The expedition of the Syndicat Commercial du Katanga did not take place until 1892, after Conrad had left the Congo, but he must have heard of the fate of Hodister and his expedition not only from his aunt but also from the English newspapers, for the expedition, after a very successful beginning, ended in disaster. It was to be described as 'the greatest of all disasters in Central Africa'.[20]

In 1891 Hodister and his group of twenty men left for the Congo, and on 10 February 1892 they sailed from Stanley Falls in the *Roi des Belges* and Hodister began establishing stations and factories on the Lomami and Lualaba. On 3 July 1892 the *Congo Illustré* referred to 'les 6 stations commerciales, qu'en compte à demi avec la société, M. Hodister fonde en ce moment sur le Lomami et le Lualaba'. Three letters from Hodister published in the *Mouvement Géographique* showed 'sa confiance en son entreprise et l'accueil absolument amical et encourageant qu'il a reçu de Rachid, le vali des Falls, et de Buana-Sefu, le sultan du Manyema'.[21]

But on 23 July 1892 the following telegram was received

in Europe from M. Hinck, agent of the Société Antiesclavagiste in the area: 'Arabes Nyangwé se sont révoltés, mission
Hodister repoussée, deux hommes tués, route Tanganika
fermée. J'arrive. Hinck.'[22] Accounts of the tragedy appeared
in *The Times* on 7 September, 3 October and 8 December
1892. Although much had been made of Hodister's good
relations with the Arabs and the natives, it was a revolt of
the Arabs which resulted in the massacre of Hodister and
his followers:

The Fate of the Hodister Expedition

Paris, Dec. 7

A letter published in the *Temps* this evening and dated Libreville,
October 15, affords circumstantial details of the disaster to the mission
of M. Hodister, organized by the Katanga Company.

M. Hodister, on the advice of Lieutenant Mikils, sent four agents—
MM. Noblesse, Touvet, Page and Doré—to establish factories at Riba
Riba and Kassongo. Lieutenant Mikils set out with them, taking four
soldiers and a black trumpeter to give the little band a sort of diplomatic air.
At Riba Riba the Lieutenant and M. Noblesse stopped, while the three
others continued their trip towards Kassongo.

The reception at Riba Riba was distinctly unpleasant. Arabs and
natives refused absolutely to recognize the Government of the Congo
State, and insisted that the flag should be hauled down. Lieutenant
Mikils wished to leave the town, but the two Europeans with him were
immediately attacked. They succeeded in getting into the bush, but
everybody was on the look out for them, and one night when M. Noblesse
was out foraging for bananas he was caught and had his head cut off.
Shortly after Lieutenant Mikils was captured and taken back to Riba
Riba, where he was brutally murdered. His head was placed at the top
of a long pole and placed by the side of that of M. Noblesse in front of
the Palace of Nserera, the chief of the tribe.

Meanwhile M. Hodister, trusting Lieutenant Mikils's assurance of
Arab friendship, had set out from Bena Kamba with three Europeans,
having spent the intervening time in establishing factories on the Lomani
at Yanga, Bena Kamba, and Lomo. Trying to parley, M. Hodister was
not listened to; he and his comrades were seized, tortured, and put to
death, and their heads were stuck on poles and their bodies eaten.

All this ghastly narrative, some details of which are too horrible for
publication, is on the authority of Lieutenant Mikils's boy slave, who is

the property of Rachid, a nephew of Tippoo Tib. His master claimed him and saved his life, and it is he who brings these details, described as having been 'investigated and verified', to Stanley Falls.

The situation on the Lomani was quite as bad. M. Pierret was assassinated at Lomo, and it was only with the greatest difficulty that M. Pauwels got back up the Congo. The Arab revolt appears to have taken very large proportions. They have from 2,000 to 3,000 Winchester, Colt, Albini, Snider and Martini rifles. 'The resources of the State', adds the *Temps*, 'in men and armament did not seem in the middle of last August at all commensurate with the situation. It is the processes adopted in collecting the ivory which have driven these people to revolt.'—Our Own Correspondent (*The Times*, 8 December 1892).

Hodister's fate was not precisely that of Kurtz, but it might be said of both men that their faith in their ability to command the 'exotic Immensity' of the Congo jungle led to their being destroyed by that same Immensity—by its inhabitants in the case of Hodister and its primitive customs in the case of Kurtz.

But certain aspects of *Heart of Darkness* appear to arise from the recriminations and inquiries that followed the Hodister disaster. The manager in the story says that as a result of Kurtz's activities 'The district is closed to us for a time', 'Mr. Kurtz's methods had ruined the district.' And it was true that the result of the Hodister massacre was a closing of the district to trade. The *Daily Graphic* of 18 October 1892 reports: 'The further prosecution of the late M. Hodister's enterprise has been temporarily abandoned, and the steamers & merchandise will be utilised by the Upper Congo Company for the benefit of the Commercial Syndicate of Katanga.' In fact, the situation was worse than is suggested here. It was some six years later that the Katanga Syndicate recovered from the blow.

And the manager's insistence in *Heart of Darkness* that Kurtz's methods had been at fault—'He did not see the time was not ripe for vigorous action...We must be cautious yet'—applies more accurately to Hodister's methods, and indeed would seem to reflect an aspect of the criticism of the expedition that came after his death. *The Times*, 15 August 1892, commented: 'In official quarters it is held that there must have been some grave mistake on the part of the commercial agents on the Upper Congo.' *Le Temps* suggested, 'It is the processes adopted in collecting the ivory which have driven these people to revolt', and in the *Daily Graphic* of 16 August 1892, a letter from a 'Late Agent, Société Anonyme Belge' suggested:

> A glance at the map will show how far Kasongo is from succour of any kind, and if the rising is serious the agents of the Katanga Company are in a critical position...It is a great mistake for trading companies to go into the interior away from the clear waterways without a large force to protect them, because where the Arab is we must always look for trouble some day.

M. van Eetvelde, Secretary of State for the Interior, stated in a letter of 28 July 1892 to the *Indépendance Belge*:

> Que cherche à prouver votre correspondant?
> Que M. Hodister n'est pas un 'fauteur de désordres'? Mais, nul plus que moi ne rend justice à ses qualités de tact et de prudence, et je n'ai pas dit ni insinué qu'il fut 'un provocateur de révolte'. J'ai fait ressortir à votre reporter — et ma pensée ne va pas au delà — que depuis trois ans l'Etat a envoyé des résidents à Nyangoué et qu'ils n'y ont pas été molestés; que pour la première fois qu'il y pénètre une mission commerciale, il survient des difficultés, et que, en tout état de cause, ces événements montrent qu'il peut être parfois nécessaire de ne pas laisser aller les particuliers dans une région où l'ordre est encore mal assuré.[23]

In *Heart of Darkness*, there is some ambiguity about the reasons for the delay in relieving the sick Kurtz, with the implication that the delay resulted in his death. The jealousy of the manager and his uncle would appear to be behind this, and while the manager insists that the delays are not his fault, he is nevertheless satisfied with the result. This possibly reflects two similar aspects of the Hodister affair. It was suggested afterwards that the agents of the State in the area, jealous of Hodister as a trading rival where the ivory was concerned, deliberately fomented Arab unrest and hatred of white agents, perhaps even of Hodister in particular.[24] And secondly, just as the delay in the steamer's reaching the Inner Station ensured that Kurtz would die of his illness, so it was suggested that the delay of Hodister's supply steamer in reaching him contributed towards the disastrous end of his expedition:

Le 19 mai, ils rencontrèrent *l'Auguste Beernaert* qui, en retard de plus d'un mois, se rendait à Bena-Kamba avec un chargement considérable en marchandises et munitions (60 fusils Mauser et plus de 5,000 cartouches); *l'Auguste Beernaert*, à l'annonce des troubles du Haut-Lomami, rétrograda et reconduisit tous les blancs à Yanga.

Nous ne pouvons nous empêcher, en passant, de déplorer le retard de *l'Auguste Beernaert* dans le ravitaillement de l'expédition Hodister. Si, en effet, le steamer était arrivé à temps, Hodister ne serait pas resté un mois à Bena Kamba, presque dans l'inaction; en se rendant plus tôt à Riba-Riba, il y serait arrivé bien avant les douloureux événements relatés plus haut, et, grâce à son intimité — qui ne fait aucun doute — avec les chefs arabes de Riba Riba, de Nyangué et de Kassongo, il eût peut-être pu conjurer la crise qui lui coûta la vie à lui-même.[25]

During the subsequent inquiries into the massacre, some rather unpleasant light was shed upon Hodister and his relationship with the natives. Two survivors of the expedition, Schouten and Hansenne, turned against him:

it appears that M. Hodister must, to a certain extent, be held responsible for the fate of the expedition, as he treated the Arabs cruelly, and his companions without the least regard for the most elementary comfort. The latter, for instance, had during the whole course of the expedition to sleep on the hard ground, whereas their camp beds were given to female favourites (*Daily Graphic*, 17 October 1892).

Whatever the truth of this might be, it had been reported that on various occasions that Hodister 'refusait l'hospitalité des directeurs des compagnies pour partager le sort de ses indigènes'.[26] And certainly, although he had a wife and daughter in Belgium and thought of the latter 'Tous les jours, de trois à quatre heures...dans sa tente',[27] he appears also to have taken a native wife and to have had children by her. *The Times*, 17 October 1892, reported: 'Moharra, chief of Nyangwe, has evinced much regret for M. Hodister's death and has adopted a child born to him by a native woman.' He had, in fact, two children who were ultimately taken from the Arabs: 'Les deux enfants d'Hodister et leur mère ainsi que les marchandises de Jourret avaient été amenés chez Mohara.'[28] Kurtz also had his native woman: 'She carried her head high; her hair was done in the shape of a helmet; she had brass leggings to the knees, brass wire gauntlets to the elbow, a crimson spot on her tawny cheek...'

Hodister, like Kurtz, found one supporter against all the charges of barbarous behaviour. M. Jacques Doré, one of his agents, defended him strenuously. The deposition of M. Doré, which was in Hodister's favour, was given the front page of the *Mouvement Géographique*; he published a reply to van Eetvelde's accusations; and the following passage is his reply to the further attacks of Schouten and others which were published in the *Etoile*:

L'opinion de M. Doré sur Hodister

J'ai pensé qu'il serait intéressant pour les lecteurs de l'*Etoile* de connaître l'avis de M. Jacques Doré sur l'interview que vous avez publié, hier matin, de M. Schouten et de ses compagnons.

Il est assez difficile de trouver M. Doré. Il paraît très ennuyé du bruit qui s'est fait autour de son nom et il a les journalistes en une sainte horreur. Grâce cependant à l'obligeance d'un ami commun, il m'a été donné de le rencontrer ce soir. M. Doré est toujours malade. Sa santé se rétablit peu à peu, mais si lentement que la moindre imprudence lui donne des rechutes. Il ne supporte pas de viande et son ordinaire se compose de poisson, de pain et de légumes. Il boit de l'eau ou du lait. Quand il a connu le but de ma visite il a d'abord manifesté le désir de prendre connaissance de l'article que l'*Etoile* a publié hier matin.

'C'est absurde', a-t-il dit. 'A lire ces lignes Hodister serait un barbare, un homme sans cœur et sans entrailles.* On lui impute des choses dont on ne devrait même pas parler. Au lieu de ne considérer que la grandeur du but final, on s'arrête aux bagatelles de la porte. Je ne veux pas approfondir le but que l'on poursuit en essayant de salir ainsi le mémoire de Hodister, mais je m'étonne cependant du portrait que trace M. Schouten de son chef, alors que dans ses lettres publiées précisément par l'*Etoile*, il fait de Hodister et de son ami Abbou un éloge éclatant et enthousiaste.

Certes, il y a eu des mécomptes. Bien des illusions sont restées en route et tout le monde a souffert. Ainsi, par example, nous n'étions pas sur un lit de roses quand nous logions à bord du steamer le *Roi des Belges*, où nous étions treize blancs et où la place manquait absolument. Il y a eu des murmures et des mécontentements. Moi, tout le premier, j'ai protesté, mais il ne nous est jamais venu alors à l'idée, à moi, ou à mes compagnons, de rendre Hodister responsable de la situation qui nous était faite. Notre malheureux chef était lui-même victime d'une situation qu'il n'avait pas créée. A la guerre comme à la guerre. On ne se promène pas en Afrique comme sur les boulevards d'Anvers. Si Hodister, à certains moments, n'a pu mieux satisfaire aux besoins de ses agents, c'est réellement, je le répète, qu'il y a été forcé par les circonstances.

Là où Hodister a pu satisfaire ses agents, il l'a fait. Toujours il a partagé nos peines comme nos agréments. Quand nous sommes arrivés à Matadi, la Compagnie des Magasins généraux a offert à Hodister de loger à l'hôtel, alors que ses compagnons devaient se contenter d'un hangar. Il a refusé. "Je ne veux pas plus que mes agents", a-t-il répondu. "Ils doivent dormir sous un hangar, je ferai comme eux." Et il l'a fait. La même scène s'est passée à Kinshassa, où il a décliné l'hospitalité de M. Camille Delcommune pour pouvoir partager le sort de ses subordonnés.

'M. Hodister', ainsi a terminé M. Doré, 'n'était pas un barbare. Ce que je viens de dire doit vous le prouver. Je veux cependant vous donner encore un détail qui achèvera de vous faire connaître cet homme d'élite. Tous les dimanches, de trois à quatre heures de relevée, il s'enfermait dans sa tente. Personne ne pouvait le déranger et il n'était visible pour personne. C'est que pendant ce temps sa petite fille qu'il avait laissée à Anvers jouait du piano à son intention; et ce barbare, ce monstre, s'isolait pour suivre par la pensée les progrès de son enfant pour laquelle il avait un véritable culte. Le public', a conclu M. Doré en guise de conclusion, 'appréciera.'

---

* The statement that Hodister was 'un homme sans cœur et sans entrailles' may have suggested to Conrad the phrase of the manager of the Central Station: 'Men who come out here should have no entrails.'

L'entretien a fini sur ces mots et je crois avoir reproduit fidèlement les idées du peintre anversois (*Mouvement Géographique*, 23 October 1892).

This indicates, I am reasonably certain, that Doré, in this aspect of his devotion to Hodister, is a source for the Harlequin. And there is further support for this in certain details of *Heart of Darkness* which suggest that Conrad knew this defence of Doré's. Of particular interest is the accusation of barbarism levelled at Hodister by Schouten and the others: 'Hodister serait un barbare', for Kurtz's corruption by the jungle turned him, in spite of his high principles, into a barbarian: 'Exterminate all the brutes.' And Doré, like the Harlequin, is defending him against such an accusation in an inadequate way. 'Notre malheureux chef était lui-même victime d'une situation qu'il n'avait pas créée', is a statement true, in different ways, of both Hodister and Kurtz. But Doré goes on: 'A la guerre comme à la guerre. On ne se promène pas en Afrique comme sur les boulevards d'Anvers. Si Hodister, à certains moments, n'a pu mieux satisfaire aux besoins de ses agents, c'est réellement, je le répète, qu'il y a été forcé par les circonstances.' This reminds us of the Harlequin's, 'You don't know how such a life tries a man like Kurtz' (p. 132). But it also reminds us of Marlow's statements, which bring out the theme of the dangers of the wilderness as opposed to the safety of civilisation, the recognition of which makes him, on his return to the sepulchral city, irritated by 'the bearing of commonplace individuals going about their business in the assurance of perfect safety' (p. 152). 'Here you all are', he says to his audience, 'each moored with two good addresses, like a hulk with two anchors, a butcher round one corner, a policeman round another, excellent appetites, and temperature normal...from year's end to year's end' (p. 114). And later:

You can't understand. How could you?—with solid pavement under your feet, surrounded by kind neighbours ready to cheer you or to fall on you, stepping delicately between the butcher and the policemen, in the holy terror of scandal and gallows and lunatic asylums—how can you imagine what particular region of the first ages a man's untrammelled feet may take him into by the way of solitude—utter solitude without a policeman—by the way of silence—utter silence, where no warning voice of a kind neighbour can be heard whispering of public opinion? (p. 116).

It would seem likely, also, that the name of the Harlequin's Dutch backer was derived from another agent of Hodister's expedition: 'It appears he had persuaded a Dutch trading-house on the coast to fit him out with stores and goods, and had started for the interior...Good old Dutchman, Van Shuyten' (p. 124). Of course there was a Dutch trading house on the coast and we have already referred to the important Dutch manager and trader, A. Greshoff, but I think it is likely that Conrad has taken up the name of the Belgian on the Hodister expedition, whose function it was to stay out of the real interior but to provide merchandise for the expedition: 'sous la conduite de M. Schouten, resté à Isanghi à cette intention, des merchandises et des provisions'.[29]

Kurtz's activities in the story are remarkable for the atmosphere of undefined and horrific vagueness that surrounds them, but in the Hodister story Conrad would have found sufficient suggestions of primitive barbarism on which to base his idea of Kurtz's activities. As for the shrunken heads on poles round Kurtz's house, these might be a macabre transference by Conrad of the fate of Hodister and his men. *The Times*, 8 December 1891, stated: 'His head was placed at the top of a long pole and placed by the side of that of M. Noblesse in front of the Palace of Nserera, the chief of the tribe.' On the other hand, a description of the use of such heads for decorations round a house was given by one of the mission, M. Hinck, in his journal when he described the station at Yanga (see map facing p. 9, above): 'Le poste est entouré de cinquante-deux têtes humaines plantées au bout de perches: elles ont encore pour la plupart le cuir chevelu et des lambeaux de chair. C'est ignoble, et dire que deux blancs doivent y séjourner! Ce poste appartient au chef Mounié-Mohara. C'est un vrai repaire de bandits.'[30]

Conrad must have learnt of the later success and tragedy of the man he had been linked with on the Congo, who had stood out so strongly with his qualities of courage, adventurousness, eloquence, influence and principle from the other agents. And he must have been Conrad's own choice of the particular nightmares offered to him in the Congo. Conrad developed the suggestions of barbarism hinted at in Hodister's story to make them the whole of Kurtz's tragedy, which was not, of course, the same as Hodister's. Kurtz's tragedy could not be a simple revolt of the inhabitants of the area. It had to symbolise the destruction of the white man through his very aspirations which led him, tainted by the greed for profit, too close to the primitive and barbarous which released those same suppressed instincts in himself. But the pattern of Hodister's life is that of Kurtz, a man of virtue and pretensions and particularly of courage who fails, partly betrayed by lesser men, partly by his own aspirations.

12

HENRY MORTON STANLEY—
THE YAWL 'NELLIE'

It is the river Thames with which *Heart of Darkness* begins—
'The sea-reach of the Thames stretched before us like the
beginning of an interminable waterway'—and with which the
story ends: 'the tranquil waterway leading to the uttermost
ends of the earth flowed sombre under an overcast sky'. And
the Thames not only encloses the action of the story which
concerns that other great river, but is shown to share some
of the characteristics of the Congo. The same kind of language
is used to describe both—'interminable waterway', 'dark',
'mournful gloom', 'flowed sombre', 'seemed to lead into the
heart of an immense darkness'—but more important, the two
rivers are drawn together by a direct comparison, a comparison
of two periods of history—an early and a late colonisation.
'And this also', says Marlow, 'has been one of the dark
places of the earth.' He goes on to show more precisely what
he means by describing the Roman legionary or 'decent
young citizen' sent out to tackle the darkness that was then
the Thames. His narrative then gives the modern example
of the pilgrims and Kurtz tackling the darkness of the Congo
—'a squeeze' in both instances, 'men going at it blind'.

This brilliant preamble to his story was suggested to
Conrad, I believe, by a speech of Stanley. This explorer and
coloniser was never far from the sidelines of Conrad's Congo
experience both in terms of his exploits and of his ideals.
The contrast between 'light' (Christian civilisation) and
'darkness' (African barbarism) was very much part of
Stanley's conception of the background against which he

acted, the two images being taken, without question, at their face value. In October 1892 Stanley was given the freedom of the city of Swansea and the following report of his speech on that occasion, in which he quoted Pitt with approval, appeared in *The Times*, 4 October 1892:

To illustrate the slow growth of ideas among nations, I will quote you a portion of a speech delivered by the great Pitt a hundred years ago. Lord Granville, Bishop Wilberforce, and Sir Bartle Frere in 1873 and Lord Salisbury in 1890 have made some effective speeches about the obnoxious slave traffic and our duties in regard to it, but they bear no comparison...with that delivered by William Pitt in April, 1792. Said he, 'Grieved am I to think that there should be a single person in this country, much more that there should be a single member of the British Parliament, who can look on the present dark, uncultivated, and un-civilized state of Africa as a ground for continuing the slave trade, as a ground for not only refusing to attempt the improvement of that continent, but even for hindering and interrupting every ray of light which might otherwise break in upon it—as a ground for refusing to it the common chance and the common means with which other nations have been blessed of emerging from their barbarism. It has been alleged that Africa labours under a natural incapacity for civilization, that it is enthusiasm or fanaticism to think that she can ever enjoy the knowledge and morals of Europe, that Providence never intended her to rise above barbarism, that Providence has irrevocably doomed her to be only a nursery for slaves. Allow of this principle as applied to Africa, and I should be glad to know why it might not also have been applied to ancient and uncivilized Britain. Why might not some Roman Senator have predicted with equal boldness—"There is a people destined never to be free, a people depressed by the hand of nature below the level of the human species, and created to form a supply of slaves for the rest of the world"? Sir, we were once as obscure among the nations of the earth, as debased in our morals, as savage in our manners, as degraded in our understandings as these unhappy Africans are at present. But in the lapse of a long series of years, by a progression slow and, for a time, almost imperceptible, we have become rich in a variety of acquirements, favoured above measure with the gifts of Providence, unrivalled in commerce, pre-eminent in arts, foremost in the pursuits of philosophy and science, and established in all the blessings of civil society. But had other nations applied to Great Britain the reasoning which some gentlemen now apply to Africa, ages might have passed without our emerging from barbarism, and we might even at this hour have been little superior in morals, in knowledge, or in refinement to the rude inhabitants of Guinea. If we shudder to think of the misery which would still have overwhelmed us had Great Britain continued to the present time as she once was, God forbid that we should any longer subject Africa to the same dreadful scourge and preclude the light of knowledge which has reached every other quarter of the globe from having access into her coasts.'

We have here the same conception of Britain as being at one time 'obscure', 'debased', 'savage' and 'degraded', 'dark, uncultivated and uncivilised' as Africa then was. It is this notion that Conrad takes up, particularising and also extending it in visual terms. At the same time, however, Conrad inverts the accepted beliefs behind the comparison. He does not accept the colonising process as one of 'improvement' and bringing in light, his story being an inquiry into the nature of 'light' and 'darkness' in this context.

Two fields of human activity that were of great significance in Conrad's work are brought together for the purpose of this inquiry—the craft of the sea and an aspect of politics—colonisation. Marlow's unusual contact with land through becoming a 'fresh-water sailor' brings him that experience of the colonising movement at the heart of darkness, and the virtues implanted in man by the craft of sea and by the desire to bring 'light' into the darkness are equally tested. Thus Marlow's story, though dealing with 'land affairs', is still 'a seaman's yarn', though, as we are told, whereas a seaman's yarn generally has a direct simplicity—'the whole meaning of which lies within the shell of a cracked nut', Marlow's tale is not typical: 'to him the meaning of an episode was not inside like a kernel but outside, enveloping the tale' (p. 48).

It is, therefore, most appropriate that his story should be told on board a 'cruising yawl' while waiting for the 'turn of the tide' on the Thames—once a dark place:

The *Nellie*, a cruising yawl, swung to her anchor without a flutter of the sails, and was at rest. The flood had made, the wind was nearly calm, and being bound down the river, the only thing for it was to come to and wait for the turn of the tide.

The sea-reach of the Thames stretched before us like the beginning of an interminable waterway (p. 45).

This appropriate setting is not fortuitous, for even here Conrad is reflecting his own experience, an experience which is to a certain extent linked with his Congo period. For there *was* a cruising yawl called the *Nellie* in which Conrad sailed on the Thames immediately before and immediately after his Congo trip, and he had, like Marlow, told stories to his fellow sailors of his past experiences. The *Nellie* belonged to his old friend, G. F. W. Hope. Conrad sailed with Hope in this yacht on several occasions during the two years of Hope's ownership of the *Nellie*.[1] I have discovered an unpublished account by Hope of his yachting days, which is now in possession of his daughter-in-law, Mrs Jean Hope, and which gives us some insight into these journeys of Conrad on the *Nellie*, and also shows how closely he was mirroring such experiences in *Heart of Darkness*. Hope himself points out, 'He [Conrad] mentions her [the *Nellie*] in *Heart of Darkness* and myself as the Director.' And he provides the following account of Conrad's first trip in the *Nellie*:

Joseph Conrad had just arrived from Australia, where he had been for two years in command of the *Otago*, owned by Simpson and Co., of Adelaide. He was waiting for his passport to go to Russia to see his Uncle, and as he had nothing to do for a few days, I asked him to come down, and spend a few days with me, and as he hadn't seen the *Nellie* to have a cruise with two other friends who were coming with me on the Saturday, and I thought this would be a good opportunity to introduce him to Keen and Mears. The latter had himself sailed 2 voyages in the *Duke of Sutherland* as an apprentice with Captain Loutit.[2] The *Duke of Sutherland* was the first British full-rigged ship that Conrad sailed in, so that there would be three out of four of us, who had sailed in the old *Duke* though at different times...The next day we went aboard the *Nellie* taking with us, a cold leg of lamb, and a bottle of mint-sauce (we always started our cruises with a leg of lamb) some bottles of Reffels Beer and sundry small stores and our gear...He [Conrad] had never been in a yawl before.

There are, of course, five men aboard the fictional *Nellie*:

The Director of Companies was our captain and our host. We four affectionately watched his back as he stood in the bows looking to seaward. On the whole river there was nothing that looked half so nautical. He resembled a pilot, which to a seaman is trust-worthiness personified. It was difficult to realize his work was not out there in the luminous estuary, but behind him, within the brooding gloom.

Between us there was, as I have already said somewhere, the bond of the sea. Besides holding our hearts together through long periods of separation, it had the effect of making us tolerant of each other's yarns— and even convictions. The Lawyer—the best of old fellows—had, because of his many years and many virtues, the only cushion on deck, and was lying on the only rug. The Accountant had brought out already a box of dominoes, and was toying architecturally with the bones. Marlow sat cross-legged right aft, leaning against the mizzen-mast. He had sunken cheeks, a yellow complexion, a straight back, an ascetic aspect, and, with his arms dropped, the palms of hands outwards, resembled an idol. The director, satisfied the anchor had good hold, made his way aft and sat down amongst us. We exchanged a few words lazily. Afterwards there was silence on board the yacht. For some reason or other we did not begin that game of dominoes. We felt meditative, and fit for nothing but placid staring (pp. 45–6).

But Conrad is not moving far from his own experience here. Hope was a director of companies,[3] and all the men on board on the occasion he describes shared 'the bond of the sea', since Hope also had at one time sailed in the *Duke of Sutherland*.[4] And the activities of the auditors in *Heart of Darkness* reflect those of the passengers on the actual *Nellie*— playing dominoes and yarning. According to Hope, on the first night of this particular trip they 'played cards till time to turn in', but on the Sunday night:

It came on very thin. We made the buoy at the Eastern end of the Swale and nearly ran into a large Brigantine at anchor. As soon as I judged we were about opposite to Faversham Creek, we let go our anchor and gave her all the chain we could. It came on to blow very hard and although we were some way up the Swale, we had no shelter and had to stop where we were. It blew very hard all night. We found we were just opposite Faversham Creek, the tide didn't ebb a bit. It was kept up by the wind...we played Dominoes most of the day. I never knew it blow harder than it did then, in this country...

Margate was very full of visitors, mostly from the East End of London. We spent a little time ashore, and then went aboard and had a yarn about the old *Duke of Sutherland*.

Hope does not record that Conrad, during these 'yarning' periods, told the story of his Congo experience, but he does recall that on Conrad's first trip with him, Conrad told the assembled group of Keen, Mears and Hope at the Lobster Arms at Hole Haven,[5] the story of his Don Carlos adventures, which he used later in *Arrow of Gold*:

Conrad told the story of when he was a youngster about eighteen, where he joined a party of four, an Englishman, an American, a Spaniard and himself, in Don Carlos's party when the Spaniards were trying to get up a revolution. They ran two cargoes but when running the third, a Spanish Revenue cruiser hove in sight and chased them, and finally they had to run their lateen ashore on the rocks and only just escaped with their lives (pp. 200–1).

There is every chance therefore that Conrad told of his Congo experiences later on board the *Nellie*.

Thus the two opposing concerns in the story—the seaman's and the coloniser's—which come together so brilliantly in the preamble, came together naturally in Conrad's life through his association with Hope and the *Nellie* on the Thames at that time, strengthened for Conrad by Stanley's speech. Although *Heart of Darkness* was written in 1899 and Conrad would then be able to see all these experiences in suitable perspective, almost all the experiences from which the story was drawn—his Congo episode, the fate of Hodister, the trips on the *Nellie*, and Stanley's speech—took place within two years of Conrad's life—1890 to 1892—a concentration of experience which perhaps accounts in part for the feeling of assurance and compactness in the tale itself.

13

'AN OUTPOST OF PROGRESS'

A study of the sources of the short story 'An Outpost of Progress' makes an interesting tail-piece to *Heart of Darkness*, although it was written almost three years earlier. This tale of two commercial agents on the Congo shows, to begin with, Conrad working over, much earlier and in a more obvious form, certain themes of *Heart of Darkness*. There is, for example, the ironic treatment of the concept of 'progress' as it is applied to the setting up of trading posts in the jungle— the story was initially called 'A Victim of Progress'. And there is also the belief in the need for the restraining effects of society upon man's instincts and in the disintegrating effect solitude and the primitive can have upon him. On a less significant level, therefore, we have a foreshadowing of the predicament of Kurtz.[1] Although Conrad claimed that 'An Outpost of Progress' was 'true enough in its essentials', I think we must conclude that while it is based firmly on the Congo Conrad knew and that the setting is realistic enough, the story itself and its details are invented for the purpose of demonstrating these themes.

The story is simple. Two commercial agents, hopelessly ill-chosen for their task—'They were two perfectly insignificant and incapable individuals, whose existence is only rendered possible through the high organisation of civilised crowds'—are settled by the managing director of 'the great Trading Company' in a post of little significance off the main river. Their predecessor who had built the outpost and then died of sunstroke lies buried in the compound. Kayerts and Carlier are happy to begin with. A certain

amount of ivory trickles in and they are befriended by the
chief of the village, Gobila, whom they call 'Father Gobila'.
Then, reluctant at first but finally acquiescing, they allow
their native assistant, Henry Price, to exchange their ten
trading-post natives for ivory. During the slaving raid, some
of Gobila's men are carried off. In retaliation, Gobila leaves
the white men entirely alone, and they quickly degenerate
in the wilderness and isolation. The steamer which should
relieve them is delayed[2] and when it does arrive, the managing
director finds Carlier shot and Kayerts, who has killed him,
hanging from the cross over the grave of his predecessor:
'he seemed to be standing rigidly at attention, but with one
purple cheek playfully posed on the shoulder. And, ir-
reverently, he was putting out a swollen tongue at his
Managing Director' (p. 117).

In a footnote to his account of 'An Outpost of Progress',
Jean-Aubry writes:

There is every reason to believe that it was Harou who told Conrad the
story of the death of the two agents of the Company in circumstances
exactly similar to those he describes in 'An Outpost of Progress'. I have
Conrad's own testimony as to the authenticity of the facts. The real
names of the characters have not been discovered; Conrad called them
Kayerts and Carlier, the actual names of two men, an agent and a captain,
whom he met in the Congo.[3]

It may be Conrad insisted that Harou told him this story
of the two agents of the Company, but I think it is unlikely
that he heard such a story from Harou or anyone else.

An essential for the working out of Conrad's story here, as
in *Heart of Darkness*, is the total isolation of the trading-post
where the action takes place. Conrad, as I have shown, had
no experience of such an isolated post, and, so far as I have
been able to discover, had no knowledge of any tributary
of the Congo where such complete isolation might have been
found, though he must have passed on the main river certain

stations which would be comparatively isolated. But Conrad could have found descriptions of the founding of such isolated stations and of the fortunes of the agents left at them in the writings of Stanley, and indeed I believe that the character of the managing director in the story is based upon Stanley himself—upon his activities, his character and his methods in establishing trading-posts. Conrad's description of the managing director is as follows:

At any rate the director of the Great Trading Company, coming up in a steamer that resembled an enormous sardine box with a flat-roofed shed erected on it, found the station in good order, and Makola [the third assistant] as usual quietly diligent...The director was a man ruthless and efficient, who at times, but very imperceptibly, indulged in grim humour. He made a speech to Kayerts and Carlier, pointing out to them the promising aspect of their station. The nearest trading-post was about three hundred miles away. It was an exceptional opportunity for them to distinguish themselves and to earn percentages on the trade... Next day...the sardine-box steamer went off, not to return for another six months. On the deck the director touched his cap to the two agents, who stood on the bank waving their hats, and turning to an old servant of the Company on his passage to headquarters, said, "Look at those two imbeciles. They must be mad at home to send me such specimens.[4] I told those fellows to plant a vegetable garden, build new storehouses and fences, and construct a landing-stage. I bet nothing will be done" (pp. 87–8).

Stanley really did make speeches of this kind to the men he left in charge of trading-posts, as he himself recorded:

The instructions, few and simple, to him are: See now, sir, this is your domain, legitimately acquired. It has become, by the power invested in you as a chief, your estate, over which you have absolute control, subject to none other than myself. I must leave you as master and sole arbiter in all questions. Let justice attend your dealings; be kind to your people, for remember you are their father and their mother. Show me on my return that a fit choice was made when I selected you. By industry you may make your place a model to be followed by others less experienced than yourself; by due care you may make it the happiest place in Africa. You have sufficient native moneys, and abundant provisions.[5]

And like the managing director, he was frequently disappointed in his expectations and regretted the type of men who were available to him:

I am absent ten months from the scene, but I find on my return that the condition of the place is far worse than when I departed. The warm promises made by him created in me an ideal paradise; but instead of my bright, and, alas! too florid an ideal, I see the wild grass has overrun our native village, so that it is scarcely visible. Not one house has been added to those structures we had raised for him. The station is also in a state of siege; a palisaded circle shows that once an alarm had bestirred him to spasmodic action; famine beleaguers the garrison; four days searching far and wide only brings enough to last a few hours; the stores are empty; there are only enough brass rods to last three days. *The natives leave him and his station so severely alone* that he is in actual risk of starvation. What a great contrast it is altogether to that beautiful ideal of mine! How very reverse to those glowing promises, letters, and reports!

'Why, how is this? Good heavens, this is a very ruin of a place!' I exclaim. 'See the village—the road, the street, the station, is buried in grass!' [my italics][6]

This is the situation in 'An Outpost of Progress': 'Gobila's people drummed and yelled to every new moon...but kept away from the station', there was nothing left to eat but rice and coffee, 'Rank grass began to sprout over the courtyard.'

Although Stanley is speaking generally in the passage quoted above, he also had a particular station in mind as the details he gives show. The history of the post at Vivi was also one of decline from a successful post to a failing one. Stanley found, on arriving at Vivi, that 'There has been a quarrel about something very trivial, and both whites and natives have seemingly agreed that they had best leave one another severely alone, in which impassive warfare the whites have suffered severely'.[7] And though this was a much larger station than the one Conrad deals with, the method by which it is brought down is the same. In 'An Outpost of Progress' Gobila decides that his people must keep away from the

European station and thus the food which his people had brought Kayerts and Carlier, 'fowls, and sweet potatoes, and palm wine, and sometimes a goat', is also stopped. The agents find that 'Gobila's people might have been dead and buried for any signs of life they gave...They [the agents] should be left alone. Perhaps in time they would disappear into the earth as the first one had disappeared. His people [Gobila decrees] must keep away from them, and hope for the best' (p. 107).

The earlier history of the station at Mswata (see map facing p. 9, above) has some relevance to the story. This station was originally established by Lieutenant Janssen who made an enormous success of it, but was accidentally drowned. Stanley writes:

He was requested to build a station a little higher up than Mswata and to show the Abbé Guyot a portion of the ground where he might have his mission-house erected. Their canoes, returning in a hurry to Mswata in the teeth of a gale of wind, foundered when opposite Ganchu's Point, and both the young Lieutenant and the Abbé, with several of the coloured men, were drowned.[8]

The predecessor at the trading post in the story, of course, died of sunstroke, and Conrad appears to have taken up here another suggestion from Stanley. The death of a Lieutenant Parfoury from sunstroke is told on the same page as is the story of Janssen: 'One of the most excellent men was Lieut. Parfoury...and yet, being a little indiscreet [notice Conrad's sound assessment here of Stanley—"at times, but very imperceptibly, [he] indulged in grim humour"] one day under a burning sun, he was gone from us.'[9]

I feel certain that Conrad put together his story from these incidents related by Stanley, and my belief is strengthened by the lack of any report of a linked murder and suicide in the area, as well as by the records of agents who died. According to the *Mouvement Géographique*, 1890, the numbers who died 'accidentally' as the Département de l'Intérieur euphemistically called it, were small: two in 1885, three in 1887, one in 1890. But one of these men did kill himself out of the anguish brought about by his isolation and loneliness, and it is possible that Conrad heard of the incident since it occurred on 13 October 1890. Jenssen-Tusch, quoting from Captain Madsen's diary, relates how Madsen visited a station deep in the Congo on the Lomami river at Bena-Kamba (see map facing p. 9, above)

where four months earlier a Belgian lieutenant had established himself with a hundred soldiers from Dahomey and Bangala. The lieutenant had cleared away 300 meters of trees along the river, but he had been quite ill and was in great distress because of the condition of anguish and loneliness. Madsen left again on the 22nd February 1890. The Chief of the station had tears in his eyes when he, Madsen, took his leave—it was indeed miserable to stay behind with wrecked health as the only white man amidst enemies only. Some time later he shot himself.[10]

I think we can accept the statement that the story is 'true enough in its essentials' if we take the conception of truth in relation to his work as Conrad intended it: 'Truly imagined from hints of things that really happened.' Certainly, when we turn from the agents and their station to the Congolese chieftain, Gobila, we find that there was such a person in the Congo at one time. Conrad writes:

At times Gobila came to see them. Gobila was the chief of the neighbouring villages. He was a gray-headed savage, thin and black, with a white cloth round his loins and a mangy panther skin hanging over his back. He came up with long strides of his skeleton legs, swinging a staff as tall as himself... How goes it, you old image? [says Kayerts] and they would smile at one another. The two whites had a liking for that old and incomprehensible creature, and called him Father Gobila. Gobila's manner was paternal, and he seemed really to love all white men (p. 95).

Gobila can be found in Stanley's account of a station he had established at Msuata (or Mswata):

The next day we leave Kimpoko, and a few hours later have entered the gates of the Upper Congo, at the head of Stanley Pool. On the evening of the third day we are alongside of the landing-place of Mswata Station. Lieutenant Janssen, brought here thirteen months ago, has by this time completed his station. His residence is like a genteel farmhouse in appearance, with a cool and shady porch, where he holds his palavers and chats twice a day with Papa Gobila...This old gentleman, stout of form, hearty and genial in manner, came up breathlessly and held out his fat hands, and welcomed Bula Matari [sobriquet given to Stanley by the natives and meaning a 'Breaker of Rocks'] after his long absence... Gobila, genial, aldermanic Gobila—Papa Gobila.[11]

Stanley established the post at Mswata on 1 May 1882, and we learn that Lieutenant Janssen made great headway both with the station and in his relationships with the chief Gobila: 'Young Lieutenant Janssen had distinguished himself meanwhile by a great progress in the construction of a commodious house, while to Papa Gobila he bore himself with filial respect. The stout old man regarded him with paternal pride.'[12]

We can see how very closely Conrad follows Stanley's account here. In both cases the white man calls the chieftain 'father' and stress is laid upon the fact that Gobila is seen as a paternal figure in his relations with the whites at the trading post. Conrad turns the well-known 'fat' chieftain into someone 'thin', but the description of the white cloth round his loins and the fact that Gobila has a 'staff as tall as himself' is derived from Stanley. Gobila was very popular with most white men, and the missionary W. Holman Bentley, referring to a trip George Grenfell took up the river Congo in 1884, acidly records: 'By noon the next day, Grenfell reached Mswata, Stanley's first station above the [Stanley] Pool. The chief Ngoibila, a very fat man. He was a shrewd man, well disposed to white men, who were doubtless considered by him to be cows worth keeping, and to be milked at pleasure.'[13] It is possible that Conrad saw, or at any rate heard of, Gobila while he was in the Congo, for the old chief was still alive at that time, according to a report in the *Mouvement Géographique*, 28 June 1891.

Other aspects of the fictional Gobila, such as his ideas about white men, probably derive from beliefs current among the Congolese on their first meeting with white men, and Conrad may have heard of these or have met examples of them:

They all appeared to him [Gobila] very young, indistinguishably alike (except for stature), and he knew that they were all brothers, and also immortal. The death of the artist [the first head of the post who died of sunstroke] who was the first white man whom he knew intimately, did not disturb this belief, because he was firmly convinced that the white stranger had pretended to die and got himself buried for some mysterious purpose of his own, into which it was useless to inquire. Perhaps it was his way of going home to his own country? At any rate, these were his brothers, and he transferred his absurd affection to them. They returned it in a way. Carlier slapped him on the back, and recklessly struck off matches for his amusement. Kayerts was always ready to let him have a sniff at the ammonia bottle. In short, they behaved just like that other white creature that had hidden itself in a hole in the ground (pp. 95–6).

It is also possible, of course, that Conrad found references to these beliefs in books about the Congo. H. H. Johnston (later Sir Harry Johnston), for example, who also met Gobila, describes the attitude of some natives at Itimba (below Tchumbiri) to Lieutenant Orban who, at a funeral, saluted a dead native by firing his Winchester:

The chief and people were delighted. Could there be greater honour for the deceased than to receive his farewell salute at the hands of a white man, with his wonderful gun from Mpüto—the mysterious region beyond the sea—the unknown—perhaps heaven itself? ('for are not these white men sons of heaven?')...and he pointed to the pale and peaceful evening sky—'you will send him back to us, will you not? you will tell him his hut is waiting for him, his wives will prepare his manioc white as cotton-cloth, and there shall be malafù in plenty, and a goat killed. You will send him back will you not?'[14]

'An Outpost of Progress'

As to the belief that white men all derived from the same mother, Herbert Ward relates:

Friday, February 3 (1888)...Some natives from the village that Selim bin Mohammed raided a few days ago visited the fort during lunch-time, and came into the mess-house to see the white men, whom they had heard of but never before seen...They asked if we were all born of one mother, and upon being told we were (for fun), they elevated their eyebrows, looked at one another, and covered their open mouths with their hands.[15]

And striking matches to interest the natives was also a recorded practice. The missionary Bentley recalls that in 1881, reaching the town of Nkio Buminu, near Stanley Pool, he and his companions were surrounded by curious natives: 'Matches were a mystery to them; they would have crowded for hours to see *mindele* [white man] strike a little stick on something, and a great flame ensue.'[16]

'An Outpost of Progress', therefore, would appear to be based much more upon Conrad's reading and much less upon his direct experience than *Heart of Darkness*, but it treats themes that were to be dealt with more fully and skilfully in the later novel.

NOSTROMO

South America

14

'GASPAR RUIZ'

The short story 'Gaspar Ruiz' shares the setting of South America with *Nostromo*, and, like the story of *Nostromo* itself, is a tale of revolution, changing loyalties and love. Unlike *Nostromo*, its literary value is slight, and as with many of Conrad's short stories it has a peculiarly grotesque quality about it. Strange also is the fact that this grotesqueness is inherent in the source—a true tale—and that Conrad has enhanced this quality rather than lessened it in the change from source to complete story. It appeared in the collection *A Set of Six* (1908) of which Conrad remarked: 'They are just stories in which I've tried my best to be *simply entertaining*.'[1] And he described 'Gaspar Ruiz' as 'the story of a South American Bandit. "The Strong Man", warlike in its feeling.'[2]

Gaspar Ruiz, son of a humble man, is pressed into the Republican army. He is of little intelligence but great strength. He is taken prisoner by the Royalist army, and then recaptured by the Republicans who claim he is a deserter and sentence him to be shot. By accident he survives, though wounded, and is looked after by a now impoverished family of Royalists, whose daughter he first saves from death during an earthquake and then carries off. Doña Erminia[3] is a woman of extremely strong will. Under her direction, Ruiz sends a letter to the Republican General Robles arranging a secret meeting, in the course of which he offers to work secretly for the Republicans to clear his name, and the offer is accepted. Ultimately, however, he quarrels with and kills the Civil Governor, and takes to the hills with his followers.

The Republican army cannot unseat him, until his wife is captured by Carreras, dictator of the nearby republic of Mendoza, and taken to the fort of Pequeña. Ruiz attacks the fort and during the attack his back is broken. The Republican army arrives and takes prisoner Ruiz, his wife and child. Ruiz dies, and his wife, giving her daughter into the care of one of the generals, commits suicide.

This story, Conrad claims, came from a book by a Captain Basil Hall, R.N.:

The hint for Gaspar Ruiz the man I found in a book by Captain Basil Hall, R.N., who was for some time, between the years 1824 and 1828, senior officer of a small British Squadron on the West Coast of South America. His book published in the thirties obtained a certain celebrity and I suppose is to be found still in some libraries. The curious who may be mistrusting my imagination are referred to that printed document, Vol. II, I forget the page, but it is somewhere not far from the end.[4]

Conrad is quite right to tell us that the hint for Gaspar Ruiz came from Hall but it is near the end of Volume I, not Volume II. Three years after writing the passage above, Conrad in a letter to Cunninghame Graham again referred to Hall as the source of the story but remarked on the limited nature of the source:

I found the seed of it in Capt Basil Hall RN. 'Journal of the years 1820, –21, –22'; a work of which you may have heard...The original of G. Ruiz is a man called Benavides, a free lance on the southern frontier of Chile during the wars of the revolution. Hall gives him a page or two—mostly hearsay. I had to invent all his story, find the motives for his changes of sides [Benavides was first a Royalist, then a Republican and later a Royalist again]—and the scenery of the tale.[5]

As this letter suggests, Conrad did have to manipulate his source slightly—particularly in terms of his hero's character, as he did in the case of Nostromo. Hall's narrative represents Benavides as a rogue with no good reason for changing sides:

The history of Benavides is curious. He was a native of Conception, and served, for some time, in the Chilian army, from which he deserted to

the Royalists, but was retaken at the battle of Maypo in 1818. He was
of a ferocious character, and as, in addition to the crime of desertion, he
had committed several murders, he was sentenced to death, along with
his brother and other delinquents.[6]

There is no suggestion here of the character Conrad gives to
Ruiz—that of a humble, innocent, good-hearted man caught
up in movements beyond his control. But the incident of
Ruiz's escape from death is taken with all its macabre detail
straight from Hall's account:

Accordingly, the whole party were brought forth in the Plaza of Santiago
and shot. Benavides, who, though terribly wounded, was not killed, had
sufficient fortitude to feign himself dead. The bodies being dragged off,
were left without burial to be destroyed by the Gallinazos, a species of
vulture. The sergeant who superintended this last part of the ceremony
was personally inimical to Benavides, for murdering some of his relations;
and to gratify his revenge, drew his sword, and while they were dragging
the body of his foe to the pile, gave it a severe gash across the neck. The
resolute Benavides bore this also, without flinching, and lay like a dead
man amongst the others, until it became dark; he then contrived to
extricate himself from the heap, and in a most miserable plight crawled
to a neighbouring cottage, the generous inhabitants of which received
and attended him with the greatest care.[7]

The narrator in '*Gaspar Ruiz*' recalls:

I heard three volleys fired, and thought that I should never hear of
Gaspar Ruiz again. He fell with the others. But we were to hear of him
nevertheless, though the sergeant boasted that as he lay on his face
expiring or dead in the heap of the slain, he had slashed his neck with
a sword. He had done this, he said, to make sure of ridding the world
of a dangerous traitor (pp. 17–18).

Ruiz is not dead, however. Wounded by two bullets, and
by the sergeant's sword, he remains 'lying stretched out with
rigid limbs' and after dark 'shaking off the dead...he crawled
away over the plain on his hands and knees' to the small
house where the Royalists looked after him.

Conrad has kept close to Hall's account here save in two
respects. According to Hall, Benavides was wounded by only

one bullet and there was no love affair with the daughter of an aristocrat. The latter is a development by Conrad, as is Ruiz's saving of Erminia during an earthquake.

Ruiz's attempt to work with the Republicans and its disastrous ending is also based fairly closely on Hall's account. Hall records how Benavides arranged a meeting with General San Martin:

It is even said that the bold ruffian himself gave information of his being alive, and invited San Martin to hold a secret conference at midnight, in the centre of the great square of Santiago. The appointed signal was to strike fire from their flints three times; a mark sufficiently conspicuous for the purpose of distinction, yet of a nature calculated to excite no suspicion. San Martin accordingly, alone and provided with a brace of pistols, went to the spot, where he encountered Benavides similarly armed. After a long conference with the desperado, whom he finally engaged in his service, he settled that Benavides should, for the present, serve in the Chilian army, employed against the Araucanian Indians in the south; but should be ready to join the army in Peru, when the expedition sailed. This was ill judged in San Martin; for Benavides soon quarrelled with the Chilian General, and once more changed sides, offering his services to the Indians, who were delighted to obtain so brave and unrelenting an associate.[8]

Conrad's Ruiz also arranges a secret meeting with General San Martin. He proposed 'to the General-in-Chief a meeting at midnight in the middle of the Plaza before the Moneta. The signal would be to strike fire with flint and steel three times, which was not too conspicuous and yet distinctive enough for recognition' (p. 43). Ultimately, however, Ruiz quarrels, not with 'a general' as Hall has it, but with the civil governor, and here Conrad has moved to his second source, the *Memoirs of General Miller*:

Unhappily Balcarce imparted his secret to Freyre, governor of Concepcion, who, in a conference at which all three were present, had the indiscretion to tell Benavides, in a moment of warm discussion, that a man of his species was not to be trusted. Fired at the insult, the stern Benavides disappeared within eight-and-forty hours, and speedily commenced a desolating war with fire and sword, committing unheard-of barbarities upon the helpless and unoffending inhabitants.[9]

Once again, however, Conrad moves from both sources to make the quarrel a much more dramatic event in which Ruiz murders the Civil Governor.

Four distinct phases of Ruiz's career as a Royalist bandit are shown by Conrad. There is the fatal affair 'long remembered afterwards as the "Massacre of the Island"'; his abduction of foreign vessels; his contact with a Spanish Governor and weapons he receives from that Governor; and Ruiz's living in a 'military barbaric state' with his aristocratic wife. All of these, except for the relationship of Ruiz and his wife, are to be found in Hall.

Conrad writes of the incident he calls the 'Massacre of the Island':

Afterwards, in the day of their greatest prosperity, this poncho was embroidered in gold, and she wore then, also, the sword of poor Don Antonio de Leyva. This veteran Chilian officer, having the misfortune to be surrounded with his small force, and running short of ammunition, found his death at the hands of the Arauco Indians, the allies and auxiliaries of Gaspar Ruiz. This was the fatal affair long remembered afterwards as the 'Massacre of the Island'. The sword of the unhappy officer was presented to her [Ruiz's mistress] by Peneleo, the Araucanian chief; for these Indians, struck by her aspect, the deathly pallor of her face, which no exposure to the weather seemed to affect, and her calm indifference under fire, looked upon her as a supernatural being, or at least as a witch (p. 48).

Conrad keeps close to Hall here but he uses the incident to draw attention to the powerful female who directs Gaspar Ruiz's barbarous career. Such a person does not seem to have inspired the career of Benavides:

On the 26th, on the banks of the River Laja he [Benavides] attacked three hundred men of the...battalion, No. 1, and some militia, which had been sent to reinforce the head-quarters...At eight o'clock next morning he addressed a despatch to Major-general Don Andres Alcazar, offering to spare the lives of all those who should give themselves up unarmed. It happened that this worthy veteran had run short of ammunition, and his people were worn out with fatigue; he therefore capitulated, giving up at once his arms and his life. The officers were immediately shot, without being allowed the consolations of religion; one person only escaped by accident, Friar N. Castro, of the order of Hermits. Major-general Alcazar, and Sergeant-major Ruiz, were then delivered over to the Indians, that they might be speared to death, along with three hundred families who had assembled on the island of Laja.[10]

The next event in the 'day of their greatest prosperity' is the decoying of vessels into harbour prior to their abduction. This is immediately followed by the demand for assistance from the remaining Royalists:

In the territory upon which he ranged, from sea coast to the Cordillera, there was a bay where the ships of that time, after rounding Cape Horn, used to resort for wood and water. There, decoying the crew on shore, he captured first the whaling brig *Hersalia*, and afterwards made himself master by surprise of two more ships, one English and one American.

It was rumoured at the time that he dreamed of setting up a navy of his own. But that, of course, was impossible. Still, manning the brig with part of her own crew, and putting an officer and a good many men of his own on board, he sent her off to the Spanish Governor of the island of Chiloe with a report of his exploits, and a demand for assistance in the war against the rebels. The Governor could not do much for him; but he sent in return two light field-pieces, a letter of compliments, with a colonel's commission in the royal forces, and a great Spanish flag. This standard with much ceremony was hoisted over his house in the heart of the Arauco country. Surely on that day she may have smiled on her guasso husband with a less haughty reserve (p. 49).

Again Conrad has followed Hall's description of these events with only negligible and insignificant changes, though of course Hall speaks with some contempt of Benavides:

Benavides, taking advantage of this favourable moment, augmented his authority amongst the Araucanians, by many successful incursions into Chili; till, at length, fancying himself a mighty monarch, he thought it becoming his dignity to have a fleet as well as an army. Accordingly, with the help of his bold associates, he captured several vessels. The first of these was the American ship *Hero*, which he surprised in the night, as she lay at anchor off the coast. His next prize was the *Herselia*, an American brig, which had sailed on a sealing voyage to New South Shetland, and after touching there, had come on to the Island of St Mary's, where she anchored in a small bay exactly opposite to the town of Arauco...

About a month afterwards, Benavides manned the *Herselia* brig, partly with his own people, and partly with her original crew, and dispatched her on a mission to the Island of Chiloe, to solicit assistance from the Spanish authorities there. The brig was placed under the command of the mate, who was given to understand, that, if he betrayed his trust, the captain and his other countrymen would be put to death. This warning had its effect: The brig went and returned as desired; bringing back a twenty-four-pound gun, four six-pounders, and two light field-pieces, with a quantity of ammunition; besides eleven Spanish officers, and twenty soldiers; together with the most complimentary and encouraging letters from the Governor of Chiloe, who, as a good and loyal Spaniard, was well pleased to assist any one who would harass the Patriots.[11]

The rest of Ruiz's story shows Conrad working rather more imaginatively upon hints from his sources, and following the details less closely. The dictator Carreras is the traitor who captures Ruiz's wife:

Now Carreras, under the guise of politics and liberalism, was a scoundrel of the deepest dye, and the unhappy state of Mendoza was the prey of thieves, robbers, traitors, and murderers, who formed his party. He was under a noble exterior a man without heart, pity, honour, or conscience. He aspired to nothing but tyranny, and though he would have made use of Gaspar Ruiz for his nefarious designs, yet he soon became aware that to propitiate the Chilian Government would answer his purpose better. I blush to say that he made proposals to our Government to deliver up on certain conditions the wife and child of the man who had trusted to his honour, and that this offer was accepted.

While on her way to Mendoza over the Pequeña Pass she was betrayed by her escort of Carreras' men, and given up to the officer in command of a Chilian fort on the upland at the foot of the main Cordillera range (p. 54).

Hall, on the other hand, gives only a passing reference to Carrera, the development here being Conrad's: 'he [Benavides] opened a communication with Carrera, one of the chiefs of the anarchists, who was laying waste the province of Mendoza, and invited him to take a share in these devastations'.[12]

Ruiz, setting off to rescue his wife from the Pequeña fort, seeks help from the Indian chief Peneleo: 'He sent, however, messengers to Peneleo, the Indian chief then ranging in the foothills, directing him to bring his warriors to the uplands and meet him at the lake called the Eye of Water, near whose shores the frontier fort of Pequeña was built' (p. 56). And when Peneleo and his braves meet outside the fort we have Conrad's first description of Peneleo with his beehive hairstyle: 'Peneleo, the Indian chief, sat by our fire folded in his ample mantle of guanaco skins. He was an athletic savage, with an enormous square shock head of hair resembling a straw beehive in shape and size, and with grave, surly, much-lined features' (p. 59). Peneleo comes from an earlier description by Hall:

At length Peneleo's door opened, and the chief made his appearance... A more finished picture of a savage cannot be conceived. He was a tall, broad-shouldered man; with a prodigiously large head, and a square-shaped bloated face; from which peeped out two very small eyes, partly hid by an immense superfluity of black, coarse, oily, straight hair, covering his cheeks, and hanging over his shoulders, rendering his head somewhat of the size and shape of a beehive. Over his shoulders was thrown a poncho of coarse blanket-stuff. He received us very gruffly, and appeared irritated and sulky at having been disturbed.[13]

Peneleo and his warriors make the first attack on the fort, which is surprisingly repulsed, and the failure of which leads Gaspar Ruiz to his last heroic deed:

The masses of Indians had begun to move upon the fort. They rode up in squadrons, trailing their long *chusos*; then dismounted out of musket-shot, and, throwing off their fur mantles, advanced naked to the attack, stamping their feet and shouting in cadence. A sheet of flame ran three times along the face of the fort without checking their steady march. They crowded right up to the very stakes, flourishing their broad knives. But this palisade was not fastened together with hide lashings in the usual way, but with long iron nails, which they could not cut. Dismayed at the failure of their usual method of forcing an entrance, the heathen, who had marched so steadily against the musketry fire, broke and fled under the volleys of the besieged (p. 58).

Nothing in the nature of this kind of Indian attack on a fort is to be found in Basil Hall and we might therefore feel that at last Conrad has allowed his imagination a freer rein. But for this passage Conrad turned to an entirely different work, one which has held its renown throughout the years, Charles Darwin's account of his journey round the world in HMS *Beagle*. Darwin recalls a story he heard of an attack made by bands of Indians:

A man present at one [an Indian attack] gave me a very lively description of what took place. The inhabitants had sufficient notice to drive all the cattle and horses into the 'corral' which surrounded the house, and likewise to mount some small cannon. The Indians were Araucanians from the south of Chile; several hundreds in number, and highly disciplined. They first appeared in two bodies on a neighbouring hill; having there dismounted, and taken off their fur mantles, they advanced naked to the charge. The only weapon of an Indian is a very long bamboo or chuzo, ornamented with ostrich feathers, and pointed by a sharp spearhead. My informer seemed to remember with the greatest horror the quivering of these chuzos as they approached near. When close, the cacique Pincheira hailed the besieged to give up their arms, or he would cut all their throats. As this would probably have been the result of their entrance under any circumstances, the answer was given by a volley of musketry. The Indians, with great steadiness, came to the very fence of the corral: but to their surprise they found the posts fastened together by iron nails instead of leather thongs, and, of course, in vain attempted to cut them with their knives. This saved the lives of the Christians: many of the wounded Indians were carried away by their companions; and at last one of the under caciques being wounded, the bugle sounded a retreat.[14]

The source of Gaspar Ruiz's final effort to save his wife—he supports a gun on his back—is not known, though Conrad in his ambiguous way seems to suggest that he had a particular source in mind:

Another document connected with this story is a letter of a biting and ironic kind from a friend then in Burma, passing certain strictures upon 'the gentleman with the gun on his back'...Yet the gun episode did really happen, or at least I am bound to believe it because I remember it, described in an extremely matter-of-fact tone, in some book I read in my boyhood.[15]

15

THE GARIBALDINO

Nostromo has been admired because it 'creates a continent [South America] which [Conrad] had only glimpsed',[1] and certainly Conrad's personal experience of South America was by his own confession a brief and distant one by the time he came to write the novel—'I just had a glimpse 25 years ago', he told Cunninghame Graham.[2] Previous studies of the sources of the novel have shown, however, that *Nostromo* depends neither upon this brief glimpse nor entirely upon Conrad's immense power of visualisation. It was from a number of books written about the South American continent that Conrad obtained certain important material for his novel. One, to which he himself refers in his Author's Note, is the tale of the stolen lighter of silver which he came across in the life story of an American sailor, a book identified by Mr John Halverson and Professor Ian Watt as Frederick Benton Williams's *On Many Seas: The Life and Exploits of a Yankee Sailor* (1897).[3] The torture of Dr Monygham was shown by Ivo Vidan and Edgar Wright to be derived from George Frederick Masterman's account of his own torture in *Seven Eventful Years in Paraguay* (1869),[4] and Jocelyn Baines and Edgar Wright pointed to the exploits of the tyrant Francisco Solano Lopez as providing suggestions for the past history of the imaginary Occidental Republic.[5]

In this section on *Nostromo*, as well as introducing some new sources, I wish to demonstrate certain aspects of Conrad's use of sources in the novel. The South American continent had been well observed and written about, and Conrad might have put himself through an intensive reading course in preparation for writing his book, had he wished.* Ultimately, though, one has to conclude that a handful of books only were of importance to the novel in the sense that one can trace them as definite sources, but the borrowings here are of a particular kind. They provide Conrad mainly with hints for characters, names, incidents, topography; rarely do we discover a substantial borrowing from any one book, and no one important source as in the case, for example, of *Lord Jim*. This use of sources would seem to reflect Conrad's need to take from authors details of which he would be ignorant himself, but it also suggests a larger imaginative freedom on Conrad's part in building up character and incident without too much reliance on any specific source. On the other hand, one must stress also that a number of books are significant as sources because they provide the suggestions for important movements within the historical, socio-economic world of the novel. And finally one becomes impressed by the influence of actual historical events—not simply the tyranny of Lopez, but historical movements and ideas, true of the continent.

I shall deal here with the borrowings that can be traced with some certainty, and with the wider and less easily demonstrated influences in the conclusion.

*

The Italian element in the novel is strong and, as Conrad pointed out, inevitable: 'the thing is perfectly credible: Italians were swarming into the Occidental Province at the time, as anybody who will read further can see', he wrote in his Author's Note,[6] and this was equally true of the South American republics. But one Italian in particular was chosen by Conrad to stand against the material interests and the revolutionaries who are inspired by them—'Giorgio

* I read about 200 books on the area in search of Conrad's sources.

Viola the Garibaldino, the Idealist of the old, humanitarian revolutions'.[7]

And Viola brings us to a relatively unexplored, and from Conrad's point of view, very personal source, whose influence cannot now easily be tapped, since, like the influence of Ford Madox Ford, it depended upon a friendship. I am referring, of course, to R. B. Cunninghame Graham's relationship with Conrad, for Cunninghame Graham's experience of South America must have had some influence upon *Nostromo* —perhaps the fundamental one of turning Conrad's thoughts to that continent as a setting for a novel. There are certain parallels between Charles Gould and R. B. Cunninghame Graham which tempt one to suggest that Conrad had his friend in mind as a model for this character in the novel. Both are given Spanish names—Don Roberto, Don Carlos; both are remarkable for their flaming hair and moustaches; both have early family connections with the country in a political sense; both met their wives on the continent of Europe; both wives sketch and both wives went on an exhausting tour of a South American country with their respective husbands.

Conrad was engaged in writing the first part of the novel between January or February 1903 and 22 August of the same year. The beginning is marked by his letter to John Galsworthy—'Only with my head full of a story, I have not been able to write a single word—except the title, which shall be, I think: *Nostromo*',[8] and the completion by his letter to Pinker sending him 'half of the book, about 42,000 or so. I send it as forming only one part, the First, entitled: "The Silver of the Mine"'.[9] But between these two dates there are two letters to Cunninghame Graham whose authority on South American matters Conrad fully acknowledged. On 9 May he wrote: 'I want to talk to you of the work I am engaged on now. I hardly dare avow my audacity—but I am placing it in Sth America, in a Republic I call Costaguana. It is however concerned mostly with Italians. But you must hear the *sujet* and this I can't set down on a small piece of paper.'[10]

His second letter on 8 July can be interpreted as showing the need for further assistance: 'I am dying over that cursed Nostromo thing. All my memories of Central America seem to slip away. I just had a glimpse 25 years ago—short glance. That is not enough pour bâtir un roman dessus.'[11] Presumably between 9 May and 8 July there was at least one discussion with Cunninghame Graham specifically on the subject of the novel and at a time when the first part of the work was being written. And it is in this first part of eight chapters that we can find convincing evidence of Cunninghame Graham's influence. Chapters 3 and 4 of Part 1 introduce Giorgio Viola and establish his character and history. I have no doubt that the first suggestion for Viola came to Conrad from Cunninghame Graham. But the character of Viola, through his loyalty to Garibaldi, leads us to another and quite significant source for the novel.

Viola is presented as 'Old Giorgio Viola, a Genoese with a shaggy white leonine head—often called simply "the Garibaldino" (as Mohammedans are called after their prophet)' (p. 16). He has a 'little hotel...standing alone halfway between the harbour and the town' (p. 15). He had been 'one of Garibaldi's immortal thousand in the conquest of Sicily' (p. 20). Conrad might have heard from Cunninghame Graham of a similar Italian innkeeper in South America, or he might have read of him in Graham's collection *Thirteen Stories* which was published in 1900. In this book, a sketch called 'Cruz Alta' contains the following account:

Two days we passed in Ytapua resting our horses, and I renewed my friendship with Enrico Clerici, an Italian, who had served with Garibaldi, and who, three years ago, I had met in the same place and given him a silver ring which he reported galvanized, and was accustomed to lend as a great favour for a specific against rheumatism. He kept a *pulperia*, and being a born fighter, his delight was, when a row occurred (which he styled 'una barulla de Jesu Cristo'), to clear the place by flinging empty bottles from the bar. A handsome, gentlemanlike man, and terrible with a bottle in his hand, whether as weapon of offence or for the purposes of drink; withal well educated, and no doubt by this time long dead, slain by his favourite weapon.[12]

The parallels between Giorgio Viola and Enrico Clerici are obvious—both are Italian, both have served with Garibaldi, both became innkeepers in South America. But in character the two men are totally different, and there is no suggestion in the sketch of Enrico Clerici of the extreme admiration Viola has for Garibaldi. But Clerici did share this admiration, as we find in another sketch by Graham which appeared later in a volume called *Hope* (1910), and it is possible that Conrad heard of this admiration from Graham in the course of conversation: 'Spaniards and Frenchmen sat side by side with an Italian, one Enrique Clerici, who had served with Garibaldi in his youth, but now was owner of a *pulperia* that he had named "The Rose of the South", and in it hung a picture of his quondam leader, which he referred to as "my saint".'[13]

Conrad takes up the implication here of intense admiration for Garibaldi which is suggested by the picture and the phrase 'my saint', and evolves the central fact of Viola's life. Unlike his Italian wife Señora Teresa, he does not believe in saints, or in prayers, or in what he called 'priest's religion'. Liberty and Garibaldi are his divinities; and as he and his family—he has two daughters—await the attack of the rioters on his isolated inn, we have evidence of his attachment to Garibaldi:

A discharge of firearms near by made her throw her head back and close her eyes. Old Giorgio set his teeth hard under his white moustache, and his eyes began to roll fiercely. Several bullets struck the end of the wall together; pieces of plaster could be heard falling outside; a voice screamed 'Here they come!' and after a moment of uneasy silence there was a rush of running feet along the front.

Then the tension of old Giorgio's attitude relaxed, and a smile of contemptuous relief came upon his lips of an old fighter with a leonine-face. These were not a people striving for justice, but thieves. Even to defend his life against them was a sort of degradation for a man who had been one of Garibaldi's immortal thousand in the conquest of Sicily. He had an immense scorn for this outbreak of scoundrels and leperos, who did not know the meaning of the word 'liberty'.

He grounded his old gun, and, turning his head, glanced at the coloured lithograph of Garibaldi in a black frame on the white wall; a thread of strong sunshine cut it perpendicularly. His eyes, accustomed to the luminous twilight, made out the high colouring of the face, the red of the shirt, the outlines of the square shoulders, the black patch of the Bersagliere hat with cock's feathers, curling over the crown. An immortal hero! This was your liberty; it gave you not only life, but immortality as well!

For that one man his fanaticism had suffered no diminution (pp. 20-1).

Not only does Conrad enlarge upon the idea of the picture of Garibaldi, describing it in detail and making it a focus in the Casa Viola, but the conception of a revolutionary striving not for personal gain but for justice, as Garibaldi did, is set immediately against the present revolution in Costaguana where the leaders are interested only in power and in the silver of the mine—'These were not a people striving for justice, but thieves.' Thus Viola, representative of the ideals of Garibaldi, takes his place significantly in the novel's design.*

The details of Viola's past history, which are given in a series of flashbacks and allusions to past events, do not derive from Clerici. Conrad here reinforces the Garibaldi theme by linking Viola's life to his hero's:

* As this book was going to press, I came upon Rosemary Freeman's article, 'Conrad's *Nostromo*: A source and its use' in *Modern Fiction Studies*, VII, no. 4, winter 1961–2, pp. 317–26, in which she also deals with the influence of Garibaldi upon *Nostromo*, pointing to parallels between the novel and Garibaldi's life, and also to the influence of Garibaldi on 'The End of the Tether'.

The Garibaldino

When quite a youth he had deserted from a ship trading to La Plata, to enlist in the navy of Montevideo, then under the command of Garibaldi. Afterwards, in the Italian legion of the Republic struggling against the encroaching tyranny of Rosas, he had taken part, on great plains, on the banks of immense rivers, in the fiercest fighting perhaps the world had ever known. He had lived amongst men who had declaimed about liberty, suffered for liberty, died for liberty, with a desperate exaltation, and with their eyes turned towards an oppressed Italy. His own enthusiasm had been fed on scenes of carnage, on the examples of lofty devotion, on the din of armed struggle, on the inflamed language of proclamations. He had never parted from the chief of his choice—the fiery apostle of independence—keeping by his side in America and in Italy till after the fatal day of Aspromonte (p. 29).

Thus through his association with Garibaldi, the life of Viola is plotted from 1842, when Garibaldi commanded the fleet of Uruguay, and 1843 when he organised the Italian Legion there, to 1860 when he invaded Sicily, and finally to 1862 when he was wounded and captured at the battle of Aspromonte. Viola was also concerned in the retreat from Rome in 1862, during which Garibaldi's wife Anita died. Conrad makes use of two specific incidents involving Garibaldi and his wife at that time, and it is possible through one of these incidents to trace a second source for Viola. Viola, we are told, 'was one of the four fugitives who, with the general, carried out of the woods the inanimate body of the general's wife into the farmhouse where she died, exhausted by the hardships of that terrible retreat' (p. 31). Of the actual event upon which this is based, we learn from Paul Frischauer's *Garibaldi: The Man and the Nation*[14] that, having attempted to escape in some stolen fishing-vessels, Garibaldi was forced to come ashore again because of his wife's illness. John Parris in his biography describes the scene thus: 'The last three to come ashore moved slowly. One of them dragged a wounded foot behind him; the other stumbled through the waters with the still figure of a woman in his arms.'[15] This third person was called Leggero. Frischauer writes: 'Only the lame

Leggero had followed Anita and Garibaldi ashore',[16] and Leggero would appear to be the source for Viola who had also been 'wounded in the defence of the Roman Republic'. Leggero was the nom-de-guerre of Giovanni Guliolo, of whom John Parris writes: 'A native of Maddalena, he had served in the Piedmontese navy for seven years and deserted in Montevideo in 1839, and had later joined the Italian Legion there.'[17] We know that Conrad's Viola had 'when quite a youth...deserted from a ship trading to La Plata, to enlist in the navy of Montevideo, then under the command of Garibaldi' and that afterwards he served 'in the Italian legion of the Republic struggling against the...tyranny of Rosas'. Starting with aspects of Clerici, Conrad has thus added appropriate historical experience of Garibaldi's campaigns together with certain experiences of Leggero, a follower of Garibaldi.

Another incident from the last illness of Garibaldi's wife Anita is used effectively in the death scene of Viola's wife Señora Teresa:

Thus Garibaldi and Anita remained together even when danger was very near, and the tiny procession took to the road once more. On the way Anita was hungry and Garibaldi implored two country lads to find her a little soup. His voice was so full of agony that the boys rushed to the nearest house and begged that a fowl might be killed and broth prepared. But when the broth appeared Anita was too exhausted to drink. Her face was deathly pale, her hair dishevelled, she could scarcely breathe. White foam formed on her lips, which her husband removed with a silk handkerchief. The August sun blazed down without mercy, and the conveyance which carried Anita could only advance very slowly. She begged for water. But there was none to be had. At last the men who were accompanying them, heard her say: 'Giuseppe—the children!' Then she became silent. The cart rolled slowly over the stony path.[18]

These words, 'Giuseppe—the children!' were not Anita's last words, but Conrad makes them the last words of the dying Teresa. Martin Decoud describes the scene in the Albergo d'Italia Una during the revolution:

Just then a shot was fired in the kitchen, which made us jump and cower as if at a thunder-clap. It seems that the party of soldiers had stolen quite close up, and one of them had crept up to the door. He looked in, thought there was no one there, and, holding his rifle ready, entered quietly. The chief told me that he had just closed his eyes for a moment. When he opened them, he saw the man already in the middle of the room peering into the dark corners. The chief was so startled that, without thinking, he made one leap from the recess right out in front of the fireplace. The soldier, no less startled, up with his rifle and pulls the trigger, deafening and singeing the engineer, but in his flurry missing him completely. But, look what happens! At the noise of the report the sleeping woman sat up, as if moved by a spring, with a shriek, 'The children, Gian' Battista! Save the children!' (p. 340).

A significant aspect of Viola is his immense admiration for the English:[19]

Giorgio Viola had a great consideration for the English. This feeling, born on the battlefields of Uruguay, was forty years old at the very least. Several of them had poured their blood for the cause of freedom in America, and the first he had ever known he remembered by the name of Samuel; he commanded a negro company under Garibaldi, during the famous siege of Montevideo, and died heroically with his negroes at the fording of the Boyana...And everywhere he had seen Englishmen in the front rank of the army of freedom. He respected their nation because they loved Garibaldi (pp. 30–1).

Although the possibility of there having been an Englishman called Samuel with a negro company fighting under Garibaldi seemed unlikely, Conrad's use of Garibaldi's history as a source for Viola made it a worthwhile line of search. And the first reference to such a man was found in a book by Rear-Admiral H. F. Winnington-Ingram in an account of the siege of Montevideo:

I will relate [a story] that went the round of the barracks in connection with the doings of...Cockney Sam...Our hero (?), one very dark night, when engaged in an outpost enterprise, found himself suddenly face to face with a Blanco sentinel. The latter was proceeding to level his musket at him, when he shouted out: 'De tengase usted un instante, estoy Samuel de Londres' (Stop a moment, I am Samuel of London). The man was paralysed with fear, and an easy victim to the assassin's knife.[20]

But the most detailed account of the siege of Montevideo so far as Garibaldi's exploits are concerned is that edited by the French novelist Alexandre Dumas. The story of Samuel is given in Garibaldi's own words:

There was between us and Ceno, a sort of muddy river, called the Bayarda [actually Boyada]. We had to cross this with the mud up to our middles. In order to endeavour to throw disorder into the passage the enemy established upon a hillock a battery of four pieces of cannon, which began playing upon us at the moment we commenced crossing. But the Italian legion was becoming more warlike every day; they took no more notice of this shower of *mitraille* than if it had been an ordinary shower of hail. It was then I saw what brave men our negroes were. They suffered themselves to be killed, awaiting the enemy one knee on the ground. I was in the very midst of them, and was able to see how they behaved. The fight lasted six hours.

There was an Englishman in the service of Montevideo. My Englishman of the last campaign has more than once reminded me of his compatriot. There was then in the service of Montevideo, who had *carte blanche* from Pacheco, who knew him well, to do everything he thought would be serviceable. He had from forty to fifty men under his command. We called him Samuel; I don't know whether he had any other name or not. I never saw a braver man than he was. After the passage of the Bayarda [*sic*], I saw him coming alone with his warrant.

'Well, Samuel,' said I, 'where is your regiment?'

'Regiment!' cried he, 'Attention!'

Nobody appeared, nobody answered; his men had all been killed from first to the last.[21]

Giorgio's Samuel is not quite the same as Garibaldi's, since the real Samuel did not die, but it is Garibaldi's assessment of Samuel—'I never saw a braver man'—that Conrad gives to Giorgio.

Clerici's portrait of Garibaldi which hung in the *pulperia* is taken up by Conrad, and Viola's portrait of his former hero, as it is described in *Nostromo*, is carefully based upon Garibaldi's appearance as a young man—the high colouring of the face, the red of the shirt, and the black patch of the Bersagliere hat are typical. But Conrad went further than this and actually based Viola's appearance and character upon Garibaldi as an old man. Viola has a 'shaggy white leonine head': he is 'the old fighter with a leonine face'. Each afternoon 'the Garibaldino could be seen...with his big bush of white hair, his arms folded, his legs crossed, leaning back his leonine head against the lintel, and looking up the wooded slopes of the foothills at the snowy dome of Higuerota' (p. 26). Old Viola is even called by the local people 'an old lion'. His character is best summed up by the following account:

The spirit of self-forgetfulness, the simple devotion to a vast humanitarian idea which inspired the thought and stress of that revolutionary time, had left its mark upon Giorgio in a sort of austere contempt for all personal advantage. This man, whom the lowest class in Sulaco suspected of having a buried hoard in his kitchen, had all his life despised money. The leaders of his youth had lived poor, had died poor. It had been a habit of his mind to disregard to-morrow. It was engendered partly by an existence of excitement, adventure, and wild warfare. But mostly it was a matter of principle. It did not resemble the carelessness of a condottiere, it was a puritanism of conduct, born of stern enthusiasm like the puritanism of religion (p. 31).

'We wanted nothing, we suffered for the love of all humanity!' he cried out furiously sometimes, and the powerful voice, the blazing eyes, the shaking of the white mane, the brown, sinewy hand pointing upwards as if to call heaven to witness, impressed his hearers (p. 32).

Almost any photograph of Garibaldi in his old age will show those aspects which Conrad reflects in his physical descriptions of Viola. Like Viola he was described as an old lion—both because of his physical attributes and because of his courage. John Parris entitled his life of Garibaldi, *The Lion of Caprera*, and David Larg in his impressive biography written in the 1930s writes: 'He looked sometimes like a lion and sometimes like the pictures of Jesus Christ.'[22] Like Viola also, Garibaldi was renowned for refusing financial rewards. After he had achieved great fame during the Montevideo siege and immediately after his victory at the Salto San Antonio, the French admiral Lainé called on him only to discover that the Garibaldis' house was in darkness, there being not a penny to buy a candle.[23]

Viola thus derives in part from the lives and careers of two followers of Garibaldi, but significantly, he is in his appearance and character Garibaldi *himself*.*

*

One of the most moving incidents in *Nostromo* would also appear to derive from the life of Garibaldi. It is an ironically comic fate that puts Hirsch, the Jewish dealer in hides, into the power of his torturer, General Sotillo. Hirsch, discovered hiding in the lighter of silver when Decoud and Nostromo are taking it out into the gulf, is swept by accident, during a collision in the dark between the lighter and Sotillo's transport, on to Sotillo's vessel. Sotillo, driven by greed, refuses to believe Hirsch's story—that the transport has collided with the lighter of silver and sunk it—and is willing to believe Dr Monygham's false story that the silver has been buried somewhere along the shore for Gould's own private purposes. Sotillo, convinced that Hirsch knows where the silver is hidden, decides to torture him into telling the 'truth' he wishes to hear. He is brought, in one of the rooms of the Custom House, into the presence of Sotillo:

Sotillo looked at him in silence. 'Will you depart from your obstinacy, you rogue?' he asked. Already a rope, whose one end was fastened to Señor Hirsch's wrists, had been thrown over a beam, and three soldiers held the other end, waiting. He made no answer. His heavy lower lip hung stupidly. Sotillo made a sign. Hirsch was jerked up off his feet,

* Hints for two other characters in *Nostromo* can be traced to Dumas's edition of Garibaldi's autobiography—Anzani, the shopkeeper and Hernandez, the bandit. Anzani takes his name and occupation from one of Garibaldi's comrades-in-arms during his South American experiences[24] and an incident in the life of the actual Anzani gave Conrad suggestions for the character of Hernandez.[25]

and a yell of despair and agony burst out in the room, filled the passage of the great buildings, rent the air outside, caused every soldier of the camp along the shore to look up at the windows...

Sotillo followed by the soldiers, had left the room. The sentry on the landing presented arms. Hirsch went on screaming all alone behind the half-closed jalousies...He screamed with uplifted eyebrows and a wide-open-mouth—incredibly wide, black, enormous, full of teeth—comical...

The sun had set when he [Sotillo] went in once more. A soldier carried in two lighted candles and slunk out, shutting the door without noise.

'Speak, thou Jewish child of the devil! The silver! The silver, I say! Where is it? Where have you foreign rogues hidden it? Confess or—'

A slight quiver passed up the taut rope from the racked limbs, but the body of Señor Hirsch, enterprising business man from Esmeralda, hung under the heavy beam perpendicular and silent, facing the colonel awfully. The inflow of the night air, cooled by the snows of the Sierra, spread gradually a delicious freshness through the close heat of the room.

'Speak—thief—scoundrel—picaro—or—'

Sotillo had seized the riding-whip, and stood with his arm lifted up. For a word, for one little word, he felt he would have knelt, cringed, grovelled on the floor before the drowsy, conscious stare of those fixed eyeballs starting out of the grimy, dishevelled head that drooped very still with its mouth closed askew. The colonel ground his teeth with rage and struck. The rope vibrated leisurely to the blow, like the long string of a pendulum starting from a rest. But no swinging motion was imparted to the body of Señor Hirsch, the well-known hide merchant on the coast. With a convulsive effort of the twisted arms it leaped up a few inches, curling upon itself like a fish on the end of a line. Señor Hirsch's head was flung back on his straining throat; his chin trembled. For a moment the rattle of his chattering teeth pervaded the vast, shadowy room, where the candles made a patch of light round the two flames burning side by side. And as Sotillo, staying his raised hand, waited for him to speak, with the sudden flash of a grin and a straining forward of the wrenched shoulders, he spat violently into his face.

The uplifted whip fell, and the colonel sprang back with a low cry of dismay, as if aspersed by a jet of deadly venom. Quick as thought he snatched up his revolver, and fired twice. The report and the concussion of the shots seemed to throw him at once from ungovernable rage into idiotic stupor. He stood with drooping jaw and stony eyes. What had he done, *sangre de Dios!* What had he done? (pp. 445–9).

For the source of this terrible incident, the attempt at forcing a confession by means of the *estrapado*, and the final heroic spitting in the face of his enemy by Hirsch, we have to go to the autobiography of Garibaldi edited by Alexandre Dumas. Garibaldi's account of being taken prisoner by Governor Don Leonardo Milan is suitably low-toned, as befits an account of one's own heroic actions:

No one will accuse me of being too tender to myself; and yet, I confess that I shudder every time that circumstance of my life is recalled to my mind. Being led into the presence of Don Leonardo Milan, I was required by him to denounce those who had furnished me with means of escape. It may be concluded that I declared I had alone prepared, and alone carried my flight into execution; then, as I was bound, and Don Leonardo Milan had nothing to fear, he came up angrily to me, and began to strike me with his whip; after which he renewed his demands, and I repeated my denials. He then ordered me to be taken to prison, adding a few words in a whisper to my conductors. These words were an order to put me to the torture.

On arriving at the chamber destined for me, my guards, in consequence of the whispered order, leaving my hands tied behind my back, passed a fresh cord round my wrists, turned the other end of it round a joist, and pulling it towards them, they suspended me at about four or five feet from the ground. Don Leonardo Milan then entered my prison, and asked me if I would confess. I could do nothing but spit in his face, and I gave myself that satisfaction.

'It is very well!' said he, leaving the chamber. 'When the prisoner shall please to confess, you will call me, and when he has confessed, he shall be let down to the ground again.' After which he went out. I remained two hours suspended in this manner. All the weight of my body hung by my bleeding wrists and my dislocated shoulders. My whole body burned like a furnace; at every instant I begged for water, and my guards, more humane than my executioner, gave me some; but the water, on entering my stomach, dried up, as if it had been thrown upon a bar of red hot iron. No idea can be formed of what I suffered but by reading the tortures inflicted upon prisoners in the Middle Ages. At the end of the two hours, my guards took pity on me, or believed me dead, for they let me down. I fell flat, at full length. I was nothing but an inert mass, without any feeling but heavy, severe pain—a dead body or nearly so.[26]

The Garibaldino

Of course, Conrad has made some radical changes here—Milan did not shoot his victim on being spat at, and the transformation of character is very great. Viola presumably might have survived, as Garibaldi his counterpart did, but Hirsch is the kind of man whom only Conrad celebrated—one who, through an excess of imagination is unmanned—and indeed Conrad deliberately compares Captain Mitchell with Hirsch in order to underline his point:

Nothing, not even a gleam of light from anywhere, interfered with Captain Mitchell's meditation. He did some hard but not very extensive thinking. It was not of a gloomy cast. The old sailor, with all his small weaknesses and absurdities, was constitutionally incapable of entertaining for any length of time a fear of his personal safety. It was not so much firmness of soul as the lack of a certain kind of imagination—the kind whose undue development caused intense suffering to Señor Hirsch; that sort of imagination which adds the blind terror of bodily suffering and of death, envisaged as an accident to the body alone, strictly—to all the other apprehensions on which the sense of one's existence is based (p. 338).

16

NOSTROMO AND DECOUD

For the character of Nostromo, Conrad was guided, as he says in his Author's Note, by the demands of this particular novel—the need for 'a man of the People' to stand by Viola. His nationality was determined by the population facts of the area; his central dilemma, the responsibility for and corrupting influence of the silver, came from the tale of the sailor 'who was supposed to have stolen single-handed a whole lighterful of silver, somewhere on the Tierra Firme seaboard during the troubles of a revolution'.[1] This 'vagrant anecdote completely destitute of valuable details' was reinforced by information which Conrad found in Frederick Benton Williams's book *On Many Seas: The Life and Exploits of a Yankee Sailor*.[2] And, Conrad adds in his Author's Note,

> In the sailor's story he [the thief] is represented as an unmitigated rascal, a small cheat, stupidly ferocious, morose, of mean appearance, and altogether unworthy of the greatness this opportunity had thrust upon him. What was interesting was that he would boast of it openly.
>
> He used to say: 'People think I make a lot of money in this schooner of mine. But that is nothing. I don't care for that. Now and then I go away quietly and lift a bar of silver. I must get rich slowly—you understand.'[3]

A comparison of Conrad's version here with the original text confirms certain aspects which appear in the novel. There is the basic situation of the plot—the silver had to be got away during a revolution. There is also the great trust his employers had in the sailor who was put in charge of the silver—a misplaced trust in the case of the original story, since the sailor was obviously a rogue. Conrad, with great perception, shows Nostromo to be worthy of that trust, indeed to live by the good word of others, and to be corrupted into the theft by his sudden appreciation of the true circumstances surrounding himself and the silver: 'His fidelity had been taken advantage of...He had been betrayed!' His employers never lose their trust in Nostromo's honesty and ability, even after he becomes rich. Conrad was able to see that the sailor 'need not necessarily be a confirmed rogue... he could be even a man of character'.[4]

Italian and a man of character—this leads Conrad to a possible source in his own experience: 'Dominic [Cervoni], the padrone of the *Tremolino*', whom he had known at Marseilles between 1874 and 1878, 'might under given circumstances have been a Nostromo'.[5] Dominic Cervoni was first mate of the *Saint Antoine*, the vessel in which Conrad sailed to the West Indies and then on to the South American continent. But he was also, if Conrad's account in *The Mirror of the Sea* can be accepted as fact, involved in Conrad's youthful adventure, gun-running for the Carlist cause in the *Tremolino*. Cervoni's fearlessness and caustic manner, specifically mentioned by Conrad, are the traits that were passed to Nostromo. And Conrad also writes in his Author's Note to *Nostromo*: 'Many of Nostromo's speeches I have heard first in Dominic's voice' (p. xxii). In this matter we have had to take Conrad's word for it since nothing very much has been known about the historical Dominic Cervoni.

Unlike Nostromo, who is Genoese, Dominic Cervoni was a Corsican, and according to Conrad he had with him in the *Tremolino* his nephew Cesar Cervoni. After much searching I was able to find the son of Cesar Cervoni* and it appears that Cesar was not Dominic's nephew—the two were not related. But Cesar did serve in the *Saint Antoine* with Dominic, and his son was able to give me some information

---

* See Plate 7 a for photograph of Cesar Cervoni.

about Dominic and about Conrad's relationship with him. What he had to say does help to confirm, I think, that Conrad did have Dominic in mind, to a certain degree, in his portrait of Nostromo:

The captain Dominic Cervoni who had travelled on all types of vessels was a very brave man on land. On board, he was indeed, the real master after God on his ship. He belonged to the Brotherhood of the Coast, a kind of Mafia. He was a filibuster and under the cover of navigation was smuggling goods from one continent to another. My countryman [Cesar's son recalls his father saying] was a fearful and feared leader, if one can go by the deference and respect which was shown to him when he met people in the course of long voyages.'[6]

Nostromo, who is younger than the Dominic Cervoni Conrad knew, certainly dresses more flamboyantly but just as Dominic 'belonged to the Brotherhood of the Coast, a kind of Mafia', Nostromo is leader of the Cargadores and later of the labour movement and is a 'fearful and feared leader': 'There was not one of them that had not, at some time or other, looked with terror at Nostromo's revolver poked very close at his face...He was "much of a man"...a tireless taskmaster, the more to be feared because of his aloofness' (pp. 14–15). Monygham comments that the revolutionaries will go for strength 'to the secret societies amongst the immigrants and natives, where Nostromo...is the great man' (p. 511).

Dominic was a smuggler, according to Cesar Cervoni's son, and Conrad gives us an account of gun-running when dealing with the *Tremolino* incident. The group Conrad was involved with chose Dominic Cervoni to command the *Tremolino* as being a man capable of outwitting customs officials and smuggling arms from Marseilles to the Spanish coast—'he was the very man'.[7] Nostromo also is chosen for difficult tasks, and is particularly involved in smuggling the silver out of Costaguana. He is 'the indispensable man', 'tried and trusty', an 'invaluable fellow'. According to

Conrad, Dominic has a physical assurance which attracted that splendid lady and Carlist intriguer, Doña Rita: 'il est parfait, cet homme', she says,[8] and Nostromo is attractive to women also—both the Viola girls are in love with him. Dominic Cervoni's character of bravery on land and sea and his qualities of leadership can be seen in the character of Nostromo. Indeed, it is particularly when he is at sea with the lighter of silver that Nostromo becomes the fearful and feared leader, superior to the educated Decoud and extravagantly threatening to put a bullet into the head of Hirsch and a knife into Decoud's heart if, during the movement of Sotillo's transport across their bows, either makes a sound. To Hirsch he shouts: 'If I hear as much as a loud breath from you I shall come over there and put a bullet through your head' (p. 274) and to Decoud: '*Por Dios*, Don Martin... if I didn't know your worship to be a man of courage, capable of standing stock still whatever happens, I would drive my knife into your heart' (p. 279).[9]

Martin Decoud, 'the brilliant Costaguanero of the boulevards' who returns home from Paris to become the 'young apostle of Separation', can be given a definite origin in terms of his name and occupation. Ivo Vidan has already pointed out that 'a certain Carlos Decoud is mentioned near the beginning [of Masterman's book, *Seven Eventful Years in Paraguay*] in an account of an unhappy incident, bearing a remote similarity to the Martin Decoud situation in *Nostromo*'.[10] Actually, two Decoud brothers are mentioned by Masterman, but the initial source of Martin Decoud lies in another Decoud brother altogether who lived outside Paraguay and was a mortal enemy of Lopez. The following reference is from R. F. Burton's *Letters from the Battle-fields of Paraguay*:

We call upon D. Juan Decoud, editor of *El Liberal*, the most advanced paper; he has fled his country (Paraguay), where he owes a long tale of vengeance. Of this distinguished family one was put to death by the elder Lopez, and another commands a Paraguayan brigade in the Allied service—D. Juan may look forward to becoming Minister and even President.[11]

Martin Decoud, like Juan Decoud, was a journalist: 'great black letters appeared painted between the windows above the arcaded ground floor of a house on the Plaza...The big black letters formed the words, "Offices of the *Porvenir*". From these offices a single folded sheet of Martin's journalism issued three times a week' (p. 159). And the title of Decoud's newspaper, *Porvenir*, no doubt derives from the *Porvenir* which was published in Cartagena, and which Conrad may well have seen during his visit there in 1876.[12] Decoud, in his paper, attacks General Montero: 'I call Montero a "gran' bestia" every second day in the *Porvenir*' (p. 177). Masterman, during his enforced confession, accused Charles S. Washburn, Minister Resident for the United States of America in Paraguay, of leading a conspiracy against Lopez and intersperses his confession 'with abuse and ridicule of "el gran bestia"'.[13] Washburn himself recalls in his *History of Paraguay*: 'The torturers had taught him that the more extravagant the denunciations of the "evil genius of Paraguay", or the "Great Beast" as the inquisitors were accustomed to call me, the more acceptable were his "declarations" to their master.'[14]

But Conrad hints in his Author's Note at a similarity between himself and Decoud which would appear to lie in the relationship between Decoud and Antonia Avellanos. Conrad states that Antonia was modelled on his first love, and that in this relationship he was 'very much like poor Decoud'. But the similarity would seem to be only in their common situation as rejected lovers, for to a considerable extent the relationship between Antonia and Decoud derives from Conrad's reading. It is doubtful whether much of

Conrad's personal experience is present here.[15] Baines has pointed to the source for Antonia in a certain Antonia Ribera whom Edward B. Eastwick met in Venezuela.[16] The fictional girl's beauty, her free, European manners, her seriousness and her intention of marrying a foreigner all derive from Antonia Ribera. However, Antonia's devotion to her father in the novel could not derive from Antonia Ribera, since her father was dead. But Conrad probably noticed in Eastwick an account of another girl, Erminia, who is particularly devoted to her father.[17]

I think it can be shown, however, that there is a closer relationship between the character of Decoud and that of Conrad than Conrad allows, and that Conrad would seem, for certain parts of the novel, to have returned to his early days in Marseilles for suggestions for Decoud. Certainly a similarity exists between Conrad and Martin Decoud if we consider the young Conrad at Marseilles and the nature of the relationship between Dominic Cervoni and Conrad at that time, and if we take into account also some of the views expressed by Conrad at a later date in letters to Cunninghame Graham. According to Cesar Cervoni's son, Cesar knew Conrad to be a Polish gentleman: 'then for the first time he [Cesar] told me he had known a Polish nobleman who had become a writer in England and who had honoured him by calling him friend'. In the same letter Cesar's son recalls his father's first meeting with the young Conrad:

One day, when my father was on board the *Saint Antoine* my father saw a slim and very distinguished man arrive in the company of his fellow countryman Dominic Cervoni. He went to the forecastle to greet them and the captain invited him to follow them to his cabin. The explanation was brief for this other Cervoni didn't like long speeches. Dominic Cervoni said that the gentleman had been put on board by the firm as super-cargo and he recommended him to my father's care. After having tidied up the small cabin in which this passenger was going to stay, my father went out for news and met the Captain who told him in patois to take care of the man and to spare him too many contacts with the other members of the crew.[18]

In *The Mirror of the Sea* Conrad describes joining the *Tremolino* in preparation for a gun-running expedition: 'He [Dominic] would raise a lantern silently to light my steps along the narrow, spring plank of our primitive gangway. "And so we are going off", he would murmur directly my foot touched the deck' (p. 162). Conrad and Dominic come together on a gun-running expedition and Decoud and Nostromo come together at night on an expedition to save the silver of the San Tomé mine. Decoud, like Conrad, is looked upon as distinguished and aristocratic, and he too is a writer of sorts. Superior in many ways, Decoud, again like Conrad, when at sea is under the command of the braver and nautically more skilled Nostromo/Dominic:

Nostromo detected the ironic tone. 'I dare say, Señor Don Martin', he said, moodily. There are very few things that I am not equal to. Ask the foreign signori. I, a man of the people, who cannot always understand what you mean. But as to this lot which I must leave here, let me tell you that I would believe it in greater safety if you had not been with me at all' (p. 301).

Decoud commits suicide, and we know that it was just after his adventures with the Cervonis that Conrad attempted suicide. Conrad's uncle wrote:

While still in possession of the 3,000 fr...he met his former Captain, Mr. Duteil, who persuaded him to participate in some enterprise on the coasts of Spain—some kind of contraband!...he lost the lot...he returns to Marseilles and one fine evening invites his friend the creditor to tea, and before his arrival attempts to take his life with a revolver... The bullet goes durch und durch near his heart without damaging any vital organ.[19]

In *The Arrow of Gold* Conrad, though he deals with this situation in a slightly ambiguous way, nevertheless does seem to be reflecting the actual course of events: 'At last came the day when everything slipped out of my grasp. The little vessel, broken and gone like the only toy of a lonely child, the sea itself, which had swallowed it, throwing me on shore after a shipwreck that instead of a fair fight left in me the memory of a suicide' (p. 256).

Conrad must have been drawing upon his attempted suicide in describing Decoud's death, and indeed the nature of the incident of the suicide supports the idea that Conrad is dealing with a personal experience here: 'his hand, feeling about his waist, unbuttoned the flap of the leather case, drew the revolver, cocked it, brought it forward pointing at his breast, pulled the trigger..."It is done", he stammered out, in a sudden flow of blood' (pp. 500–1).

And in Decoud Conrad drew close to presenting something of his own nature. Like Decoud, Conrad was in his early youth 'intellectually well developed...with a sarcastic smile on his face [he made] frequent critical remarks on everything'.[20] Decoud beholds the universe 'as a succession of incomprehensible images' (p. 498) and ultimately entertains 'a doubt of his own individuality' which 'had merged into the world of cloud and water, of natural forces and forms of nature'. And then follows the final statement of man's position in the universe and, it would seem, the only strategy for dealing with the helpless human condition: 'In our activity alone do we find the sustaining illusion of an independent existence as against the whole scheme of things of which we form a helpless part' (p. 497). Decoud 'had recognized no other virtue than intelligence', and waiting in solitude on the Great Isabel finds 'his intelligence' is 'swallowed up easily in this great unbroken solitude of waiting without faith' (p. 498). In a letter to Cunninghame Graham of 14 January 1898 Conrad wrote:

The attitude of cold unconcern is the only reasonable one. Of course reason is hateful—but why? Because it demonstrates...that we, living, are out of life—utterly out of it. The mysteries of a universe made of drops of fire and clods of mud do not concern us in the least. The fate of a humanity condemned ultimately to perish from cold is not worth troubling about...Life knows us not and we do not know life—we don't know even our own thoughts. Half the words we use have no meaning whatever and of the other half each man understands each word after the fashion of his own folly and conceit. Faith is a myth and beliefs shift like mists on the shore; thoughts vanish; words, once pronounced, die.[21]

Father Corbelàn's condemnation of Decoud fits the creator of Decoud: 'You believe neither in stick nor stone' (p. 197).

17

SIR JOHN AND 'MATERIAL INTERESTS'

The 'vagrant anecdote' of the theft of the silver which gave Conrad the initial inspiration for the novel led inevitably to the conception of the silver mine, and the theme of 'material interests'. But although the emphasis here is upon the mine and its influence, it should not be forgotten that 'material interests' are present in the novel in many other forms—they are represented by the loan to the State, the construction of the railway, the Gould concession from the Government, the influence of Holroyd the financier. And it is not only Gould and Nostromo who are corrupted by wealth. The whole background of the finances and economy of the country is one of a Government corrupted through greed, of leaders enriching themselves through concessions and bribes, of revolutions begun with the idea of personal aggrandisement in mind.

A figure important to this theme of 'material interests' in the novel is Sir John, the great financier, 'the chairman of the railway company board (from London)'. Sir John comes from Europe to smooth the path for his railway, but as 'he worked always on a great scale' there was also 'a loan to the State, and a project for the systematic colonization of the Occidental Province' involved. This 'loan to the State' takes us to Edward B. Eastwick's book on Venezuela, a book already recognised as a source,[1] but whose significance in the world of the novel has not been fully explored. For Eastwick's *Venezuela* provided the suggestion for Sir John and his visit and business, and also for a pattern of events within the novel connected with the theme of 'material interests' generally.

The financial affairs of Venezuela over a period of many years provide examples of the kind of corruption demonstrated in *Nostromo*; but especially the rule of Guzman Blanco[2] is relevant for it was during the period of Blanco's influence that Eastwick became concerned in the economic affairs of the country. Eastwick went to Venezuela in 1864 as financial commissioner for the General Credit Company which had floated an immense loan for Venezuela. Guzman Blanco had negotiated the loan in London and the principal and interest were secured on the revenue derived from export duties from the ports of La Guaira, Puerto Cabello, and Ciudad Bolívar. Eastwick's job was to see whether Venezuela could keep up the payments and whether the customs duties could be collected by the Credit Company. Although Eastwick's book is largely an account of his travels in Venezuela, incidents concerned with the negotiations with Government ministers are recorded, some analysis of the failure of Republican economics is given, a chapter is devoted to the history of the loan, and another to Venezuelan economic history in terms of foreign loans. An appendix gives a full account of the negotiations for this particular loan. The book would provide, in fact, a detailed commentary on the 'material interests' of this land for Conrad.

Eastwick was earnest in trying to impress upon the Government the necessity of fulfilling their obligations in the matter of the loan: 'I tried to impress upon every one in authority that any infraction of the conditions of the contract would strike a fatal blow at the national credit' and even to General Falcon, the President himself: 'I dwelt on the importance of a scrupulous adherence to the conditions, and of the government's maintaining its character for good faith.'[3] Thus Sir John in *Nostromo* as the representative of 'material interests' from abroad is based upon Eastwick and his similar function. Like Eastwick, Sir John is concerned about the safety of the loan: 'Good faith, order, honesty, peace, were badly wanted for this great development of material interests' (p. 117); 'The Government was bound to carry out its part of the contract with the board of the new railway company' (p. 37).

Sir John is helped a great deal in his business trip by 'the agent of the San Tomé mine', the 'very clever advocate', Moraga. Moraga possesses 'an extraordinary influence in the highest Government spheres': 'It was known that he had easy access to ministers, and that the numerous Costaguana generals were always anxious to dine at his house. Presidents granted him audience with facility' (p. 93). The name Moraga was taken by Conrad from Maurice H. Hervey's book *Dark Days in Chile*.[4] The actual Moraga was a sea-captain of real distinction who fought tenaciously on the Government side during the revolution in Chile in 1891. But the function of Moraga, the agent of the San Tomé mine, is taken from a man, referred to as C., by whom Eastwick was introduced to Government ministers in Venezuela. It was through the influence of C. that Eastwick was invited to breakfast with several ministers, and he gives an account of one of these occasions which proves to be a significant source for *Nostromo*. The breakfast is given by the acting President, General Trias, who had demanded a share of the loan that Guzman Blanco had negotiated, and who was now entertaining the man come to make enquiries regarding the safety of the loan:

The Sunday following, the scene was repeated, but on this occasion it was the acting president who gave the breakfast. At last the meal reached its termination, and the president, filling his glass, looked round the table, and then at me, and said, 'Brindo al señor qui nos ha llevado treinte mil libras.'—'I drink to the gentleman who has brought us thirty thousand pounds.' I was somewhat disconcerted by the wording of the toast, and thinking that it spoke for itself, judged it unnecessary to rise to respond. Presently, filling his glass again, the old general said, 'I drink now to the English government, which has always been the protector of Venezuela, and has set the best example for free states to follow.' This, of course, compelled me to reply, and I expressed the pleasure I had had in visiting that beautiful country, in which Nature had been so lavish of her gifts, and whose inhabitants, by their gallant struggle for liberty, had shown themselves worthy of such a fair inheritance. England, I said, was the friend of all free nations, and would no doubt support the Venezuelans in maintaining their independence, as warmly as she had aided them in acquiring it. These, and many other things, I was obliged to say in English, not having sufficient Spanish at command for an oration. A friend, however, translated what I had said into pure Castilian and his version seemed to give great satisfaction.[5]

Conrad has made use of and heightened the various aspects of this scene. It becomes the basis for the banquet on board the *Juno*, and the minister (General Trias) is paralleled by the corrupt General Montero. In each instance, the object is to flatter and reassure the visiting financier, and in each case the financier is disconcerted by the tacit insinuation by the minister that the loan is regarded as a gift through his crude toast to the financier and the money he brings:

'General Montero is going to speak', he [Sir John] whispered, and almost immediately added, in comic alarm, 'Heavens! he's going to propose my own health, I believe.'

General Montero had risen with a jingle of steel scabbard and a ripple of glitter on his gold-embroidered breast; a heavy sword-hilt appeared at his side above the edge of the table. In this gorgeous uniform, with his bull neck, his hooked nose flattened on the tip upon a blue-black, dyed moustache, he looked like a disguised and sinister vaquero. The drone of his voice had a strangely rasping, soulless ring. He floundered, lowering, through a few vague sentences; then suddenly raising his big head and his voice together, burst out harshly:

'The honour of the country is in the hands of the army. I assure you I shall be faithful to it.' He hesitated till his roaming eyes met Sir John's face, upon which he fixed a lurid, sleepy glance; and the figure of the lately negotiated loan came into his mind. He lifted his glass. 'I drink to the health of the man who brings us a million and a half of pounds.'

He tossed off his champagne, and sat down heavily with a half-surprised, half-bullying look all round the faces in the profound, as if appalled, silence which succeeded the felicitous toast. Sir John did not move.

'I don't think I am called upon to rise,' he murmured to Mrs. Gould. 'That sort of thing speaks for itself.' But Don José Avellanos came to the rescue with a short oration, in which he alluded pointedly to England's goodwill towards Costaguana—'a goodwill', he continued, significantly, 'of which I, having been in my time accredited to the Court of St James, am able to speak with some knowledge.'

Only then Sir John thought fit to respond, which he did gracefully in bad French, punctuated by bursts of applause and the 'Hear! Hears!' of Captain Mitchell, who was able to understand a word now and then (pp. 120–1).

Conrad makes direct use of statement and reaction here:

Trias. 'I drink to the gentleman who has brought us thirty thousand pounds.'

Montero. 'I drink to the health of the man who brings us a million and a half of pounds.'

Eastwick. 'I was somewhat disconcerted by the wording of the toast, and thinking that it spoke for itself, judged it unnecessary to rise to respond.'

Sir John. 'I don't think I am called upon to rise,' he murmured to Mrs. Gould. 'That sort of thing speaks for itself.'

Trias's speech is partly objectionable (the toast to Eastwick) and partly acceptable (the praise of England). Conrad divides appropriately these two aspects between the objectionable Montero and the sympathetic Avellanos. The loan negotiated by Guzman Blanco, moreover, was £1,500,000, although Eastwick brought only £30,000 of it with him.

Eastwick had sound reasons for demanding assurances of good faith: the background of Venezuelan affairs did not inspire confidence. The rule of Guzman Blanco was corrupt. Apart from concessions and grants to members of his family, the commissions he exacted from the loan amounted to a personal fortune. Moreover, the loan was of interest to various other members of the Government who wanted a share of it. Indeed the seeds of revolution were present at the gathering at General Trias's that Eastwick describes. He commented upon the presence of a 'red-hot republican who discoursed with immense fluency on the rights of man assuring us that, as all obstacles to perfect freedom were at length removed, Venezuela would now enjoy permanent tranquillity'.[6] Eastwick then adds: 'Ten days afterwards, one of the ministers and a number of leading men were arrested and thrown into prison, while, at the same time, an insurrection with which it was supposed they were connected, broke out in several of the provinces.'[7] And shortly after the celebration on board the *Juno* in the novel we learn of General Montero's attempted revolt:

Less than six months after the President-Dictator's visit, Sulaco learned with stupefaction of the military revolt in the name of national honour. The Minister of War, in a barrack-square allocution to the officers of the artillery regiment he had been inspecting, had declared the national honour sold to foreigners. The Dictator, by his weak compliance with the demands of the European powers—for the settlement of long outstanding money claims—had showed himself unfit to rule. A letter from Moraga explained afterwards that the initiative, and even the very text, of the incendiary allocution came, in reality, from the other Montero, the ex-guerrillero, the Commandante de Plaza (p. 145).

It is this background of corruption that is reflected in Decoud's comment to Antonia Avellanos about the Monterist revolution:

And Moraga has miserably mismanaged this business. Perhaps your father did, too; I don't know. Montero was bribeable. Why, I suppose he only wanted his share of this famous loan for national development. Why didn't the stupid Sta. Marta people give him a mission to Europe, or something? He would have taken five years' salary in advance, and gone on loafing in Paris, this stupid, ferocious Indio! (p. 182).

*

Sir John and 'Material Interests'

Apart from the broader issues of material interests and their effects, Conrad also borrowed from Eastwick certain details which lend authenticity to the revolutionaries in *Nostromo*, a book of which authentic detail is the hall-mark.

Pedro Montero, after his ride over the mountains, arrives in Sulaco with his victorious, and ragged, army:

Behind the rabble could be seen the lances of the cavalry, the 'army' of Pedro Montero. He advanced between Señores Fuentes and Gamacho at the head of his llaneros, who had accomplished the feat of crossing the Paramos of the Higuerota in a snow-storm. They rode four abreast, mounted on confiscated Campo horses, clad in the heterogeneous stock of roadside stores they had looted hurriedly in their rapid ride through the northern part of the province; for Pedro Montero had been in a great hurry to occupy Sulaco...*Emaciated greybeards rode by the side of lean dark youths, marked by all the hardships of campaigning, with strips of raw beef twined round the crowns of their hats*, and huge iron spurs fastened to their naked heels...A haggard fearlessness characterized the expression of all these sun-blacked countenances; they glared down haughtily with their scorched eyes at the crowd, or, blinking upwards insolently, pointed out to each other some particular head amongst the women at the windows (pp. 384-5) [my italics].

This episode is based upon a description by Eastwick of the entry of the Venezuelan army into the Gran Plaza at Valencia in early September 1864:

It was a bright hot forenoon in the first week of September when, as I was lazily swinging in my hammock in the Calle de Constitucion at Valencia, the unusual sound of martial music reached my ear. Starting up, I hurried to the Gran Plaza, and was in time to see the Venezuelan army enter...Some of the officers, indeed, were tall and well-made; but the men were the strangest figures—*lean old scarecrows and starveling boys not five feet high, the greater number half naked, with huge strips of raw beef twisted round their hats or hanging from their belts*. Their skins seemed to have been baked black with exposure to the sun, and their arms and accoutrements were of the most wretched description. Yet they were not contemptible—far from it—but rather weird, repulsive—a sight to make one shudder [my italics].[8]

Pedro, determined to take possession of Sulaco in the name of the democracy, makes many pointed inquiries as to the silver mine. But, having made a speech in the square, he retires to the Intendencia where his sensibilities, finer than those of his brother, and his taste for beautiful things, are hurt by the destruction that has been wrought in that building:

Upstairs Pedrito Montero walked about rapidly from one wrecked room of the Intendencia to another, snarling incessantly:

'What stupidity! What destruction!'

Señor Fuentes, following, would relax his taciturn disposition to murmur—

'It is all the work of Gamacho and his Nationals'; and then, inclining his head on his left shoulder, would press together his lips so firmly that a little hollow would appear at each corner. He had his nomination for Political Chief of the town in his pocket, and was all impatience to enter upon his functions...

'The brute!' observed his Excellency Don Pedro Montero through clenched teeth. 'We must contrive as quickly as possible to send him and his Nationals out there to fight Hernandez.'

The new Géfé Político only jerked his head sideways, and took a puff at his cigarette in sign of his agreement with his method for ridding the town of Gamacho and his inconvenient rabble...

'We shall organize a popular vote, by yes or no, confiding the destinies of our beloved country to the wisdom and valiance of my heroic brother, the invincible general. A plebiscite. Do you understand?'

And Señor Fuentes, puffing out his leathery cheeks, had inclined his head slightly to the left, letting a thin, bluish jet of smoke escape through his pursed lips. He had understood.

His Excellency was exasperated at the devastation....He would get even with Gamacho by-and-by. And Señor Gamacho's oration, delectable to popular ears, went on in the heat and glare of the Plaza like the uncouth howlings of an inferior sort of devil cast into a white-hot furnace...

His opinion was that war should be declared at once against France, England, Germany, and the United States, who, by introducing railways, mining enterprises, colonization, and under such other shallow pretences, aimed at robbing poor people of their lands, and with the help of these Goths and paralytics, the aristocrats would convert them into toiling and miserable slaves. And the leperos, flinging about the corners of their dirty white mantas, yelled their approbation (pp. 390–2).

Effective detail for this scene has been borrowed from Eastwick's book. The mannerisms of Fuentes in his response to Pedro are the same as those of the superintendent of the Custom House of Puerto Cabello. Eastwick records: 'My first visit in the morning was to the custom-house, which I found under the superintendence of the brother of the Secretary of State for Finance: a small, taciturn man, who replied to all remarks that were not direct questions by a violent puff of his cigarette, and a very slight inclination of his head.'[9] And the references to the Goths and paralytics in Gamacho's speech appear to derive from the following passage in Eastwick—an account of an incident related by Eastwick's servant:

Why, when this gang marched into Carácas, they were very near shooting a lady—Madame R.—because her little boy had a red riband in his cap. You know, red's the colour of the aristocratical party, the same as these chaps call the Godos and Epilepticos, the 'Goths' and 'Epileptics'. Well, sir, there were above a hundred muskets pointed at the balcony where Madame R. was. 'Down with the oligarchs!' 'Down with the red!' they kept shouting.[10]

The phrase 'Down with the oligarchs' is referred to by the railway engineer in *Nostromo* when he tells how, during a pause in Gamacho's harangue, 'the rabble below yelled, "Down with the Oligarchs"' (p. 321).

Pedro Montero does not profit from the riches of Sulaco, being driven out by General Barrios and his forces, and Sotillo's experience is equally frustrating. Sotillo is 'a handsome fellow, with a soft voice' who talks to the *señoritas* at the windows of the houses, 'showing his white teeth all the time'. But he is also said to have had 'a man...flayed alive in the remote Campo' (p. 281). He is, we are told, of 'no convictions of any sort upon anything except as to the irresistible power of his personal advantages...The only guiding motive of his life was to get money for the satisfaction of his expensive tastes, which he indulged recklessly, having no self-control. He imagined himself a master of intrigue,

but his corruption was as simple as an animal instinct'
(pp. 285–6).

Sotillo had his counterpart in Venezuelan politics at the
time of Eastwick's visit in the person of a General Sotillo,
a person as sanguinary and greedy as the fictional character.
A Dane with whom Eastwick dined in a *posada* told him
'he had just returned from the province of Apure, and that
Sotillo, who reigns there after the fashion of Paez, had been
enquiring for his share of the loan, and would probably raise
disturbances unless a considerable portion were set aside
for him'.[11] And Eastwick also comments: 'The other great
revolutionary leaders have been sanguinary, too, and even
those associated with Falcon, as Sotillo, are no exception to
the rule' (p. 198). Sotillo's determination to find the silver
from the mine results in the terrible torturing of the cowardly
Hirsch, one of the most ruthlessly cruel scenes in the novel,
and an act equal to the ferocity of the original Sotillo as
described by Charles Dance in *Recollections of Four Years
in Venezuela*:

Who was General Sotillo? Well, I never heard his friends speak of him.
But if you are willing to take his character from the description given
by the Maturineros who did not profess ardent friendship for the
General—Sotillo had sold his soul to the devil, who had given in exchange
for it the heart of a tiger. He had risen to the rank of general by the force
of his ferocity. Sent to arrest some political prisoners, he brought in
their heads in a bag attached to his saddle. In his massacres the first
blood on his sword was wiped off on his fingers and placed in his mouth,
while he exclaimed that 'La sangre de un enemigo es dulcé', the blood
of an enemy is sweet. His vengeance included the lives of innocent
women and children.

This then was the man leading thousands of men, including his
favourite regiment of Caribé Indians called 'Sotillo's bloodhounds', to
punish the rebellious Maturineros.[12]

And then in a later chapter Sotillo makes his triumphant
entry into Maturin:

The sound of horses' feet was distinctly heard, and presently came Sotillo, a very tall and powerful looking man, but exceedingly fat. He was very dark complexioned, and had a fierce countenance. A savage scowl passed over his face as he came by, and said loudly—'The foreigners who came to the country to earn bread should be ashamed to encourage the natives in their disaffection to a patriotic government; and that they deserved, every one of them, to have short work made with them.'[13]

Quite clearly, Conrad has made use of only certain characteristics of the original Sotillo, and these he allows to function appropriately within the tale of the silver.

18

DR MONYGHAM AND DON JOSÉ AVELLANOS

The past history of Costaguana has been carefully plotted by Conrad—a past of exploitation, tyranny, and the misrule of corrupt government. Of some importance in the novel is the effect of this past upon particular individuals. The Garibaldino is entirely moulded by the past influence of Garibaldi; Gould cannot escape the influence of the history of the mine as it was impressed upon him by his father; and Don José Avellanos and Dr Monygham are permanently affected by their experiences under the tyranny of Guzman Bento. The influence of humanitarian ideals, of material interest, and of sheer physical cruelty, are thus constants in the novel.

Dr Monygham has been permanently crippled by the torture he suffered under the rule of Guzman Bento: 'He hobbled about the room... Many years ago both his ankles had been seriously damaged in the course of a certain investigation conducted in the castle of Sta. Marta by a commission composed of military men' (pp. 370–1). The source of this event has been traced to George Frederick Masterman's *Seven Eventful Years in Paraguay* (1869) and the incident of the torturing has been well documented.[1] Baines writes: 'Conrad based his account of Dr Monygham's torture and confession on that of Masterman himself',[2] and Vidan gives us close parallels between Masterman's book and *Nostromo*. Masterman was put to the torture of the 'cepo uruguayana' and his portrait of Padre Roman is the source for the infamous Padre Beron to whom Monygham made his confession. I shall give one example of such parallels from Vidan's article and one from the thesis by Edgar Wright:

> He was, as an army chaplain, dressed in lieutenant's uniform, and wore a sword; all that pointed out his clerical character being a small red cross on his left breast, and the little stubbly tonsure on his crown (Masterman, p. 287).

> That priest was a big round-shouldered man, with an unclean-looking, overgrown tonsure on the top of his flat head, of a dingy, yellow complexion, softly fat, with greasy stains all down the front of his lieutenant's uniform, and a small cross embroidered in white cotton on his left breast (*Nostromo*, p. 371).

> Then turning to the priest [Falcòn] told him to take me out and put me in the rack [musket torture] the priest meanwhile, in a monotonous voice, as if he were repeating a formula he had often gone through, urged me to confess (Masterman, p. 257).

> Dr. Monygham could by no manner of means forget the zeal of Father Beron, or his face, or the pitiless, monotonous voice in which he pronounced the words, 'Will you confess now?' (*Nostromo*, p. 371).

It should be observed, however, that Monygham's experience is not exactly that of Masterman, and that Masterman's book has been used a great deal more extensively than these quotations alone would suggest. The forceful picture which Masterman shows of human misery caused by the tyrant is an inescapable part of the landscape of *Nostromo*.

The details of Monygham's torture are deliberately and effectively left vague by Conrad, who does not state that the doctor was put to the torture of the 'cepo uruguayana', though this torture is referred to—'a few muskets in combination with a length of hide rope'. In the same way there is the comment, 'A simple mallet of heavy, hard wood applied with a swing to human fingers or to the joints of a human body is enough for the infliction of the most exquisite torture' (p. 373).[3] Masterman writes of his meeting with a certain Dr Carreras who tells him, 'That terrible Father Maiz... tortured me in the *uruguayana* on three successive days, and then smashed my fingers with a mallet!' Masterman adds: 'He...held out his maimed hands as testimony.'[4]

Masterman, unable to stand more torture, confesses what is required of him, but confesses in 'agony and shame', and fully expecting that he will afterwards be executed:

When I recovered, I was lying on the grass utterly exhausted, and felt that I could bear no more; that it would be far preferable to make a pretended confession, and be shot, than suffer such cruel torture. So, as they were about to again apply the *uruguayana*, as it is called by them, I said, 'I am guilty; I will confess': and they immediately unbound me. The priest said, 'Why were you such an obstinate fool?...' There was no help for it, but God knows with what agony and shame I repeated that wretched tissue of fables and misrepresentations. I felt that I ought rather to have suffered any martyrdom than purchase life on such terms, and until I was put to the question I hoped and believed I should have done so; it was that, however, and not death, I feared.[5]

Monygham, also breaking down under torture, has a much stronger hope than does Masterman that he will be executed —for him this is a 'consolation':

When making his extorted confessions to the Military Board, Dr. Monygham was not seeking to avoid death. He longed for it. Sitting half-naked for hours on the wet earth of his prison, and so motionless that the spiders, his companions, attached their webs to his matted hair, he consoled the misery of his soul with acute reasonings that he had confessed to crimes enough for a sentence of death—that they had gone too far with him to let him live to tell the tale (p. 374).

Neither man was executed. Masterman was released three months later. On the morning of 3 December he was sent for and a Father Maiz lectured him on the need for consistency in his story 'in all places and under all circumstances'. Masterman promised to 'make the truth fully known' and 'A blacksmith was then called, my fetters were knocked off'.[6] Monygham suffered further by being left 'for months to decay slowly in the darkness of his grave-like prison'. His release comes much later, and under different circumstances, after Guzman Bento's death:

Dr Monygham and Don José Avellanos

His fetters were struck off by the light of a candle, which, after months of gloom, hurt his eyes so much that he had to cover his face with his hands. He was raised up. His heart was beating violently with the fear of this liberty. When he tried to walk the extraordinary lightness of his feet made him giddy, and he fell down. Two sticks were thrust into his hands, and he was pushed out of the passage. It was dusk; candles glimmered already in the windows of the officers' quarters round the courtyard; but the twilight sky dazed him by its enormous and overwhelming brilliance. A thin poncho hung over his naked, bony shoulders; the rags of his trousers came down no lower than his knees; an eighteen months' growth of hair fell in dirty grey locks on each side of his sharp cheek-bones (pp. 374–5).

Masterman gives no such details of his release, simply commenting upon his weakness and relating how he was taken on horseback to a ship and so left Paraguay. What Conrad has done here is to return to an earlier period of imprisonment which Masterman suffered. On that occasion he was put into 'a grave-like prison' for eleven months, and his condition on release after that first imprisonment is the same as Monygham's:

I remained there, in that horrible place, in a dim twilight or total darkness, a fetid atmosphere, surrounded by prisoners dying from Asiatic cholera, and without once leaving it or seeing sunlight, for *eleven months*. I left it sick, weak, and half blind, and so changed in appearance that my most intimate friends scarcely knew me. On the evening of the 22nd of September, 1867, a sergeant told me to get ready, for I was to see the Mayor-de-Plaza; and about half an hour afterwards I was taken across the great patio, at almost the same hour at which I had entered it so long before. The sun had set, and candles were to be already seen in the officers' quarters; but to me the light was brighter than my eyes could bear, and in a dazed and half-dreamy state, doubting the reality of what I saw, I walked slowly through the guard-room... Shortly afterwards, I saw myself in a looking-glass. A more spectral figure is scarcely imaginable: my face was almost fleshless and as colourless as that of a corpse; indeed, I resembled one more than a living man. My hair, uncut for thirteen months, hung over my shoulders and mingled with my beard, both quite grey; whilst my eyes, with the pupils widely dilated by the darkness, seemed to have concentrated within themselves the life which had deserted the rest of my body.[7]

It was during his first experience as a prisoner in the Colegio[8] that Masterman developed a habit of walking out the night in his underground cell.

When tired of reading, and during the long interval between the close of my day and the arrival of the lanthorn, which announced the beginning of the outer night, I used to pace from end to end of my prison, and I formed thus a broad beaten path. The sentries were greatly amused at my restlessness, for a native would never think of making any exertion merely to pass time away; if he could not get a cigar, he would lie down, and sleep like a dormouse: so they cried out to passers-by, '*Mirè que quartì*, what a racoon that fellow is! never still; he prowls about half the night.'[9]

Masterman found it useful at first to deliver silent lectures during his walking sessions but this excited him too much for sleep: 'I could get no rest, and used to pace the whole night away, weary and worn out, but unable to remain still a moment.'[10] This compulsive walking is Monygham's later reaction to his memories of his torturer, Father Beron: 'He remembered that priest at night, sometimes, in his sleep. On such nights the doctor waited for daylight with a candle lighted, and walking the whole length of his rooms to and fro, staring down at his bare feet, his arms hugging his sides tightly' (p. 372).

Masterman's book gives no suggestion that he is permanently affected by his experiences, either physically or mentally. He was not a broken man and was very much concerned with retaining his dignity, as his attitude to the master of the gunboat *Wasp* that took him from Paraguay shows:

I had expected a warm welcome; but the captain, without replying to my salute, called the master-at-arms, and said, 'Take these men forward, and put a sentry over them.' I was thunderstruck; Mr. Bliss was fawning as usual, hat in hand. 'Put your hat on, man', I said to him angrily, and then to Commander Kirkland, 'You surely will not send us forward as prisoners. Mr. Bliss is the son of a Baptist minister, and I have held the rank of lieutenant for many years.'[11]

Dr Monygham and Don José Avellanos

So Masterman left Paraguay. In his perception of a different consequence of Masterman's experience, Conrad has moved far from his source.

Doné Jos Avellanos was also imprisoned by Guzman Bento and suffered a great deal, but his character has not been ruined by his experience. Avellanos's sufferings appear to have been based by Conrad upon those of Dr Carreras, and his information about that man also comes from Masterman. Avellanos suffers for many years:

For years he [Guzman Bento] had carried about at the tail of the Army of Pacification, all over the country, a captive band of such atrocious criminals, who considered themselves most unfortunate at not having been summarily executed. It was a diminishing company of nearly naked skeletons, loaded with irons, covered with dirt, with vermin, with raw wounds, all men of position, of education, of wealth, who had learned to fight amongst themselves for scraps of rotten beef thrown to them by soldiers, or to beg a negro cook for a drink of muddy water in pitiful accents. Don José Avellanos, clanking his chains amongst the others, seemed only to exist in order to prove how much hunger, pain, degradation, and cruel torture a human body can stand without parting with the last spark of life (pp. 137–8).

Masterman, after his torture, joins a crowd of other wretched prisoners who are forced upon a long march to a camp in Pikysỳrỳ, and the passage above would seem to be based on the condition of these prisoners. The following is particularly close:

some prisoners of war...were not fettered, but were in the last stage of misery, almost, some quite, naked, covered with wounds, and the majority too feeble to walk...a stalwart negro, assisted by several prisoners, prepared the food for all the guardias around, and little enough it was; a small allowance of boiled meat and broth in the morning, and at night a handful of parched maize and the bones and scraps left by the soldiers. I saw poor Dr. Carreras, once the most influential man in Uruguay, an ex-prime minister, eagerly gnawing the gristle from a few well-picked bones contemptuously thrown him by a passer-by. Can I give a more vivid picture of our miserable condition?...Horn-spoons were coveted treasures, I found; and when a prisoner died who had had one, there used to be a furious contention amongst the survivors for its possession, often leading to a severe thrashing administered indiscriminately to all within reach. As I had only just been sent there, nothing was given to me until late, when the negro cook came by with a piece of roast meat he was eating, and gave me part of it.[12]

The method by which the number of prisoners was occasionally reduced in *Nostromo* is also paralleled in Masterman's book. Conrad writes:

Sometimes interrogatories, backed by some primitive method of torture, were administered to them by a commission of officers hastily assembled in a hut of sticks and branches, and made pitiless by the fear for their own lives. A lucky one or two of that spectral company of prisoners would perhaps be led tottering behind a bush to be shot by a file of soldiers. Always an army chaplain—some unshaven, dirty man, girt with a sword and with a tiny cross embroidered in white cotton on the left breast of a lieutenant's uniform—would follow, cigarette in the corner of the mouth, wooden stool in hand, to hear the confession and give absolution; for the Citizen Saviour of the Country (Guzman Bento was called thus officially in petitions) was not averse from the exercise of rational clemency. The irregular report of the firing squad would be heard, followed sometimes by a single finishing shot; a little bluish cloud of smoke would float up above the green bushes, and the Army of Pacification would move on over the savannas, through the forests, crossing rivers, invading rural pueblos, devastating the haciendas of the horrid aristocrats, occupying the inland towns in the fulfilment of its patriotic mission, and leaving behind a united land wherein the evil taint of Federalism could no longer be detected in the smoke of burning houses and the smell of spilt blood.

Don José Avellanos had survived that time (p. 138).

And Masterman:

On the 27th September, a guard, with fixed bayonets, led off Dr. Carreras and Don Gumisindo Benitez to the little copse where Don Benigno had been taken four days before; a couple of priests and some men with spades followed them. I prayed that they might soon be despatched, and their sorrows be ended. But I now know that a more terrible fate was in store for them; they were inhumanly tortured for a long time before their execution. I waited with feverish anxiety for the end; but it was late ere a volley of musquetry and a thin cloud of smoke rising over the bushes told that all was over, that 'the wicked had ceased from troubling, and the weary were at rest'.[13]

According to Masterman, the final camp in the area of Pikysỳrỳ was to be the grave of all save two of his companions. Avellanos, however, survives his torture and lives to write his 'Fifty Years of Misrule'. Though, like Monygham, he was ruined in every way and rendered timid by his horrible experience, he has greater compensation—'a man possessed of passion is not a bankrupt in life', and Avellanos has a passion to see his country at peace. The motif is repeated when Dr Monygham develops his devotion to Mrs Gould and it proves a regenerative force.

19

COSTAGUANA AND SULACO

Costaguana is an imaginary South American republic, but the extraordinary concreteness and precision of detail with which it is described have encouraged a certain amount of speculation as to whether it is not, in fact, based upon a particular state. Perhaps Conrad took an actual setting and described it with great accuracy (as with the Berau river, the 'Eastern Port' of Singapore, the Congo river). But Conrad himself said of Costaguana that it was all of South America,[1] and indeed when particular aspects of the republic are traced to their sources, Costaguana, and particularly Sulaco, are seen to be made up of hints from areas all over South America.

The name of the imaginary state itself, Costaguana, is derived from Costa Rica and Guano (manure), as was seen by Gustav Morf long ago.[2] The Peruvian–Chilean war, referred to by Holroyd in the novel, arose over the possession of rich guano deposits. It is understandable, then, that many of the names Conrad uses should come from that long western coastline of South America. Zapiga, for instance—'Señor, if you are forced to leave this island before anything can be arranged for you, do not try to make for Zapiga. It is a settlement of thieves and matreros', says Nostromo before he leaves Decoud on the Great Isabel—is to be found in Chile in the region of Tarapaca, east of the coastal town of Pisagua. Cayta, the principal port of Costaguana—'The Monteristos were besieging Cayta, an important postal link' (it is this port that Nostromo reaches after his 'marvellous ride—four hundred miles in six days')—is derived from the coastal port of Payta in the northern part of Peru. Esmeralda, where Sotillo commands the garrison, is in Ecuador. The name Sta Marta comes from the Colombian port of the same name and in *Nostromo* is seen as the capital of Costaguana.

There is little need to comment on the use Conrad makes of Puerto Cabello (see map facing p. 137, above) for the topography of the port of Sulaco since Jocelyn Baines has done this effectively: 'Puerto Cabello...is situated in the Golfo Triste, which became the Golfo Placido in *Nostromo*' and 'the reefs of Punta Brava' become in *Nostromo* 'the cape of Punta Mala'.[3] Describing the origin of the name of the gulf, Conrad writes: 'the two outermost points of the bend which bears the name of Golfo Placido, because never a strong wind had been known to blow upon its waters' (p. 5) and W. E. Curtis, writing of Puerto Cabello harbour in 1896, provides us with a further indication of the reputation for safety Puerto Cabello had: 'The place is called Puerto Cabello (the Port of the Hair), on the pretence that ships are so safe in its harbour as to be tied with a single hair to their moorings.'[4]

The Ivie Pass over the Cordilleras through which Ribiera, the fleeing dictator, and later Pedro Montero make their way is derived from a pass of the same name which Masterman explored:

The day after, I was amongst the hills again, and recrossed the cordillera by the Paso Iviè (the bad pass), which fully deserved its name. I had been told that it was too bad for bullock-carts, and therefore expected one of the very worst kind; for those lumbering waggons, with their huge broad wheels, get over roads which we should deem utterly impracticable.[5]

Describing Ribiera's defeat and retreat over the pass, Conrad writes:

His remaining forces had melted away during the night. Bonifacio and he rode hard on horses towards the Cordillera; then they obtained mules, entered the passes, and crossed the Paramo of Ivie just before a freezing blast swept over that stony plateau, burying in a drift of snow the little shelter-hut of stones in which they had spent the night (p. 241).

The town of Sulaco itself is also put together from various sources. Details of the port are taken from Eastwick's book and of the town itself from the town of Asunción in Paraguay and Carácas and Valencia in Venezuela. It is of particular interest that Conrad created from these details a complete and accurately plotted town, whose topography and history can be traced through descriptions and comments within the novel. The town of Sulaco becomes a place whose streets and buildings we know not only by name but intimately in the details of their interiors and in the history they represent. Often one can see Conrad placing a detail within this setting, but altering and adapting it to his particular use.

Conrad's Sulaco takes its name from the town of Sulaco in Honduras,[6] but it is of Valencia that Eastwick comments: 'I could not help asking myself how it was that in three centuries it had made so little progress in wealth, population and importance.'[7] Sulaco is also 'an inviolable sanctuary from the temptations of a trading world', though the novel itself is a demonstration of the encroachment of the outside world as a result of the mine's development and the coming of the railway.

The mine, situated near the village of Rincon along the Camino Real, we see in its several stages of growth, but for details of the site before the mine is developed Conrad united several suggestions. The mine is in the San Tomé mountain, which is notable for its unusual shape:

In a high ravine round the corner of the San Tomé mountain (which is square like a blockhouse) the thread of a slender waterfall flashed bright and glassy through the dark green of the heavy fronds of tree-ferns. Don Pépé, in attendance, rode up, and, stretching his arm up the gorge, had declared with mock solemnity, 'Behold the very paradise of snakes, señora'...

The waterfall existed no longer. The tree-ferns that had luxuriated in its spray had dried around the dried-up pool, and the high ravine was only a big trench half filled up with the refuse of excavations and tailings. . .

Only the memory of the waterfall, with its amazing fernery, like a hanging garden above the rocks of the gorge, was preserved in Mrs. Gould's water-colour sketch; she had made it hastily one day from a cleared patch in the bushes, sitting in the shade of a roof of straw erected for her on three rough poles under Don Pépé's direction (pp. 105–6).

Masterman tells of an exploring journey he made into Paraguay, during which he reaches Paraguari (see map facing p. 137, above) which lies 'beneath the shade of a certain mountain': 'There was another long ride through rough copses and meadow-land, around the flanks of the cordillera, till we reached its termination in the Cerro Santo Tomàs, a bold square mountain, almost vertical on its western face.'[8] Masterman makes no reference to snakes but Eastwick describes a place which, because of snakes and because of the fact that it is similarly named, may well have caught Conrad's eye:

North of the city, I found only one other place worth a visit. This is the Toma, or reservoir, which supplies Carácas with water. It is situated in a thickly-wooded ravine, and a very narrow path among the bushes leads to it. It is necessary to tread with caution here, as, on account of the dense thickets, and the place being so little frequented, snakes abound in incredible numbers. I was assured that, on a little rocky terrace where the shrubs will not grow, sometimes forty or fifty rattle-snakes and other serpents might be seen basking in the sun.[9]

Though it has not been possible to find a silver mine comparable with Gould's mine, part of its violent history is derived from a copper mine which again appears in Eastwick. In *Nostromo*, we learn that

An English company obtained the right to work it, and found so rich a vein that neither the exactions of successive governments, nor the periodical raids of recruiting officers upon the population of paid miners they had created, could discourage their perseverance. But in the end, during the long turmoil of pronunciamientos that followed the death of the famous Guzman Bento, the native miners, incited to revolt by the emissaries sent out from the capital, had risen upon their English chiefs and murdered them to a man (p. 52).

And Eastwick writes:

If I went to San Felipe, I could easily go on to the copper-mines of Aroa, which I was desirous of visiting. These mines were worked for a time under the superintendence of Englishmen with good results; but unfortunately one fine day the native miners took it into their heads that they had a grievance against the foreigners, so they fell on them suddenly, split their skulls with hatchets, and decamped with their property. For this cruel and cowardly deed some of the guilty parties were afterwards executed, but the mines were for a time abandoned.[10]

Thus details chosen apparently haphazardly from a number of diverse sources are brought together to give the concreteness of factual detail needed to create a convincing mine with a convincing situation and history.

It has been observed that the plan of Sulaco appears to be based upon that of Valencia as described by Eastwick,[11] and certainly it shares with Valencia a Gran Plaza with similarly designated buildings surrounding it, and a Calle de la Constitución. But Conrad has added to this, not only the other aspects of Sulaco—the O.S.N. building, the Casa Viola, the old Spanish gateway, the Camino Real that leads to the village of Rincon and the silver mine—but details of these streets and buildings. We are told, for example, of how, on the occasion of mass being said for the troops in the Gran Plaza of Sulaco, 'They brought outside [the Cathedral] all the painted blocks to take the air. All the wooden saints stood militarily in a row at the top of the great flight of stairs' (p. 187). Masterman, rather deprecatingly, recalls the church at Humaità: 'The church was a rather favourable specimen of native architecture, gaily painted outside, and with a double row of life-sized wooden saints within.'[12]

The Sala of the Provincial Assembly (in the Municipal

Buildings of Sulaco), situated in the Gran Plaza, derives from Eastwick: 'The south side of the [Gran Plaza] is entirely taken up by public offices and the Government house of Carabobo, of which state Valencia is the capital' (p. 155). Conrad transforms this into a significant part of the Sulaco setting by making it the room where Don José Avellanos's renowned eloquence is practised in the service of the Ribiera Government, a room which also contains emblems from Sulaco's past history:

The Sala of the Provincial Assembly (in the Municipal Buildings of Sulaco), with its portraits of the Liberators on the walls and an old flag of Cortés preserved in a glass case above the President's chair, had heard all these speeches...and when the provinces again displayed their old flags (proscribed in Guzman Bento's time) there was another of those great orations, when Don José greeted these old emblems of the war of Independence, brought out again in the name of new Ideals (p. 136).

It is interesting to see from what material Conrad has built this up. After some days in Carácas, Eastwick visited the Municipal Hall:

Round the room are hung some very tolerable portraits. Among these are that of the ecclesiastic who filled the archiepiscopal chair of Carácas in 1813, and those of President Monagas and his brother. There are also portraits of Bolivar, of Count Tovar, and Generals Miranda and Urdaneta, and one remarkable picture of the reading of the Act of Independence, with likenesses of the leaders in the revolution...But the great curiosity of all is the flag of Pizarro, sent from Peru in 1837, and enshrined in a case. All the silk and velvet are eaten off, but the gold wire remains, with the device of a lion, and the word Carlos...There are also two flags of Carlos the Fourth, taken from the Spaniards.[13]

Conrad has made use here of the portraits—'portraits of the Liberators' as he calls them, and of the old flag in its frame, though attributing it to Cortés. The reference to Carlos the Fourth is taken up in another context when he places this king's statue at the entrance to the Alameda:

13-2

for the big equestrian statue of Charles IV at the entrance of the Alameda, towering white against the trees, was only known to the folk from the country and to the beggars of the town that slept on the steps around the pedestal, as the Horse of Stone. The other Carlos, turning off to the left with a rapid clatter of hoofs on the disjointed pavement—Don Carlos Gould, in his English clothes, looked as incongruous, but much more at home than the kingly cavalier reining in his steed on the pedestal above the sleeping leperos, with his marble arm raised towards the marble rim of a plumed hat (pp. 48–9).

The idea of an equestrian statue would seem to derive from the equestrian statue 'of the Great Liberator', which is modelled after that of Andrew Jackson in front of the White House and which stood in the Plaza Bolívar in Carácas.[14]

Even such a minor detail as the name of a particular sculptor is picked up by Conrad to lend greater credence to his fictional setting. Within the patio of the Amarillo Club we are told by Captain Mitchell that there is a 'Fine old bishop with a broken nose...Remarkable piece of statuary, I believe. Cavaliere Parrochetti—you know Parrochetti, the famous Italian sculptor—was working here for two years—thought very highly of our old bishop... There! I am very much at your service now' (pp. 474–5). And Masterman, referring to his seeing a Mr Monygham tortured, writes:

One afternoon I saw them about to put a foreigner in the *uruguayana*; I am almost sure it was Mr. Monygham, an English sculptor, formerly an assistant to Baron Marochetti, and who had been employed by Lopez to carve some figures for his new palace. I only saw his face for a moment: he was deathly pale, and was holding out his hands as if praying for mercy.[15]

Conrad has simply substituted Parrochetti for Marochetti.

The Goulds' household in Sulaco gives an impression of convincing solidity to the reader, though a careful study of the text shows that the impression is built upon a very few details. Some of these details appear to derive again from

Masterman's book in which he describes the house of Mr Washburn, the American ambassador. There is a suggestion, indeed, of Dr Monygham in Masterman's concern for Mrs Washburn and his obvious dislike of her husband. Washburn is the man whom Masterman, under torture, calls the 'gran' bestia' in the plot against Lopez.

In one passage, Masterman makes a reference to a servant called Basilio in the Washburn's house, and Washburn, in his history of Paraguay, describes Basilio as 'the ever-faithful Paraguayan servant'.[16] Basilio then is Washburn's special servant at the American legation and we find Basilio in *Nostromo* is head servant in the house of Gould: '"No, señor", said behind Mrs. Gould the soft voice of Basilio, the head servant of the Casa' (p. 211).

Masterman also recalls how a number of tame parrots sought the hospitality of the American legation in Asunción:

> One of them astonished us by croaking out 'Viva Pedro Segundo!' (the Emperor of Brazil). 'Hullo!' cried Mr. Washburn, looking round in amazement, 'what's that?' 'Viva Pedro Segundo!' repeated the parrot, turning her head on one side to look at him. 'Wring that bird's neck directly!' said he to Mr. Meinke, his secretary, 'or we shall all get into trouble.' And in truth it was perilous enough.[17]

Perilous indeed, when a maniac like Lopez was President and when Paraguay was at war with Brazil! No doubt the parrot had his neck wrung, but in *Nostromo* the parrot appears as a respected member of the household of the Goulds: 'A big green parrot, brilliant like an emerald in a cage that flashed like gold, screamed out ferociously, "Vive Costaguana"' (p. 69).[18]

The Casa Gould is an old Spanish house:

> Mrs. Gould loved the patio of her Spanish house...Subdued voices ascended in the early mornings from the paved well of the quadrangle, with the stamping of horses and mules led out in pairs to drink at the cistern...Barefooted servants passed to and fro, issuing from dark, low

doorways below; two laundry girls with baskets of washed linen; the baker with the tray of bread made for the day...Then the old porter would hobble in, sweeping the flagstones...All the lofty rooms on three sides of the quadrangle opened into each other and into the *corrédor* ... whence...she could witness from above all the departures and arrivals of the Casa, to which the sonorous arched gateway lent an air of stately importance (p. 68).

This would seem to be based partly on Masterman's description of the Washburn home: 'I found the minister located in a large house in the Plaza Vieja, old square, of Asunción, a place big enough for a barrack...It occupied almost all one side of the square, had a large garden in the centre, with a huge *algibe*, or tank, and storerooms of immense capacity.'[19] But Masterman also remarks upon the houses in Asunción generally: 'I was greatly struck with the remarkably Pompeii-like appearance of many of the old Spanish houses...the wide and lofty doorway, not opening into the house, but into a broad vestibule, and showing the pillared courtyard beyond...the handsome reception rooms...the dark and sooty kitchen...the arrangements for an almost out-of-door life...'[20] One could not imagine that Mrs Gould's house would have a 'dark and sooty kitchen', but the idea of the arrangement of the house providing for 'an almost out-of-door life' is demonstrated in the novel by the amount of domestic activity that goes on in the courtyard of the Goulds' house.

The Casa Gould is, though, a house of great beauty, filled with flowers and elegantly furnished and ordered. 'Rows of plants in pots, ranged on the balustrade between the pilasters of the arches, screened the *corrédor* with their leaves and flowers'; 'the dimly lit corridor had a restful mysteriousness of a forest glade, suggested by the stems and the leaves of the plants along the balustrade of the open side. In the streaks of lights falling through the open doors of the reception-rooms, the blossoms, white and red and pale lilac, came out vivid' (pp. 209–10). The largest drawing-room in its loftiness dwarfs 'the mixture of heavy, straight-backed Spanish chairs...and European furniture...There were knick-knacks on little tables, mirrors let into the wall... square spaces of carpet...smaller rugs scattered all over the floor of red tiles; three windows from ceiling down to the ground, opening on a balcony' and overlooking the street (p. 51). For these aspects of the impressive Casa Gould, Conrad seems to have used W. E. Curtis's *Venezuela*. We find there that houses in Carácas have wide arched gateways, patios with bronze fountains and tessellated corridors, palms and roses, orange-trees and oleanders. And one house is described in detail and has

a patio or courtyard...in which are growing and blossoming in their natural luxuriance plants...The atmosphere is laden with the odour of flowers...Around...is a corridor fifteen feet wide, upon which the windows of all the apartment open...The corridor is paved with blue and white marble tiles, upon which Persian rugs are spread...The front room, that which looks upon the street, is about twenty or thirty feet inside and is used for a drawing-room. The floor is tiled and covered with a large rug. In the centre is a handsome table...In one corner is a grand-piano, scattered around are easy chairs, Turkish divans...and other articles of furniture and decoration...[21]

We are, by the end of *Nostromo*, familiar through repeated references with the main features of the town of Sulaco, but it is Captain Mitchell's conducted tour of the city for the 'privileged passenger' at the end of the novel that draws the city together with its history and its inhabitants. For most of the details given here, Conrad drew upon Eastwick's account of the city of Valencia. Conrad took not only topographical detail from Eastwick but also the whole conception of Captain Mitchell and his conducted tour for the 'privileged passenger':

'We enter now the Calle de la Constitution. Observe the old Spanish houses. Great dignity. Eh? I suppose it's just as it was in the time of the Viceroys, except for the pavement. Wood blocks now. Sulaco National

Bank there, with the sentry boxes each side of the gate. Casa Avellanos this side, with all the ground-floor windows shuttered. A wonderful woman lives there—Miss Avellanos—the beautiful Antonia. A character, sir! A historical woman! Opposite—Casa Gould. Noble gateway. Yes, *the* Goulds of the original Gould Concession, that all the world knows of now...'

And all day Captain Mitchell would talk like this to his more or less willing victim—

'The Plaza. I call it magnificent. Twice the area of Trafalgar Square.' From the very centre, in the blazing sunshine, he pointed out the buildings—

'The Intendencia, now President's Palace—Cabildo, where the Lower Chamber of Parliament sits. You notice the new houses on that side of the Plaza? Compañia Anzani, a great general store, like those co-öperative things at home...'

Thus Captain Mitchell would talk in the middle of the Plaza, holding over his head a white umbrella with a green lining; but inside the cathedral, in the dim light, with a faint scent of incense floating in the cool atmosphere, and here and there a kneeling female figure, black or all white, with a veiled head, his lowered voice became solemn and impressive (pp. 475–7).

Conrad has made use here of Eastwick's first impressions during his initial exploration of Valencia, and of his conducting his friend George Hayward round the town at a later date to point out the homes of the various Creole beauties. Eastwick's interpolations and forceful directives to his friend—'Now, mark me', 'You see the large house on the right hand'—are very like Captain Mitchell's 'We enter now...', 'Observe the old Spanish houses', and both men make use of white-covered umbrellas:

The Calle de la Constitución is one of the central streets that run from the Gran Plaza at Valencia, as straight as a die, on and on, till the houses begin to be interpolated with gardens and orchards, and at last cease altogether.[22]

On the left of the posada is an enormous mansion belonging to Señor A., who was once secretary to the Venezuelan Government, and is something of a poet, philosopher, and statesman. The south side of the square is entirely taken up by public offices and the Government House of Carabobo, of which State Valencia is the capital.[23]

The posada of La Belle Alliance, at Valencia, is situated in the centre of the eastern side of the Gran Plaza: a square which is as large as any in London, and which looks larger from the surrounding buildings, except the cathedral, being only one story high.[24]

Now mark me; the white Creoles live at this end of the street, near the Plaza...You see the large house on the right hand, with the two little maidens seated at the first window? They are the younger sisters.[25]

Accordingly, next day after breakfast we hoisted umbrellas with white covers as a protection against the vertical sun, and crossing the Gran Plaza, found ourselves, after passing a cuadra to the west of it, at the girls' school.[26]

THE SECRET AGENT

20

'THE INFORMER'

Conrad chose anarchism for his subject-matter on three separate occasions—in the two short stories 'The Informer' and 'An Anarchist', and in the novel *The Secret Agent*. What is unusual in this choice of subject is Conrad's own lack of any direct personal experience of the anarchist movement or of anarchists; and he is surprisingly specific, in his Author's Note to *The Secret Agent*, about his ignorance of such matters. All his comments insist upon his own lack of direct personal contact, the importance of suggestions arising from conversations on the subject of anarchism with an 'omniscient friend', and the reading of the 'rather summary recollections of an Assistant Commissioner of Police'. Of anarchists he confesses that 'as a matter of hard fact, I had seen even less of their kind than the omniscient friend who gave me the first suggestion for the novel'.[1] Despite the emphasis here upon lack of intimate knowledge and the importance rather of meditation and imagination in the origin of the novel, there is a ring of considerable pride and satisfaction in the general acknowledgement which his apparently intuitive accuracy in this matter of revolutionary activity received.

Such accuracy came, however, from Conrad's extensive knowledge of this area of human activity, a knowledge which depended a good deal upon the 'omniscient friend' and to a greater degree upon a wide course of reading in the field of anarchist polemical literature and commentary upon the movement, from which specific details of revolutionary activity, attitude and character were derived.

Consideration of Conrad's personal contact with his source

material for the three anarchist stories brings us to the question of his relationship with Ford Madox Ford, the 'omniscient friend', and the nature of the assistance Conrad had from him: 'the subject of *The Secret Agent*—I mean the tale—came to me in the shape of a few words uttered by a friend in a casual conversation about anarchists or rather anarchist activities'.[2] Conrad went on to show how slight was the information that he derived in this instance from his friend, and to stress that friend's very limited and casual knowledge of anarchists:

my friend...remained silent for a while and then remarked in his characteristically casual and omniscient manner: 'Oh, that fellow [an anarchist] was half an idiot. His sister committed suicide afterwards.' These were absolutely the only words that passed between us; for extreme surprise at this unexpected piece of information kept me dumb for a moment... It never occurred to me later to ask how he arrived at his knowledge. I am sure that if he had seen once in his life the back of an anarchist that must have been the whole extent of his connection with the underworld.[3]

Ford, in his book *Joseph Conrad: A Personal Remembrance*, recognising the reference to himself here, gave a very different impression of the part he had played:

That passage is curiously characteristic Conrad...For what the writer really did say to Conrad was: 'Oh that fellow was half an idiot! His sister murdered her husband afterwards and was allowed to escape by the police. I remember the funeral...' The suicide was invented by Conrad. And the writer knew—and Conrad knew that the writer knew—a great many anarchists of the Goodge Street group, as well as a great many of the police who watched them. The writer had provided Conrad with Anarchist literature, with memoirs, with introductions to at least one Anarchist young lady who figures in *The Secret Agent*...Indeed the writer's first poems were set up by that very young lady on an Anarchist printing-press.[4]

If the first quotation is characteristic Conrad, the second is characteristic Ford, and, given the doubts generally held of Ford's veracity, it is Conrad's account of Ford's influence that has been accepted. Mrs Hay, in her study of Conrad's political novels, questions Ford's testimony generally, and points out the specific error of fact it contains:

> The whole passage in *A Personal Remembrance* is questionable, if for no better reason than Ford's remark that his 'first poems were set up' by 'one Anarchist young lady who figures in *The Secret Agent*'. Since no one of this description is in *The Secret Agent*, the lady referred to can only be the upper-class young English-woman, possibly a Rossetti, who appears in Conrad's story 'The Informer'.[5]

Ford's attitude to 'truth', which is of some relevance here, is explained in the following passage from David Garnett's *The Golden Echo*. Garnett recalls an occasion on which, while his father, Edward Garnett, was lunching with Ford, a successful journalist came to their table and Ford began to talk of the success of his (Ford's) last novel:

> The journalist inquired about its sales. 'It has sold twelve thousand copies in three weeks', drawled Ford, 'and it is still heading the list of best-sellers.' After the journalist had gone away, Edward asked Ford: 'How can you tell him such awful lies? You know we have only sold just over a thousand copies.' 'My dear Edward', said Ford, in his very slow drawl and in his most dégagé manner, 'truth is relative. You and I know that my book has done extraordinarily well to have sold twelve hundred copies, but that fellow would never have understood that. When I told him it had sold twelve thousand copies it astonished him just to the same degree that you and I are astonished by its having sold twelve hundred. Truth is relative.'[6]

And Ford's cousin, Mrs Helen Rossetti Angeli, had this to say on the subject of Ford's attitude to truth: 'truth and untruth about mere facts are so inextricably mixed that it is almost impossible to disentangle them...whatever he did talk or write about he saw in a light shimmering between fact and fiction, which is illuminating.'[7]

In considering Ford's claims to an influence on Conrad's work, we will be on guard against Ford's view of fact as a substance to be manipulated in terms of the effect he was aiming at. We must concede also that he was guilty of a total and obvious inaccuracy in confusing 'The Informer' with *The Secret Agent*, though this was most probably unintentional. But we are left with certain truths. Ford *had* had contact with anarchists, and most likely a fairly wide contact, and his first poems *were* set up by an anarchist young lady on an anarchist printing-press. I think it can be shown that Ford meant to say, and quite truthfully, in the passage quoted above, that this same anarchist young lady figures in 'The Informer', and it can be accepted that Ford provided Conrad with an introduction to her, and that he also provided Conrad with anarchist literature and stories.

Certainly Conrad was in close contact with Ford during the writing of 'The Informer', 'An Anarchist' and *The Secret Agent*. On 26 December 1905 Conrad wrote to Galsworthy: 'And tomorrow I must start another short story' (presumably 'The Informer'),[8] and on 29 December: 'Yes, I wrote the Anarchist story and now I am writing another of the sort.'[9] By mid-February he was writing what he thought would be a third short story, first entitled 'Verloc', and he had completed thirteen pages.[10] Evidence that Conrad was in contact with Ford just before this spate of creative activity appears in Conrad's letter to H. G. Wells of 20 October 1905: 'If I haven't been to see you...I haven't been to see anyone else —except Ford...As to Ford he is a sort of lifelong habit— of which I am not ashamed.'[11] And there was a period of equally close and equally important contact with Ford, so far as the anarchist stories are concerned, during the previous year, 1904. From January to March of that year, the Conrads lived close to the Fords in London, and Ford obviously helped Conrad in certain ways during the writing of *One Day More* and *The Mirror of the Sea*. And again, in October of that year, the Conrads were in London.

Given Ford's earlier and quite genuine association with

anarchists, it would seem likely that he had not a little influence upon the conception of Conrad's stories dealing with anarchism—he might indeed have been responsible for turning Conrad's thoughts towards the subject as a possible theme. His function in all this would be 'introductory' in every sense, and the further research and development would be Conrad's; but it was a sufficiently important function for Conrad to make some acknowledgement of it in an Author's Note and, I believe, to introduce a fictional figure actually based on Ford into one of the stories, a figure who performs precisely the same function in the story as did Ford in real life.

It is at the beginning of 'The Informer' that Ford appears, I think, in his particular role. The narrator of the story refers to a friend of his who first introduced to him Mr X, who is both a famous anarchist—'the mysterious unknown Number One of desperate conspiracies' (p. 74)[12]—and also 'an enlightened connoisseur of bronzes and china' (p. 74):*

My friend in Paris is a collector, too. He collects neither porcelain, nor bronzes, nor pictures, nor medals, nor stamps, nor anything that could be profitably dispersed under an auctioneer's hammer. He would reject, with genuine surprise, the name of a collector. Nevertheless, that's what he is by temperament. He collects acquaintances. It is delicate work. He brings to it the patience, the passion, the determination of a true collector of curiosities...he has met with and talked to everyone worth knowing on any conceivable ground. He observes them, listens to them, penetrates them, measures them, and puts the memory away in the galleries of his mind...his collection is pretty complete, including objects (or should I say subjects?) whose value is unappreciated by the vulgar, and often unknown to popular fame' (p. 73).

* There was an actual anarchist who was a collector of antiques: 'a notorious Anarchist named Parmeggiani. When the Anarchists first established themselves in any force in London, Parmeggiani was one of the most prominent men in the Anarchist agitation, and his house and his movements were frequently kept under observation. Though an Anarchist he had a fine taste in matters artistic, for the antique, and for curios of all sorts. Of these he possessed a fine collection' (John Sweeney, *At Scotland Yard*, London, 1904, pp. 84–5).

There is a similarity between Conrad's conception of a collector of acquaintances here and his comments about Ford in the Author's Note to *The Secret Agent*: 'He was, however, a man who liked to talk with all sorts of people, and he may have gathered those illuminating facts at second or third hand, from a crossing-sweeper, from a retired police officer, from some vague man in his club, or even, perhaps, from a Minister of State met at some public or private reception.'[13] Now I do not wish to suggest that the contact between the narrator of the story and the famous anarchist, engineered by the collector of acquaintances, parallels an actual instance in which Ford was instrumental in introducing Conrad to a leading anarchist. But the fact that Conrad twice makes a reference to Ford's role as one who introduced him to anarchists and anarchism supports rather Ford's view of his influence than Conrad's playing down of it.

*

What is of interest in 'The Informer', from the point of view of Conrad's contact with the anarchist movement, is the Hermione Street group of anarchists and the young lady anarchist. The young lady anarchist is the daughter of 'a distinguished government official' and, having discovered the group 'while exploring the poor quarters of the town', she has offered her home in Hermione Street to them as a centre. On the ground floor of the house is an Italian restaurant run by the anarchists; on the first floor 'a shabby Variety Artists' Agency' run by a man called Bomm (presumably Conrad's attempt at a pun), and the top floor is also occupied by the anarchists. In the basement 'two printing-presses were established' which produced 'a lot of revolutionary literature'. 'The brother of our anarchist young lady found some occupation there. He wrote articles, helped to set up type and pull off the sheets.' The anarchist young lady's 'usual task was to correct the proofs of the Italian and French editions of the *Alarm Bell* and the *Firebrand*.'

It is the anarchist press in the basement with its young operators that brings us to Conrad's source. There never was an anarchist publication called the *Alarm Bell* (though there was the *Alarm*), but the *Firebrand* was advertised regularly in the English anarchist publication *The Torch*. *The Torch* was published by the children of William Michael Rossetti, then a government official, and printed on a press in his home in London. And the Rossetti children were cousins of Ford. It is clearly *The Torch* offices and its publishers that Conrad has in mind here, and it is through the *Torch* that we find the link between Ford and the anarchist young lady and Conrad.

In his little-known book of reminiscences, *Ancient Lights and Certain New Reflections*, published four years after *The Secret Agent*, Ford refers to the *Torch* office, 'which upon the death of my aunt Rossetti left the house of William Rossetti'.[14] And in giving a more detailed account of the *Torch* offices in *Return to Yesterday*, Ford describes the premises Conrad had in mind:

Until my aunt's death, the Rossettis' house being her property, my juvenile relatives carried on their activities at home. Why my aunt permitted them to run in her basement a printing press that produced militant anarchist propaganda I never quite knew...In any case the world was presented with the extraordinary spectacle of the abode of Her Majesty's Secretary to the Inland Revenue so beset with English detectives, French police spies and Russian *agents provocateurs* that to go along the sidewalk of that respectable terrace was to feel that one ran the gauntlet of innumerable gimlets.[15]

Ford's 'juvenile relatives' were Olive, Helen and Arthur Rossetti, who published *The Torch: A Revolutionary Journal of Anarchist Communism* from 3 St Edmund's Terrace in the 1890s. Ford's sister, Juliet Soskice, recorded in her *Chapters from Childhood*: 'We had an anarchist printing press down in the front room of the basement. We printed an anarchist newspaper on it. Olive and Arthur wrote most of the articles themselves...The paper was called *The Torch*, and we used to sell it in Hyde Park on Sunday, and on the platforms of the biggest railway stations.'[16] The young lady anarchist in Conrad's story corrects the proofs of the Italian and French editions of the anarchist publications, and the Rossettis were, naturally, closely connected with Italian anarchists in particular. Emma Goldman, the famous anarchist, recalled:

The Torch was a little paper published by two sisters, Olivia and Helen Rossetti. They were only fourteen and seventeen years old, respectively, but developed in mind and body far beyond their age. They did all the writing for the paper, even setting the type and attending to the press work themselves. *The Torch* office, formerly the nursery of the girls, became a gathering-place for foreign anarchists, particularly those from Italy, where severe persecution was taking place. The refugees naturally flocked to the Rossettis, who were themselves of Italian origin.[17]

Thus we have the house of 'a distinguished government official', William Michael Rossetti, being used as a centre for anarchists, particularly Italian anarchists, and the children of that official running an anarchist press in the basement. Conrad would not, of course, have known the house and its activities at that time, but he was obviously given the salient and incongruous facts by Ford.

The most striking aspect of the Rossettis' activity was the youth of the anarchist writers. When *The Torch* was established Olive was sixteen, Arthur fourteen, and Helen twelve.[18] Conrad does not mention this, and he reduces the three teenage anarchists to one young lady of about twenty and her brother. This was, no doubt, partly to remove the extraordinary aspect of the anarchist children, partly to enable him to deal with a young woman who, at the age of twenty, might be expected to have some sense of what she was about—an important part of the story. There is, also, the matter of the love interest between the young lady and the secret agent,

Sevrin. However, I believe Conrad limited the amateur anarchist field to one young lady anarchist almost certainly because he met only one of the Rossetti children, and that was Helen, who was about twenty at that time. The 'young Lady Amateur of anarchism' is almost certainly based on her.

Mrs Helen Rossetti Angeli recalled that she met Conrad on two occasions. 'I remember Conrad visiting my father in his little library to discuss the meaning of "Nostromo"', she wrote to me in a letter of 7 February 1967 and, when I interviewed her on 2 July 1967, she said that she met Conrad twice—once when he visited her father and a second time when she visited Ford's house. She was sure that Conrad did not meet either her sister Olive or her brother Arthur. As to the date of these meetings, Mrs Angeli's daughter, Mrs Dennis, wrote: 'My mother is evidently not certain when Conrad called at 3 St Edmund's Terrace but thinks she must have been about twenty at the time—this would bring Conrad's visit to the very end of the last century. Olive would not be there, being already married, while Arthur would already have been at work in the North of England.'[19] According to William Michael Rossetti's autobiography, Olive married Antonio Agresti in December 1897 and went to live in Florence. Arthur 'was placed as a student in the large engineering works' in Salford toward 1896.[20] But if Conrad visited William Michael Rossetti in order to discuss the meaning of *Nostromo*, his visit must have taken place during the writing of that novel at some time between the beginning of 1903 and August 1904.

Apart from her anarchist activities, Helen Rossetti's appearance appears to have impressed Conrad. A photograph of her taken at the end of the century (Plate 7*b*) shows those qualities of character and physical beauty which she shares with the young lady in the story:

The girl, a fine figure, was by no means vulgarly pretty. To more personal charm than mere youth could account for, she added the seductive appearance of enthusiasm, of independence, of courageous thought (p. 80).

...her big-eyed, broad-browed face and the good carriage of her shapely head, crowned by a magnificent lot of brown hair done in an unusual and becoming style (pp. 84–5).

Conrad refers to his young lady anarchist as the author of many articles, 'sentimental articles with ferocious conclusions', and this was true also of Helen Rossetti. Indeed, a study of *The Torch* indicates that under pseudonyms the Rossetti children wrote a great deal of the publication themselves. But what particularly disturbs the narrator in the story is that the young lady, in correcting the proofs of the anarchist publications, is reading material unsuitable for a young woman's eyes:

I had been shown once a few copies of these publications. Nothing, in my opinion, could have been less fit for the eyes of a young lady They were the most advanced things of the sort; advanced, I mean, beyond all bounds of reason and decency One of them preached the dissolution of all social and domestic ties; the other advocated systematic murder. To think of a young girl calmly tracking printers' errors all along the sort of abominable sentences I remembered was intolerable to my sentiment of womanhood (pp. 89–90).

Anarchist publications of the time were 'advanced' enough. This passage appeared in *The Torch* a few weeks after Helen Rossetti's sixteenth birthday: 'Wretched women:—Be sterile, close your wombs; abort!'[21]

It is in 'The Informer' that we first meet the Professor of *The Secret Agent*, or rather, Conrad's first sketch of that character. He has his laboratory at the top of the house in Hermione Street: 'The top floor caused considerable anxiety [during the mock raid]...There...a comrade, nick-named the Professor (he was an ex-science student) was engaged in perfecting some new detonators...we were afraid that under a mistaken impression he would blow himself up and wreck the house about our ears' (p. 88). It would seem that the initial inspiration for the Professor came also from the Rossetti household. In *A Girl among the Anarchists*, the Rossetti sisters wrote of their experiences under the pseudonym of Isabel Meredith, and this description, which is very similar to that of the Professor, appears in that book:

[My father] was a chemist and a man of advanced ideas on most things... He was a devoted and enthusiastic student, and for days, nay, weeks together, we would see but little of him. He had fitted himself up a small laboratory at the top of our house on which he spent all his available money, and here he passed nearly all the time he could dispose of.'[22]

The Rossetti girls made certain modifications to the facts in their book, no doubt in the cause of anonymity, and this description does not, of course, apply to their father who had no interest in science or chemistry. They are actually describing their brother Arthur, the only Rossetti to take to mathematics and science. His father stresses this point in his memoirs: 'Arthur is the only Rossetti (within my knowledge) who showed a scientific turn. In boyhood he had plenty of opportunity for reading poems, romances, histories, biographies, etc...but studies of chemistry, algebra, and other matters of science, engaged his chief personal attention; for a spell of light reading he would take up the Differential Calculus.'[23] Arthur Rossetti probably worked, therefore, like the Professor, in a laboratory at the top of the house, and a passage from Juliet Soskice's books suggests that his interest, at least at times, was, like the Professor's, in explosives. She recalls a particular incident in Arthur Rossetti's boyhood: 'He liked to fill a tin with gas and close it and hold it over a flame until the lid flew off with a tremendous bang, and once he blew his hair and eyebrows off by an experiment with gunpowder, which nobody ever knew how he got.'[24]

'The Informer' gives us the first indication of Conrad's

disapproval of anarchists, but it is directed here at the leaders, not at the rank and file, at upper class amateurs of revolution, and at the cynicism which he sees as lying at the root of the movement.

The narrator of the story is told of the incident concerning the Hermione Street group by Comrade X. The anarchists 'at the centre' in Brussels having become suspicious that information was being leaked to the police through this group, Comrade X comes to London to investigate and meet the 'young Lady Amateur of anarchism'. He organises a mock police raid on the Hermione Street house, and as a result the secret agent, Sevrin, is tricked into revealing himself as a traitor. Comrade X narrates the story in order to show that much of the support for the anarchist movement comes from the very class the anarchists are out to destroy: 'Don't you know yet...that an idle and selfish class loves to see mischief being made, even if it is made at its own expense?' (p. 78). And he is very critical of the young lady anarchist who, he says, had 'acquired all the appropriate gestures of revolutionary convictions—the gestures of pity, of anger, of indignation against the anti-humanitarian vices of the social class to which she belonged herself' (p. 81). Similar criticism was levelled at the Rossettis, as the two sisters record in their book. At a meeting at Chiswick, an anarchist called Kosinski objected to 'Isabel Meredith' as 'a mere bourgeois, attempting to play the part of lady patroness to the revolution'.[25] This particular point of view is not simply left to Comrade X in the story, but becomes the theme about which the ironies and ambiguities of the tale centre.

Comrade X is himself an example of the upper class anarchist whom he is criticising in the figure of the young lady anarchist. She may be an irresponsible amateur, safely locked in her upper class world of 'accomplished and innocent gestures', of 'conventional signs', 'the consummate and hereditary grimaces that in a certain sphere of life take the place of feelings', but X himself 'belonged to a noble family, and could have called himself Vicomte X de la Z if he chose', collected bronzes and china and 'took his meals in a very good restaurant'. Both, therefore, are of the same kind, but Comrade X is no amateur; and he is, moreover, more vicious: a destroyer of society, an impostor, a secret agent, hiding his true revolutionary activities beneath his appearance and his reputation as a revolutionary writer—'a kind of rare monster', just as some Chinese bronzes are 'monstrously precious'. It is surely the figure of Comrade X that the narrator is referring to when he says that he has been 'utterly unable to discover where in all this the joke comes in'.

The narrator's friend in Paris, the collector of acquaintances, is also criticised. If the irresponsible dabbling of the young lady and the fundamental cynicism of Comrade X are disapproved of, so is the essentially frivolous nature of the collector of acquaintances who lacks serious discrimination when he includes such pieces as Comrade X: '"Isn't X well worth knowing?" he bubbled over in great delight. "He's unique, amazing, absolutely terrific." His enthusiasm grated upon my finer feelings. I told him curtly that the man's cynicism was simply abominable. "Oh, abominable! abominable!" assented my friend, effusively' (pp. 101–2).

So much of the story and its attitudes appear to derive from the Rossettis and Ford, and Conrad's view of their anarchist activities. But what arises from this is a more general condemnation—the suggestion of a basic and cynical deceit which lies at the heart of anarchism, and is revealed in the irreconcilable paradox that undermines the position of the collector of acquaintances, the young lady amateur of anarchism and the unknown Number One of desperate conspiracies. The collector of acquaintances sees all round

Comrade X—'He has scalped every venerated head, and has mangled at the stake of his wit every received opinion and every recognised principle of conduct and policy...[he is also] a veteran of many subterranean campaigns' (p. 74)—without understanding the full implication of the portrait he paints. The young lady is shaken by her contact with the secret agent—'Has ever any one been exposed to such a terrible experience? To think that he had held my hand!' (p. 99)—without understanding Sevrin's 'terrible experience' (he has taken poison). Comrade X says: 'There's no amendment to be got out of mankind except by terror and violence' (p. 77) as he drinks his champagne, breaks bits of white bread, and attacks impassively a *bombe glacée* in a good restaurant. The narrator concludes:

Anarchists, I suppose, have no families...Organization into families may answer to a need of human nature, but in the last instance it is based on law, and therefore must be something odious and impossible to an anarchist...Does a man of that...persuasion still remain an anarchist when alone, quite alone and going to bed, for instance? ...I am sure that if such a faith...once mastered my thoughts I would never be able to compose myself sufficiently to sleep or eat or perform any of the routine acts of daily life. I would want no wife, no children; I could have no friends, it seems to me; and as to collecting bronzes or china, that, I should say, would be quite out of the question (p. 75).

And it is this paradox which is taken up in *The Secret Agent*.

I think one can justifiably conclude from this study that Ford and the Rossettis had a strong influence upon Conrad at this point in his writing career. His connection with them probably suggested the subject of anarchism to him, and they probably provided him, in one way and another, with ideas for situations, characters, and attitudes to the subject. Moreover, from their relationship with the anarchist movement, Conrad would seem to have derived his own critical attitude towards amateurs and their part in a revolutionary activity whose nature they only half appreciated.

21

'AN ANARCHIST'

The subject of 'An Anarchist' is again anarchism, but with
the interest shifted from the leaders and intelligentsia of the
movement to the working man who becomes involved with
it. The story is homiletic, moral in aim and symbolic in
technique. Paul, the hero, a working man with a warm heart
and a weak head, is forced to join the anarchists, having lost
his job after a term of imprisonment; as a result he takes
part in a bank robbery, and is committed to the penal settlement on St Joseph's Island, one of the Iles de Salut, French
Guiana. Escaping, he eventually becomes equally a prisoner
in 'a sort of penal settlement for condemned cattle', the
principal cattle estate of a famous meat-extract manufacturing
company, his position being exploited by the representative
of capitalism there, the manager of the station. Paul is thus
the innocent victim of a harsh justice, of anarchism, and of
capitalism. The theme is 'gullibility': the gullibility of mankind in the face of modern devices of advertisement which
in the story are used to sell the meat-extract Bos; and the
gullibility of the working man in the face of anarchist propaganda. The person in the story who does not suffer from that
'popular form' of 'mental degradation', gullibility, is the
narrator, a lepidopterist, unallied to either cause, and with
a pure scientific interest in nature.

The story is built round the central incident of the convict
mutiny on St Joseph's Island, a mutiny which enables Paul
to escape and also to avenge himself on the anarchists who
brought about his downfall. The narrator tells us that he
has checked this part of Paul's story: 'I have turned up the

files of French newspapers, and I have also talked with the officer who commands the military guard on the *Ile Royale*, when in the course of my travels I reached Cayenne. I believe the story to be in the main true' (p. 136); and later: 'From personal inquiry I can vouch that the story of the convict mutiny was in every particular as stated by him' (p. 161).

Remarks of this kind have all the effect of persuading the reader of the story's reality, but Conrad did have an actual mutiny in mind, the only one which took place in the penal settlement of the Ile St Joseph. This happened on 21 October 1894. When the actual and the fictional mutinies are compared, we find that Conrad kept unusually close to the original, though the changes he makes are significant. An incidental proof of Conrad's use of the incident is his adoption of the name Simon called Biscuit for one anarchist from Simon called Biscuit in the original incident.

It is most likely that Conrad first came upon references to the Cayenne mutiny during his reading of anarchist literature in preparation for the writing of *The Secret Agent*, for brief accounts of the mutiny appeared at different times in the anarchist press—in *The Torch* in 1894, in *La Sociale* in 1896, in the *Anarchist* in 1895. But we can best reconstruct the events of the original mutiny on St Joseph's Island from two main sources—the confidential report made to the Director of Prisons by the *commandant en chef* of the Iles de Salut, M. Bouchet,[1] and the account which appeared in Liard-Courtois's *Souvenirs du Bagne*.[2] These two accounts provide on the one hand the official interpretation and on the other a florid piece of anarchist special pleading. As Conrad makes use of the incident, the attitude of neither of these accounts is adopted, but the reader's sympathy is not directed towards the anarchists, except for Paul who takes no part in the mutiny. In this way the mutiny falls into

place in the story with the rest of Conrad's condemnation
of anarchism and anarchists.

The mutiny planned in Conrad's story is, in its essentials,
simple. St Joseph's Island, we learn, is the prettiest of the
Iles de Salut. Six warders, armed with revolvers and carbines,
are responsible for the convicts, and the only communication
is between St Joseph's Island and the Ile Royale, a quarter
of a mile away, where there is a military post. Contact is
made twice a day, at 6 a.m. and 4 p.m., by means of an
eight-oared galley. Escape is impossible: 'From that time
till next morning the island of St Joseph remains cut off
from the rest of the world', the warders patrol the island,
and 'a multitude of sharks' patrol the waters all round (p. 151).
Nevertheless, a mutiny is planned, though '*such a thing had
never been known in the penitentiary's history before*' [my
italics]. The convicts intend to take the warders by surprise
at night, kill them and, with the aid of their arms, get
possession of the galley the following morning and 'row away
up the coast'.

Conrad's close adherence to the facts of the original
situation in the penal settlement is shown in this account of
it by Michel Bourdet-Pléville: 'There were three of these
islands: the largest, Royale, some fifty-two acres in area,
Saint Joseph, thirty-five acres, and Diable (Devil's Island)
the smallest, covered only some seventeen acres. The islands
formed a separate convict station, the headquarters of which
were on Royale.'[3] Liard-Courtois, recalling the original
mutiny, states that the anarchists on St Joseph's Island had
a plan which was simple to establish and easy to carry out:

On choisirait un jour où le petit vapeur qui faisait pour l'administration
le trajet entre les îles, Cayenne et le Maroni — le *Capy* — serait en rade.
On supprimerait le gardien de nuit de service sur le plateau ainsi que
les deux contremaîtres de route afin qu'aucune alarme ne pût être
donnée. Ensuite, au moyen d'un radeau construit à l'avance et soigneuse-

ment caché dans les rochers, on se rendrait à bord du *Capy*, dont l'équipage, peu nombreux et surpris en pleine nuit, serait en un tour de main mis hors d'état de résister. Et l'on gagnerait la haute mer.[4]

Bourdet-Pléville writes simply 'they conceived a plan to seize the Cayenne mailboat and to get away to Brazil or to Dutch Guiana',[5] and he adds that this attempted escape was 'a very rare event in the annals of the *bagne*'.[6]

In Conrad's story, the plan goes at first without a hitch:

> At dusk the two warders on duty mustered the convicts as usual. Then they proceeded to inspect the huts to ascertain that everything was in order. In the second they entered they were set upon and absolutely smothered under the number of their assailants. The twilight faded rapidly. It was a new moon; and a heavy black squall gathering over the coast increased the profound darkness of the night. The convicts assembled in the open space, deliberating upon the next step to be taken, argued amongst themselves in low voices (pp. 151–2).

The murder of these two warders is followed by the killing of the chief warder and another three of his men:

> At last they [the convicts] divided into two parties and moved off... The path to the warders' house was dark and silent...Presently I saw a faint thread of light before me. The chief warder, followed by his three men, was approaching cautiously. But he had failed to close his dark lantern properly. The convicts had seen that faint gleam, too. There was an awful savage yell, a turmoil on the dark path, shots fired, blows, groans: and with the sound of smashed bushes, the shouts of the pursuers and the screams of the pursued, the man-hunt, the warder hunt, passed by me into the interior of the island. I was alone...I walked on along the path till I kicked something hard. I stopped and picked up a warder's revolver (pp. 152–3).

The original mutiny followed similar lines, although it was less bloody in its initial stages, only two of the warders being killed, and the head warder being unharmed. He had, in fact, been warned of the conspiracy in advance by a convict informer named Flista, and so had sent two overseers to muster the convicts that evening instead of the customary one. Bouchet's report shows that the two warders, Cretallaz and Mosca, inspected without incident huts 1, 3, 4, 5, 6 and 7 in succession and then approached hut 2:

M. Cretallaz qui a les clefs ouvre la serrure et se retire un peu en arrière le condamné, Boubout...contre-maître tire le verrou. A ce moment la porte est violemment tirée de l'intérieur et les anarchistes se précipitent dehors Garnier et Marpeaux se jettent sur Boubout...Garnier cherche à enlever le fanal dont le contre-maître est porteur le fanal est briseé... déjà Thiervoz, Simon et un troisième armés de poignards se sont élancés sur le surveillant qui après avoir crié 'Halte-là!' fait feu cette première balle tue le condamné Garnier. M. Cretallaz brûle encore trois cartouches et il tombe percé de coups. On l'entend crier avant de mourir: 'Assez! Assez!' la voix de Simon répond avec un accent de sauvagerie 'Non! Non!' — Simon qui s'est emparé des clefs court ouvrir la porte de la 6 case dans laquelle il crie:...'Vite, tout le monde dehors.'[7]

Twelve convicts obeyed the summons, and a convict called Richard incited the entire hut by shouting 'Allons! Allons! mes amis...ne nous laissons pas assassiner!' The second overseer was also murdered:

Pendant ce temps, le surveillant M. Mosca...est assailli de son côté et bat en retraite en faisant feu sur ses aggresseurs. Acculé contre le mur de soutènement il est saisi à la gorge par Thiervoz et jeté à terre par Mamert...et il est lardé de coups de poignards par Mamert...et par d'autres...son cadavre est jeté dans le ravin.[8]

Once this double murder had been committed, half the anarchist convicts rushed back to their huts, throwing their weapons away and hoping, as a result of the darkness, to escape punishment. Undoubtedly one of the leaders was '25607 Simon dit Biscuit': 'Simon apercevant Mamert se cacher dans la case pour se soustraire au châtiment se précipite à la porte de cette case...et la ferme en disant d'une voix très forte que personne ne rentre...Simon qui paraît être celui des révoltés qui a déployé la plus grande énergie avait les mains ensanglantées.'[9]

Up to this point, Conrad has followed the report of the actual mutiny very closely indeed. In each case, two warders have been set upon and murdered; the time is similar—8 p.m. in the actual case, dusk in the story. In the story 'the convicts kept on quarrelling over their plans. The leaders could not get themselves obeyed', and in the official report, once the two warders have been murdered, Simon 'Biscuit', though energetic, had little control over the convicts, half of them rushing back to their huts.

In describing the next stage of the mutiny, Conrad follows the *pattern* of events as they actually happened, but alters the details, and returns in part to the original plan of the mutineers, which involved an escape by sea. Conrad treats the mutiny as falling ironically into two parts, first a 'warder-hunt', then a 'convict-hunt'. And this is what took place. In the actual mutiny the convicts were quickly dispersed by a non-commissioned officer called Dard who arrived while Simon was attempting to open the door of hut number 8 and who fired 'several times' on the convicts outside their huts, scattering them 'in the direction of the plateau'. Help was then obtained from the Ile Royale. The official report states:

Le surveillant chef Billet réunissait déjà les surveillants, leur assignait leur poste et après avoir prescrit de faire des signaux à l'Ile Royale, courait au camp — le condamné Lôle...lampiste agitait sur le quai, un fanal pour demander du secours en armes, — Madame Billet, femme du surveillant chef, pendant que son mari allait au danger où était sa place accourait auprès du condamné Lôle, s'emparait de la corne et essayait de corner. Le condamné Lôle voyant que Madame Billet ne pouvait tirer aucun son s'est emparé de la corne et tout en continuant d'agiter son fanal d'une main il a corné jusqu'au moment où il a aperçu une embarcation venant de l'Ile Royale — conduite par le surveillant M. Le Goff l'embarcation amenait 3 surveillants. Après avoir essuyé un coup de feu auquel il a répondu le surveillant Le Goff est rentré à l'Ile Royale pour prévenir le commandant que sa présence était nécessaire et pour ramener de nouveaux renforts en surveillants et en troupe.[10]

Of these events, Conrad took over the heroic gesture of the chief warder's wife in summoning help:

Suddenly, a big light ran across my path very low along the ground. And it showed a woman's skirt...I knew that the person who carried it must be the wife of the head warder. They had forgotten all about her, it seems. A shot rang out in the interior of the island, and she cried out to herself as she ran. She passed on. I followed, and presently I saw her again. She was pulling at the cord of the big bell which hangs at the end of the landing-pier, with one hand, and with the other she was swinging the heavy lantern to and fro. This is the agreed signal for the *Ile Royale* should assistance be required at night...She went on without stopping...A brave woman, monsieur...we must believe the signal was seen, for the galley from *Ile Royale* came over in an astonishingly short time. The woman kept right on till the light of her lantern flashed upon the officer in command and the bayonets of the soldiers in the boat...Some soldiers were only in their shirt-sleeves, others without boots, just as the call to arms had found them. They passed by my bush at the double. The galley had been sent away for more (pp. 153–4).

There are certain obvious differences here, but reports of the mutiny which appeared in the *Anarchist* of 20 January 1895 mention that 'the wife of a warder gave the alarm, a revolver in one hand, a lantern in the other', and Liard-Courtois states that 'Un garde-chiourme, du nom de Dard, ordonna à sa femme de se tenir à la cloche et de l'agiter sans discontinuer, afin de prévenir à l'île Royale que l'heure du massacre était sonnée.'[11] Conrad appears to have noticed the part played by the convict Lôle who assisted the warder's wife in giving the signal to the Ile Royale. Paul, in the story, does not play the same positive role, but he does stand guard over the head warder's wife while she rings the bell (although she does not know he is there), prepared to take action if she is molested: 'I made up my mind that if a body of my fellow-convicts came down to the pier—which was sure to happen—I would shoot her through the head before I shot myself. I knew the "comrades" well' (pp. 153–4). So Paul, like Lôle, is on the side of law and against the anarchists.

In the case of the actual mutiny, the convict-hunt began with the arrival of the soldiers from the Ile Royale. The reprisals taken against the mutineers were extreme—none escaped from the island, and they were either shot or beheaded:

Les condamnés Garnier, Mattei et Boasis avaient été tués; on constate l'absence des condamnés: Thiervoz, Mazarquil, Léauthier, Simon dit Biscuit, Chevenet, Meyruesis, Lebeau et Marpeaux. Sauf Marpeaux tous étaient tués dans le matinée, Chevenet dans les roches du plateau, Simon et Meyruesis sur un arbre (plateau), Thiervoz dans une des carrières du plateau, Léauthier, Lebeau, et Mazarquil au milieu des roches bordant la côte-est de l'île, ces trois derniers sont tombés en criant: 'Vive l'anarchie!'[12]

Liard-Courtois describes the death of Simon called Biscuit:

'...les soldats aperçurent Simon dit Biscuit qui s'était juché jusqu'au faîte d'un cocotier.
— Où veux-tu que je te tire? lui cria l'un d'eux. Dans la tête ou dans le c...?
— Vive l'anarchie! répondit simplement Biscuit.
Et le corps de cet enfant de vingt ans s'abattit sur le sol. Ils s'étaient mis quatre pour le tuer.'[13]

Conrad covers this part of the incident by the sentences 'I heard firing, shouts. Another hunt had begun—the convict-hunt', but whereas our sympathy has been aroused for the murdered warders, no sympathy is suggested for the hunted convicts. And that this is a deliberate omission on Conrad's part is shown by his omission also of those suggestions of severe punishments and maltreatment of convicts that appeared in some reports and which were given as the reason for the mutiny.

Ignoring the massacre that followed the arrival of help, then, Conrad turns to the plans the mutineers had for their escape. They were to have left the island by means of a raft and the steamer *Capy*, and Conrad takes up this idea, substituting the finding of a boat left by two late-arriving soldiers. Paul, and the two anarchists Simon the Biscuit and Mafile, escape in the boat, but, just as they are in sight of a ship, Paul shoots both his comrades, seeing them as the men responsible for his downfall: 'I remembered their lies, their promises, their menaces, and all my days of misery. Why could they not have left me alone after I came out of prison? ...A black rage came upon me—the rage of extreme intoxication' (pp. 158–9). From the hints contained in Lôle's action, Conrad developed the character of Paul. His method is, as in *The Secret Agent*, to personalise an event which he knew only in its public, official, and de-personalised form.

So far as I have been able to discover, the events in the first part of the story leading to the hero's imprisonment have their source in Conrad's imagination, though they may have been suggested by his reading about the anarchist movement.[14]

'An Anarchist' is a strange story, crude and uncomfortable in some of its implications, but it gives us a foreshadowing of Conrad's methods and attitudes in *The Secret Agent*. As in that novel, he takes as his central incident an actual and horrible event, and remains fairly close to the details of that event, but the modifications and changes he makes and the manner in which the characters are developed show a deliberate attempt to present anarchists as contemptible creatures and to deny them the reader's sympathy.

22

THE BOMB OUTRAGE

The source for the basic incident of *The Secret Agent* was, as in the case of 'An Anarchist', an actual episode from anarchist history. The bomb outrage in the novel, which is carried out by Verloc on the prompting of Vladimir and which results in Stevie's death, was based upon the Greenwich Bomb Outrage which took place in 1894, twelve years before Conrad wrote his novel. That this was his source has never been denied except by Conrad himself, and he was not consistent about his denial.

In his earlier statements about the novel, Conrad emphasized that his story arose from the historic event. He wrote in the Author's Note to *The Secret Agent*:

the subject of 'The Secret Agent'—I mean the tale—came to me in the shape of a few words uttered by a friend in a casual conversation about anarchists or rather anarchist activities...Presently, passing to particular instances, we recalled the already old story of the attempt to blow up the Greenwich Observatory....*This* book is *that* story, reduced to manageable proportions, its whole course suggested and centred round the absurd cruelty of the Greenwich Park explosion.[1]

And in a letter to Sir Algernon Methuen of 7 November 1906 he says: 'it is based on the inside knowledge of a certain event in the history of active anarchism'.[2] But in 1923, replying to Ambrose J. Barker who had sent him a pamphlet on the subject, he denied all knowledge of the Greenwich Bomb Outrage which he had previously claimed as his source: 'As a matter of fact I never knew anything of what was called ...the "Greenwich Bomb Outrage". I was out of England when it happened, and thus I never read what was printed in the newspapers at the time. All I was aware of was the mere fact—my novel being, in intention, the history of Winnie Verloc.'[3] It looks very much as though Barker had stumbled upon one of Conrad's source books for the novel in this pamphlet and that Conrad's denial arose from a desire to conceal his sources of information. 'It was a matter of great interest to me', Conrad continued, presumably referring to the subject of the pamphlet, 'to see how near actuality I managed to come in a work of imagination.'

But Conrad's imagination required always a firm basis of fact, and he certainly had this in the case of *The Secret Agent*. The novel derives undoubtedly from Conrad's knowledge of the bomb outrage and of anarchist activity in London at that time. In spite of his statement to the contrary, Conrad was, during January and February of 1894, living at 17 Gillingham Street, London, engaged in the writing of *Almayer's Folly*[4] and must have read the accounts of the Greenwich Park incident which appeared in the London newspapers. Whatever part his imagination later gave to Winnie Verloc, his initial conception derived from the bomb outrage: the first draft of the novel was called *Verloc* after the protagonist, and Winnie's part in the first version to be published[5] is small.

His sources were most certainly the contemporary newspaper accounts of, and speculation about, the incident. His 'inside knowledge' must have been in part derived from anarchist publications of the kind sold by Verloc in his shop: 'a few apparently old copies of obscure newspapers, badly printed, with titles like *The Torch*, *The Gong*—rousing titles' (p. 3). And I believe that Conrad's source material can in part be traced to one anarchist newspaper, the *Anarchist*, and to two pamphlets on the Greenwich incident. One of these pamphlets—'The Greenwich Mystery', published in 1897 at Sheffield—may well be the one which Barker sent to

Conrad and which until now has not been identified.[6] The *Anarchist* was at that time edited by a David Nicoll, who was also author of the pamphlets.

The bomb outrage in the novel is instigated by a foreign embassy at the time of an anti-anarchist conference in Milan, with the object of discrediting the anarchists who have taken refuge in England and so persuading the English to take stricter measures against them. The incident thus becomes the work of an *agent provocateur* (Verloc), which takes the anarchists and also the police, by surprise, arouses some concern among the ruling class, and results in the entirely accidental death of the catspaw, Stevie. It achieves none of its aims and thus has the appearance of a mysterious and absurd cruelty. All of these aspects of the fictional incident are to be found in the actual incident of the Greenwich Bomb Outrage. The initial reports of the incident in the newspapers were as brief and as mysterious as that read out by Comrade Ossipon in the novel. *The Times* wrote:

EXPLOSION IN GREENWICH PARK

Last evening an explosion was heard by a keeper of Greenwich Park on the hill close to the Royal Observatory. Proceeding thither he found a respectably-dressed man, in a kneeling posture, terribly mutilated.

One hand was blown off and the body was open. The injured man was only able to say, 'Take me home', and was unable to reply to a question as to where his home was. He was taken to the Seamen's Hospital in an ambulance, and died in less than half an hour.

A bottle, in many pieces, which had apparently contained an explosive substance, was found near the spot where the explosion took place, and it is conjectured that the deceased man fell and caused its contents to explode.

The deceased, who was not known in Greenwich, is a young man of about 30, supposed to be a foreigner. The only evidence of identification was a card bearing the name 'Bourbon' [*sic*] (16 February 1894).

The *Morning Leader* reported the incident more sensationally, its headlines being:

The Bomb Outrage

BLOWN TO PIECES!
Victim an Anarchist (?)
Was he a member of a gang
who had fell designs on
London's Safety?

A man who carried a terrible explosive blown to pieces at Greenwich—it is declared that he was the chief of a gang of anarchists, and was seeking to conceal his bombs—was he an associate of Emile Henry?[7] (16 February 1894)

The victim's name was Martial Bourdin (see Plate 8*c* for a photograph of Bourdin).

Although in *The Secret Agent* the reader has been prepared by the interview between Verloc and Vladimir for an attempt to blow up the Greenwich Observatory, the explosion is introduced with as much shock and mystery as was the actual explosion. Comrade Ossipon reads the first newspaper report of Verloc's attempt to the Professor—it is brief, and gives no explanations:

Bomb in Greenwich Park. There isn't much so far. Half-past eleven. Foggy morning. Effects of explosion felt as far as Romney Road and Park Place. Enormous hole in the ground under a tree filled with smashed roots and broken branches. All round fragments of a man's body blown to pieces. That's all. The rest's mere newspaper gup. No doubt a wicked attempt to blow up the Observatory, they say. H'm. That's hardly credible (pp. 70–1).

The two anarchists are unprepared for anything like this. Ossipon knew of no such plan to blow up the observatory, and the Professor knew only that there was 'to be a demonstration against a building'. He had supplied Verloc with the explosive. They conclude that the shattered body is that of Verloc. This misunderstanding is only cleared up when Inspector Heat discovers, among the remains of the body, the velvet collar of a coat bearing a label on which is written Verloc's address. Through this he eventually learns that the body is that of Stevie, Verloc's witless brother-in-law.

It is obvious that the basic situations are the same. In both incidents there is an initial mystery as to the identity of the victim, and much speculation as to what happened to him in the park and as to why he was there. The major initial differences between the actual and fictional incident are in the fate of the victim and in the cause of the accident.

Stevie is blown to pieces ('All round fragments of a man's body blown to pieces') and Conrad seems to have taken the sensational headline of the *Morning Leader*: 'Blown to Pieces' and for the purposes of his fiction treated this as fact. Bourdin, on the other hand, though badly wounded, was alive and able to speak when he was discovered. The description of Bourdin's mutilations were made much of in the *Morning Leader*: 'His left hand and wrist were blown away, his face and the rest of his body were covered with wounds, and his stomach was blown open, a portion of the intestines protruding' (16 February 1894). In its report of the inquest, the paper gave such details as:

On one of the iron bars of the fence, on the second bend from the bottom, witness [a detective inspector] found a tendon of sinew, fresh [*sic*], which had, by the force of the impact, been twisted round the railing. Above that, and to the left of the railing, he found five pieces of apparently human skin. At a subsequent examination he found on the right of the path two bones, apparently the knuckle-joints of the thumb.

Conrad's descriptions of Stevie's death are not, therefore, out of place:[8] 'Another waterproof sheet was spread over that table in the manner of a tablecloth, with the corners turned up over a sort of mound—a heap of rags, scorched and bloodstained, half concealing what might have been an accumulation of raw material for a cannibal feast' (p. 86). The list of details in the report of the inquest reflects the unmoved compilation of facts, however intolerable, by the police mind; and the attitude of Conrad's constable is the same:

'You used a shovel', he remarked, observing a sprinkling of small gravel, tiny brown bits of bark, and particles of splintered wood as fine as needles.

'Had to in one place', said the stolid constable. 'I sent a keeper to fetch a spade. When he heard me scraping the ground with it he leaned his forehead against a tree, and was as sick as a dog' (p. 87).

'Well, here he is—all of him I could see. Fair. Slight—slight enough. Look at that foot there. I picked up the legs first, one after another. He was that scattered you didn't know where to begin' (p. 89).

The effect in both newspaper and novel is macabre, but the newspaper reports also aroused sympathy in the reader for the condition and suffering of the mutilated man, Bourdin —who was conscious, after all, when found. This sympathy is denied Stevie by the fact that he is quite dead, and quite scattered. Heat's reflections that even instantaneous death might involve a moment of intense suffering cannot arouse our sympathies in face of the constable's descriptions, and the image of Heat as 'an indigent customer bending over what may be called the by-products of a butcher's shop with a view to an inexpensive Sunday dinner' (p. 88).

Views on the cause of Bourdin's blowing himself up varied. The *Morning Leader* and *The Times* both suggested at first that Bourdin had stumbled, and that his death was, therefore, due to this accident:

He reached Greenwich about half an hour before dusk, and, turning to the left on leaving the station, he walked to the park by way of London-street and Stockwell-street. Walking along the main avenue lined with great trees on both sides, he reached the top of the hill, near the Observatory. Across the pathway the roots of the older trees protrude through the gravel, and it may be assumed that, it now being quite dusk, the man stumbled and fell, with the result that the infernal machine or machines which he was carrying exploded on his own person (*The Times*, 16 February 1894).

But at the inquest on Bourdin, Colonel Majendie, a Home Office expert on explosives, rejected this theory: 'Beyond all doubt the man was standing up at the time of the explosion, which was not the result of an accidental fall on the part of either the deceased or the bomb. There was no disturbance on the gravel such as would have been found had any explosion occurred on the ground' (*Morning Leader*, 27 February 1894). Colonel Majendie went so far as to reconstruct what occurred. He concluded that Bourdin had been holding the explosive in his left hand at a short distance in front of his body, while ascending the path; that he had taken the bottle of sulphuric acid out of his pocket, used as much of its contents as was necessary to ignite the bomb; and from some mischance, miscalculation, or clumsy handling, the explosion which was intended to occur very shortly, occurred prematurely.

In *The Secret Agent*, both the Professor and Verloc are convinced that Stevie had had plenty of time to deposit the bomb and leave the park before it exploded: 'It was set for twenty minutes...He either ran the time too close, or simply let the thing fall' (p. 76). But Conrad leaves us in no doubt as to why the bomb exploded, and he takes as the reason the view first put forward by the newspapers to explain Bourdin's accident—that he stumbled over the roots of trees in the dusk and fell. Conrad's constable, the 'first man on the spot after the explosion', draws this same conclusion: 'Them roots do stick out all about the place. Stumbled against the root of a tree and fell, and that thing he was carrying must have gone off right under his chest' (p. 89).

Whereas Colonel Majendie gave elaborate evidence to prove that Bourdin could *not* have stumbled and fallen, Conrad goes to the trouble of giving equally convincing evidence that Stevie *must* have fallen. It was dusk when Bourdin died, and though Conrad's explosion takes place in the morning, it is a foggy morning to account for Stevie stumbling. Majendie pointed out that if Bourdin had stumbled, his legs would have been wounded and there would have been disturbance to the ground beneath him. Stevie is blown to pieces, and there is a large hole where the explosion occurred.

The noise of the explosion is mentioned, as a piece of dramatic background material, in the *Morning Leader* report: 'The stillness of the park...was rent by the sound of the explosion with such violence as to be heard by creditable witnesses as far away as the Chatham and Dover Railway Station in Stockwell-street on the west and Maze-hill station on the South-Eastern Railway on the east' (16 February 1894). This is paralleled by Conrad's: 'Effects of explosion felt as far as Romney Road and Park Place' (p. 70).

The events immediately following the explosion, and the subsequent investigation, are closely followed by Conrad. Two schoolboys were first on the spot in the actual case, followed by a park-keeper, Patrick Sullivan: 'He declared that the report was followed by a volume of smoke...and [he] immediately ran in the direction of the smoke' (*Morning Leader*, 20 February 1894). A local constable, Patrick Tangey, was soon on the scene, and he went afterwards to the Seamen's Hospital where Bourdin had been taken. Constable Tangey searched the body there, on the afternoon of the explosion, and a list of the articles he found was given in the *Morning Leader* (27 February 1894). In *The Secret Agent* it is the constable, of course, who arrives first though he is provided with a shovel by a park-keeper. Stevie is also carried to a nearby hospital, and Chief Inspector Heat started 'immediately to begin his investigation on the spot [that is, at Greenwich] ...Then he had walked over to the hospital.' He inspects the mangled remains and listens to the local constable's report. Heat searches the body and takes away an address.

Heat has been called from Scotland Yard to investigate the incident: '[He] had had a disagreeably busy day since his department received the first telegram'. In the same way, the newspapers report: 'The local police officers quickly realised that they had more than an ordinary case to deal with, and Scotland Yard was communicated with by telegraph.' The report continues: 'One of the chiefs of the Criminal Investigation Department proceeded at once to Greenwich' (*Morning Leader*, 16 February 1894).

These aspects of the investigation—the presence of the local constable, the taking of the remains to the hospital, the searching of the body, the sending for a Yard man by telegraph, are I believe too close to the original for Conrad not to have been working with that original in mind.

At the inquest on Bourdin, two witnesses gave evidence of his journey by tram to the park:

The tram conductor who issued the ticket, William Smith, stated that last Thursday week he was working on the Westminster to East Greenwich Route. He only issued one through ticket...He issued it to a young man whom he believed to be the deceased. The man sat about half-way down on the left hand side when he got in first. As the people gradually got out he moved up to the front end of the car, nearer to the driver. He did not appear to be carrying anything in particular. He travelled right down to the terminus at East Greenwich (*Morning Leader*, 27 February 1894).

John Bone, a timekeeper, stated that while he was checking the conductor's time, the deceased asked the conductor the way to Greenwich Park. Stevie, on the other hand, travelled by train, but evidence of the journey is also given by two witnesses:

'The porter who took the tickets at Maze Hill remembers two chaps answering to the description passing the barrier. They seemed to him two respectable working-men of a superior sort—sign painters or house-decorators. The big man got out of a third-class compartment backward, with a bright tin can in his hand. On the platform he gave it to carry to the fair young fellow who followed him' (p. 101).

'The old woman who spoke to the sergeant noticed a fair-haired fellow coming out of Maze Hill Station...She noticed two men coming out of the station after the uptrain had gone on...She couldn't tell if they were together. She took no particular notice of the big one, but the other was a fair, slight chap, carrying a tin varnish can in one hand...' (p. 88).

The nature of the evidence and the way in which it is presented by Conrad is similar to that of the actual case.

The explosion was immediately connected with the anarchist movement and many reasons were put forward to explain Bourdin's presence with the explosive in Greenwich Park.[9] But Conrad adopted the explanation which had the support of the Government, that Bourdin was out to destroy the Greenwich Observatory. *The Times* of 17 February 1894 argues very forcefully for the view that Martial Bourdin was going to demonstrate against the Observatory:

Whether his actual intention was to blow up the Observatory at Greenwich or not is one of those questions which can be judged from probabilities only, since the person who could have spoken with certainty upon the point is dead; but the facts certainly show that he intended some serious mischief when he entered Greenwich Park; and the path which he followed, a narrow, zigzag, and secluded path, leads practically nowhere except to the Observatory.

Moreover, at the inquest on Bourdin, Colonel Majendie, when asked by the coroner what he thought was the man's intention, answered: 'Probably against the Observatory, or its contents, or its inmates. That is my opinion. I can arrive at no other conclusion' (*Morning Leader*, 27 February 1894).

One of Conrad's major changes from source to novel would appear to be that Stevie was accompanied by his brother-in-law, Mr Verloc, to Greenwich Park whereas Bourdin made the journey to Greenwich alone. However, as the investigation into Bourdin's movements before he blew himself up got under way, new information appeared. It was discovered that 'he lunched at about two o'clock with his brother...at the International Restaurant, Bennett St., Fitzroy Square...It was ten minutes to three when he left'

The Secret Agent

(*Morning Leader*, 17 February 1894). Two days later, an interview with Mr Samuels, Bourdin's brother-in-law, was published in the *Morning Leader*. The newspaper headlines were as follows:

MR. SAMUELS INTERVIEWED: *What Bourdin's brother-in-law has to say of his Purpose.*

Mr. H. B. Samuels, the editor of one of the Anarchist papers, has, of course, been interviewed. He is, besides being an Anarchist leader, a brother-in-law of Bourdin. He stated that on Thursday last he met Bourdin in the West-end about two o'clock, and remained in his company a considerable time. During the conversation he asked Bourdin whether he had succeeded in finding work. The latter replied in the negative, and added that he did not particularly want any at that time. Mr. Samuels told him that probably if he accompanied him to the place he worked at he would be able to get some work, as they were very busy...They walked about 20 or 30 yards together in the direction of Mr. Samuel's workshop, when Bourdin suddenly exclaimed, 'No, I'm not going to-day. I shall go back.' They then parted. Mr. Samuels thinks it very unlikely that he had anything of an explosive nature on his person at that time. He thinks Bourdin must have had an appointment to meet someone soon afterwards, from whom he obtained the explosive. By the way, Mr. Samuels subsequently said he had an idea that the manufacture of bombs for Continental use has been going on for some little time. He feels convinced Bourdin did not go to Greenwich with any intention of blowing up the Observatory. His object was, he believes, either to buy the explosive or to experiment.

The Anarchist leader was greatly surprised to learn that a sum of £13 in gold had been found in his brother-in-law's possession, and it was a complete mystery to him as to where he obtained the money. He was quite certain, he said, that when Bourdin left him he had scarcely any money on him, and only the previous night at the restaurant where it was their custom to have supper he left without paying and the same thing had occurred the day before that. Mr. Samuels declared that Bourdin was quite unacquainted with the neighbourhood of Greenwich, and therefore he considered it probable that whoever gave him the explosives also gave him definite instructions as to where to go and what to do.

Here we have the same basic situation as that involving Verloc and his brother-in-law. Samuels was married to Bourdin's sister, Bourdin was the victim of the explosion in Greenwich Park—an explosion surrounded by mystery—and Samuels was in the company of Bourdin not long before the explosion took place. Moreover, Samuels, like Verloc, was a leading anarchist.* Thus the pattern of events and people immediately surrounding the disaster was completed in substantially the form in which Conrad was to present it in his novel.

Up to this point, we can conclude that Conrad was making the kind of use of the actual incident that one would expect of him since he worked close to facts and obviously knew the facts in some detail in this instance. Certainly the initial impact of the Greenwich mystery, the nature of the incident, and even the 'flavour' imparted to the inquiry through newspaper reports, is there in *The Secret Agent*.

*

The Greenwich mystery remained the Greenwich 'mystery' to the public. No real background information as to Bourdin's anarchist activities appeared. And the speculation in the newspapers is a reflection of the mysteriousness of the event. Thus the quality of the initial incident which attracted Conrad was its inexplicableness, as he records in his Author's Note:

a blood-stained inanity of so fatuous a kind that it was impossible to fathom its origin by any reasonable or even unreasonable process of thought. For perverse unreason has its own logical processes. But that outrage could not be laid hold of mentally in any sort of way, so that one remained faced by the fact of a man blown to bits for nothing even most remotely resembling an idea, anarchistic or other.[10]

But Conrad could have found a suggested explanation of the actual mystery in the anarchist press, and particularly in David Nicoll's pamphlet, *The Greenwich Mystery*,† where,

---

* Samuels wrote an obituary of his brother-in-law which appeared in the Anarchist journal the *Commonweal*, 10 March 1894.

† See Appendix D, pp. 379–94, below for a transcription of the pamphlet *The Greenwich Mystery* (Sheffield, 1897).

with much indignation, it was claimed that a police plot to bring the anarchists into disrepute in England lay behind the affair. Nicoll's purpose in writing his pamphlet was partly to unmask Samuels as the police agent in the case. The plot was one in which Samuels played the part of a double agent and in which the tool used by him was accidentally killed.

So far as Nicoll was concerned, the Greenwich Mystery had *not* been solved by the time he wrote his pamphlet of 1897, three years after the event: '. . .the Greenwich Mystery is still a mystery', he stated, and he asked: 'What was the object of Bourdin in going to Greenwich Park?' For Nicoll the solution of the Greenwich Mystery and the reason for Bourdin being in the park lay with Samuels. According to Nicoll, Samuels sent Bourdin off with the explosive, intending that he should be arrested by the police with the explosive on him—a more ruthless action than that of Mr Verloc, who intended only that Stevie should act as a carrier. Conrad stresses that Verloc 'never meant Stevie to perish with such abrupt violence' (p. 229) and we must assume, in spite of the radical differences that appear between the apathetic Verloc and the aggressive Samuels, that Samuels did not anticipate that *his* brother-in-law would 'perish with such abrupt violence'.

Nicoll's evidence against Samuels begins with Samuels's statements about his meeting Bourdin immediately before the explosion:

Mr. Samuels told the *Central News*, 'he was in Bourdin's company at two o'clock, and remained in his company for *a considerable time*.' How long is a considerable time? Forty minutes! If so, Bourdin must have left him to start on his journey to Greenwich. As it is known Bourdin travelled by tram, it would have taken him from 2.40 to 4.20 p.m., one hour and forty minutes to reach Greenwich from Hanover Square. We have tested this by actual experiment. He was in Samuels' company at 2 p.m., and arrived at Greenwich at 4.20 according to the evidence of the tram conductor.[11]

Nicoll draws the conclusion that Samuels must have been in Bourdin's company 'a considerable time after 2 p.m.' If this was the case it makes nonsense of Samuels's own story that he walked only '20 or 30 yards' with Bourdin before Bourdin left him and casts doubt on his further suggestion that 'Bourdin must have had an appointment to meet someone soon afterwards, from whom he obtained the explosive' and that 'whoever gave him [Bourdin] the explosives also gave him definite instructions as to where to go and what to do'. Nicoll also quotes a Press Association report: 'In the course of the same afternoon he [Bourdin] was observed in company with another man, in the neighbourhood of Hanover Square, and later on the two parted company in Whitehall, Bourdin then walking over Westminster Bridge and taking the tram to Greenwich.'[12] Inevitably he asks the question: 'Did the mysterious stranger, in Hanover Square, and Whitehall, bear any resemblance to Mr. Samuels? How did he escape arrest?'

It is Nicoll's belief that Samuels gave the explosive to Bourdin: 'My opinion is, that he was asked by Samuels to take the money and the "brown paper parcel" to some mysterious "comrade", whom he was to meet in that neighbourhood. He was too weak to refuse; but showed some reluctance, so the tempter was forced to go with him part of the way "to give him courage".'[13] And at a later date, it seems, Samuels admitted that he supplied Bourdin with explosive and that he had accompanied him for a considerable distance on his journey. Nicoll records that, at a weekly meeting of the 'Commonweal' group, Samuels made the following statement:

As to the Bourdin affair, he declared he had stolen the explosives out of the house of a comrade D——, who had them for use in his business, and given them to Bourdin...Further, he admitted that he went with Bourdin on his way to Greenwich, nearly as far as Westminster Bridge. That they were pursued by detectives and parted there. One to go to his death, while the other returned peacefully home, unmolested by the police.[14]

Apparently, Samuels had been giving explosives to his fellow anarchists, and then informing on them, so that they could be arrested by the police for being in possession of explosives. Nicoll quotes an incident to prove this:

But that night, in the street, he [R—] met an acquaintance who was evidently in a high state of excitement. 'Have you heard the news', he exclaimed, 'Samuels has been giving explosives to J—, *and two days after J—'s house was raided by the police.* They evidently expected to find something, for *they tore up the boards of the floor.*'[15]

Samuels was not simply intending to betray his fellow anarchists by these methods. The implications of his actions went much further, as Mrs Bevington, a well-known anarchist, pointed out in a letter to Nicoll after the appearance of, and in reply to, his pamphlet. She accepts Samuels's guilt, considers him to be a traitor, and also to be in league with the police in order to bring the anarchist movement into disrepute:

Dear Comrade, — You have got the Bourdin history wrong. The facts were that Samuels having, as it is said on good authority, supplied him with the *new compound*, suggested to him to take it somewhere for the purpose of *experiment*. Well, Bourdin, in all good faith, thought 'experiment' *meant* experiment; and hit on Epping Forest as a place where he would have a good chance of exploding his compound against a big tree without great danger of its being heard, or of him seen before he could get away. *This would, however, have obviously been of little use to the police; quite obviously a mere experiment—or else a mere bit of foolish mischief...for a big lucrative scare and scandal* [my italics]. Well, as the fates had it, Samuels met him just as he was starting with his ingredients. 'I'm going', says Bourdin, touching his pockets significantly. 'Where to?' 'Epping Forest.' 'Oh, don't go there, go to Greenwich Park.' 'All right', and they went together as far as Westminster, and were seen; and one of them accordingly was made the butt of the police. How do I know Samuels told him where to go? Because Mrs. Samuels [this is Bourdin's sister], whom I used to see very often at that time, *told me.* Why do I report that conversation above? Because Samuels himself, before he was suspected by the Group, and while he was still desirous of seeming an important character in the eyes of sundry gaping comrades, boastingly related it.[16]

Mrs Bevington's account of the mystery is therefore that Samuels gave Bourdin a compound to experiment with but in order that the experiment should produce 'a big lucrative scare and scandal' for the purpose of bringing disgrace upon the anarchist movement, he deliberately directed Bourdin to Greenwich Park. Thus the mere fact of Bourdin being discovered near the observatory in possession of an explosive would be taken to be an attempt upon the observatory. This is the basis of Conrad's plot. Vladimir's decision that Verloc should bomb the observatory stems directly from Samuels's attempt to discredit the anarchists in England. Conrad did not find a prototype for Verloc's character in Samuels, but he did find a prototype of the double agent and the *agent provocateur*. The sinister double agent behind the death of Bourdin was his brother-in-law, Samuels.

Nicoll quotes Samuels's suggestion (which appeared in the *Sheffield Daily Telegraph*, 19 February 1894) that the Bourdin incident was '*the commencement of an extensive plot*' and this suggestion, Nicoll argues, 'spread terror among the timid middle class. And Conservative Newspapers...raised at once an outcry'. He quotes from the *Globe* leader: 'Society is asking how long the British metropolis will be content to afford a safe asylum for gangs of assassins, who there plot and perfect atrocious schemes for universal murder on the Continent.' And Nicoll comments that 'The enemies of the right of asylum saw at once that the Greenwich explosion, and the statements of Mr. Samuels were a great help to them in the agitation.' Thus, the agitation which gathered as a result of the Greenwich Outrage, and which is commented upon here, is made the source of Vladimir's speculation as to how the middle classes can be stirred in England. As Mrs Bevington says, 'a big lucrative scare and scandal' indeed!

An example of the kind of reaction that was hoped for from the Greenwich Park explosion appears in Chapter 10 of *The Secret Agent* when the lady patroness, after having spoken to Vladimir, turns to the assistant commissioner and says: 'He [Vladimir] has been threatening society with all sorts of horrors...apropos of this explosion in Greenwich Park. It appears we all ought to quake in our shoes at what's coming if those people are not suppressed all over the world. I had no idea this was such a grave affair' (pp. 223–4).

And Conrad may have derived the idea of Vladimir and the foreign embassy as providing the initial impetus for the bomb outrage from the following passages taken from the *Anarchist* which was edited by the author of *The Greenwich Mystery*, David Nicoll:

The Russian and other Continental despotisms are very anxious to lay hands on the refugees from their tyranny, men whose names are known throughout the civilised world for their courage and high character.

A few dynamite explosions in England would suit the book of the Russian police splendidly, and, might even result in terrifying the English bourgeoisie into handing over the refugees to the vengeance of the Russian Czar.[17]

...the victims of one of the numerous foreign police spies with which London abounds. The Russian Government alone are said to have some thirty of these busy gentlemen in their pay, and they must do something to earn their money.

England is now almost the only country where the rebels against the tyranny of the despots of the Continent can find refuge, and the despots would like very much to see the right of asylum swept away. 'Plots to blow up the Royal Exchange' are very useful for this purpose.[18]

It is interesting that words used here by Nicoll: 'they [the foreign police spies in London] must do something to earn their money' are like those used by Vladimir to the secret agent Verloc: 'I tell you plainly that you will have to earn your money' (p. 26).

The reaction in the novel of the anarchist Ossipon to the

explosion is one of fear, and is based fairly accurately on the reaction of contemporary anarchists to the Greenwich explosion:

No doubt a wicked attempt to blow up the Observatory, they say. H'm. That's hardly credible...I hadn't the slightest idea—not the ghost of a notion of anything of the sort being planned to come off here—in this country. Under the present circumstances it's nothing short of criminal ...this business may affect our position very adversely in this country... I assure you that we in London had no knowledge (pp. 71–4).

The *Morning Leader* on the 19 February 1894 carried the opinions of certain anarchists: 'there has been a seemingly very frank confession on their part that the occurrence took them completely by surprise'. A young German anarchist put it as follows:

comrades from the Continent—whatever might be their intentions abroad—had found a safe shelter in London, and it was hardly likely, he added, that they would commit themselves to a line of desperate action in this country, which could only result in their losing the protection and immunity from arrest which they now enjoyed...Anarchists were not so blind to their own interests and well-being as to forgo by their conduct the right to the asylum which England so generously offered to political refugees...As to Bourdin's plan, he personally had not the slightest knowledge, but he did not for one moment think that the deceased ever intended to make an attempt to blow up the Observatory.

According to the anarchists, therefore, they had no part in the Greenwich Bomb Outrage which they regarded as a plot, probably instigated by the police, to bring the movement into disrepute in England. Conrad enhanced the inanity of the event by making the victim the half-witted and unallied Stevie, and he also took over this innocence of the anarchist movement with regard to the affair—save, of course, for the Professor's generosity with explosives. But instead of taking up the suggestion of a police plot, he strengthened the hidden motivation behind the affair by having it stem from the desire of certain European powers to bring pressure on the

British government to deal harshly with the anarchists. Vladimir wants a supposed anarchist event in England because of the 'Conference in Milan': 'What we want is to administer a tonic to the Conference in Milan...Its deliberations upon international action for the suppression of political crime don't seem to get anywhere. England lags' (p. 29). No such conference was taking place in Europe in 1894 at the time of the Greenwich Outrage, but one did take place four years later, with the same aim and the same reason for failing to achieve it, as Vladimir's Conference in Milan. *The Times* reported on 1 October 1898:

The *pourparlers* which since the assassination of the Empress of Austria have been going on between the European Cabinets on the subject of an international congress to discuss means for the repression of Anarchism have resulted in all the Powers expressing approval of the proposal of the Italian Government. Formal invitations to such a congress were consequently issued yesterday by the Italian Foreign Office. It is proposed that diplomatic, legal, and administrative representatives of each Government be instructed to assemble at a time and place to be determined hereafter for the purpose of concerting such international measures as may appear best calculated for the suppression of Anarchist associations and the prevention of Anarchist outrages.

The conference was eventually held in Rome and the proceedings lasted one month, from 24 November to 21 December. Britain sent three delegates, one of whom was the then head of the Criminal Investigation Department, Sir Howard Vincent. The conference proved abortive principally because of the attitude taken up by Britain over a proposal urged by the continental powers that all anarchists should be surrendered on demand to the authorities of their countries of origin. This proposal clashed with Britain's belief in the right of asylum—she saw herself still as a country whose shores were open to the oppressed of all nations.

In both the actual and fictional plots, therefore, the suggested aim of the plot was the same—to bring the anarchist movement into disrepute. But in neither circumstance was the plot notably successful in this aim. In the actual case there was a mob demonstration against the anarchists,[19] a question in the House of Commons, and certain murmurings in the press, but generally the affair was played down. Mr Asquith, in answer to Colonel Howard Vincent's question whether 'in the circumstances of the day, the Government proposed to place any limit upon foreign immigration', said: 'Her Majesty's Government are not of opinion that, in this respect, any necessity has arisen for a change in the law which has so long prevailed in Great Britain, and which they believe to be sufficient both for our own protection and for the due performance of our international duties' (*The Times*, 20 February 1894). And Conrad in *The Secret Agent* plays it down by means of his Assistant Commissioner: it 'is not the work of anarchism at all, but of something else altogether—some species of authorized scoundrelism...I call it an episode, because this affair...is episodic; it is no part of any general scheme, however wild' (pp. 140–1).

We can say, then, that Conrad's bomb outrage was based in nearly all its aspects upon the truth behind the Greenwich Outrage; the truth, we should note, as it was put forward in the national and in the anarchist press. Conrad transformed this basic situation into a domestic tragedy, as he said, by the introduction of Winnie and her maternal passion, but he also produced a representation of anarchists and anarchism which was anything but flattering, in spite of their impotency in the world he draws. It is this aspect of his novel we must consider next.

23

THE ANARCHISTS

The Greenwich Bomb Outrage, the actual event itself, provided Conrad with an example of a certain kind of 'anarchy': the 'inanity' and 'perverse unreason' exhibited by the ironic universe of *The Secret Agent* was ready to hand. From his reading about the outrage, Conrad obtained a whole series of related events based upon the secret workings of police and anarchists in London, and also some indication of the attitudes and motives of anarchists at that time. But the novel reveals a greater knowledge of anarchist attitudes and anarchist types than he could have gained from a study of the Greenwich incident alone or, for that matter, from the introductions Ford was able to arrange for him.

Conrad's representation of anarchists has drawn down upon the book on the one hand Irving Howe's complaint that Conrad denies them 'the mildest claims to dignity and redemption',[1] and on the other the comment from a 'visitor from America', 'that all sorts of revolutionary refugees in New York would have it that the book was written by somebody who knew a lot about them'.[2]

From our previous study of 'The Informer' and 'An Anarchist' we would hardly expect that in *The Secret Agent* Conrad would exhibit any approval of anarchy or anarchists, but certain things stand out in his portrayal of them here. First, his revolutionists are condemned equally as being 'enemies of discipline and fatigue'; they have a 'dislike of all kinds of recognised labour' and 'the remaining portion of social rebels is accounted for by vanity' (p. 53). Laziness and vanity are, therefore, the rather unlikely vices attributed to them generally. Second, the anarchists here are limited in number to four, excluding, of course, Verloc. And these four are carefully distinguished so that they stand out clearly in terms of personal appearance, history, and beliefs. Their delineation suggests that they are types, and a study of revolutionary literature suggests that Conrad put these characters together from a course of very wide reading, not only in anarchist literature but also in the history of the revolutionary Fenian movement. The ideas and attitudes the anarchists express are seen to reflect the more extreme forms of revolutionary thinking.

Conrad's choice of certain aspects of revolutionary character was influenced by his own disapproval of such activity; at the same time his method of character presentation is such that he draws extreme types to whom the human aspect is denied. In response to Cunninghame Graham's comments on the appearance of the first instalment of *Heart of Darkness* in *Blackwood's Magazine*, Conrad wrote: 'You must remember . . . I don't start with an abstract notion.'[3] It would seem, at least in writing *The Secret Agent*, that Conrad did begin with 'an abstract notion' of what extreme anarchists were like and, what is more, kept a tight check on his material in order to prevent his 'abstract notion' developing into a living character. Quite clearly, Mr Valdimir is not the only character in *The Secret Agent* whom Conrad thought of as 'fair game for a caricatural presentation'.[4] It is possible, therefore, to accept both of the comments quoted above on Conrad's anarchists—that he had great knowledge of a certain kind, and that he used that knowledge in order to produce extreme and unsympathetic types. The convictions that determined Conrad's presentation of anarchists might have been supported by or drawn from published commentary upon the movement. Six years before Conrad began writing *The Secret Agent*, there appeared a new monthly column in *Blackwood's Maga-*

zine entitled 'Musings without Method'. It was contributed under the name of Charles Whibley but the views expressed were those of William Blackwood. Blackwood had been extraordinarily kind to Conrad; Conrad's own attachment to him is shown by Meldrum's letter to Blackwood: 'he [Conrad] considers himself. . . bound to you in his work',[5] and his attachment to the magazine by '*Blackwood's* is the only periodical *always* open to me—and the only one for which I really care to work.'[6] In the issue of October 1901, there appeared the following account of the anarchist: 'we shall never find a proper remedy for Anarchism until we understand what an Anarchist is, and what he wants. He is an indolent monster, diseased with vanity, whose first and last desire is advertisement.' Indolence and vanity!—Conrad's insights are similar to those of, and perhaps derived from, *Blackwood's Magazine*.

But *Blackwood's Magazine* was not alone in commenting upon this aspect of contemporary anarchists. There are other accounts of London anarchists, and at least two of these lay stress upon their excessive laziness. And these accounts are especially relevant since they are by ex-anarchists commenting upon the 'Commonweal' group to which H. B. Samuels and Martial Bourdin belonged. The first to appear was *A Girl among the Anarchists*; the second, *Confessions of an Anarchist*, by W. C. Hart,[7] appeared while Conrad was at work on *The Secret Agent*. Isabel Meredith remarks: 'Short and Simpkins were typical figures [they are the laziest creatures we meet in Miss Meredith's book] of the rank and file of the English party. . . Communism, as they conceived it, amounted pretty nearly to living at other people's expense.'[8] And W. C. Hart queries: 'Will anyone be surprised to learn that the Anarchist has strong objections to hard work? Many Anarchists I have met abstain from work "on principle".'[9]

These writers also attempted to categorise the anarchists of the 1890s. Olive and Helen Rossetti's division of anarchists is fourfold. There were 'a whole host of cranks, who, without being Anarchists in any real sense of the word, seemed drawn towards our ranks; there were noble dreamers, incorrigible idealists, men whom experience could not teach nor disappointment sour. Men who lived in a pure atmosphere of their own creation, whom the worldly wise pity as deluded fools, but who are perhaps the only really enviable people in the world'; then there are '"the fanatics", stern heroic figures who seem strangely out of place in our humdrum world, whose practical work often strikes us as useless when it is not harmful'; 'and finally a considerable sprinkling of the really criminal classes'.[10] And W. C. Hart provides us with Liebknecht's classification which corresponds to Olive and Helen Rossetti's: (1) criminals and semi-criminals who throw an anarchist cloak over their crime; (2) police agents; (3) the defenders of so-called 'propaganda by deed'; and strictly speaking, there is another section: (4) that of the 'perfect beings'.[11] We can see that each of Conrad's five anarchists approximates to a particular class. Michaelis stands out as one of Hart's 'perfect beings' and the Rossettis' 'noble dreamers, incorrigible idealists'; the Professor is the fanatic; Verloc, the police agent; Karl Yundt, defender of the 'propaganda by deed'; and Ossipon, a petty swindler really living off the savings of silly girls.

This classification determined in some degree the kind of verbal conflict which Conrad could present in *The Secret Agent*; that is, in Chapter 3, a conflict between an idealist and visionary (Michaelis) and the defender of propaganda by deed (Karl Yundt), and, in Chapter 4, between a genuine fanatic (the Professor) and the petty crook (Ossipon).

Clearly, Conrad did not have far to seek to find assessments of anarchists which approximated to, or which helped to influence, his own attitude towards them. But was there a particular source for individual anarchists as they appear in the novel? They are such freaks, what Professor Guerard has called 'Soho crackpots',[12] such stage villains, that a source seems unlikely, and yet, once the search into anarchist history has begun, it is suprising to find how closely Conrad modelled his anarchists on historical types. In his treatment of such sources, Conrad deliberately excludes the human and intimate aspects of his historical originals in order to condemn his anarchists by a caricatural presentation.

24

KARL YUNDT

The character of Karl Yundt, the 'terrorist', is based upon an obvious and ironic incongruity. He is malevolent but extinguished, a 'moribund murderer'. His passion is 'worn-out', his fierceness 'impotent'. Set against his bloodthirsty images of violence is physical degeneracy—painfully slow movements, gouty swellings, quivering hand, dried throat and toothless gums. In the design of the novel he obviously reinforces, along with Michaelis and Ossipon, the futility and impotence of anarchism.

A figure so melodramatic and incongruous, demonstrating an ironic intention on Conrad's part, suggests the stereotype of the extreme anarchist of the popular imagination, a deliberately constructed Aunt Sally. Yet Yundt is more than this, for he can be related, in a particular fashion, to actual revolutionary history.

One of the striking characteristics of Yundt is his partiality for violent and vitriolic language; the effect of the law upon the people is seen by him in the following terms: 'And what about the law that marks him still better—the pretty branding instrument invented by the overfed to protect themselves against the hungry? Red-hot applications on their vile skins —hey? Can't you smell and hear from here the hide of the people burn and sizzle?' (pp. 47–8). Yundt clearly enjoys his own eloquence and is, as Conrad says, a 'venomous evoker of sinister impulses'. His last words, which end the evening's discussion at Verloc's, are irrelevant but blood-thirsty: 'Do you know how I would call the nature of the present economic conditions? I would call it cannibalistic.

That's what it is! They are nourishing their greed on the quivering flesh and the warm blood of the people—nothing else' (p. 51). Did such an anarchist, using this sort of extreme rhetoric of blood, exist? Conrad describes Yundt's character with some care and perhaps from the following description we can find a clue to Yundt's original:

The all but moribund veteran of dynamite wars had been a great actor in his time—actor on platforms, in secret assemblies, in private interviews. The famous terrorist had never in his life raised personally as much as his little finger against the social edifice. He was no man of action... he took the part of an insolent and venomous evoker of sinister impulses which lurk in the blind envy and exasperated vanity of ignorance, in the suffering and misery of poverty, in all the hopeful and noble illusions of righteous anger, pity, and revolt (p. 48).

It seems most probable that Conrad had in mind here a well-known extremist, one who symbolised in himself all that terrified the ordinary and the rich citizen alike—the German anarchist, Johann Most.

Most was indeed 'a great actor in his time—actor on platforms, in secret assemblies, in private interviews' and also it could be said of Most, albeit a little unkindly on Conrad's part, that 'the famous terrorist had never in his life raised personally as much as his little finger against the social edifice'. He was repeatedly imprisoned, in Europe, in England and many times in the United States, but he did not on any known occasion do more than incite 'direct action' by means of dynamite, did not himself take part in such action. George Woodcock strikes a similar note to Conrad: 'Most discussed with the sinister enthusiasm of a malevolent and utterly irresponsible child [the making and use of bombs, the praise of dynamite, the value of burglary and arson for the cause]. He never used and probably never intended to use such methods himself; he recommended them to others instead.'[1] While in London, Most came under the influence of Bakunin, and in March 1883 he published a portion of the *Revolutionary Catechism* in his journal *Die Freiheit*. The emphasis is upon a band of dedicated revolutionaries utterly ruthless in their dedication to the task of creating revolution:

For him [the revolutionist] there is only one pleasure, one comfort, one recompense: the success of the revolution. Day and night he may cherish only one thought, only one purpose, viz., inexorable destruction. While he pursues this purpose without rest and in coldblood, he must be ready to die, and equally ready to kill everyone with his own hands, who hinders him in the attainment of this purpose.[2]

Johann Most was a consistent and 'venomous evoker of sinister impulses', and passages from his pamphlet *Beast of Property*[3] parallel Karl Yundt's homily on present economic conditions: 'I would call it cannibalistic...they are nourishing their greed on the quivering flesh and the warm blood of the people,' says Yundt and Johann Most writes of capitalists' appetites:

Should the people finally contemplate rebellion, an unceasing howl of rage raised by the gold tigers will be heard throughout the world—they pant for massacres and their thirst for blood is insatiable. The life of the poor is valued as nothing by the rich man.

Women are cheaper than men: for this reason the capitalistic vampires, with insatiate rapacity, seek their blood. Besides, female labour procures them cheap mistresses.

Child flesh is the cheapest; what wonder, then, that the cannibals of modern society continually feast upon juvenile victims?[4]

Language of this kind surely moved Conrad, in his Author's Note, to write of 'a brazen cheat exploiting the poignant miseries and passionate credulities of a mankind always so tragically eager for self-destruction'.[5]

Ironically, Most's early ambition was to be an actor; and this is what he might well have become if it had not been for an unfortunate childhood and an early jaw infection which left him with a serious facial deformity. Near the end of

Most's life, the famous anarchist Emma Goldman recalls going to the Thalia Theatre in 1904 to see Most playing in Hauptmann's *Weavers*. He gave 'a brilliant performance... his interpretation of Baumert was a superb piece of acting that brought back the memory of all he had told me of his passionate yearning for the theatre'.[6]

Most was not then, in the anarchist sense, active himself; yet, by the extremity of his language he made himself the stimulator of extreme deeds and he undoubtedly became the most famous example of a modern day ogre, the Victorian era's most frightening spectre. He died on 17 March 1906, while Conrad was writing his novel, and the *New York Times*'s obituary (where final kindness might not have been out of place) referred to Herr Most as 'an enemy of the human race' and as a 'mad dog'[7] (this last opprobrious term is applied by Inspector Heat to the 'perfect anarchist', the Professor, in the novel).

But Yundt's other ideas would appear to derive from a number of other sources. After Michaelis has stated his belief: 'History is dominated and determined by the tool and the production', Karl Yundt provides us with his entirely irrelevant but impressive statement of his extreme position:

'I have always dreamed,' he mouthed, fiercely, 'of a band of men absolute in their resolve to discard all scruples in the choice of means, strong enough to give themselves frankly the name of destroyers, and free from the taint of that resigned pessimism which rots the world. No pity for anything on earth, including themselves, and death enlisted for good and all in the service of humanity' (p. 42).

And he ends in a slightly despondent fashion: 'And I could never get as many as three such men together' (p. 43).

It is difficult to trace with certainty the exact source of Yundt's statement. The notion of 'death being enlisted for good and all in the service of humanity' could be derived

Karl Yundt

from *Blackwood's Magazine*. In *Musings Without Method* (May 1900, p. 688) appeared the following reference: 'So the discontent which he fondly construes into a general love of the human race, drives the Anarchist to attempt reform, and for him reform means death.' On the other hand, Isabel Meredith refers to 'the knights of death, as an Italian comrade had named a certain section of the Anarchists.'[8] But perhaps the clue lies unexpectedly in front of us. Michaelis, in answer to Yundt's charge, 'So much for your rotten pessimism', states that on the contrary he is optimistic and that his optimism does not depend on 'metaphorical lurid suns of vengeance rising above the horizon of a doomed society' (p. 43). In providing Michaelis with this statement, Conrad may have had in mind a passage from Bakunin's famous pamphlet *Appeal to the Slavs*, where he wrote: 'the star of revolution will rise high and independent above Moscow from a sea of blood and fire, and will turn into the lodestar to lead a liberated humanity'.[9] It may well be that Conrad has Bakunin in mind also for Yundt's ideas. The following passage comes from that extraordinary pamphlet, *Revolutionary Catechism*, which Bakunin wrote in Geneva in collaboration with (and while under the influence of) the young psychopath and terrorist Nechaev:

The revolutionary despises and hates present-day social morality in all its forms and motives. He regards every thing as moral which helps the triumph of revolution...All soft and enervating feelings, of relationship, friendship, love, gratitude, even honour, must be stifled in him by the cold passion for the revolutionary cause...Day and night he must have one thought, one aim—merciless destruction.[10]

The idea of the revolutionary dedicated without scruples of pity or morality to destruction for the good of humanity is the basic philosophy of this passage and of Yundt's beliefs.

Yundt's desire for a small band of revolutionaries 'absolute

in their resolve to discard all scruples in the choice of means...
No pity for anything on earth, including themselves' can
also be traced to Bakunin: 'Three men alone if they stand
united already form an important beginning of strength. Now
what will happen when you organize your country to the
extent of some hundreds...they will be enough to reorganize
the revolutionary power of the people.'[11]

There is one danger in seeing Bakunin as a *direct* influence
on the make-up of Conrad's terrorist. Bakunin's influence
in the anarchist movement was endemic and in reading
anarchist journals one is constantly meeting statements,
written by minor leaders of the movement, which in substance
and tone echo Bakunin. Thus we have to treat with some
scepticism the idea of Bakunin as an immediate source for
some notion which appears in *The Secret Agent*. And it is
likely that Yundt's pronouncement comes more directly from
articles and letters which appeared originally in the anarchist
journal *Commonweal*. In response to an article by William
Morris[12] there appeared a letter from a Charles Mowbray
which put forward Yundt's point of view: 'I feel confident
that a few determined men—and when I say determined,
I mean men who are prepared to do or die in the attempt—
could paralyse the forces of our masters, providing that they
were acquainted with the power [dynamite] which nineteenth
century civilisation has placed within their reach.'[13] And in
the same journal, a letter from Dr Creaghe places before us
the two sides of the debate that Michaelis and Yundt are
involved in:

[Social Democrats] act the part of good Socialists by looking on at the
awful misery and suffering around and doing nothing but waiting for
evolution of Capital itself to end them!!...Give me Anarchists willing
to die *now*, if necessary for Anarchy, and if you can find me 15 or 20 to
join me, I promise you we will make an oppression on the enemy and
do more to make recruits to our cause than all the rest who only preach
and write verses.[14]

Michaelis 'saw already the end of all private property coming along logically, unavoidably'; Yundt 'had always dreamed of a band of men absolute in their resolve to discard all scruples in the choice of means, strong enough to give themselves frankly the name of destroyers'.[15] 'Since the beginning of the Anarchist movement', wrote Frank Kitz in the *Commonweal*, 26 December 1891, 'two chief factors have disputed the ground. The idea of both being how to win the masses more rapidly to our views. By which means are we able to reach the common goal soonest? The preaching of anarchist philosophy, and the preaching of violence.' In Chapter 3 Conrad had this continuing anarchist debate in mind. And the crudity of the anarchists' response in the novel to the problems of revolution, although it may be taken to be a deliberate attempt to present them as mere word-mongers, denying them, as Howe puts it, 'the mildest claims to dignity', can be shown to be an exact mirroring of the response to the political situation made by unlettered anarchists in such journals as the *Commonweal*, the *Sheffield Anarchist*, *Alarm*, and even the Rossetti journal, *The Torch*.

Karl Yundt—'the terrorist, as he called himself'—while he clearly retains aspects of the stage anarchist, is most certainly derived from Michael Bakunin, though not necessarily by any direct route. He also corresponds to Johann Most; but in this instance Conrad did not need to make too many changes in the direction of caricature since Most was surprisingly like a 'grimy lunatic...a cartoon'.[16]

25

MICHAELIS

In contrast to the other anarchists, the figure of Michaelis is surrounded by suggestions—though ironic ones—of saintliness and innocence. Michaelis has been and still is being put through a process of martyrdom; he is 'the ticket-of-leave apostle'. In spite of the irony, the emphasis is upon the innocence of Michaelis and his role as a victim of popular sentiments, first furious indignation, and then outraged sympathy for his sufferings. The term of imprisonment which brought about extreme physical and mental changes in him was a harsh sentence imposed for a comparatively trivial offence.

From the point of view of Conrad's source material, the interest here lies not in the irony of the saintly anarchist, but in the fact that he is a representative anarchist while being in origin part Fenian, part anarchist, and part socialist.

Michaelis was imprisoned because he had taken part in an attempt to rescue some prisoners from a police van. The short account of the incident given in the novel brings out all the accidental nature of an event governed by a malignant fate. In the 'mad attempt' Michaelis is merely present, as a locksmith, to force open the door of the van. The 'accidental death' of the policeman, the resulting outburst of public indignation, Michaelis's own sincerity in expressing his feelings, contribute to his receiving a life sentence, a punishment greatly in excess of the crime:

Michaelis had been the object of a revulsion of popular sentiment, the same sentiment which years ago had applauded the ferocity of the life sentence passed upon him for complicity in a rather mad attempt to rescue some prisoners from a police van. The plan of the conspirators had been to shoot down the horses and overpower the escort. Unfortunately, one of the police constables got shot, too. He left a wife and three small children, and the death of that man aroused through the length and breadth of a realm for whose defence, welfare, and glory men die every day as matter of duty, an outburst of furious indignation, of a raging, implacable pity for the victim. Three ring-leaders got hanged. Michaelis, young and slim, locksmith by trade, and great frequenter of evening schools, did not even know that anybody had been killed, his part with a few others being to force open the door at the back of the special conveyance. When arrested he had a bunch of skeleton keys in one pocket, a heavy chisel in another, and a short crowbar in his hand: neither more nor less than a burglar. But no burglar would have received such a heavy sentence. The death of the constable had made him miserable at heart, but the failure of the plot also. He did not conceal either of these sentiments from his empanelled countrymen, and that sort of compunction appeared shockingly imperfect to the crammed court. The judge on passing sentence commented feelingly upon the depravity and callousness of the young prisoner (p. 106).

This attack on a police van is given as an anarchist incident, but Conrad is actually making use of a Fenian incident—the then famous and now century-old event of the Manchester Martyrs, which involved an attack on a police van by Fenians in Manchester. It is possible that the term Manchester Martyrs suggested to Conrad the idea of Michaelis's martyrdom, but certainly the incident in which he was involved reads as a summary of the actual historical event. The *Annual Register* of 1867[1] records under the title 'Rescue of Fenian Prisoners at Manchester':

One of the most audacious outrages that have occurred in this country for many years was perpetrated in open day, within the limits of the City of Manchester, by a party of Irish desperadoes... The object was to effect the rescue of two persons believed to be leading members of the Fenian Conspiracy, who were on their way to the city gaol in the police-van [these were two well-known Fenians, Colonel Kelly and Captain Deasy]. The van...was drawn by two horses....The doors of the inner compartments having been locked, police-sergeant Brett took his seat inside the van; the outer door was then locked, and the keys returned to Brett through a small aperture at the top of the door...About midway between the city and the gaol the van had to pass under a railway arch which crosses the Hyde-road...The moment the van approached the arch, Allen [the leader of the Fenians] stepped into the roadway, and presenting a revolver at the driver, called upon him to stop. Immediately, before the driver had time to decide what to do, a volley of pistol-shots was fired at him. Then followed a scene as extraordinary as it was unexpected. One of the horses was shot and commenced plunging, and the second horse, frightened, turned aside; and from that moment the Fenians were masters of the situation. When the pistol-shots were fired, the officers upon the top of the van scrambled down as quickly as they could, and the driver was knocked off by a large stone. The second horse was then shot. One of the leaders climbed to the top of the van; and...about twenty labourers, who had been hiding in the clayfield, clambered up after him. The armed men formed a circle round the van, and menaced every one that approached with their pistols.

Conrad states: 'Unfortunately, one of the police constables got shot, too', and this was the case at Manchester, Sergeant Brett, the policeman inside the van, being the victim:

The men on the roof gradually pounded it to chips. They saw Brett below; and in answer to their demands he refused to deliver up the keys. Stones were thrown upon him, which injured his head and face, but still he refused to betray his trust. Then a panel of the door was broken open; Allen presented a pistol at Brett's head, and demanded the keys. They were still refused. Allen immediately placed his revolver to the lock of the door, and firing, blew it open. There was Brett, bleeding and wounded in his seat, the doors of the two compartments still locked. Allen once more demanded that the keys should be given up to him. Brett's answer was a flat refusal, whereupon Allen deliberately fired at him, and Brett rolled mortally wounded on to the roadway... His keys were taken from him, the inner compartments unlocked, and the prisoners released.

Public reaction to the incident was strong. Conrad, in his fictional account, uses the terms 'ferocity', 'an outburst of furious indignation'. The *Illustrated London News*, 28 September 1867, commented: 'In the first place—and this, indeed, is what we most fear—should such outrages as that which

has surprised the metropolis of the north be repeated elsewhere, there is reason to fear that they may have the effect
of goading the public mind into a temporary but extremely
harmful state of fierce exasperation.' *The Times*, in its editorial
of 25 November 1868, referred to 'The contest between
crime and justice which has now occupied the public mind
for two months, and almost thrown into the shade invasions,
hurricanes, and expeditions'.

Sergeant Brett, like the police constable who is killed in the
novel, had a wife and three children, and *The Times*, 18
November 1867, refers to a fund being raised in order to
'place the widow of Sergeant Brett in a similar position
to that which she would have occupied had he been still
alive'.

Just as in the novel 'three ring-leaders got hanged', so
Allen, Gould and Larkin were publicly executed for the
death of Sergeant Brett on 23 November 1867. And a fourth
man, Condon (alias Shore),[2] initially condemned with them,
was given a last-minute reprieve, his sentence being commuted
to that received by Michaelis—life imprisonment.[3] The reason
given for this reprieve was that 'Condon...had not been
proved to have had a revolver in his hands' and this 'led
the Government to listen to the intercessions on his behalf'
(*The Times*, 25 November 1867).[4] Now Michaelis also was
unarmed: 'When arrested he had a bunch of skeleton keys
in one pocket, a heavy chisel in another, and a short crowbar
in his hand: neither more nor less than a burglar', the implication being that he was equipped only to force open the
door of the van.

Michaelis was not left unmoved by the death of the
constable, and he expressed his feelings in court, but he
also regretted the failure of the attempt: 'The death of the
constable had made him miserable at heart, but the failure
of the plot also. He did not conceal either of these sentiments

from his empanelled countrymen, and that sort of compunction appeared shockingly imperfect to the crammed court' (p. 106). Thus, his sentiments only ensure the harshness of the sentence he receives, and this again parallels the trial of the Manchester Fenians. According to *The Times*, Condon had 'excelled all the other convicts in his zeal for the Fenian cause', but while Allen, Larkin and Condon had all three expressed regret at the death of Brett, it was Larkin whose sentiments come closest to those of Michaelis:

My Lords and gentlemen, I am only going to say a word or two concerning Sergeant Brett...I believe no one in court regrets the man's death as much as I do...Certainly, my lords, I do not want to deny but I did go to the aid and assistance of them two noble heroes that was lying in that van, Colonel Kelly and Captain Deasy. I did go to them and did as much as lay in my power to extricate them out of the bondage they lay in at present time; but I did not go for to take life, nor, my lords any one else. It is a misfortune there was life taken, but if it was taken, it was not done intentionally.

*

In *The Secret Agent* this incident has taken place many years before the present time of the novel. Michaelis is now notable, not for his part in the early anarchist plot, but for the fact that he has been released from prison on ticket-of-leave, and his release has been marked by 'a revulsion of popular sentiment'. The ferocity with which his imprisonment was applauded is changed to sympathy: 'the fame of his release was made for him...by people who wished to exploit the sentimental aspect of his imprisonment either for purposes of their own or for no intelligible purpose' (pp. 106–7). Moreover, Michaelis is now patronised by elegant society. None of these circumstances was true of Condon on his release from prison on 10 September 1878, after having served eleven years of his sentence.[5] No fuss was made in the English newspapers, there were no expressions of public sympathy, and indeed Condon left the country in the greatest secrecy.[6]

But there was another Fenian whose experiences on being released from prison parallel those of Michaelis; and Conrad, in his reading of Fenian history, must have known of him. The most famous ticket-of-leave political prisoner of the day was Michael Davitt, second only to Charles Stewart Parnell in the Irish leadership. Davitt, a working-class boy, joined the Fenians in 1865 and assumed the role of a commercial traveller in firearms as a cloak for his revolutionary work of buying arms and shipping them to Ireland. On 14 May 1870 he was arrested at Paddington while awaiting a consignment of arms from Birmingham and sentenced to fifteen years penal servitude—the period of time served by Michaelis. Davitt did not serve the full sentence but like Michaelis he was released on ticket-of-leave, on 19 December 1877. When Davitt came out of prison he was not met by his family, for his father had died and his mother and sister had emigrated to America, and this in part parallels Michaelis's position. 'His parents are dead: the girl he was to marry has died while he was in prison.'

Very little comment is to be found in the newspapers of the day either on the occasion of Davitt's first arrest or on his release. But Davitt did become famous during the years he was out of prison on ticket-of-leave. He had suffered great hardship in prison, and the pamphlet he wrote about his prison experiences attracted attention:

To find black beetles in soup, 'skilly', bread, and tea, was quite a common occurrence; and some idea may be formed of how hunger will reconcile a man to look without disgust upon the most filthy objects in nature, when I state as a fact that I have often discovered beetles in my food, and have eaten it after throwing them aside, without experiencing much revulsion of feeling at the sight of such loathsome animals in my victuals....It was quite a common occurrence in Dartmoor for men to be reported and punished for eating candles, boot oil, and other repulsive articles; and, notwithstanding that a highly offensive smell is purposely given to prison candles to prevent their being eaten instead of burned, men are driven, by a system of half-starvation, into an animal-like voracity, and anything that a dog would eat is nowise repugnant to their taste. I have seen men eat old poultices found buried in heaps of rubbish, and have seen bits of candle pulled out of the prison cesspool and eaten after the human soil was wiped off them.[7]

Davitt had lost an arm, which made his life in prison even more onerous for him, and this mutilation, which became to the public a symbol of his suffering although it had taken place years before his imprisonment, together with his ability as a public speaker, ensured his popularity with audiences. In the novel it is Ossipon who exclaims: 'I must lay hands on Michaelis at once, and get him to speak from his heart at one of our gatherings. The public has a sort of sentimental regard for that fellow' (pp. 77–8), and certainly the British public had a sentimental regard for Davitt.

By 1881 he was a prominent political figure, and when, in the February of that year, his licence was withdrawn and he was again arrested, there was an outcry. The arrest was called by M. M. O'Hara 'essentially a mean manœuvre. Davitt had not repeated the offences of which he had been guilty in the 'sixties. He was now engaged in an admittedly constitutional movement and he had been active in denouncing crime and outrage. He had incurred Fenian hostility by departing from the old lines of political conspiracy.'[8] And D. B. Cashman expressed 'popular sentiment' when he wrote:

Davitt, the noble-hearted, gifted, and honoured champion of his country's cause against oppression, who had already suffered long years of torture, dragged back to a British dungeon on a contemptible pretext of having violated the terms of his ticket-of-leave—the civilised world cried shame! on the miserable tyrants who could stoop to so paltry a trick of *State policy* to serve an ignoble purpose.[9]

Just as in the case of Michaelis there was an attempt 'to exploit the sentimental aspect of his imprisonment', so a similar campaign was launched to exploit Davitt's second and unjustified imprisonment. In Parliament, Mr Kettle moved 'that we record our emphatic protest against the arrest by a Liberal Ministry of Mr. Michael Davitt, by cancelling his ticket-of-leave, as a violation of personal liberty so gross that a Tory Government, while anxious to imprison him, shrank from perpetrating it' (*The Times*, 5 February 1881). Sympathy for Davitt did not come from his own supporters alone but was felt among many members of the House of Commons, and Major Nolan was able to forward to Sir William Harcourt, then Home Secretary, a Memorial signed by 105 Members of Parliament asking that 'Mr. Davitt should be exempted from all personal hardships not inevitably arising from his detention'.

After the bomb outrage in the novel, Inspector Heat wants to re-arrest Michaelis immediately: 'A man like that has no business to be at large, anyhow...The rules of the game did not protect...Michaelis, who was an ex-convict. It would be stupid not to take advantage of legal facilities, and the journalists who had written him up with emotional gush would be ready to write him down with emotional indignation' (pp. 113 and 122). The opportunity which Inspector Heat did not want to miss—that of putting Michaelis back in jail—was one which was not missed by the Liberal Government in the 1880s in Davitt's case.

In 1885 Davitt published *Leaves from a Prison Diary or Lectures to a Solitary Audience*. His solitary audience was a blackbird provided by the prison governor during Davitt's second period of detention. The suggestion of solitariness here, of lectures spoken in a void, perhaps gave Conrad the notion of Michaelis appearing always to be talking to himself, indifferent to the presence of listeners, 'the habit... of thinking aloud hopefully in the solitude of the four white-washed walls of his cell'. And though the titles of their books are different, it is likely that the notion of Michaelis writing the memoirs of his prison life comes from Davitt: 'Michaelis was writing night and day in a shaky, slanting hand that "Autobiography of a Prisoner".'

His prison experiences appear to have brought out the unique character of Davitt. As his biographer says, 'All this was endured, too, without his being either daunted or soured; that is the supreme marvel'.[10] He was 'strengthened and remoulded in nobler shape by the calamity which must have irretrievably ruined a nature of less intrinsic grandeur'.[11] Undoubtedly his experiences left him 'unstained by the faintest trace of personal animosity or vindictiveness'.[12] M. M. O'Hara offers the same judgement:

The almost shrinking purity of Davitt's life and the nobility and kindliness of his nature made it an exquisite ordeal to be compelled to associate with the vilest of England's seething life...That Davitt came uncontaminated from the ordeal, his heart as pure, his mind as clean...his temperament as unsoured...was little short of a miracle of human nature. No words of anger against them [his jailers] escaped him when he was once again free, with the whole world as an audience. And surely this is the most wonderful fact of all, for he had great cause for the sternest resentment.[13]

In the same way, it is Michaelis's saintliness, optimism, and resignation on coming out of prison that are stressed. He has an innocent heart and a simple mind. His 'unembittered faith' has been strengthened by the solitude of his imprisonment. And just as he is 'confident of the future, whose secret ways had been revealed to him within the four walls of a well-known penitentiary' (p. 107), so something of the same sort of transformation took place during Davitt's incarceration. From being a Fenian believing in secret conspiracy, he came to see the need for an open organisation and open agitation:

The Prison University had moulded him into a man, of wide outlook, keen insight into the heart of things Irish and universal, unfailing sympathy for the wretched. In prison he had thought out the whole history of Ireland's long and comparatively ineffective struggle. Searching for the hidden flaw which had rendered all the ideals and all the sacrifices of Fenianism of no avail, he found it in the secrecy which stamped its proceedings and prevented it from obtaining the adhesion of the masses of the people. Davitt therefore rejoined the ranks of the Brotherhood with the definite object of doing away with this secrecy and persuading his associates in it to abandon the devious paths of secret conspiracy for an open agitation.[14]

The implication here is, of course, that a change of outlook was brought about by the intellectual processes of learning and reflection, the prison becoming Davitt's university. Conrad, while retaining the idea of the change of character, outlook, and belief in the prisoner, presents the process as being akin to a divine revelation—the coming universal ruin had been 'revealed to Michaelis', and he has become 'a saintly man', who has his 'apostle' in the lady patroness. Nevertheless, it seems clear that in terms of his purity of spirit, his gentleness and his optimism, all the result of his term of imprisonment, Michaelis is based upon Davitt. Yet those aspects of Michaelis which were drawn from a Fenian incident and a Fenian leader allow us to identify him with a definite type of anarchist.

*

The political philosophy of Michaelis is derived from a number of writers, socialist as well as anarchist. In the last chapter of *The Secret Agent*, the Professor makes fun of the 'apostle Michaelis' and his idea of the world of the future: 'He is elaborating now the idea of a world planned out like an immense and nice hospital, with gardens and flowers, in which the strong are to devote themselves to the nursing of the weak' (p. 303). This looks like a summary by the Professor of Prince Kropotkin's *Mutual Aid*,[15] in which Kropotkin argued against Huxley's paper on the 'Struggle for Existence and its Bearing Upon Man'.[16] Huxley saw life as a continuous fight in which 'the Hobbesian war of each against all was the normal state of existence'. Kropotkin argued that 'mutual aid' was an important factor in the life of animals and of man throughout their long history:

In the practice of mutual aid, which we can retrace to the earliest beginnings of evolution we thus find the positive and undoubted origin of our ethical conceptions; and we can affirm that in the ethical progress of man, mutual support—not mutual struggle—has had the leading part. In its wide extension, even at the present time, we also see the best guarantee of a still loftier evolution of our race.[17]

And so, inadvertently, the novel bears tribute in the character of Michaelis to Prince Kropotkin's faith in the innate goodness of humanity. Perhaps we have, in the expressions of the Professor, Conrad's sad rejection of Kropotkin's too easy acceptance of man's goodness. Yet, though *Mutual Aid* may have played a part—and I think that Kropotkin's recognised angelic nature is also being made fun of by Conrad in the figure of his apostle Michaelis—I nevertheless believe that Conrad turned to another writer for a *concrete* vision of Michaelis's future world. I suspect that, like so many other persons during the 1890s, he read a book then receiving widespread attention, Edward Bellamy's *Looking Backward: 2000–1887*[18] which was an immensely popular account of life in the year 2000, as envisaged by its author in the year 1887. In Bellamy's Utopia we discover that the weak and the crippled are to be cared for by the strong:

'the right of a man to maintenance at the nation's table depends on the fact that he is a man, and not on the amount of health and strength he may have'.

'I am to understand, then, that the lame, the blind, the sick, and the impotent, are as well off as the most efficient, and have the same income?'

'Certainly', was the reply.[19]

And later, in Chapter 19, we learn that prisons having been abolished, criminals are treated in hospitals as persons mentally ill.

Michaelis

A central characteristic of Michaelis is his childlike optimism, and this optimism is due to his belief in the way society will automatically develop:

His optimism had begun to flow from his lips. He saw Capitalism doomed in its cradle, born with the poison of the principle of competition in its system. The great capitalists devouring the little capitalists, concentrating the power and the tools of production in great masses, perfecting industrial processes, and in the madness of self-aggrandizement only preparing, organizing, enriching, making ready the lawful inheritance of the suffering proletariat (p. 49).

This is so generalised that it might be dangerous to say more than that it has a Marxian flavour. One has the feeling that though some aspects of Marx are here, it is all too crude, and that the author of the passage is using Marx for his own purposes. Again, I think that Conrad found Michaelis's basic expression of his philosophy in Bellamy's book, though Bellamy's own source was probably Marx.[20] At any rate, he could have found the following passage there:

the era of small concerns with small capital was succeeded by that of the great aggregations of capital...the absorption of business by ever larger monopolies continued...In manufactories, every important staple was controlled by a syndicate. These syndicates, pools, trusts...fixed prices and crushed all competition except when combinations as vast as themselves arose. Then a struggle, resulting in a still greater consolidation, ensued...The movement toward the conduct of business by larger and larger aggregations of capital, the tendency toward monopolies, which had been so desperately and vainly resisted, was recognized at last, in its true significance as a process which only needed to complete its logical evolution to open a golden future to humanity.[21]

Michaelis, given his belief in the inevitable changes that are to take place in the organization of society, seems to leave the assembled revolutionaries very little scope for their abilities. Comrade Ossipon points to the irrelevancy of any effort on the part of revolutionaries to bring about a change in the society, to be answered by Michaelis with the need for revolutionary propaganda:

Michaelis pronounced the great word 'Patience'...Comrade Ossipon's face twitched with exasperation.

'Then it's no use doing anything—no use whatever.'

'I don't say that,' protested Michaelis, gently...Preparation for the future was necessary...he argued that revolutionary propaganda was a delicate work of high conscience. It was the education of the masters of the world. It should be as careful as the education given to kings (pp. 49–50).

This is not derived from Bellamy but from William Morris, who was a stern critic of Bellamy's book. In the *Hammersmith Socialist Record*, May 1892, he wrote:

To make the workers conscious of the disabilities which beset them; to make them conscious of the dormant power in them for the removal of these disabilities; to give them hope and an aim and organization to carry out their aspirations. Here is work enough for the most energetic: it is the work of patience, but nothing can take the place of it.

And in his final article for the *Commonweal*, a journal which he had founded and which was now in the hands of the anarchists, he commented: 'I say for us *to make Socialists* is the business at present and at present I do not think we can have any other useful business' (15 November 1890).

The popularity of Edward Bellamy's *Looking Backward* brought in its train pamphleteers who attempted to modify and combat his ideas. One of these pamphlets was entitled *A Sequel to Looking Backward* and it was written by a Richard Michaelis.[22] It seems likely that from just such a little known pamphleteer Conrad found a name for his 'ticket-of-leave apostle'.

Finally, Michaelis has one aspect which is derived from the Russian anarchist Bakunin, but not a political conviction or attitude. The most striking thing about Michaelis is his size, an obesity which is the result of a long term of imprisonment. He 'had come out of a highly hygienic prison round like a tub, with an enormous stomach and distended cheeks of a pale, semi-transparent complexion' (p. 41). He had entered prison 'young and slim' and left it at 'eighteen stone', fifteen years later. Conrad makes a great deal of this obesity of Michaelis, transforming him into a comically pathetic, and at the same time, repulsive being. He is 'round like a distended balloon', his 'round and obese body seemed to float low between the chairs', he is 'pathetic in his grotesque and incurable obesity'. This appears to be inspired by Bakunin, whose imprisonment left him bloated and toothless. When Bakunin was first imprisoned, he had been a 'handsome young dandy of thirty five' but on his release twelve years later he had 'aged and coarsened, almost beyond recognition ...he had swelled enormously in bulk, and now weighed twenty stone'.[23] He reminded Herzen 'of a mastodon' and Karl Marx 'of a bullock'.[24] Michael Bakunin was rather proud of his title 'Apostle of Destruction', and it could be that Conrad took the phrase 'ticket-of-leave apostle' from this.

In Michaelis, therefore, a character put together from a number of sources, we nevertheless have a character who is 'real' in the sense in which Conrad insisted upon. Every aspect is taken from some revolutionary personage, and every aspect is so moulded that Michaelis can become a further demonstration of the theme of the futility of such revolutionary activity and of the fickle and hysterical attitude of society to it. Maimed physically and mentally by society, Michaelis can thus be accepted by society, by publisher and patroness, as a martyr and a saint: 'If that's the stuff revolutionists are made of some of us may well go on their knees to them', says the lady patroness. Such a combination of fate, conviction, persecution and suffering is required to form 'this grotesque incarnation of humanitarian passion'.

26

THE PROFESSOR

Writing to Cunninghame Graham about *The Secret Agent*, Conrad distinguished between the Professor and the other anarchists: 'All these people are not revolutionaries—they are Shams. And as regards the Professor I did not intend to make him despicable. He is incorruptible at any rate. In making him say "madness and despair—give me that for a lever and I will move the world" I wanted to give him a note of perfect sincerity.'[1] In his devotion to his anarchist beliefs, the Professor is, in his way, incorruptible and perfectly sincere. But the note of perfect sincerity can be applied also to Conrad's scrupulous adherence to a certain kind of fact in creating this particular character.

The Professor appears first, very briefly, in 'The Informer', and I have suggested that the idea of the experimenter with explosives working in his laboratory at the top of the house was probably derived from the habits of Arthur Rossetti. But this first description of the Professor shows also that Conrad had already in mind the completed conception of the Professor's nature and character: 'His was the true spirit of an extreme revolutionist. Explosives were his faith, his hope, his weapon, and his shield' (p. 88). In *The Secret Agent* this conception is expanded and, within the limits of the caricatural method Conrad adopted, developed by gathering suggestions from a surprisingly wide number of sources for the Professor's origins, psychology, beliefs and revolutionary methods.

The Professor was apparently intended by Conrad to demonstrate through his appearance and psychology the theories of two contemporary writers, Cesare Lombroso, the Italian criminologist, and Max Nordau, the author of *Degeneration*. Physically, the Professor has not changed in the transition from one story to another. As in 'The Informer' he is a 'dingy little man' and there is a constant stress on his spectacles: 'the dome of the forehead seemed to rest on the rim of the spectacles', 'the large round spectacles, which gave a look of staring self-confidence to the sallow face' parallels the reference in 'The Informer' to 'an abstracted, self-confident, sallow little man, armed with large round spectacles'. But Conrad now draws our attention to the Professor's ears: 'His flat, large ears departed widely from the sides of his skull' (p. 62). This last addition to the portrait of the Professor is evidence, I think, that Conrad did not have a particular individual in mind, but a particular *type* of individual. Lombroso believed that such physical features —the large ears and limited vision—were typical of the anarchist and the criminal. In his book *Criminal Man*[2] we learn that the born criminal is marked by 'the external ear often of large size...twenty-eight per cent. of criminals have handle-shaped ears standing out from the face as in the chimpanzee'; also 'many criminals have a restricted field of vision'.

If I am right in thinking that Conrad's choice of features for the Professor was influenced by Lombroso, then it is an indication of his ironical intention where this anarchist is concerned. It is an ironical intention which might not, of course, be recognised by the general reader, but certainly it indicates Conrad's personal attitude to his anarchists. And there are, in fact, other indications in the novel that Conrad had Lombroso's theory in mind and was using it. Lombroso is, after all, specifically mentioned, and his theory indicated, so that the close reader can, if he wishes, apply this theory within the novel.

No doubt with a further sense of irony, Conrad allows Ossipon to introduce the subject of Lombroso's theory with regard to Stevie, for Conrad appears also to have constructed 'the robust anarchist' with Lombroso's theory in mind. Ossipon comments of Stevie: 'That's what he may be called scientifically. Very good type, too, altogether, of that sort of degenerate. It's enough to glance at the lobes of his ears. If you read Lombroso—', and Yundt retorts: 'Lombroso is an ass...this imbecile who has made his way in this world of gorged fools by looking at the ears and teeth of a lot of poor, luckless devils? Teeth and ears mark the criminal? Do they?' (pp. 46–7). The answer is that Lombroso thought that they did, and Conrad chooses ironically to prove him right in the case of Ossipon, as well as of the Professor.

Ossipon has 'a flattened nose and prominent mouth cast in the rough mould of the negro type': the nose of the born criminal, writes Lombroso, 'is frequently twisted, up-turned or of a flattened, negroid character in thieves'.[3] 'Comrade Ossipon's thick lips accentuated the negro type of his face'; 'The lips of the violators of women...are fleshly, swollen and protruding, as in negroes', writes Lombroso.[4] Moreover, Lombroso finds 'Curly and woolly hair in swindlers',[5] and Ossipon possesses a 'bush of crinkly, yellow hair'; 'As to Ossipon', reflects Mr Verloc, 'that beggar was sure to want for nothing as long as there were silly girls with savings-bank books in the world' (p. 53).

In attempts to explain and account for the psychology of such men as the Professor, Conrad's reading went beyond Lombroso. 'Ego-mania' as it was called by Max Nordau in his book *Degeneration*[6] appears to have influenced Conrad's conception of the character of the 'perfect anarchist'. Nordau gives the following account of the cause and effects of this disease, and its application to the beliefs and actions of revolutionaries, anarchists and dynamitards:

the being incapable of self-adaptation is for this reason far less able to procure agreeable, and avoid disagreeable, sensations than the normal being; he runs up against every corner, because he does not know how to avoid them; and he longs in vain for the luscious pear, because he does not know how to catch hold of the branch on which it hangs. The ego-maniac is a type of such a being. He must, therefore, necessarily suffer from the world and from men. Hence at heart he is bad-tempered, and turns in wrathful discontent against Nature, society and public institutions, irritated and offended by them, because he does not know how to accommodate himself to them. He is in a constant state of revolt against all that exists, and contrives how he may destroy it, or at least, dreams of destruction. In a celebrated passage Henri Taine indicates 'exaggerated self-esteem' and 'dogmatic argument' as the roots of Jacobinism. This leads to contempt for and rejection of institutions already established, and hence not invented or chosen by himself...as a revolutionary...he does not clear the ground with conscious aim, but blindly destroys...the ego-maniac raves against everything that stands upright, whether useful or useless, and does not think of clearing the building-ground after the devastation...he never troubles himself to question what will replace the things destroyed...discontent as the consequence of incapacity of adaptation, want of sympathy with his fellow-creatures...and the instinct of destruction as a result of arrested development of mind, together constitute the anarchist, who...has recourse to a dynamite bomb.[7]

In outlining the Professor's development into an anarchist of the extreme kind, Conrad would appear to have had this history of ego-mania in mind. The Professor's career begins in frustration of his ambitions:

Of humble origin, and with an appearance really so mean as to stand in the way of his considerable natural abilities, his imagination had been fired early by the tales of men rising from the depths of poverty to positions of authority and affluence. The extreme, almost ascetic purity of his thought, combined with an astounding ignorance of worldly conditions, had set before him a goal of power and prestige to be attained without the medium of arts, graces, tact, wealth—by sheer weight of merit alone...this moral attitude translated itself into a frenzied puritanism of ambition. He nursed it as something secularly holy. To see it thwarted opened his eyes to the true nature of the world, whose morality was artificial, corrupt, and blasphemous (pp. 80–1).

The injustice of the world becomes a constant factor for him: 'His struggles, his privations, his hard work to raise himself in the social scale, had filled him with such an exalted conviction of his merits that it was extremely difficult for the world to treat him with justice' (p. 75). In his extreme egoism, he turns against society and the revolutionaries alike: 'The terrorist and the policeman both come from the same basket. Revolution, legality—counter moves in the same game' (p. 69). But he is different, standing, as he does, alone, and consequently superior: 'There are very few people in the world whose character is as well established as mine'; '. . . I am deadly'; '[My character] stands free from everything artificial. . . I depend on death. . . My superiority is evident' (pp. 67–8); 'It is I who am the true propagandist' (p. 70). And the Professor's wish is for destruction without thought of what might follow: 'I told him that I dreamt of a world like shambles, where the weak would be taken in hand for utter extermination' (p. 303); 'What's the good of thinking of what will be!. . . To the destruction of what is!' (p. 306). Thus, the Professor's enmity towards society is seen to be the result of the crippling of his personality, and his desire for total destruction of that society, with dynamite as his means, is viewed as the characteristic attitude of the ego-maniac.

But these extreme views, appropriate to his ego-mania, nevertheless reflect some anarchist beliefs of the time. It is never easy to pinpoint a source for these with certainty, but extremist views similar to those of the Professor can be found running like a continuous thread through such anarchist publications as the *Commonweal* and *The Torch*. Of the two opposing views discussed by Michaelis and Yundt, the Professor supports that of Yundt. He rejects Michaelis's belief that capitalism will inevitably destroy itself—for him, the only solution is force, taken to the extreme of total destruction. 'You plan the future, you lose yourselves in reveries of economical systems derived from what is; whereas *what's wanted is a clean sweep*[8] and a clear start for a new conception of life. That sort of future will take care of itself if you will only make room for it', he says (p. 73) [my italics]. Felix Dubois commented in 1894: 'The anarchist doctrine comprises two very distinct conceptions. The first, which is entirely negative, involves the destruction of all existing institutions. *A clean sweep is to be made* of the entire fabric of society' [my italics].[9]

One of the objects of the Professor's passion for destruction would be the masses themselves:

The weak! The source of all evil on this earth!...I told him [Michaelis] that I dreamt of a world like shambles, where the weak would be taken in hand for utter extermination...They are our sinister masters—the weak, the flabby, the silly, the cowardly, the faint of heart, and the slavish of mind. They have power. They are the multitude. Theirs is the kingdom of the earth. Exterminate, exterminate! That is the only way of progress. It is! Follow me, Ossipon. First the great multitude of the weak must go, then the only relatively strong. You see? (p. 303).

This seems to be a long way from any anarchist teaching, yet the famous anarchist Malatesta, in the Rossettis' anarchist publication *The Torch*, 18 April 1895, quoted some of the extraordinary ideas current in certain anarchist circles—though Malatesta himself objected to them strongly: 'The masses allow us to be oppressed; let us revenge ourselves on the masses'; 'The more workers one kills the fewer slaves remain.'[10]

The prime enemy for the Professor is law: 'To break up the superstition and worship of legality should be our aim' (p. 73), 'to destroy public faith in legality was the imperfect formula of his pedantic fanaticism' (p. 81). At the Anarchist Congress held at Geneva, 12–14 August 1882, a manifesto was drawn up which directed attention to the anarchist's attitude to law: 'Our enemy is the law which oppresses the weak by the strong, to the justification and apotheosis of crime...According to our strength, we will work for the annihilation of all legal institutions.'[11]

The Professor's is a determined individualism. '...if you met a man who could give you for certain ten years of time, you would call him your master', says Ossipon, and the Professor replies sententiously: 'My device is: No God! No master!' *Ni Dieu, Ni Maître* was the title of an important paper published by Blanqui, the prominent French Jacobin, in 1881. This might well be Conrad's source for the Professor's motto, but he could also have found it nearer at hand, for it appears in the anarchist journal, the *Commonweal*: 'Anarchy must then necessarily have for its motto *Neither God nor master*' (9 July 1892), and it appeared also on the banner of a certain Dr Creaghe.[12] Mat Kavanagh, born in 1876 but still active in the anarchist movement in the 1950s, publishing his account of the anarchists he had known, said of Creaghe: 'Small in stature, he was the very embodiment of mental and physical energy, and every Sunday, wet or fine, he was to be found on the old Monolith with his black and red banner bearing the inscription in bold letters, "No God nor Master".'[13]

The Professor's means of destruction, his passion, is dynamite. It is dynamite which gives him his power and force of character, it is the weapon which he ranges against the ordered ranks of society. Because of it, he is free from social order and conventions as neither the police nor the other anarchists are:

Their character is built upon conventional morality. It leans on the social order. Mine stands free from everything artificial. They are bound in all sorts of conventions. They depend on life, which, in this connection, is a historical fact surrounded by all sorts of restraints and considerations, a complex, organized fact open to attack at every point; whereas I depend on death, which knows no restraint and cannot be attacked. My superiority is evident' (p. 68).

By means of dynamite he can keep in check the Chief Inspector who is 'armed with the defensive mandate of a menaced society'. The 'force of law, property, oppression, and injustice' in the person of Heat can be thus 'fearlessly confronted'. This defiant stance against society, based on the power of explosives, can be found in the writings of at least two anarchists, Johann Most being one of them. Most published the following glorification of dynamite in *Die Freiheit*:

In giving dynamite to the downtrodden millions of the globe science has done its best work. The dear stuff can be carried in the pocket without danger, while it is a formidable weapon against any force of militia, police, or detectives that may want to stifle the cry for justice that goes forth from the plundered slaves...A pound of this good stuff beats a bushel of ballots all hollow—and don't you forget it. Our lawmakers might as well try to sit down on the crater of a volcano or on the point of a bayonet as to endeavour to stop the manufacture and use of dynamite. It takes more than justice and right than is contained in laws to quiet the spirit of unrest.[14]

And Auberon Herbert in his article 'The Ethics of Dynamite'[15] expresses on behalf of extreme anarchists similar feelings of power as a result of the new weapon:

we, too, have power. It is not like your power, disguised under innumerable forms and ceremonies...mine is the power that can be carried in the pocket of any ragged coat, if the owner of the ragged coat is sufficiently endowed with courage and ideas...I am not magnificently equipped as you are; I have no court as you have, no army, no public institutions, no national treasury, no titles, no uniforms resplendent with decorations... and yet, perhaps, as regards the true test of power, I can command the fears of men and possess myself of their obedience quite as effectually as you can.

The Professor is willing to distribute dynamite to whoever asks for it. 'Do you', asks Ossipon...'give your stuff to anybody who's up to asking you for it?' 'My absolute rule is never to refuse anybody', replies the Professor. And seven pages later, still in conversation with the 'robust anarchist', the Professor reaffirms: 'Yes, I would give the stuff with both hands to every man, woman, or fool that likes to come along' (p. 71). It would seem to be from Samuels, the brother-in-law of Bourdin, that Conrad obtained the idea of a man who was in the habit of distributing explosives and of showing people how to use them. Samuels was accused of giving sulphuric acid to two comrades at a meeting of the 'Commonweal' group in May 1884: 'Samuels was dumb-founded, he could only ejaculate "They asked me for it"... The accusers told their tale, the question too was raised as to his share in the Bourdin conspiracy. Whereupon he made a remarkable statement. He admitted he had given away sulphuric acid, but said it had been done at the request of his accusers.'[16]

But the most startling aspect of the Professor's attachment to dynamite lies in his always carrying explosive with him in his pocket. The idea of the ragged coat concealing the death-dealing weapon occurs, of course, in the passages given above by Most and Herbert. 'The dear stuff can be carried in the pocket without danger', says Most, and 'mine is the power that can be carried in the pocket of any ragged coat', writes Herbert. And these statements might have suggested to Conrad the character of a dynamite-carrying anarchist. Moreover, one of the more sinister aspects of the Bourdin case was suggested by the *Morning Leader* in similar terms: 'They [the Criminal Investigation Department] will have to decide as to the character of the explosive which the dead man so recklessly carried on his person along thronged thoroughfares and in crowded railway carriages, risking death to himself and his fellow creatures' (16 February 1894).

But there is considerable development from the casual and isolated example of bomb-carrying in the case of Bourdin to the sensational and melodramatic figure of the man who constantly carries an explosive with the intention of destroying himself and anyone who attempts to arrest him.

'But they could send someone—rig a plant on you. Don't you see? Get the stuff from you in that way, and then arrest you with the proof in their hands' [says Ossipon].

'Proof of what? Dealing in explosives without a licence perhaps... I don't think they could get one of them to apply for a warrant. I mean one of the best. Not one' [says the Professor].

'Why?' Ossipon asked.

'Because they know very well I take care never to part with the last handful of my wares. I've it always by me.' He touched the breast of his coat lightly. 'In a thick glass flask', he added '...I shall never be arrested...I walk always with my right hand closed round the india-rubber ball which I have in my trouser pocket. The pressing of this ball actuates a detonator...A full twenty seconds must elapse from the moment I press the ball till the explosion takes place'...With a slight turn of the head the glitter of the spectacles seemed to gauge the size of the beer saloon in the basement of the renowned Silenus Restaurant.

'Nobody in this room could hope to escape', was the verdict of that survey. 'Nor yet this couple going up the stairs now' (pp. 65–7).

Such a conception, appropriate enough to the Professor and his dedication, would seem to be an imaginative invention of Conrad's, since no such explosive-carrying person existed in anarchist circles in spite of the melodramatic and sensational image which anarchists had in the minds of the general public. But such a man *did* exist among the Fenians. Like the Professor he worked severely alone, and for that reason he was not generally known and no reference to him appears in any of the memoirs of retired policemen and secret service men who were concerned with both the Fenian dynamite outrages of the 1880s and the anarchist troubles of the 1890s. The person Conrad seems to have used as a source here was Luke Dillon, an Irish terrorist who, though involved in the dynamite outrages that shook London, was not (at least at this time) caught by the police, though surely he must have been known to them.

An article appearing in *An Phoblacht*, 18 January 1930, and entitled 'Sixty Years' Service: The Life-Story of a Revolutionary who never saw his native land', awards Dillon the nickname (and it was well earned) of 'Dynamite Dillon', and provides an account of his activities in the London dynamite campaign.[17] From this article we learn that Dillon was involved in two explosions—the dynamiting of the Junior Carlton Club and of the House of Commons. But when contemporary accounts of these incidents are consulted, strangely enough Dynamite Dillon does not appear as a terrorist in any way connected with them, for in spite of the vigorous and active part he took in the Clan-na-Gael's war against Britain, Luke Dillon was not discovered. He seems to have had a charmed life. The reason he was not arrested, according to Desmond Ryan,[18] was that, like the Professor, he carried dynamite on his person with the intention of destroying anyone who attempted to capture him: 'Luke Dillon was one of the dynamiters of the 'Eighties who was never captured. He told his Irish-American friends...the reason was that he had worked on his own, and worn off duty a belt of explosives which it was his intention to touch off with a lighted cigar if any attempt was made to capture him.' There is, so far as I have been able to discover, only one further published reference to Dillon's unique method of avoiding arrest. This appears in Le Roux's account of Tom Clarke:

It is in vain that Devoy tried to wash his hands of this terrorism business, for Dillon was on Devoy's Executive, and he was also the most efficient of the dynamitards who came from America to Great Britain. Dillon had gone twice to England to do dynamiting, and it was he who blew up the Carlton Club on one trip. Writing to the author of this book, Dr. Pat McCartan states: 'I heard him tell how he took the dynamite wrapped round his body with a fuse in the button of his vest. He smoked a cigar with the intention of touching the fuse with the cigar in case of arrest.'[19]

Now Ryan's book was published in 1937 and Le Roux's in 1936, thirty years after the appearance of *The Secret Agent* and clearly, therefore, Conrad did not use either of these written sources for his Professor. Yet I have not been able to discover any account of Dillon published early enough for Conrad to have made use of it. Furthermore, although Conrad had contact with the anarchist movement through Ford Madox Ford and his cousin Helen Rossetti, he had no similar contact, so far as is known, with the Fenians. His only Irish friend would appear to have been T. P. O'Connor, the famous Irish journalist, one of the first men to proclaim Conrad's genius in his review of *Almayer's Folly* in the *Weekly Sun*. There is a possibility, however, that Conrad learnt of Dynamite Dillon from Roger Casement, with whom he had contact in 1890, in 1903 and 1905. Conrad met Casement on the river Congo. Thirteen years later, writing to R. B. Cunninghame Graham, Conrad enclosed two letters he had presumably just received from Casement: 'I send you two letters I had from a man called Casement, premising that I knew him first in the Congo.'[20] Jessie Conrad records that, while they were living at Pent Farm, 'Sir Roger Casement, a fanatical Irish protestant, came to see us, remaining some two days our guest.'[21] It may well have been from Casement that Conrad heard of Luke Dillon. But it is possible that R. B. Cunninghame Graham, who knew Parnell and Davitt,[22] also knew of Dillon and told Conrad about him.

The 'perfect anarchist' is, therefore, based upon certain psychological theories about criminal types, and is given a history derived from the personal background of at least two anarchists (Most and Creaghe) and one Fenian (Luke Dillon). Again, in spite of the wealth of information Conrad apparently had about revolutionaries, he chooses those aspects which deny sympathetic response in the reader, and which lead to the presentation of an extreme type.

27

LAW AND ORDER:
SIR ETHELRED THE HOME
SECRETARY

The novel's debt to actuality in its portrait of the revolutionaries is repeated in the figures representing law and order.
These are presented with skilled economy in three characters
—Sir Ethelred, the Home Secretary, the Assistant Commissioner of Police, and Chief Inspector Heat. This simple
structure of the law was put together from a considerable
number of sources, though Conrad gives no hint of this
complexity in his comments on the novel.

In the novel, information is passed along the line from
Verloc, the secret agent, to Inspector Heat, to the Assistant
Commissioner, to the Home Secretary. Conrad makes this line
of communication an integral part of the action, but I believe
that this basic arrangement itself leads us to one of his sources.
The suggestion for so limiting the characters on the side of the
law to these three with this particular relationship came from
certain comments in the reminiscences of Detective Sergeant
Patrick McIntyre. McIntyre belonged to the Special Crimes
section under an Inspector Melville. His memoirs were not
published in book form, but appeared in *Reynolds News*, 3
February to 5 May 1895, and in them he writes:

all information that [a particular secret agent] supplied was taken possession of by Melville, who submitted it to Mr. Anderson, the Assistant
Commissioner of Police. Anderson would direct whatever action was
to be taken in the matter...In serious cases every iota of information
has to be reported to the Assistant Commissioner...And he, in his
turn, was responsible to one man only, the Home Secretary, whom he

had to inform of all matters of this character which border on State questions, and which are in no sense matters of ordinary criminality.[1]

*

Referring to one of his sources—'the rather summary recollections of an Assistant Commissioner of Police'—Conrad mentions a meeting between this Assistant Commissioner and the Home Secretary, in the lobby of the House of Commons. The Home Secretary, Conrad says with his customary vagueness, was, he thought, Sir William Harcourt then, and he believed the Assistant Commissioner's name was Anderson. Conrad implies that the influence of this recorded incident upon the novel, although a stimulating one—'There must have been, however, some sort of atmosphere in the whole incident because all of a sudden I felt myself stimulated'—was vague and minor—'I won't even try to explain why I should have been arrested by a little passage of about seven lines.'[2]

The book which he refers to was Sir Robert Anderson's *Sidelights on the Home Rule Movement*[3] and the Home Secretary involved *was* Sir William Harcourt, and a study of Anderson's book reveals that Conrad made use not of one short passage but of two, echoes of which appear at different times in the novel. Moreover, the stimulation which he describes must have been sufficient to take him on a course of inquiry into the character of Sir William Harcourt, for a comparison of Sir William Harcourt with Sir Ethelred, the Home Secretary in the novel, shows that, far from being vague about the then Home Secretary, Conrad clearly had him very much in mind.

Sir William Harcourt was Home Secretary in Gladstone's Government from 1880 to 1885 during which period he had to deal with the Fenian dynamite outrages. The *Dictionary of National Biography* provides us with the following account of the part Harcourt played in stamping out the famous dynamite campaign against London: 'The London campaign of the Irish dynamite conspirators in the spring of 1883 greatly increased Harcourt's responsibilities...On 9 April he introduced into the House his explosives substance bill, which inflicted the severest penalties for the unlawful possession and illegal use of explosives.'[4] It is, therefore, appropriate that Conrad's Home Secretary, Sir Ethelred, should, in face of the Greenwich explosion, greet his Assistant Commissioner of police with the words: 'I would like to know if this is the beginning of another dynamite campaign' (p. 136).

Sir Robert Anderson was never Assistant Commissioner while Sir William Harcourt was Home Secretary, but he was concerned as a policeman with the Irish side of the Fenian campaign, as S. H. Jeyes's *Life of Vincent* shows:

In the autumn [1880] Harcourt began to stir himself. It would be tedious to reproduce the official memoranda exchanged and describe the obstructions which had to be surmounted before it was arranged that Anderson (who had special source of information on Fenianism, and peculiar skill in dealing with it) should attend to the Irish side of the expected campaign, while Vincent should have supreme authority in Great Britain.[5]

Thus during the greater part of Harcourt's term of office Sir Howard Vincent, not Anderson, was the Assistant Commissioner.

The piece of dialogue from Anderson's book which Conrad gives in his Author's Note is said to have taken place in the lobby of the House of Commons: 'the author...reproduced a short dialogue held in the Lobby of the House of Commons after some unexpected anarchist outrage, with the Home Secretary...He was very much irritated and the official was very apologetic. The phrase, amongst the three which passed between them, that struck me most was Sir W. Harcourt's angry sally: "All that's very well. But your idea of secrecy over there seems to consist of keeping the Home Secretary in the dark.'''[6] As Anderson describes the incident it *does not* take place in the lobby of the House of Commons, but it does arise, as in *The Secret Agent*, as a result of police 'methods of dealing with informants'. Anderson's refusal to reveal anything of his sources of information irritated Harcourt into the accusation: 'Anderson's idea of secrecy is not to tell the Secretary of State.' In the novel, this is transferred with slight modification to the Assistant Commissioner as a retort to Inspector Heat's 'I must do my work in my own way...There are things not fit for everybody to know.' The Assistant Commissioner replies: 'Your idea of secrecy seems to consist in keeping the chief of your department in the dark' (p. 132).[7]

But the second incident that Conrad takes from Anderson's book *did* take place in the lobby of the House of Commons. It occurred some years later, at the time of the Parnell Commission,[8] in March/April 1889. At this time Anderson was Assistant Commissioner, and, the Liberal party not being in power, Harcourt was no longer Home Secretary but Gladstone's chief lieutenant on the opposition benches. In 1889, Harcourt and Anderson disagreed over Anderson's attitude with regard to a particular secret agent in police employ. In spite of their strenuous disagreement, Anderson admired Harcourt tremendously, and was therefore delighted when Harcourt returned his salutation in the lobby of the House of Commons:

One afternoon shortly after this Supply debate, I was in the Members' lobby, and seeing him come out of the House, I went forward to speak to him. He failed to recognize me, however, and brushed me aside as he passed. An hour later the incident was recorded, with a sensational headline, in the 'Special Editions'. A few days afterwards I met him again as I was leaving the House by the Members' staircase. He was engaged in close conversation with Mr. Childers, and leaning on his arm. I saluted him in passing, but again he failed to notice me. Before

I reached the bottom of the flight, however, I heard him calling after me, and on my retracing my steps he greeted me with all the old cordiality. He shook me warmly by the hand, said he was glad to see me, and that '*he hoped I was getting on well at Scotland Yard*'.[9]

Harcourt's solicitous: 'he hoped I was getting on well at Scotland Yard' was appropriate since Anderson had been Assistant Commissioner for little more than six months at this time and it is appropriately spoken in the novel by Sir Ethelred to the comparatively new Assistant Commissioner there: 'You are still rather a novice in your new berth. And how are you getting on over there?' (p. 137) and also 'I hope you'll get on over there' (p. 144).

Another aspect of the Anderson/Harcourt meeting which seems to have impressed Conrad is the fact that Harcourt was in close conversation with Mr Childers and 'leaning on his arm'. This would appear to be the suggestion for Toodles, Sir Ethelred's secretary, and his having the Home Secretary leaning on his arm:

'It's all the exercise he can find time for while this session lasts...I rather enjoy these little strolls. He leans on my arm' (p. 135).

'This fight [over his Bill for the Nationalization of Fisheries] takes it out of him frightfully. The man's getting exhausted. I feel it by the way he leans on my arm as we walk over' (p. 145).

'I say, these foreign scoundrels aren't likely to throw something at him —are they? It would be a national calamity. The country can't spare him.' [In his answer to the young secretary the Assistant Commissioner has his tongue in his cheek.]

'Not to mention yourself. He leans on your arm...You would both go' (p. 145).

A further remark of Toodles is also appropriate to Sir William Harcourt. Speaking of Sir Ethelred he says: 'And, I say, is he safe in the streets? Mullins has been marching his men up here this afternoon. There's a constable stuck by every lamp-post, and every second person we meet between this and Palace Yard is an obvious 'tec' (p. 145). According to the *Dictionary of National Biography* at the time of the Fenian troubles, 'Harcourt...was never without police protection.'[10]

Apart from these slight borrowings from Anderson's book, Conrad obviously thought it worthwhile to discover more about Sir William Harcourt as a source for his own Home Secretary, and he picks out certain obvious features of Sir William in presenting Sir Ethelred. First Conrad stresses Sir Ethelred's vast bulk and his aristocratic look and bearing:

Vast in bulk and stature, with a long white face, which, broadened at the base by a big double chin, appeared egg-shaped in the fringe of thin greyish whisker, the great personage seemed an expanding man... From the head, set upward on a thick neck, the eyes, with puffy lower lids, stared with a haughty droop on each side of a hooked, aggressive nose, nobly salient in the vast pale circumference of the face (p. 136).

We are then told of this 'great personage's' astonishingly long family tree: 'the unbroken record of that man's descent surpassed in the number of centuries the age of the oldest oak in the country' (p. 136). Also, he has one physical defect, the weakness of his eyes, and this is dramatically revealed to the Assistant Commissioner when he goes to see the Home Secretary to report his findings on the Greenwich affair: 'Shades of green silk fitted low over all the lights imparted to the room something of a forest's deep gloom. The haughty eyes were physically the great man's weak point. This point was wrapped up in secrecy. When an opportunity offered, he rested them conscientiously' (p. 217).

A photograph of Harcourt which appears as the frontispiece to the second volume of A. G. Gardiner's *The Life of Sir William Harcourt*[11] reveals in particular some aspects which Conrad stresses. It shows Sir William Harcourt 'vast in bulk', and noticeable is the big double chin with its fringe of whisker around the double chin. He could fairly be described as 'an expanding man'. The photograph is a side view and very apparent is 'the head set upward on a thick neck ,the eyes, with puffy lower lids'. A second photograph[12] of Sir William, which is a front view (this is reproduced in this volume as Plate 7*c*), reveals the other aspects Conrad stresses—a face which appears 'egg-shaped' and the nose 'hooked, aggressive' 'nobly salient in the vast pale circumference of the face'. And indeed his bulk, his general size, was noted by commentators of the day. E. T. Raymond in his *Portraits of the Nineties* records: 'the pride of Sir William Harcourt was as much a feature of him as his almost gigantic height, his portentous under lip, and his keen enjoyment of his own jokes';[13] and again: 'what remained as the motive power sufficing to propel the vast bulk of this political galleon through the cross-currents of over thirty years of varied navigation?'[14] The *Dictionary of National Biography* also stresses the physical size of the man: 'In his youth remarkably handsome, Harcourt assumed, later in life, robust proportions which were eminently suited to his vigorous and aggressive temperament.'[15]

The statement that 'the unbroken record of that man's descent surpassed in the number of centuries the age of the oldest oak in the country' indicates again that Conrad had Harcourt in mind. The *Dictionary of National Biography* records: 'Harcourt was proud of a descent which was traceable through many noble houses to the Plantagenet Royal Family',[16] and Raymond, in his portrait, also stresses this aspect of Harcourt: 'this parson's son, jests about whose Plantagenet blood seemed rather unmeaning to the uninitiated, was in very fact enormously interested in his genealogy. He could boast of a descent as noble as any in Europe.'[17] One can conclude that not only is Sir William Harcourt the source of Sir Ethelred but that it was on reading one particular account of Harcourt that Conrad's attention was directed to his possibility as a Secretary of State in *The Secret Agent*.

Conrad's previous novel, *Nostromo*, was serialised in *T.P.'s Weekly*, the last issue of the serial appearing on 7 October 1904. In the same issue there was an appraisal of Sir William Harcourt under the title 'The Great Englishman who has just passed away':

There is no doubt that he was immensely and justly proud of his high ancestry. It was certainly a wonderful ancestry to come from and to produce such a sturdy specimen. There are family trees that end in time in nothing but decayed branches, and thus are amongst the most mournful and tragic proofs of the impermanence of things human. But in the magnificent frame of Sir William Harcourt there was all the sturdiness of an oak that had ages of strength behind it, and ages of splendid strength before it as well (p. 462).

Even the passage referring to the great man's weak point, his eyes, is based on fact. A. G. Gardiner refers to Harcourt's visit to Pagenstecker, the oculist at Wiesbaden, 'who assured him...that his defective eye was so much improved';[18] and again in the same volume, Gardiner states, 'Apart from his concern about his eyes, he was no friend to the doctors.'[19]

Physical features, physical disabilities, incidents in his life as recorded by officials who came into contact with him—these are aspects of Sir William Harcourt which Conrad used. Of course, Harcourt was never given the unfortunate nickname Sir Ethelred, but he was such a powerful and individual politician, so outspoken in his politics and prejudices, that he could not avoid during his life being made a butt by his journalistic enemies. *Punch* called him the 'Squire of Malwood'—he acquired a country residence in the New Forest in 1885. In the 14 May 1892 issue *Punch* provided the headline: 'Get your Harcourt' and in the 4 June 1892 issue appears a comic poem: 'Harcurtius of the triple chin.'

At the time of the Greenwich Outrage, Harcourt was constantly in the news. A Liberal Government was again elected in August 1892 with Gladstone as Prime Minister and Harcourt as Chancellor of the Exchequer, but now Gladstone's age and infirmities kept him away from the House and Harcourt had the task of leading there. On 1 March 1894 (a fortnight after the Greenwich Bomb Outrage) Gladstone made his last speech in the House and it was expected that Harcourt would become Prime Minister, but the appointment went to Lord Rosebery. It may well be that Conrad's determination to use Harcourt as a source for Sir Ethelred was reinforced by the constant attention he was receiving in the national press at the time of the Greenwich Outrage.

There is a further piece of evidence which lends credence to this view. Conrad's Home Secretary, Sir Ethelred, is involved in the House of Commons in a tremendous effort to bring about the nationalisation of fisheries. His secretary Toodles says to the Assistant Commissioner of Police: '"But, seriously, you can't imagine how irritated he is by the attacks on his Bill for the Nationalization of Fisheries. They call it the beginning of social revolution. Of course, it is a revolutionary measure. But these fellows have no decency. The personal attacks—" "I read the papers", remarked the Assistant Commissioner' (p. 145). Not only did the Assistant Commissioner read the papers but Conrad also read them, for *The Times* of 17 February 1894 (two days after the Greenwich Bomb Outrage) reports long sessions in Parliament, not over a bill to nationalise the Fisheries—this is a Conrad innovation, a bill before its time—but over the 'Sea Fisheries Regulation Bill'. Reference to this bill appeared on page six, and on page five were three columns about the Greenwich Outrage. And the *Daily Graphic* of 17 February 1894 whilst carrying an editorial referring to the 'horrible occurrence in Greenwich Park on Thursday afternoon' also referred in the same column to the fact that 'the House of Lords has actually dared to throw out a second time certain clauses which are essential to the Scotch Fisheries Bill'.

Law and Order: The Home Secretary

Though there is much macabre humour in *The Secret Agent*, Sir Ethelred escapes it. As the supreme representative of the British Government in the novel he is treated in a delicate, chiding fashion and the humorous criticisms of him, the fact of his descent reaching beyond the 'age of the oldest oak', his physical resemblance to an oak tree—'this big and rustic Presence', 'a reed addressing an oak'—chime with contemporary accounts of Harcourt.

It seems strange, given Conrad's own reference to Harcourt in his Author's Note to *The Secret Agent*, that the parallels between Sir Ethelred and Sir William Harcourt have escaped notice. Indeed, Conrad showed himself conscious of the possibility of discovery when he further wrote in his Author's Note: 'The suggestions for certain personages of the tale, both law-abiding and lawless, came from various sources which, perhaps, here and there, some reader may have recognized.'[20]

Conrad was delighted with R. B. Cunninghame Graham's general praise of the novel and particularly pleased that Cunninghame Graham had singled out Sir Ethelred: 'I am extremely flattered to have secured your commendation for my Secretary of State.'[21] This pleasure is understandable, but, since we now know Sir Ethelred to be closely based on an actual person, we might feel inclined to take issue with Conrad's further statement in the same letter, given his method of work, that 'it was very easy there (for me) to go utterly wrong'.

28

THE ASSISTANT COMMISSIONER

The Assistant Commissioner is a minor but completely drawn character, who is seen both in his official capacity and as a private individual. In a novel concerned with the melodrama of revolutionaries and secret agents, he is the only character to adopt a disguise and go in search of information, and it is he and not the Chief Inspector who gets from Verloc the truth that Michaelis is not involved in the bomb outrage but that Vladimir is the moving power behind it. He is notable for certain eccentricities, of wishing to take part in detective work personally, and of understanding, and in part sharing, Verloc's predicament as a married man: '"He [Verloc]...would have thrown everything up...would have tried to...leave the country, only he felt certain his wife would not even hear of going abroad. Nothing could be more characteristic of the respectable bond than that", went on, with a touch of grimness, the Assistant Commissioner, whose own wife, too, had refused to hear of going abroad' (p. 221). Conrad based this character carefully upon historical precedents in police history.

The Department of Special Crimes with which Conrad deals in the novel is the Criminal Investigation Department which, by the time of the Greenwich Bomb Outrage, had been established sixteen years. Inspector Heat, during his interview with the Assistant Commissioner, reflects that 'There had been three [Assistant Commissioners] in his time', and he goes on to describe them. And it is an interesting reflection of Conrad's method in the novel that there should have been, since the establishment of the CID, three holders of the office of Assistant Commissioner who were Directors of the CID. The first was Colonel Howard Vincent (later Sir Howard Vincent), who was Director from 1878 to 1884, and in charge during the Fenian disturbances in London. The second was James Munro, Assistant Commissioner for four years, from 1884 to 1888, during a less hectic period. The third was Dr (later Sir) Robert Anderson who dealt with the anarchist disturbances of the 1890s. Conrad appears to have drawn characteristics from Sir Howard Vincent and Sir Robert Anderson in evolving the characters of the second and third commissioners in the novel. Munro does not appear to have contributed to the portraits at all.

The second Assistant Commissioner, Heat reflects, was 'a perfect gentleman, knowing his own and everybody else's place to a nicety, on resigning to take up a higher appointment out of England got decorated for (really) Inspector Heat's services. To work with him had been a pride and a pleasure' (p. 119). Certain characteristics of Sir Howard Vincent seem to be present in this brief sketch. Vincent was a 'a perfect gentleman' and Jeyes and How, recording the reactions of his subordinates to Vincent, write: '"He is a gentleman", was the verdict, "and never comes airs over a fellow as some of the bigwigs do."'[1] This characteristic, and that of 'knowing his own and everybody's place to a nicety', were true also of Vincent who managed successfully to hold the anomalous position of Assistant Commissioner and Director of the CID, but was also nominally subordinate to the Chief Commissioner even though told to act independently of him. Sir Robert Anderson wrote of him: 'nobody but Vincent could have worked successfully in so ambiguous a position'.

Vincent did receive a knighthood on leaving the CID, and mainly as a result of the achievements of a subordinate, Superintendent Williamson: 'It was the string of notable successes achieved by "Dolly" Williamson and his new school detectives that was very largely responsible for Howard Vincent receiving a knighthood.'[2]

But the character of Howard Vincent comes out more strongly in certain aspects of the reigning Assistant Commissioner in the novel. As a new man in the post of Director, Vincent was at first unpopular: 'A subordinate Officer in the Criminal Investigation Department after a brief experience of the new Director, seems to have summed up the general opinion of Scotland Yard. He had made a lot of enemies at first, declared this witness.'[3] The Assistant Commissioner in the novel is also new to his job: 'You are still rather a novice in your new berth', Sir Ethelred says to him, and the immediate reaction of his subordinate, Heat, is one of dislike: '...you, my boy, you don't know your place and your place won't know you very long either, I bet', Heat reflects. The reason for this animosity lies in that trait of the Assistant Commissioner which is responsible for his leaving his desk and going out to make his own inquiries. He is 'a square peg forced into a round hole' because, although he has administrative abilities, they are combined with an adventurous disposition. Moreover, he resents 'the necessity of taking so much on trust', of being supposed 'to hold all the threads' in his hands yet having to hold whatever is put into his hands —'they can fasten the other ends of the threads where they please' (p. 115). And so he decides not to instruct Heat to go on with the case, but to take over the inquiry himself. It was this same characteristic in Howard Vincent which initially made him unpopular—'he would do things in his own way'.[4] George Dilnot recalls Vincent's nature and method: 'It was one of Vincent's defects that he would meddle and direct when he should have left matters entirely to a man deputed to carry out an investigation. This in all probability was one of those cases in which the detective inspector in charge of the case suffered from too much instruction.'[5]

The Assistant Commissioner

The Assistant Commissioner's adoption of a disguise, and the nature of that disguise, derive also from Vincent. The Secretary of State asks him: '"And how do you propose— Will you assume a disguise?" "Hardly a disguise! I'll change my clothes, of course"' (pp. 143–4). The Assistant Commissioner then returns to Scotland Yard and dresses himself in a '*short jacket* and the *low, round hat*' [my italics]. He goes by hansom cab and enters a cheap Italian restaurant and there he receives a 'sudden inspiration' and raises the collar of his jacket and turns up the ends of his moustache: 'He was satisfied by the subtle modification of his personal aspect caused by these small changes' (p. 149). He then calls at Mr Verloc's shop. During a visit to this country, the Belgian Minister, Van de Velde, asked Colonel Howard Vincent to take him to hear the anarchist, Johann Most, speak. The minister disguised himself, but Vincent 'just wore a *pea jacket* and a *pot hat*' [my italics] and as he went in 'he had his hat slouched over his eyes and his collar upturned with the result that one of his own Inspectors failed to recognise him'.[6]

The Assistant Commissioner is concerned not to offend the lady patroness, the influential society woman, who is a friend of his wife. This relationship is paralleled by a similar relationship between Vincent and the famous Victorian philanthropist Baroness Angela Burdett-Coutts, whose assistance and sympathy Vincent enjoyed while he was chairman of the Metropolitan and City Police Orphanage.[7]

Certain characteristics of the Assistant Commissioner, however, apparently derive from the third Director of the CID, Sir Robert Anderson, whose memoirs were one of Conrad's acknowledged sources for the novel.

Heat sees the third Assistant Commissioner as being 'a bit of a dark horse from the first' and 'at the end of eighteen months something of a dark horse still to the department'.

It was in fact said of Sir Robert Anderson that 'he is the most discreet, the most silent and reserved of public functionaries. Someone said he was a mystery even to himself.'[8] The Assistant Commissioner has a particular ability at detective work: 'A mistrust of established reputations was strictly in character with [his] ability as detector.' His intuition as a detective enables him to perceive immediately that Inspector Heat is concealing something from him during their interview: 'debarred by his position from going out of doors personally in quest of secrets locked up in guilty breasts, [he] had a propensity to exercise his considerable gifts for the detection of incriminating truth upon his own subordinates. That peculiar instinct could hardly be called a weakness. It was natural. He was a born detective' (p. 117). It was similarly said of Sir Robert Anderson that he was 'an ideal detective officer, with a natural bias for the work and endowed with gifts peculiarly useful in it. He is a man of the quickest apprehension, with the power of close, rapid reasoning from facts, suggestions, or even impression. He seizes on the essential point almost by intuition, and is marvellously ready in finding the real clue.'[9]

The source of the Assistant Commissioner's physical appearance has raised some speculation. Mrs Hay[10] suggests that he resembles Anderson 'most strongly in looks' and she refers to the photograph of Anderson which appears in his volume *The Lighter Side of my Official Life* as evidence. I suspect this is too easy an identification, though since Anderson provided Conrad with certain vital information and was himself an Assistant Commissioner, the identification is understandable enough. The Assistant Commissioner's appearance—'His black, narrow figure, with the white band of the collar under the silvery gleams on the close-cropped hair at the back of the head' (p. 113), 'a long, meagre face with the accentuated features of an energetic Don Quixote'

(p. 115)—seems to have been derived in part from the famous cartoon of Sir Howard Vincent drawn by the artist Spy (see Plate 8*a*) which first appeared in *Vanity Fair* in 1883 and was later reproduced in Vincent's biography.[11]

29

CHIEF INSPECTOR HEAT

Chief Inspector Heat is the central police figure in *The Secret Agent*. He stands in a special relation to Verloc, and is the only policeman we see in any direct contact with the 'perfect anarchist', the Professor. There is such assurance in the novel as to Heat's status, methods and opinions, that it might be concluded that Conrad had one particular police officer in mind as a source. But following the method of characterisation in this novel, Chief Inspector Heat is made up of suggestions from a number of different sources.

We can start the search with certain fundamentals of the character in mind. To Winnie Verloc, Heat introduces himself as 'Heat. Chief Inspector Heat of the Special Crimes section', and in the novel he is in charge of the investigation into the Greenwich Bomb Outrage: '[Chief Inspector Heat started] immediately to begin his investigation on the spot [at Greenwich].' Since the bomb outrage in the novel is based upon the actual Greenwich Bomb Outrage, we might well begin our investigation at this spot. The *Morning Leader* of 16 February 1894, reporting on the Greenwich explosion, stated: 'One of the chiefs of the Criminal Investigation Department proceeded at once to Greenwich', and in the next day's issue we learn who the particular inspector was: 'Inspector Melville was at Greenwich' (17 February 1894). Inspector Melville, therefore, seems an obvious 'suspect', and in some important aspects he approximates to Conrad's Inspector Heat. Inspector Heat's name, Conrad tells us, 'printed sometimes in the papers, was familiar to the great public as that of one of its zealous and hard-working protectors'

(p. 101). He is also the 'principal expert in anarchist procedure'. Of all the members of the Special Branch of the police force operating during the 1890s, only of Inspector Melville could this claim be made. Melville's reputation was known to the public by way of the newspapers—he was only too well known by the anarchists, whose name for him was 'le vil Melville'.[1] A book written in 1904 by Major A. G. F. Griffiths refers to 'the officer who is nowadays our chief mainstay and defence against these [anarchist] outrages, Inspector Melville',[2] and the following report appeared in the *Daily Graphic* of 23 February 1894: 'Chief Inspector Melville, of whom we give a portrait today,* has made Anarchism and Anarchists a speciality for many years. He is one of the ablest members of the Scotland Yard force, gifted with a *sangfroid* in moments of danger which is to be envied, and one of the most genial of men in his dealings with criminals.'

Inspector Heat is restricted by the law in his methods of dealing with the anarchists, so that he must rely upon keeping them under close surveillance: 'It may yet be necessary to make people believe that some of you ought to be shot at sight', he tells the Professor, but also, 'When I want you I will know where to find you.' It has been Heat's boast that he had his finger on the anarchists and that there was nothing they could do without his knowing of it. Inspector Melville was similarly restricted in the methods he could use against the anarchist. An editorial in *Blackwood's Magazine*, October 1901, states: 'That our method is the best we would not

---

* For a photograph of Chief Inspector Melville see Plate 8*b*. Conrad appears to make use of Melville's physical appearance on one occasion in describing his Assistant Commissioner. The view of the Assistant Commissioner as he is seated at his desk— 'pen in hand, bent over a great table bestrewn with papers...Speaking tubes resembling snakes were tied by the heads to the back of the Assistant Commissioner's wooden armchair' (p. 97)—is similar to a sketch of Chief Inspector Melville in the *Westminster Budget*, 23 February 1894. Melville is shown 'bent over a great table bestrewn with papers' with 'speaking tubes resembling snakes...tied by the heads' just behind, though not to, the Chief Inspector's wooden armchair.

assert; but until sterner measures are taken Inspector Melville's device is not to be despised.' Inspector Melville's 'device' was Inspector Heat's, and his surveillance is well attested. The same editorial goes on:

True, the Anarchists are allowed the freedom of Soho, but it is a freedom sternly tempered by the knowledge and control of Inspector Melville. The Anarchists frequent their cafes and attend their clubs, under the wise restriction that all they say is known to a vigilant police. With the worst intention in the world, they can do nothing, for once they move they are checked on the threshold of action and then a prison receives them.

Immediately after the Greenwich Bomb Outrage, Melville led a raid on the Autonomie Club, a famous haunt of London anarchists at the time. The reporter for the *Morning Leader* recorded an interview with Melville at the club during the raid:

I had at last an opportunity of a few quiet words in a corner with the famous and courteous chief-inspector, who at this moment was enjoying the well-earned luxury of a cigar...

'Do you think you will make any complete arrests?' [asked the reporter and Melville replied:] 'That will have to be seen; I cannot say just yet. But we know the whereabouts and movements of all these fellows, and can always put our hands on them when we want them' (*Morning Leader*, 17 February 1894).

Similarly Inspector Heat tells the high government official: 'There isn't one of them, sir, that we couldn't lay our hands on at any time of night and day. We know what each of them is doing hour by hour' (p. 84). And further confirmation of Melville's method appears in a book by McNaughton, one-time Chief Constable of London, and also involved in the suppression of anarchist activities. He writes:

In anarchist circles our information was always so good that, had a plot been in the hatching, I think the Yard would have got wind of it within twenty-four hours; but what neither the King's horsemen nor all the

Metropolitan Police can guard against is the individual initiative of some crank, who, with a very elementary knowledge of chemistry, could fashion a dangerous bomb out of an empty sardine box and some nitroglycerine.[3]

What is particularly mortifying to the Chief Inspector after the discovery of the remains of Stevie's body is that he had assured an important government official that 'nothing of the sort could even be thought of without the [Criminal Investigation] department being aware of it within twenty-four hours'. And Conrad comments: 'A given anarchist may be watched inch by inch and minute by minute, but a moment always comes when somehow all sight and touch of him are lost for a few hours, during which something (generally an explosion) more or less deplorable does happen' (p. 85). The Greenwich Bomb Outrage, both in the actual case and in the novel, revealed the weakness of surveillance; this weakness was recognised by McNaughton and referred to by Inspector Melville's superior, Assistant Commissioner Sir Robert Anderson, in connection with the Greenwich Outrage. Anderson describes how Bourdin, Stevie's counterpart, escaped surveillance at the crucial moment:

I never spent hours of greater anxiety than during one afternoon in February, 1894, when information reached me that a French tailor named Bourdin had left his shop in Soho with a bomb in his pocket. To track him was impracticable. All that could be done was to send out officers in every direction to watch persons and places that he might be likely to attack. His actual objective was the very last place the Police would have thought of watching, namely Greenwich Observatory.[4]

Police methods of dealing with anarchists in England were thus a matter of some public concern in the 1880s and 1890s, and 'surveillance' was the recognised, if not entirely satisfactory, method employed. In the novel, the true but reluctantly acknowledged source of information for the police is the secret agent. For Heat, the secret agent is the necessary tool; for the Assistant Commissioner, the use of such men is dangerous and wrong: secret agents will fabricate evidence particularly in the 'sphere of political and revolutionary activity', and particularly when they are in the pay of foreign governments. The presence of such spies destroys the efficiency of police supervision since they can manufacture incidents unknown to the police. Conrad's Assistant Commissioner speaks forcefully on the subject:

> In principle, I should lay it down that the existence of secret agents should not be tolerated, as tending to augment the positive dangers of the evil against which they are used. That the spy will fabricate his information is a mere commonplace. But in the sphere of political and revolutionary action, relying partly on violence, the professional spy has every facility to fabricate the very facts themselves (p. 139).

and later on he argues: 'A spy of that sort can afford to be more reckless than the most reckless of conspirators. His occupation is free from all restraint' (p. 140).[5] On the political side, the action of the novel revolves round this argument between Heat and his superior, and it goes to prove the Assistant Commissioner right. All the anarchists are under Heat's eye, but his power and control are undermined by the *agent provocateur* under the payment and orders of a foreign government.

It has been suggested that in this matter the Assistant Commissioner seems almost to assume Conrad's voice, and that the condemnation of secret agents represents Conrad's considered point of view. It must also be taken into account, however, that during the 1880s and 1890s (the political period Conrad studied for the novel) there was a ground-swell against the use of such agents. Sir William Harcourt, the Home Secretary, criticised Vincent for using an *agent provocateur*, and stated in the House of Commons (January 1881): 'the police ought not to use artifice of the sort practised in this case...the police ought not to set traps for people'. During the Parnell Commission of 1896 Le Caron declared himself a secret agent, and, through the Commission, it was revealed that the letters used by *The Times* to accuse Parnell of complicity in the Fenian outrages were forged by Richard Pigott.[6] In July 1906, when *The Secret Agent* was being written, the equally sensational Dreyfus Affair again came before the public, and it was revealed that Dreyfus had been condemned to life imprisonment on Devil's Island on the evidence of a letter forged by Major Henry of the Counter-Espionage Bureau. And the following condemnation of the use of such agents appears in McIntyre's articles in *Reynolds News* as part of his warning against the lavishing of public money on informers, 'who for the most part, are worthless, and some of whom even provoke crime instead of preventing it':

In all the others [plots] the hand of the spy, or *agent-provocateur* is clearly visible. These people see their opportunity when any Government is in a perturbed state of mind. They seize the 'flowing tide that leads to fortune'. Their intrigues produce conspiracies. There is this difference between a detective and an *agent-provocateur*—that, whereas the former is paid by salary, and has no interest in increasing crime, the latter is paid by results and has to depend on the rise and fall of the 'crime' thermometer. What does the 'provocating agent' do when he finds the prevailing danger is diminishing in quantity. He manufactures more 'danger' (*Reynolds News*, 3 March 1895).

In developing Heat's defence of his use of a secret agent, Conrad has also drawn upon a publicly expressed opinion of the time. The conception of there being 'rules of the game' applying between the law and the criminal, and of the revolutionary as breaking those rules and being, therefore, fair game for unorthodox treatment, was expressed on several occasions. Interestingly, Sir Robert Anderson and the fictional Inspector Heat share this view. Anderson believed that 'uniformed police upon the streets can deal with ordinary law-breakers, but they are wholly incompetent to grapple with the crime plots of professional criminals. And the

307

attempt to deal with crime of the kind here in view, under "ordinary law" and by ordinary methods, is the merest trifling.' And he goes on:

> The rules of the prize ring are held to apply to the struggle between the law and those who break the law. Everything must be done openly and above board. A legitimate principle in regard to crimes that are committed openly and above board, but utterly inapplicable to crimes such as these [Fenian bomb outrages]. For a mine can be reached only by a counter-mine.[7]

This is Anderson's justification for employing secret agents, this was his method of dealing with the Fenians as it is Inspector Heat's method of dealing with anarchists: '"I must do my work in my own way", declared the Chief Inspector. "When it comes to that I would deal with the devil himself, and take the consequences"' (p. 132), and the Assistant Commissioner says of him: 'He told me virtually that he must have tools to work with' (p. 140).

Blackwood's Magazine took up the same idea:

> Meanwhile the odds are all in favour of the anarchist. He faces society at the gambling-table with loaded dice. How shall the world prevail against a bomb furtively hidden and suddenly hurled? And because the odds are in his favour, the anarchist should be treated with the utmost severity. He should be given no advantage in that *curious game* called law. At present he pursues his avocation in Soho without let or hindrance. The policeman, who knows well that he is scheming murder, that he *even has a bomb in his pocket, hesitates to arrest him, because he deems it against the rules of the sport in which they are both engaged*...The detectives to whose vigilant care Soho is committed should be encouraged not only to watch the anarchists but to expel or imprison them [my italics].

This appeared in July 1906 while Conrad was writing *The Secret Agent*; but as early as September 1900, *Blackwood's Magazine* had been stressing the limitations placed on the police of the special branch by the rules of the game:

> Accordingly he is free to plot and suborn as he will...if they openly conspire to murder a king, they are politicians whose liberty is sacred.

And though the police know both their habit and intent, the police is prevented by a *rule of the game* from arresting their bodies. When the harm is done, then punishment may follow, but until the blow be struck, the officers of the law seem powerless [my italics].

Meeting the Professor unexpectedly, Heat says 'I'll have you yet', and the Professor replies:

'Doubtless...but there's no time like the present'...
   'If I were to lay my hands on you now I would be no better than yourself.'
   'Ah! The game!'
   'You may be sure our side will win in the end. It may yet be necessary to make people believe that some of you ought to be shot at sight like mad dogs' (pp. 94–5).

And, their meeting over, Heat compares anarchists with the ordinary criminal indulging in more conventional activities: 'Catching thieves was another matter altogether. It had that quality of seriousness belonging to every form of open sport where the best man wins under perfectly comprehensible rules' (p. 97). And he returns to the same topic, in his thoughts, while being interviewed by the Assistant Commissioner: 'The perfect anarchist was not recognised as a fellow-creature by Chief Inspector Heat...he meant to have him some day. But not yet: he meant to get hold of him in his own time, properly and effectively, according to the rules of the game' (pp. 122–3).

Heat has strong opinions about the criminal mind. Thieving to him is 'a form of human industry', comparable with other legal ways of earning a living:

It was a form of human industry, perverse indeed, but still an industry exercised in an industrious world; it was work undertaken for the same reason as the work in potteries, in coal mines, in fields, in tool-grinding shops. It was labour, whose practical difference from other forms of labour consisted in the nature of its risk, which did not lie in ankylosis, or lead poisoning, or fire-damp, or gritty dust, but in what may be briefly defined in its own special phraseology as 'Seven years hard'.

Chief Inspector Heat was, of course, not insensible to the gravity of moral differences. But neither were the thieves he had been looking after. They submitted to the severe sanctions of a morality familiar to Chief Inspector Heat with a certain resignation. They were his fellow-citizens gone wrong because of imperfect education, Chief Inspector Heat believed; but allowing for that difference, he could understand the mind of a burglar, because, as a matter of fact, the mind and the instincts of a burglar are of the same kind as the mind and the instincts of a police officer. Both recognize the same conventions, and have a working knowledge of each other's methods and of the routine of their respective trades (pp. 91–2).

A similar point of view was put forward in the *Contemporary Review* in 1896, and Conrad may well be indebted to it. The relevant passage occurs in an article entitled 'Crime and Punishment', in which the writer attacked the views of Lombroso as they had been stated in his book *La Doña Delinquente*. Lombroso viewed the criminal as one who 'is a product of pathological and atavistic anomalies', but the article here expresses the theory that the criminal is an ordinary person, and that crime is simply another aspect of human industry:

the criminal is, after all, a man of like passions with ourselves, swayed by similar motives, aiming at the same ultimate ends, recognising for the most part the same maxims of morality, imbued with the same social traditions as other members of his class...

Born criminals no doubt there are in plenty, just as there are born greengrocers; that is to say, men and women whose circumstances and associations from birth have been such as to impel them towards a career of dishonesty, just as other men's opportunities and limitations lead them to a livelihood by greengrocery. It may be admitted that there are men born into the world to whom fate scarcely offers any career but one of crime, but this no more establishes the existence of a 'criminal type' than the existence of a 'greengrocer type' would be established by the accumulation of instances in which men have scarcely had a choice of living except by the adoption of the one particular trade that circumstances have combined to offer them. The man who commences greengrocer because he is obliged to earn his living, and the shop his father has left him affords the only or the most convenient means of doing so, acts on precisely the same motive as the thief who, finding that among his relatives and intimates thieving is practically the sole means of subsistence in vogue, takes to it naturally as the most obvious means of gaining his own livelihood.[8]

*

Whatever public opinion was on the subject, secret agents were employed by the police against the anarchists. Sir Robert Anderson and Inspector Melville made use of them, and Conrad appears to have drawn upon both these instances in treating the relationship between Heat and Verloc.

Chief Inspector Heat's secret agent has been in contact with him for seven years, and Heat has not 'seen him to speak to three times in the last two years'. Moreover, Heat is reluctant to admit to Verloc's existence, since it has, until then, been a closely guarded secret:

'Of course,' said [Inspector Heat], 'the department has no record of that man.'

'Did any of my predecessors have any knowledge of what you have told me now?' asked the Assistant Commissioner...

'No, sir; certainly not. What would have been the object? That sort of man could never be produced publicly to any good purpose. It was sufficient for me to know who he was, and to make use of him in a way that could be used publicly' (p. 127).

And later on in the same interview:

He would not be much good to anybody but myself. One has got to know a good deal beforehand to make use of a man like that. I can understand the sort of hint he can give...I know how to manage our relations. I haven't seen him to speak to three times in the last two years. I drop him a line, unsigned, and he answers me in the same way at my private address (pp. 131–2).

Sir Robert Anderson's contact with his agent was even more remarkable. Le Caron, until he declared himself a secret agent before the famous Parnell Commission of 1896,[9] had worked under Anderson's special guidance, completely unknown to other officials, for twenty-one years. Anderson says in his book *Sidelights on the Home Rule Movement*, 'I never violate a confidence'[10] and this was because 'the first Fenian who ever gave me information was murdered on his arrival in New York'. Firmly, Anderson goes on: 'Never again would I give an informant's name to any one, and no man who afterwards gave me information was ever betrayed.'[11] Anderson had a stock answer to give to high-ranking officials when they questioned him: 'I will tell you, of course, if you ask me. But is it wise?'[12] This is reflected in Heat's reply to the Assistant Commissioner: 'What would have been the object [of disclosing Verloc's existence]? That sort of man could never be produced publicly to any good purpose' (p. 127). Anderson staunchly refused to betray Le Caron in any way, even to the extent of refusing to hand over his letters to the Government. Almost sixty years later Sir Robert Anderson's son recalled that 'Le Caron's letters had always been deemed private... The letters had never been on record in any government office; they had indeed been kept in our own home.'[13] Conrad's Assistant Commissioner is proud to have extracted successfully the name of Chief Inspector Heat's secret agent from him: 'The only thing I've discovered by myself is that he has been making use of that man privately.' No such success attended the efforts made to discover Sir Robert Anderson's secret agent. Le Caron writes:

If my identity remained undiscovered, it was not for want of attempts on the part of colleagues of Mr. Anderson to find it out. It was but natural, of course, that those associated with my chief should seek to penetrate his reserve regarding such a voluminous correspondent as myself, and to gain, at first hand, possession of the many important pieces of information which he alone appeared to be able to supply.[14]

Chief Inspector Heat's reputation owes much to his contact with his secret agent, Mr Verloc: 'I will take the liberty to tell you, sir, that it makes me what I am' (p. 128), and later the commissioner represses a smile 'at the fleeting thought that the reputation of Chief Inspector Heat might possibly have been made in a great part by the Secret Agent Verloc' (p. 131). David Nicoll said of Inspector Melville that he employed a secret agent and 'became famous'. The suggestion that Melville made use of a secret agent and that the agent's identity should be kept secret was made at the trial of the Walsall Anarchists in 1892. Though there were a number of anarchist incidents in Britain, it would be true to say that there were only two important ones—the Walsall Affair (1892) and the Greenwich Outrage (1894). In the former incident, three anarchists were imprisoned for ten years and one for five years for manufacturing bombs for use against the Russian despot. It was believed in anarchist circles that a well-known anarchist had acted, in this case, as *agent provocateur*. Melville, who was involved in the case, was questioned at the trial, but the part of the agent involved was not allowed to be investigated on the ground of 'public duty'. David Nicoll took up the subject in his pamphlet *The Walsall Anarchists* but just as Heat is reluctant to prosecute the Greenwich affair in a direction that will reveal his secret agent, so Melville appears to have avoided implicating his secret agent.

But the same accusations about the use of a secret agent came up during Melville's investigation of the Greenwich Bomb mystery, and in this instance more information about this 'tool' of Melville's came to light. I think it can be shown that Conrad made use of this information when he came to deal with Verloc.

30

VERLOC

Turning finally to the secret agent himself, Adolf Verloc, we have already ample evidence that there were sufficient suggestions of the presence and activity of such a figure in the revolutionary and police activity of the time, and especially in the case of the Greenwich Bomb Outrage. It is acceptable, I think, that Verloc's part in the fictional bomb outrage stems from the part played by Samuels in the actual event. Whether or not Samuels was instrumental in bringing about his brother-in-law's death as was implied, and whether or not he was a police agent, Conrad took these possibilities and developed them in his novel. The suggestion that Samuels gave Bourdin the explosive and guided him to Greenwich Park as a good place to experiment with it, being in his company beforehand, becomes Verloc's deliberate use of Stevie to take the bomb to the observatory and his accompanying Stevie as far as the park. And there is also the family relationship between Samuels and Bourdin which is paralleled by that between Verloc and Stevie. Moreover, there were suggestions that Bourdin was not particularly bright. The anarchist Leggatt, writing in the *Star* about Bourdin's death, commented that he was a bit of a simpleton. Bourdin was also reputed to have had a great admiration for his brother-in-law. Nicoll in his pamphlet recalls: 'I can remember well, at a conference, held at the Autonomie, at Christmas, 1893, little Bourdin sitting at the feet of Samuels, and looking up into his eyes with loving trust. To the little man he was evidently a hero to be loved and revered.'[1] In the novel, Winnie says to Verloc, 'That boy [Stevie] just worships you'

(p. 186), and we are told that Stevie had a 'great and awed regard for his sister's husband. He directed at him glances of respectful compassion...because Mr. Verloc was *good*' (p. 175).

Conrad insisted upon the domestic aspect of Verloc's story, and this is something which he had in mind in writing 'The Informer'—the irony of an anarchist, or of a secret agent working among anarchists, being encumbered by domestic ties. Mr Vladimir is shocked at the idea of Verloc having a wife: 'Anarchists don't marry. It's well known. They can't. It would be apostasy' (p. 38). Conrad's extension of the Greenwich tragedy into the domestic relationship was no doubt suggested by the same relationship in the original incident. Samuels was an example of an anarchist and possible secret agent who was firmly married. We have the following description of Mrs Samuels's behaviour in rescuing her husband from a meeting at which he was accused of being a traitor, the name 'Myers' being used by Isabel Meredith instead of 'Samuels':

''Ear, 'ear! Down with...' commenced Elliot again, and Jacob [Myers] opened his mouth to speak, but he was saved from any further need of self-defence or explanation, for at this moment the door of the office was broken rudely open and there entered like a hurricane a veritable fury in female form—a whirlwind, a tornado, a ravening wolf into a fold of lambs. This formidable apparition, which proved to be none other than the wife of the suspected Myers, amid a volley of abuse and oaths delivered in the choicest Billingsgate, pounced down on her ill-used husband, denounced Anarchy and the Anarchists—their morals, their creeds, their hellish machinations; she called on Jehovah to chastise, nay, utterly to destroy them, and soundly rated her consort for ever having associated with such scoundrels. And thus this formidable preacher of dynamite and disaster was borne off in mingled triumph and disgrace by his indignant spouse.[2]

Winnie is obviously not based upon Mrs Samuels, who does not seem to have been particularly moved by her brother's death, but the idea of the presence of a Mrs Verloc was no doubt derived from the existence of Mrs Samuels.

In character, however, Verloc does not resemble Samuels, who was inclined to be vociferous and quarrelsome. Describing a meeting of the Socialist Democratic Federation in 1886, Nicoll recalls:

When the meeting was over, as the audience was pouring out from the hall, I was attracted by a group evidently in hot discussion. Samuels was in the midst of it, quarrelling with a Social Democrat, and he wound up by taking off his coat and offering to fight his opponent. We have often seen that coat taken off since, but we have never seen a fight yet.[3]

And on another occasion he condemned Samuels's 'highly explosive' eloquence, which was not only unpopular with the 'mass of the party' but was 'calculated to impress the public with the impression that Anarchists are simply a gang of thieves and cut throats, which was exactly the impression that Mr. Robert Anderson, Inspector Melville of Scotland Yard and the lying Scribes of the Capitalist press were endeavouring to produce'.[4] Verloc, on the other hand, is notable for the power of his voice, for which reason he 'was always put up to speak by the leaders at a critical moment ...There was no uproar above which he could not make himself heard' (p. 23).

In appearance also the two men differ. *A Girl among the Anarchists*, by Isabel Meredith, gives the following description of Samuels, again under the name of Myers:

The man Myers, round whom the interest of the meeting was principally centred this evening, was to all appearances a mean enough type of the East End sartorial Jew. His physiognomy was not that of a fool, but indicated rather that low order of intelligence, cunning and intriguing, which goes to make a good swindler. The low forehead, wideawake, shifty little eyes, the nose of his forefathers, and insolent lock of black hair plastered low on his brow—all these characteristics may frequently be met with in the dock of the 'Old Bailey' when some case of petty swindling is being tried.[5]

Thus only certain aspects of Samuels were used by Conrad in creating Verloc, but it is possible to trace further sources which enabled Conrad to develop the political aspect of Verloc.

Verloc is a secret agent who has operated successfully for many years, has succeeded in implicating many anarchists, but who has not drawn suspicion upon himself by advocating too bloodthirsty and outrageous a doctrine in the press and at meetings.[6] There was an actual secret agent who was operating at the time of the Greenwich Outrage who shares some of these traits with Verloc, and who claimed to have been associated with Bourdin. And if Conrad saw the account of the inquest on Bourdin in the *Morning Leader*, he might well have learnt of that agent from an interview printed in the same issue:

A SECRET POLICE AGENT

Interviewed at Deptford by a 'Morning Leader' *Representative.*

'I had followed Bourdin in all his movements, and had relied on his remaining quiescent until Saturday. Otherwise I should have shadowed him carefully on Friday.'

So spoke a representative of the International Secret Police whose quarters are fixed in Deptford. In a street by no means betokening wealth may be found an unpretentious dwelling with the single word 'jeweller' lettered across its window. The window contained a few clocks and some watches, and behind the counter a young man—a Swiss—was seemingly busy at work.

'Yes, he is at home.' This was in reply to a question by the *Morning Leader* representative as to the whereabouts of the principal, and was supplemented by the query, 'Have you a card?' A card was submitted and secured a reception. The squalid surroundings of the street and the penurious appointments of the shop were agreeably contrasted with the tasteful decoration of an inner room.

'Oh, yes, I suppose you are astonished at my surroundings?' and the *Morning Leader* representative silently acquiesced in the criticism of his expression by the rapid change from slum-land into a cultured habitation. 'Yes', continued the speaker, 'I am responsible for the information placed in the hands of the English police as to foreign Anarchists. You will understand at once that my present business does not keep me and my family, but situated in the neighbourhood of Deptford, I am in a position to acquire valuable information as to the movements of imported Anarchists. I am in the service of the International Secret Police, which is subsidised by the Russian, German, and French Governments, and there is no movement of any of the members of the Anarchist party in London that is not duly communicated to these Governments.'

'Did you know anything of Bourdin?' A smile of ineffable disdain was the only response to this query. The speaker silently motioned me to his library, and taking down an index volume passed over the names of the Anarchists that had become prominent during the last five years. The name of Emile Henry was noted.

'Did you know the latest French assassin? Did you apprise the English police of his presence in England.

'Yes', came the calm rejoinder; 'I not only knew of his movements, not only apprised the English police of his dangerous mission, but indicated that it was his intention to commit his outrage in the French capital.'

'Did they do nothing?'

'No. Feeling confident that no harm would result to English property they ignored the injury, the destruction he was likely to accomplish in a foreign country. I am glad, however, to notice that the English Government has decided to place a quarantine upon the Anarchical Continental refuse, and that they are taking steps to cleanse from their midst the criminals that now infest London. Too long has England been an asylum for European murderers, forgers, and thieves.'

'As to Bourdin?'

'All the information in this direction obtained by the English police was from members of the International Secret Service.'[7]

The 'unpretentious dwelling' with the single word 'jeweller' lettered across its window, the window containing 'a few clocks and some watches', the 'squalid surroundings' of the street and 'the penurious appointments' of the shop contrasting with the 'tasteful decoration of the inner room' would seem to parallel Verloc's establishment—'a grimy brick' house, the shop 'a square box of a place' with its 'shady wares' and the parlour beyond 'in all essentials of domestic propriety and domestic comfort a respectable home'.*

* However, Hugh Walpole records in his journal a conversation he had with Conrad when staying with him in January 1919: '[Conrad] said Verloc's shop was where Leicester Galleries now are' (Rupert Hart-Davis, *Hugh Walpole*, London, 1952, p. 179).

Verloc

This secret agent's confession is not only reminiscent of Verloc's statements to Winnie:

Some of the highest in the world got to thank me for walking on their two legs to this day. That's the man you've got married to, my girl!...

There isn't a murdering plot for the last eleven years that I hadn't my finger in at the risk of my life. There's scores of these revolutionists I've sent off, with their bombs in their blamed pockets, to get themselves caught on the frontier (p. 238)

but is also in many ways a statement of Verloc's own position. The secret agent here is in the employ of the International Secret Police, which is subsidised by the Russian, German and French Governments, and Verloc is an agent of one of the foreign embassies in London, and has been subsidised by them for eleven years. 'You'll get your screw every month, and no more', Mr Vladimir tells him. This is his means of livelihood, and not his shop which had 'very little business at any time', just as the secret agent in the interview comments: 'my present business does not keep myself and my family'. But the situation of his business allows him to acquire 'valuable information as to the movements of imported Anarchists', and Verloc's shop in Soho is valuable for the same reason: 'Certain people who come there are watched.' The secret agent in the interview also supplies information to the English police, as does Verloc, and he boasts, 'there is no movement of any of the members of the Anarchist party in London that is not duly communicated', as Verloc boasts of the anarchists, 'I have them all under my eye'.

*

David Nicoll took it upon himself to find out the identity of this Secret Police Agent at Deptford. Two-and-a-half months after the Greenwich Outrage, he published the following:

Perhaps our readers would like to know who this gentleman is. Here is his card:

The Secret Agent

Coulon lives at Balham not at 'Deptford'. But it was not well to publish his real residence, the English people have strong objection to spies who inveigle men into dynamite plots. But the 'secret agent' is evidently Coulon, his pretended occupation, 'jeweller'. 'His smile of ineffable disdain' when poor Bourdin's name was mentioned, and the still more 'ineffable conceit' of the spy which leads him to claim the whole credit of all the police spying done in London: all point to Coulon.[8]

Coulon was the secret agent particularly connected with Inspector Melville, who was in charge of the Greenwich investigation and had also been responsible for the arrest of the Walsall Anarchists. The relationship between Melville and Coulon was described by Detective Sergeant McIntyre in his memoirs and it closely parallels that between Heat and Verloc:

Some time previous to what was known as the Walsall bomb conspiracy, Coulon wrote a letter to Scotland Yard offering his services to the police. Now, the police generally take advantage of any offer of this kind, in view of the necessity of keeping secret political agitators under surveillance... Coulon's offer was accepted, and he forthwith set to work... At the time that Coulon wrote to the 'Yard', Melville was senior officer, and the letter was handed over to him, and it fell to him consequently to go and see Coulon. And Coulon afterwards became his 'property'— that is to say, all information that Coulon supplied was taken possession of by Melville, who submitted it to Mr. Anderson, the Assistant Commissioner of Police... Of course, Coulon himself was never arrested.[9]

Just as Heat is reluctant to prosecute the Greenwich affair in a direction that will reveal his secret agent, so Melville appears likewise to have avoided implicating his secret agent Coulon. McIntyre's memoirs provide something of Coulon's background:

I know little of this man's antecedents, but I believe that he was at one time connected with some Catholic seminary, and figured later on as a journalist. His father was a Frenchman and his mother an Irishwoman. My experience has often shown that if you want dirty work done, it is best to employ a 'mongrel'. He is not, as a rule, particularly afraid of stooping to what is mean or contemptible.[10]

Coulon's background, then, parallels in part Verloc's. Speaking to Vladimir, Verloc insists: 'I am English...A natural-born British subject...But my father was French' (p. 22). We know from Nicoll's pamphlet that he had some connection in France with the Possibilist Party[11] and an early biographer of William Morris, J. Bruce Glasier, states that Coulon was 'a spy in the pay of the French government'.[12]

Verloc makes his contact with anarchists by being a vice-president of the Future of the Proletariat Society which published pamphlets—'prophetic bosh in blunt type on this filthy paper', as Vladimir describes them. Coulon also had his connections with an anarchist group in London, by teaching at their school, and he edited the so-called anarchist journal, the *Internationale*. Nicoll wrote:

How do English workmen like the introduction of Continental police methods into England by agents of International Secret Police? How do they like dynamite sheets like the *Internationale* edited and subsidised by police spies, with plenty of bombs and plots provided by the same gentlemen? This is what we are coming to under the rule of Inspector Melville and his friends of the International Secret Police 'subsidised by the Russian, German, and French Governments'.[13]

We can return again to Ford's claim about the information he provided Conrad with for *The Secret Agent*, particularly with regard to Bourdin, Samuels, and Mrs Samuels: 'For what the writer really did say to Conrad was: "Oh that fellow was half an idiot! His sister murdered her husband afterwards and was allowed to escape by the police. I remember the funeral." The suicide was invented by Conrad.' Ford would have had it in his power to tell Conrad something of the inside story of the affair, and of the people involved. Given Leggatt's statement about Bourdin, it would be understandable that Ford might say of Bourdin that he was 'half an idiot'. But he is unlikely to have told Conrad that Mrs Samuels murdered her husband and was allowed to escape, for according to Samuels's death certificate, he did not die until 31 October 1933. Nor did his wife commit suicide or leave the country—she survived her husband. But Ford must have known something of the Samuelses since the Rossettis were connected with them, as *A Girl among the Anarchists* shows. And Ford may have been recalling, again in an inaccurate and muddled fashion, not the fate of Samuels but the fate of the other secret agent, Coulon.

Although I have found it impossible to discover more of the background and ultimate fate of Coulon, who was a very secret secret agent, it is not unlikely that Conrad heard more of him through Ford who would get his information from his cousins, the Rossettis. Mrs Helen Rossetti Angeli told me during an interview on 2 July 1967 that she knew Samuels and his wife and she described them as 'a bad lot'. She knew the victim of the Greenwich bomb explosion—'poor devil' —and she also knew Auguste Coulon. Mrs Angeli's daughter, in a letter of 29 January 1968, wrote: 'Mother can only remember that "the filthy brute came to a bad end"', and when I interviewed Mrs Angeli that gentle old lady said: 'Disgusting looking man. He was French and was mixed up in a murder and bolted off to France. The police let him escape.'

I have not been able to discover what Coulon's fate was, and therefore we cannot conclude that Ford was speaking of him. There does seem, however, to be some similarity between Ford's comments and Mrs Angeli's, and Conrad was perhaps in possession of the truth about Coulon through Ford and made use of it in his novel.

Although Conrad drew quite strongly on Fenianism for some of his anarchists, only one aspect of Verloc seems to derive from this source. While he is interviewing Verloc at the foreign embassy, the First Secretary reflects:

This was then the famous and trusty secret agent, so secret that he was never designated otherwise but by the symbol △. in the late Baron Stott-Wartenheim's official, semi-official, and confidential correspondence; the celebrated agent △. whose warnings had the power to change the schemes and the dates of royal, imperial, grand-ducal journeys, and sometimes cause them to be put off altogether' (p. 27).

Sir Henry James recalls in his account of the Parnell Commission that

the Clan-na-Gael had been discussed throughout the civilised world. Mr. Alexander Sullivan's policy was, 'Shut out that name; call us by some other name...and instead of using any designation of name or even of alphabetical description, we will call ourselves the Triangle': and from that time we are dealing with this hidden body of murder, which described itself by the Triangle and no other description.[14]

And in his Victorian best-seller, *Twenty-five Years in the Secret Service*, Le Caron recalls: 'Three members formed the executive [of the Clan-na-Gael], and they were now known as the Triangle—a name taken from the △ sign which was used by way of cypher signature on all documents coming from head-quarters.'[15]

Conrad's secret agent was, apparently, like the other characters in the novel—'both law-abiding and lawless'—based quite carefully upon reports of the nature and activities of various secret agents working in England during the Fenian and anarchist disturbances. Yet it can be said, I think, that although Mr Verloc is treated with ironic humour, he does not become, like the anarchists, a grimy cartoon. The possibilities of melodrama inherent in a secret agent's occupation are played down by Conrad, partly by the introduction of Verloc's domestic life, and partly by the development of his own nature, his inherent laziness, which places him in the position of a man under threat of being sacked from his job if he does not do something to justify his salary. The more convincingly human portrayal of Verloc results, I think, from the fact that in dealing with him Conrad approached more closely his own experiences—an unusual occurrence in this novel—and these experiences begin with Verloc's relationship with the foreign embassy; but this is more speculative material, concerned more closely with Conrad biography, and must be treated in a separate chapter.

31

A. P. KRIEGER—A SPECULATION

Mr Verloc's visit to the foreign embassy at the beginning of the novel is an extremely significant event. His instructions from Mr Vladimir there set in motion the rest of the plot, and these instructions must have derived imaginatively from certain aspects of the Greenwich affair and the International Congress in Rome. But there are two other aspects of the incident whose sources, I believe, can be found in Conrad's experience. The first is the embassy itself with its First Secretary, Mr Vladimir; the second is Mr Verloc's character, pursuits and appearance.

Conrad did indicate his source for Vladimir: 'Mr Vladimir was suggested to me by that scoundrel Gen. Seliwertsow whom Padlewski shot (in Paris) in the nineties. Perhaps you will remember as there were peculiar circumstances in that case.'[1] Jocelyn Baines, commenting on Conrad's remarks here, writes: 'The outstanding feature of the Seliwertsow, or Seliwerstow, case was its obscurity.'[2] Having traced the account in *The Times*, 19 November 1890 *et seq.*, which dealt with Seliwertsow's murder by Padlewski, Baines concluded, 'there may well be more relevant details connected with this case but I have not been able to discover them',[3] and 'Conrad no doubt had recourse to other background material, but this has not yet come to light.'[4] I found more sensational accounts of the murder in the *Daily Graphic*, the social democrat newspaper, *Justice*, and the anarchist journal, the *Commonweal*. None of them produced anything further which could be remotely connected with Conrad's portrait of Vladimir. Mr Verloc's visit to the foreign embassy at 'No. 10

Chesham Square' might very well, however, be based upon Conrad's personal experience. Conrad had some business with the Russian embassy in London because of a visit he wished to make to his uncle in Poland, and it is possible that in the novel he has in mind not Seliwertsow, but the Russian consul at the embassy during the 1880s. According to the Foreign Office list for the years 1880–90, the Russian Consul General, Attaché and Chamberlain from 1884 to 1887 was Vladimir Weletsky. The similarity of name suggests that Conrad had this person in mind, but I have not been able to trace any direct contact between him and Conrad.

Conrad became a British subject on 19 August 1886 and it is particularly after this date that we find in the Bobrowski correspondence references to the Russian embassy in London. On 9 November 1886, writing to Conrad in London, his uncle stressed: 'Also, before leaving, take the necessary steps at the Russian Embassy, particularly as you are leaving for several months. By the time you return the permission will be granted, and the sooner you get it, the quicker will be the moment of our meeting in our country.'[5] And in the next letter (26 November 1886), Bobrowski returned to the subject: 'Once again I shall repeat my remark, or even my demand, that you must before departing take the necessary steps at the Russian Embassy to obtain release from their citizenship.'[6]

Whether Conrad himself visited the Russian embassy is not known. The visitors' book, I was told on making inquiries, though held in this country until long after the Russian revolution, was returned to Russia in the 1930s. But we do know that Conrad applied for release from Russian citizenship for, while he was sailing in Australian waters, his uncle, referring to Conrad's possible return to London, wrote:

I doubt very much if on your return to London you will find an answer from Petersburg—for the reason that the question of naturalization is at present *à l'étude* and it is customary here to postpone the settlement of such issues till legislation is actually in force. Anyhow, Panie Bracie,[7] don't let the grass grow under your feet, and when in London knock at the door of the Russian Embassy or Consulate and renew your application if need be.[8]

But Conrad was to remain in Australian waters for another year—he left Adelaide for Europe on 3 April 1889—and with this possibility in mind, Tadeusz Bobrowski suggested in his letter of 24 September 1888: 'Could you not ask Mr. Krieger to make inquiries for you at the Russian Embassy in London whether they have news concerning your application for your discharge from subjection?'[9] Clearly Conrad took up his uncle's suggestion, since we find Bobrowski writing in his next letter, 3 January 1889: 'You have done well to write to Krieger and instruct him to make inquiries at the Embassy.'[10]

According to the Russian official gazette *Senatskie Wiedomosti* (no. 49), 20 May 1889, Conrad was released from allegiance, but he did not visit his uncle until early in the following year. Presumably this was due, as Jean-Aubry suggests, to the need for Conrad to apply for the consent of the Governor of the province where he was born before entering Russian territory again,[11] and this might well have entailed further visits to the Russian embassy in London. I think it is extremely likely that Conrad, in writing of Verloc's visit to the foreign embassy, was making use of either Krieger's and/or his own visits to the Russian embassy in London during the 1880s, and that Mr Vladimir is based upon the Russian consul at that time. This would be particularly likely if, as I believe, Adolf Verloc is in part based upon Conrad's friend Adolf Krieger.

Very little has been known about Adolf Krieger. There are occasional references to him in the Bobrowski letters and there is Jean-Aubry's account of his efforts to help Conrad to get a job as captain of a steamer on the river Congo. It was through Krieger that Conrad entered the German hospital at Dalston after his return from the Congo to recover from malarial gout. We know also that Krieger lent Conrad some money and that their friendship apparently died as a result of Krieger's demands for the repayment of this loan. Information that I have discovered about Krieger helps us to trace the development and fading of their relationship and also suggests something of its nature and why Conrad might have had reasons for treating Krieger as he appears to have done in the figure of Verloc.

G. F. W. Hope in his unpublished manuscript recollections of Conrad writes: 'At this time [when Hope met Conrad for the first time, January 1880] Conrad had rooms with a Mr. Ward at Tollington Park and here got to know A. P. Kruger [*sic*].' Krieger was unmarried, and also living at Mr Ward's. But on 4 September 1881, Krieger, then aged thirty—he was seven years Conrad's senior—married Mary Penelope Reynolds. The marriage certificate shows that Krieger had then moved to Stoke Newington. Now according to Jean-Aubry, Conrad lived at 6 Dynevor Road, Stoke Newington, when he was in London between voyages over a period of at least five years from 1881 to 1886.[12] Given that Krieger lived in Stoke Newington from the time of his marriage in 1881, and that there was a very close association between the two men at this time, I think it is very likely that Conrad lodged with the Kriegers between 1881 and 1885. Certainly there are aspects of Mr and Mrs Verloc which seem to be derived from Mr and Mrs Krieger, and which suggest close observation on Conrad's part. I am indebted to Mrs Ogilvie, granddaughter of the Kriegers,[13] for the information I have about them.

Both the Kriegers were taciturn; Adolf Krieger was stolid, though kindly, and his wife a strong and silent person. She was passionately fond of Felix, the youngest of her three sons, particularly since he had suffered from meningitis when he was young. Krieger seems to have had a number of occupations during the 1880s, according to his marriage certificate and the birth certificates of his children. When he married, he gave his occupation as a commercial clerk. A year later he was a foreign correspondent, two years later a commercial clerk again, and finally a continental carrier. The extent of his journeys on the Continent is shown by the number of postcards he sent home while he was travelling. When Conrad refers to Verloc's mysterious journeys to the Continent—'Mr. Verloc was an intermittent patron. He came and went without any very apparent reason. He generally arrived in London (like the influenza) from the Continent' (p. 6)—he probably had Krieger's continental visits in mind. Mrs Ogilvie told me a story which her mother, still alive but very old and infirm now, told her. It was that her father-in-law had once been employed as a spy. No further information was available and it may well be that his spying was linked not with anarchy but with American Fenian activities, since Krieger though of German origin was, according to his passport, born in Knox City, Indiana, USA.

Finally, I think that Conrad had Krieger's physical appearance in mind when he described Verloc. The photograph of Krieger I have obtained (see Plate 7*d*) suggests this when it is compared with the descriptions of Verloc. Mr Verloc is 'undemonstrative and burly', his cheeks 'freshly shaven, had a sort of gloss'. His 'heavy-lidded eyes... sent out glances of comparative alertness'; they are 'big, prominent eyes...not well adapted to winking' (pp. 11–13). Inspector Heat describes him as 'a big fellow in a heavy overcoat sitting all alone on a chair, and holding his hat and stick in one hand' (p. 129); 'he wore his blue cloth overcoat unbuttoned; his boots were shiny' (p. 11). 'Under his hat, worn with a slight backward tilt, his hair had been carefully brushed into respectful sleekness; for his business was with an Embassy. And Mr. Verloc, steady like a rock...marched now along a street' (p. 13).

Conrad owed a great deal to Krieger (not simply in a monetary sense) and no doubt to Mrs Krieger also, and yet the portrait of Krieger (if that is what it is) in the novel is not a kindly one, and it is possible that this is the result of a decline in the friendship. Evidence of their disagreement has come mainly from Conrad and he is not very informative, at least in those accounts which have survived, but I have discovered some additional information. The relationship which appears to have begun in 1880 and to have been particularly strong in 1890, seems to have begun its decline in 1897. The first indication of a rift between the two friends comes from Conrad in a letter to Edward Garnett dated 5 December 1897:

My soul is like a stone within me. I am going through the awful experience of losing a friend. Hope [G. F. W. Hope] comes every evening to console me...When life robs one of a man to whom one has pinned one's faith for twenty years the wrong seems too monstrous to be lived down. Yet it must. And I don't know why, how, wherefore. Besides there are circumstances which make the event a manifold torment. Some day I will tell you the tale. I can't write it now. But there is a psychological point in it.[14]

But this process of 'losing a friend' seemed in this instance to go on for some time. Certainly Conrad's contact with Krieger by no means ended at this point, and we have evidence of it continuing at least until 1900.

The account of this matter is well treated in Blackburn's introduction to his edition of the Conrad/Blackwood letters,[15] but the details derive mainly from a letter from Meldrum to Blackwood, dated 9 February 1899, and a letter of 10 February written by Conrad to Meldrum. To Blackwood, Meldrum wrote:

A city friend, some two or three years ago, lent him £150, till he should make a name and with it so much of a future as a writer dare hope for. The very morning the *Academy* cheque arrived, arrived also a letter from this friend [Krieger], telling of disaster to his house, and asking if it was possible to get back his loan. Conrad had nothing but the £50 cheque, scarce out of its envelope; he endorsed it, and posted it immediately to his friend, thankful that Fate should have put it into his power to relieve himself of some of the anxiety of owing money to a man distressingly in need of it.[16]

Conrad's letter suggests quite strongly that Krieger was putting pressure upon him, but we should not feel critical of Krieger for this, as I hope to show:

My dear Mr. Meldrum.
I got your good letter this morning and at the same time the enclosed which please read. This is the third message of the sort since I saw you. Either the man is nervously anxious or he wants to put pressure on me—or he is in a bad way. In any case this kind of thing will drive me crazy. I can't work after I get such letters. I did send him the £50 of the Academy and I owe him ⟨ 100 ⟩ * 130 yet...You know the whole absurd and painful story of the broken friendship—without provocation and even any cause I could remotely guess at. Their business which he started 14 years ago with my money is very good—perfectly sound. And here I am worried with these miserable letters.[17]

In a later letter to Meldrum dated 13 February Conrad speaks of sending Krieger another £50. Receiving £60 from Blackwood, he 'sent on £50 to the man and kept 10' for himself.[18] Conrad had thus paid out £100 and if he assessed his debt accurately he then owed Krieger a mere £80. According to William Blackburn, 'Within a period of less than a month—from the middle of January until mid-February 1899—Krieger wrote Conrad four times, imploring him for aid.'[19] And Conrad thought of escaping his difficulties by taking out an insurance policy. Blackburn continues: 'Almost two years later, in December 1900, Conrad returned to the idea; he would take out an insurance policy for £1,000 and borrow the sum of £250 against it',[20] in Conrad's words 'to clear up generally my financial situation and to discharge a certain obligation which weighs on me the more, because

* Overscored in the original letter.

331

it cannot be legally enforced'.[21] This seems a strong measure if all he owed Adolf Krieger was £80. Mr William Blackburn commenting on this letter speaks of 'the frantic Krieger' returning 'for help'. We know that Conrad dedicated his collection of short stories *Tales of Unrest* to Adolf Krieger: 'for the sake of old days'. This collection was published in 1898, and Mr Blackburn refers to this as something of a manœuvre on Conrad's part: 'an obvious attempt to placate Krieger'.[22]

Thus Conrad first complains of losing a friend because of a loan of money as early as 1897, yet in spite of the smallness of the sum involved and the repayments made, he seems still to be in debt to Krieger in December 1900. One is tempted to conclude that the loan was larger than has been believed, or that Krieger continued to lend Conrad money over this period.

Three pieces of evidence in the possession of Krieger's descendants extend the period of Conrad's relationship with Krieger in a way which is of relevance to *The Secret Agent*, and they also suggest something of the discomfort Conrad felt over his debt to Krieger. There is first a document consisting of a letter written by a Frenchman called Ortinari and dated simply 28 June, followed by a note from Conrad to Krieger written on the same sheet of paper (see Appendix E for transcriptions of these documents in full):

Dear Sir,

I am very sorry to hear from Paris that the enclosed cheque has been kept for nearly three weeks by the fault of one of my clerks. I thought it had reached you long ago.

I hope you will excuse the mistake.

Yours very sincerely,
F. Ortinari

Dear Boy. This is Ortinari's sweet note. Wish he would write every day —or at least every month. Send me a cheque for £7 so that I may pay my rent. No sooner one gets something pretty than one must break into it. This is a brutal world—my masters!...

A. P. Krieger—a speculation

The dating of this document is not difficult, I think, since there is a reference to the *Saturday Review* notice of Conrad's story 'in the *Cosmo*'. This will be the *Cosmopolis*, which published 'An Outpost of Progress' in June/July 1897. The first letter here must be dated 28 June 1897, and thus antedates the process of loan repayment with its attendant distress by some six months. It is not so easy to understand what is being referred to in Conrad's letter, but it would seem that he had been expecting a cheque from Paris which would help him to reduce his debt to Krieger, that the arrival of this cheque had been delayed, but that, on receipt of it, part or all of the money had been sent to Krieger. The enclosing of Ortinari's letter would seem to indicate that Conrad felt the need to prove to Krieger that the delay was not on his side.

The second document is a letter written seven years later, five months before *Nostromo* was completed, again extending the period of the relationship and of Conrad's indebtedness.

15 March 1904. 17 Gordon Place, Kensington W.
My dear Krieger,
  Pardon the delay, but now you may take this bill as absolutely safe. In fact I shall take it up before it matures. It is made payable at Pinker's office because I've no banker after Watson's failure. Two fifty gone in one fell swoop. I am nearly out of my mind with worry and overwork. My nerves are all to pieces.

It seems likely that Conrad had at this point received help from his agent Pinker in repaying more of his debt to Krieger (we know that Conrad eventually owed Pinker £1,000).[23]

Whether or not this marks the full repayment of the loan I have not been able to discover. One final piece of evidence shows that the relationship had certainly not ended by September 1904, for this was the publication date of *Nostromo* and Krieger's descendants have a copy of the novel inscribed: 'To A. P. Krieger from his affectionate friend Joseph Conrad

1904'.[24] I would not wish to press too far the influence of Krieger on *The Secret Agent*, but I think it likely that by the time Conrad began writing the novel in 1906 he was released from his indebtedness to Krieger, and that he discharged some of the complex emotions their relationship had involved by making him in part the source for Verloc.

CONCLUSION

32

CONCLUSION

'Imagination, not invention, is the supreme master of art as of life.' This statement from *A Personal Record*[1] sums up the theory of creation so far as Conrad was concerned. 'Invention', in the sense of making up or devising themes, plots and characters, had never been his method, which was generally one of close and imaginative analysis of his own experience (*The Shadow-Line*) or of the experiences of others which were closely linked to his own (*Lord Jim*, 'The Secret Sharer'). In the latter instances, the observer/narrator figure would seem to be an essential part of the creative process, allowing Conrad to project himself, again imaginatively, into another's experience. But in the major works considered here Conrad can be seen moving further and further from his own experience and from the experience of others linked to his own. Kurtz, unlike Jim or Falk or the Secret Sharer, was not a seaman; Conrad had a mere glimpse of South America; he had no part in the world of the London anarchists. But this movement away from his own experience still does not turn him towards 'invention', but towards an extension of the faculty of 'imagination'. More and more he is involved in an immersion of the mind and spirit in the experiences of others, in the history of peoples, and in the growth of ideas as he found them recorded in books. Increasingly, the absence of any direct personal experience made the process a more difficult and a more remarkable one. It is this initial stage of reading and total and sympathetic involvement that must have formed the beginning of the creative process for each book. Its completeness and its mentally exhausting nature is revealed in his Author's Notes to *Nostromo* and to *The Secret Agent*, in his letters, and also in his record of how a lady visitor interrupted him in the composition of *Nostromo* and he 'jumped up from [his] chair stunned and dazed, every nerve quivering with the pain of being uprooted out of one world and flung down into another'.[2] The total nature of this immersion obviously accounts for his ability to construct a completely convincing fictional world, but it did more than this.

Such immersion is for him the requisite of 'a great magician' —'one must surrender oneself to occult and irresponsible powers, either outside or within one's breast'.[3] But such immersion is also, in its absolute form, distasteful to him: 'I have a positive horror of losing even for one moving moment that full possession of myself which is the first condition of good service.'[4] The immersion, the identification, of a difficult enough nature, had to be tempered wisely, therefore, with the equally difficult need to retain 'full possession'. I think that we can here understand something of the emotional difficulties Conrad went through in imaginatively grasping the experience of Kurtz, of Decoud, or of Winnie Verloc, the difficulty of deliberately allowing oneself 'to be carried away beyond the bounds of [one's] normal sensibility', without 'becoming the victim of [one's] own exaggeration, losing the exact notion of sincerity':[5] 'In that interior world where [the artist's] thought and his emotions go seeking for the experience of imagined adventures, there are no policemen, no law, no pressure of circumstance or dread of opinion to keep him within bounds. Who then is going to say Nay to his temptation if not his conscience?'[6]

But '"Il y a toujours la manière"... The manner in which, as in the features and character of a human face, the inner truth is foreshadowed for those who know how to look at their kind.'[7] This is the ultimate extension of the imaginative process for Conrad, the kind of remote control exerted throughout the process of sympathetic immersion by the belief that the features of truth can be traced within an area of experience foreign to one's own, because they *do* exist. It is not so much moulding one's material into a preconceived pattern as allowing the topographical lines to emerge—'the proper wisdom is to will what the gods will without, perhaps, being certain what their will is—or even if they have a will of their own'.[8] Thus from the sympathetic and imaginative immersion in his material would come not invented but derived characters, themes and plots, revealing themselves within the material, foreshadowing the 'inner truth' that existed there, and finally arranged, bound together by that power of full self-possession which would impose order upon material and imagination.

It seems to me that in the three major works dealt with in this book we can see how Conrad allowed the essential features of the truth within his material to emerge, and manipulated the details of his sources to emphasize those features.

Conrad's basic material for *Heart of Darkness* was a short personal experience of conditions on the Congo in 1890–1, and on the face of it this experience was a personal disaster. Disease, hardship, the pettiness of the activity and of the prevailing attitudes of the colonisers, the evidences of cruelty and exploitation and finally the active hostility of the Delcommunes and their refusal to allow him even his rights as a fully qualified sea-captain—all of these must have made it an exasperating, frustrating and humiliating experience. The 'loot' he brought out of Africa was certainly in part sickness and a sense of failure, and he must have brooded over what there was in it that was not simply a personal account of failure or a view of a contemporary abuse. And yet, if we consider the matter closely, we can see that the whole of

Conclusion

Heart of Darkness lies in a dormant form within that unsatisfactory experience, and Conrad, as he considered it, must have been conscious that the 'features and character' did exist there if they could be brought out.

The essential development at that early stage was for Conrad to be able to see that his personal *emotional* development through his Congo experience could be related to a central truth of human nature, with regard to the exploitation of the Congo and with regard to the colonising activity generally. The development for Conrad was obviously from a strong idealism to an intense disillusionment. His comments upon the Congo outside the story suggest the strong desire he had to go there, as do the efforts he made to get a job there, and the nature of the desire is hinted also in the pleasure he felt at the prospect of being one of an exploring party. He later referred to his African trip as the end to 'the idealized realities of a boy's daydreams'.[9] It was to have been part of the adventure of African exploration, of geographical discovery, and it must have been linked in his mind with the exploits of Henry Morton Stanley.

In 'Geography and Some Explorers', Conrad refers to Livingstone, with his 'unappeased desire for the sources of the Nile' which had 'changed him in his last days from a great explorer into a restless wanderer refusing to go home any more'.[10] He does not refer to Stanley in this context, but it was Stanley who in 1871 searched out Livingstone, and who in 1888 found Emin Pasha (a man equally reluctant to leave Africa). It was Stanley whose prayer on Livingstone's death was that he might be allowed to open up Africa to the light of Christianity and whose exploration filled up the blank spaces on the map that Conrad had gazed at as a boy. It was Stanley who founded the Congo Free State and the trading-stations on the river for King Leopold of the Belgians. It must have been with these achievements in mind that

Conclusion

Conrad went to the Congo only to find that it was all 'the vilest scramble for loot that ever disfigured the history of human conscience and geographical exploration', 'a prosaic newspaper "stunt"'.[11] It is the movement from idealism to knowledge and disillusionment which is suggested by the movement within the story from the narrator's comments on the famous men who had sailed from the Thames—'What greatness had not floated on the ebb of that river into the mystery of an unknown earth!...The dreams of men, the seed of commonwealths, the germs of empires' (p. 47)—to Marlow's comment on the Roman occupation of Britain that it was 'men going at it blind—as is very proper for those who tackle a darkness' (p. 50).

Because he had been aware of the truth underlying the pretensions of men in a certain field of endeavour, Conrad was able to move his story from the area of mere personal disappointment: 'I don't want to bother you much with what happened to me personally', Marlow says (p. 51), for it is 'the effect of it' on him that was important, just as it was in the case of Conrad. Considering the matter later, the personal disappointment and suffering became insignificant compared with the wider understanding that had been opened to him.

It must have been apparent to Conrad that he had material in plenty to demonstrate the process of 'men going at it blind', the ignorance, cruelty and grasping nature of the general run of the colonists. But these were men who had not voiced 'high ideals', who did not claim to see themselves as 'bearers of a spark from the sacred fire' (p. 47); yet, after all, this suggestion of idealism had been a significant part of the whole, both in Conrad's experience and in the propaganda of colonisation. Such a historical process with its marked fracture between man's stated intentions and the results of those intentions had to be presented concretely and individually.

Conclusion

Hodister's story, a part after all of Conrad's Congo experience, must have appeared to him as the right vehicle, an actual and strong example of that movement from idealism to the grotesque actuality. Hodister shared with Stanley an intense egoism, prodigious energy, idealism, and unwavering purpose. Like Stanley, he obtained the maximum publicity. And Hodister was obviously overcome by treachery on the part of envious men and by his own egoism which forced him to venture too far. It is an aspect of Conrad's genius that he was further able to see Hodister in the light of an earlier and more generally applicable myth—he was not only a colonist, he was also a Faust who, in a particularly dangerous field, had allowed 'his unlawful soul' to be beguiled 'beyond the bounds of permitted aspirations' (p. 144).

Conrad's perception of the 'inner truth' of his material— not of his personal experience but what that experience had allowed him to perceive—and his obtaining of the right example, enforced upon him all the necessary further steps in the moulding of his own material. Conrad was fortunate here in two respects. His experience had partaken of the archetypal one for Stanley and indeed for the area generally— the journey up-river to bring off a man who was in some kind of danger. And on this journey Conrad was intimately connected with a traditional figure of some importance in that situation—the man who was in charge of the steamer making the journey. For the rest, in order to bring out the 'sombre theme' two major changes were necessary in moulding his source material.

The first was the necessity to take back several years the Congo he had known. The Hodister story, Stanley's explorations, the theme of the possible corruption of a man of high ideals, all required the isolation of the primitive to be possible. The Congo that Conrad knew was just a little too close to the idea of the 'two good addresses' and a policeman round the corner. And so large settlements disappear, to be replaced by native villages and small, lost trading-posts.[12] Navigation is a matter of discovering the right channel, feeling one's way through an unknown waterway. The Inner Station became not a Stanley Falls but an isolated trading-post. For the same reason the fate of Freiesleben became the fate of a man involved with the natives at an isolated village, his body left to rot, and no European, let alone a military expedition, coming near until Marlow made his difficult journey up the same isolated stretch of water.

Conrad has gone to some trouble to recreate the story of Freiesleben in a form suited to Marlow's narrative by going beyond the events to give that 'sinister resonance' he desired. To begin with, the story deftly illustrates in advance the kind of human activity we are to find on Marlow's river, and it becomes a revelation in little of what happens to Kurtz on a much greater scale. Fresleven 'was the gentlest, quietest creature that ever walked on two legs', but two years there 'engaged in the noble cause' had changed the 'supernatural being' 'and he probably felt the need at last of asserting his self-respect in some way' (p. 54). This reconstruction of the captain's character makes him an image in miniature of Kurtz. Moreover, Conrad fixes on the most trivial cause for the incident—provisions—enhancing and particularising this by stating that it was 'two black hens'. And given the conditions he wishes to establish on Marlow's river, he omits the punitive force of 370 soldiers and six white officers, which would be fatal to the sense of isolation he wishes to create. By ignoring the official burial of the remains, and particularly by substituting the more primitive spear for the gun actually used, he is enhancing those particular aspects of primitive isolation, of chance cruelty and neglect in the relations between white and black, which are a significant part of his story.

Conclusion

In spite of his encounters with corpses, Conrad's journey did not, I believe, bring him face to face with the cruelty that was traditionally part of the history of the Congo.[13] One of his lasting impressions must have been rather that which he brings out in such figures as the manager of the Central Station, the brick-maker and the company's chief accountant, of a great deal of bureaucratic activity and posturing, operating incongruously in the midst of the jungle. But mainly, he was following the thin and uncertain line of civilisation up the Congo. The bureaucratic attitude was necessary to his theme—it was the alternative nightmare to Kurtz's, but the impression of the primitive had to be enhanced by an inclusion of the cruelty he knew existed in the history of the Congo. Thus what he had personally seen and heard had to be transformed by re-grouping and by the addition of material outside his experience which was, nevertheless, 'true' to that experience. His treatment of his rather uneventful stay at Matadi is interesting here since, following the necessities of his theme, Conrad re-works it to form Marlow's experience of the Company Station. Marlow's first close encounter with the 'devil' that exists in the heart of darkness is made dramatic and impressive, as it must be, because Conrad finds a forceful and representative image for the cruelty he knew existed. The cumulative effect of the 'grove of death' achieves more of the 'resonance' he desired than a mere recording of scattered and factual examples. The Company Station is Conrad's imaginative working over of those impressions of cruelty, waste, and selfish hypocrisy which must have been general during his stay but which are here clustered about three particular aspects—the railway, the loss of life, and the figure of the accountant—of what he observed in the area.

A further example of this 'distortion' of his material in the direction of an 'inner truth' can be seen by comparing

344

the manuscript and the completed text. Conrad writes in *Heart of Darkness*: 'I avoided a vast artificial hole somebody had been digging on the slope, the purpose of which I found it impossible to divine' (p. 65). This appears in the manuscript first as 'I avoided an hole somebody evidently had been digging and the purpose of which I could not divine.' The addition of the adjectives 'vast' and 'artificial' transform a simple situation into a bizarre and extraordinary one.

The second development of Conrad's source material was in relation to the pattern of Marlow's experience. Conrad's experience of the Congo does not appear to have had a culmination in the sense of an illuminating point of climax, though one of its features had been a process of gradual enlightenment—he did say that before the Congo episode he was a mere animal. The process was maturing for him; not a maturing through exertion, growth, the satisfaction of a job well done and one's confidence in oneself justified (as in *The Shadow-Line*), but a maturing through disillusionment, insight into and recognition of the malice, the pettiness, the cruelty and the evil of which mankind is capable in certain circumstances. This general illuminating process, the increase of perception and understanding, becomes Marlow's, paralleling, as it did in Conrad's case, the movement up-river. To this extent, Conrad's experience underlines Marlow's and is the shape of its 'inner truth'.

The choice of nightmares given to Marlow existed also in Conrad's experience, although he did not meet personally with the nightmare of his particular choice. Like Marlow, Conrad rejected the petty corruption of the 'pilgrims', because he had shared, to some extent, the idealistic vision of a Hodister. He had sacrificed a good deal to make it materialise, and the materialisation had been, in a different way, equally disastrous for him.

But Conrad must have realised that that process of maturing, that journey into disillusionment and understanding, must, dramatically, have a 'culminating point' for Marlow, so that the whole effect of his own experience could be represented in a definite and climactic way. Kurtz's death could not come to Marlow by hearsay as Hodister's came to Conrad. Kurtz had to be present as an example, an example in its terminal stages, an example capable of being aware of what had happened, in order that the theme might be concretely presented in its movement from idealism to corruption, and in order that Marlow might experience the full 'effect'. Conrad's much less significant experience of Klein came in most appropriately as a part of the plot. To bring out the final clarification and maturing process for Marlow, therefore, the imaginative accretion of his meeting with the Hodister figure, Kurtz, was essential, the 'culminating point' of his experience.

But for the 'effect' of the whole experience upon Marlow to be brought out significantly, he could not have the minor and frustrating role that was assigned to Conrad by the Delcommunes, and so a major change to Conrad's experience comes about in the development of the figure of Marlow. Marlow is given the legacy of Conrad's hard-gained insight— he is sceptical from the first. Brussels is 'sepulchral', the two women concierges are fates at the door of hell, he is suspicious of the jargon that is applied to him, given the insignificance of the part he is to play—'an emissary of light', 'a lower sort of apostle'. Conrad is taking his revenge upon his own gullibility, and at the same time making his hero a man not easily gulled by the heroics of colonisation. Marlow, again unlike Conrad, is given considerable status within the world of the story, a status at once functional and moral, but on both these levels his status depends upon actions and events which are, in the main, imaginative additions to Conrad's own experience. Marlow is comparatively unimportant as skipper of a steamboat, and yet much depends upon him in that capacity. He is the man with skill in seamanship who alone can salvage the vessel that is essential to the saving of Kurtz, he is the only man who can safely take her up to the Inner Station and back. On the moral level, Marlow is the man from the outer world, secure in his beliefs and his job. Ultimately, Marlow is the only one sensitive enough to appreciate the forces at work in the jungle, the nature of the two nightmares that are open to Kurtz and the pilgrims—the blindness of greed and self-deception, or the high but empty ideals that make one vulnerable in face of savagery and the lure of the primitive. Marlow alone forces Kurtz back ultimately from his nightmare into the real world of sickness, disillusionment and death. And in other smaller ways, we can see Conrad bending his experiences to enhance Marlow. Conrad had no part in the tragedy of Freiesleben, but he no doubt saw the ruins of Tchumbiri; and in making Marlow the person who attempted to recover Freiesleben's remains he is enlarging Marlow's stature in the story as one of the few who retain their humanity on the river, and contributing to the idea of Marlow's limited but moral victory over circumstances.

Yet, because of his superiority, Marlow is rejected by the pilgrims as Conrad was rejected by the Delcommunes. Conrad's own rejection therefore becomes the essence of Marlow's right-mindedness amidst the 'squeeze'. Like Conrad, he is not of the wrong party. We might conclude, therefore, that in Marlow Conrad is compensating for his own failure, and doing it very skilfully, for Marlow still remains merely the steamboat skipper, a modest, practical man, with a devotion to his craft.

Most interesting with regard to Marlow's significance in the story is the elevation of the homely river-steamboat. Conrad had eulogised ships before—the *Otago* is a case in point. But there he did have a command and the ship had her own beauty and courage. The steamer is a different matter, but it is an essential part of the theme of the story and of Marlow's role. It is the weapon Conrad ought to have had in face of his experience and was denied. It represents honest work and effort as opposed to the rapacious indolence of the pilgrims or the loudly acclaimed brilliance and ideals of Kurtz. While the 'pilgrims' intrigue and slander in order to be appointed to a lucrative trading-post, Marlow is at work on the 'battered, twisted, ruined tin-pot steamboat', which is nevertheless his 'influential friend', which gives him the chance to find himself in work. And the steamboat also is linked with the sombre theme of the river and the jungle, of whose threat only Marlow is aware, for Marlow has hauled the steamer out of the river 'like the carcass of some big river animal', smelling of 'primeval mud'. Given the truth of Conrad's slender actual responsibility for a river-steamer on the Congo, one must see this as a good example of Conrad moulding his experience to fit the 'inner truth'.

There is a further aspect of Conrad's experience which he introduces successfully into the story in order to bring out the 'resonance'. Part of the nightmare that Marlow rejects is the determination in the midst of the jungle to stick to the forms of European society, however irrelevant, in terms of status. And so there is an emphasis upon titles—'manager', 'chief accountant', 'brick-maker'. That this was part of Conrad's experience is suggested by the emphasis laid in the *Mouvement Géographique* on such status-indicating labels. Conrad, of course, twists them ironically, and adds his own 'pilgrims' equally ironically. Appropriate forms of expression are used by the manager after Kurtz has been found and are evidence of the need for self-deception (and for self-protection) from the actualities of their situation, on the part of the 'pilgrims'. For even in the face of the horrors that have been discovered the aim is to conceal the truth, denying its existence. References to minor issues, but issues which can equally well serve the purpose of damning Kurtz, are safer: 'the time was not ripe for vigorous action'; 'the district is closed'; the 'ivory—mostly fossil'; 'the method is unsound'. And when Marlow suggests 'no method at all', the manager seizes upon this as a better approach, indicating 'complete want of judgement'—very useful for a damning and face-saving report. These were the kind of criticisms that were levelled at Hodister after his death, and the attitude must have been common among the people Conrad met. It is an attitude he consciously develops, as we can see by his altera-tions to the manuscript. His comment that the touch of insanity 'was not dissipated by somebody on board assuring me earnestly that there was a camp of natives—he called them enemies!—hidden out of sight somewhere' (p. 62) was initially in the manuscript: 'which was not dissipated by somebody telling me there was a camp of "niggers"'. 'Nig-gers' has been crossed out and the word 'natives' substituted, followed by the interpolation 'he called them "enemies"' (MS, p. 40). It is most likely that 'niggers' was the term Conrad heard used, and for which he substituted the less objectionable 'natives', and then brought in his own development of the idea, 'enemies'. This introduces the theme of self-deceptive 'definitions' used by the colonists to give justification to their actions. Later, the natives become 'criminals', and the skulls on poles round Kurtz's home belonged to former 'rebels'; 'Rebels! What would be the next definition I was to hear? There had been enemies, criminals, workers—and these were rebels' (p. 132). To Marlow, the nightmare of full self-realisation is preferable to the nightmare of self-deception.

Conrad had had a direct personal experience in the Congo of what lay behind the elevation of colonisation there. He was fortunate in that he was able to go beyond the apparent truth of that activity to the 'inner truth' and achieve an awareness which allowed his characteristically ironic approach to man's activity to permeate 'truthfully' his account of Marlow's journey. And Conrad is being quite honest when he borrows a metaphor from the conception of *Heart of Darkness* and speaks of the 'loot' he brought out of the Congo, for this story depends not upon his personal experience so much as upon impressions and ideas related to the area, a view which was permitted to him of man's activity there. The distinction is between 'adventures' in the sense of personally acted and felt incidents and 'experiences' which include a wider area of activity—a personal view of the adventures of others, impressions of a place and a people.

*

In seeking the 'inner truth' of his Congo episode, Conrad was able to move from the particularities of his own experience to the general truths of human nature and their historical expression, and from there into the dateless and eternal themes and situations of myth and legend which ultimately underlie the story in sombre movements and suggestions. The journey by water into a kingdom of darkness, the attempted rescuing of a soul from Hades, the notion of desperate and strange adventures in unknown lands whose characteristics are drawn from the subconscious, carry suggestions of Orpheus and Odysseus and Gulliver, and particularly of Faust. This effect is assisted by Conrad's dropping of proper names which would have tied the story to a specific area.[14]

The writing of *Nostromo* involved a different set of circumstances, though the imaginative process would appear to be the same. The source-material for the novel lay almost entirely in books, and, given the paucity of Conrad's personal experience of his subject and the detailed nature of the completed fictional landscape, one might be led to expect a wide and precise reliance upon a number of source books. I have shown, however, that this is not the case. What *is* remarkable is the small number of books from which it can definitely be stated that Conrad drew specific material. In addition, the actual incidents or suggestions for character drawn from these sources are again surprisingly small in number. Against this we have to set the significant use Conrad can make of a minor or undeveloped incident, for example, the *estrapada* torture undergone by Garibaldi, or Eastwick's breakfast with General Trias. But there is more to be said about Conrad's use of sources for this novel.

What does strike one in reading about South American affairs of the period is the repetitive nature of the experience one is discovering. The books, written by European, generally English, expatriates then working in various republics, or by visiting speculators, newspaper correspondents, or simply curious travellers, all throw up a similar landscape and pattern, a similar reaction to people, places and events. The idea, for example, of Mrs Gould's long ride with her husband all over the province in search of labour, with its accompanying description of the country and the people, might have been derived from any or all of the books on South America. The authors, almost without fail, make similar journeys during which similar, though not precisely the same things, are observed and commented upon.[15]

Conrad would find particularly well documented the political, economic and social movements of the continent. The pattern of exploitation, whether benevolent or totally repressive in its nature; of revolution that involved treachery and was based upon the desire for power and personal gain or that which involved the desire for a people's liberty and was based upon humanitarian beliefs; the influx and influence of numerous different races; the monotonous nature of the landscape; the repetitive theme of potential riches and potential development thwarted by revolution or labour unrest: all this would be found again and again repeated in Conrad's reading on South America.

It would be true to say, then, that Conrad's 'experience' for this novel was the generalised picture of South American affairs that he obtained from his reading. And in spite of his lack of personal experience, the establishing of the 'features and character' of this source material, at least at one level, must have been less difficult than in the case of *Heart of Darkness*. The true protagonist of *Nostromo* is the province of Sulaco, the 'twilight country...with its high shadowy Sierra and its misty Campo for mute witnesses of events flowing from the passions of men short-sighted in good and evil'.[16] And the characteristics of Sulaco must have risen in general and shadowy form in his imagination in the early stages of the creative process from a vast hinterland of reading, from an array of characteristic towns, houses, people, customs, historical, political and economic events and enterprises. His task then was not one of relating a personal experience to wider and more permanent issues, but of reflecting accurately what was geographically, socially and historically typical in a specific but fictional example, the republic of Costaguana. Conrad assembled a country and its history from the whole of a continent. The map of South America opposite p. 137 shows how he drew place names for his republic from all over the continent. There is the care with which the geography of Costaguana and the topography of the town of Sulaco have been worked out, with aspects also taken from a number of actual republics and cities. Equally carefully planned are the agriculture, occupations, natural resources and communications of the area. But, as might be expected, Conrad's reading in the *history* of the area was of the greatest significance for the novel.

The history of Costaguana is a summation of that of the continent as a whole, but this distillation was planned carefully by Conrad to give a quite individual history of the State. Thus there are references to the earliest Spanish conquerors, the rule of Guzman Bento, the fifteen years of corrupt government that followed, the benevolent if brief government of Ribiera, the Monterist revolution, the separation of Sulaco, and, in the future, labour trouble in the silver mine. The historical pattern of successive exploitation, of successive attempts at progress contending with rebellion and revolution must have arisen, as a fairly obvious 'inner truth' from his source material. This pattern, which needed a stretch of many years to demonstrate it fully, imposed the method of narration, with its constant back-tracking in explanatory excursions from present to past.

The population of this 'twilight country' would be determined by various factors. Not only did Conrad lack personal experience of the continent but he also lacked personal knowledge of the characters—of their individual natures and, except perhaps in the case of Nostromo and Captain Mitchell, of their function in society. The characters also had to be built up in all their aspects from his reading. In so far as it has been possible to discover the sources for the characters in *Nostromo* the most remarkable aspect of these is the paucity of suggestion Conrad had to work on in terms of the individual character. Dr Monygham clearly derives from Masterman and his experiences, but fundamentally all Conrad took from his source was the fact of the torture, and perhaps the suggestion of a profession. From this he created the doctor, with his limp, his cynicism, his guilt, his poverty. Don José Avellanos comes together from several sources, none of them extensive. There is Dr Carrera in Masterman's book, and again it is a particular view of the man at a particular moment—a man driven to the extremes of hunger and distress. The suggestion of his recovery, his daughter's devotion, comes from Eastwick. And for a special incident to bring out the man's character at a specific time, Avellanos is given a part of General Trias's speech—the part most appropriate to Conrad's conception of the statesman. It is remarkable that Conrad's imagination has been able to work upon such hints and still bring out convincing traits of character, attitude and feeling.

But Conrad's sources and the theme he drew from them imposed certain definite limitations upon his method of character presentation, limitations which, given the nature of the book, are not necessarily to be viewed as faults. His characters are generally strong representative types in terms of race, status, occupation and history, and they are types which stand out clearly in the history of South America. There are the racial types—the Spanish families, the people of mixed native and Indian blood, the representatives of European countries. Added to these characteristics are the typical kinds of men that he found in his sources—the army commander who attempts a coup, the bandit who is won over to the community, the liberal-minded statesmen who were at the mercy of a strong general or a powerful dictator, the keepers of inns and shops, the workers on the docks, the muleteers. And the Europeans also are seen in terms of their likely occupations—the Italian workmen, innkeepers and sailors, the English financiers, doctors, engineers, miners, superintendents of navigation companies. It is notable, for example, that Conrad says of the Gould family, who are English, that they have been 'liberators, explorers, coffee planters, merchants, revolutionists' in the country, and a book entitled *The English in South America*[17] shows Englishmen fulfilling all these functions on the continent. Characters are generally seen also in terms of their past lives, lives which are again related to historical events and themes. Thus Viola is seen in terms of his life with Garibaldi; Don José Avellanos in terms of his past life as a politician, diplomat and patriot, closely involved in his country's history; Charles Gould in terms of the history of the mine which is an important part of the affairs of Costaguana.

From his sources, Conrad took certain suggestions for characters which inevitably tended to typify them by race, social position and history. The sources provided little in terms of individual character—what little there was Conrad used, but he was clearly affected here both by his lack of personal experience and by the nature of his sources. And an outcome of this is the presentation of characters in almost allegorical postures. Thus Gould is noted for his strongly English characteristics: 'spare and tall, with a flaming moustache, a neat chin, clear blue eyes, auburn hair, and a thin, fresh, red face, Charles Gould looked like a new arrival from over the sea' (p. 46). Typical of English interest in the area, he is a representative of progress and material interests through the silver mine with which he is constantly associated. He is generally seen either going to it or coming back from it: 'either just "back from the mountain" or. . .on the point of starting "for the mountain"' (p. 112) as Conrad himself comments, and throughout the book this is his main posture (cf. pp. 48, 50, 69, 208). Don José Avellanos, the statesman whose active participation in politics is past but who is still influential, is constantly seen, again with symbolic appropriateness, seated in the rocking-chair in Mrs Gould's drawing-room commenting upon the affairs of the country (cf. pp. 50, 86, 99, 112, 141). Nostromo, until his experiences change him into a 'less picturesque figure', is constantly seen on his silver-grey horse, active, vigorous, a leader of men (cf. pp. 22, 95, 124, 185).

Conclusion

In terms of geography, history, economic growth, political events, the population in general and the main characters in particular, Conrad, true to his theory of imagination, derived the 'inner truth' from his source material. And a general impression of the human and the social condition would appear also to have arisen from his view of South America, that of 'events flowing from the passions of men short-sighted in good and evil'. The constant changes of direction in government, the revolutions, abortive attempts at 'progress', the periods of tyranny which were recorded in the books he read, suggested the 'inner truth' of his particular view of the area.

But this is too general a view for the purpose of moulding the source material he had in his possession. It is a force in the book, just as the influence of the 'typical' is a force. The most significant theme in the novel, however, a theme which derives from the protagonist, the province of Sulaco, is that of the dominance of 'material interests' and 'material progress' in this society. As Conrad continued to study the available literature on the South American continent it would gradually be impressed upon him (this was my own experience as I waded through the literature of the period) that the central concern of many of the books was 'material interests' and he must have seen therefore that this must form the 'features and character' of his novel; the silver mine had to be sited in the Occidental Province and the characters and events grouped about the mine, the symbol of 'material interests'. The plot demonstrates the struggle to protect 'material interests' in the shape of the mine, the success of those interests in terms of material progress, and the effect of such interests upon the various characters. Largely, there is little questioning by the characters in the novel of the value and rightness of a devotion to material interests—but the sacrifice of a Decoud and a Hirsch, the corruption of

356

a Nostromo, the empty life of Mrs Gould, the deaths in the revolution are the facts which ultimately militate against the general optimism that surrounds the material progress of Sulaco. The optimism is seen particularly in Captain Mitchell's comments to the 'privileged passenger' in which everything and everybody in Sulaco is of the best: 'the "Treasure House of the World"...was saved intact for civilisation—for a great future, sir'. It is Dr Monygham who most firmly and ominously sounds the other side of the theme: 'There is no peace and no rest in the development of material interests. They have their law, and their justice. But it is founded on expediency, and is inhuman; it is without rectitude, without the continuity and the force that can be found only in a moral principle.'

From several sources Conrad might have found the phrase 'material interests', the theme of economic progress, the idea of that progress being connected with foreigners and their capital, and the sense of unquestioning optimism surrounding it. Writing of Brazil in 1863, Thomas Woodbine Hinchliff comments: 'Roads and railroads in many directions, are affording immense assistance to the material progress of Brazil.'[18] An article in the *Proceedings of the Royal Geographical Society* on a proposed railway route across the Andes deals with the evidence supplied by Mr Wheelwright (himself a possible source for Holroyd in the novel), and there is the comment: 'his paper was not the production of a mere speculator, but contained the project of a man thoroughly acquainted with the material interests of the South-American continent'.[19] Wilfred Latham's book, *States of the River Plate*,[20] has as its thesis the optimism about material progress that is questioned by Dr Monygham. He writes of the influence of returning political exiles who 'had come in contact with a more advanced civilisation, and learned in adversity to appreciate constitutional order and industrial development...

[they] understood...the application of the principles of political progress and economic science', having been with men born to 'the knowledge and habit of material progress and constitutional freedom'.[21] And he also states 'foreigners have exercised a direct material influence on...these countries'.[22] He sees the material progress deriving from 'the influences of an essentially practical age' in terms of investment, industrial development, establishing of railways, development of steamer services, and considers that 'confusion and disorder' cannot now recur.[23] The Governor, he records, helps to further 'the material interests of his province'. Thomas J. Hutchinson[24] comments:

unless in time of civil (?) war, men with stout hearts and strong hands, keeping themselves clear of the political squabbles of the peoples, can get on in the River Plate territories to a position of independence as well as in any new state of the world. Every day's experience shows us this. For a convincing proof whereof, I can point to the fact, that nine-tenths of the material progress and industrial development of these fine territories are entirely owing to the introduction of foreign capital, energy, industry, and intelligence,—an amalgam of items, in which I regret to say, the native element is sadly deficient.

The unquestioning optimism surrounding the idea of material progress here is obviously a reflection of a contemporary attitude, but Conrad could not use it in such an unquestioningly optimistic way. It may very well be that his questioning of the movement of material interests derived from Garibaldi's own attitude to progress and its relentlessness. Reflecting upon the effects of Spanish suppression on the people, Garibaldi comments: 'the Indians bequeathed ...enemies much more tenacious, much more dangerous... than the destroyed savages, seeing that they were not sustained by a religious belief...but...by a material interest, which went on augmenting every hour'.[25]

Conrad's source books in this instance, therefore, provided

not only hints for characters and situations but also suggestions for the significant themes of the novel. I have pointed out earlier how Eastwick's book contributes to the background of 'material interests', Garibaldi's life to the theme of selfless humanitarianism, and Masterman's book to the ever-present corruption of tyranny and cruelty. Conrad's own contribution to these aspects of the novel appears in muted but significant form—Monygham's views on material interests, the sweep of the plot itself with its movement towards restlessness and change and strife, and the author's own comment on the great variety of activity of the *Nostromo* canvas: 'In our activity alone do we find the sustaining illusion of an independent existence as against the whole scheme of things of which we form a helpless part' (p. 497).

And so, just as when he was dealing with the colonisation and exploitation of Africa he was able to perceive the truth that lay behind the contemporary glorification of a certain political movement and as a result bring out the underlying irony of the situation, in dealing with the contemporary devotion to material progress he was able to observe the delusion that lay at the heart of that devotion and again to bring it out in ironic commentary.

*

Nostromo is remarkable for its objective presentation of the affairs of Costaguana. Apart from a certain delighted absorption in the fictional republic, its concerns and people, Conrad's 'sojourn' appears to have been one during which the quality of sympathetic imagination was working freely, and we have to note what is in reality a personal involvement in his fictional world through the figure of Decoud. Perhaps by this projection Conrad was more able to make real an experience which was drawn almost entirely from reading.

Conclusion

That the process of 'imagination' which involved such complete exploration by Conrad of his source material was essential to him for the creation of the 'true' fiction is shown, in a negative fashion by its absence, in the short stories. Those short stories based upon the same source material as the major works—anarchy, the Congo, South America—are inferior productions partly because Conrad kept very close to the original source without a great deal of transmutation. As a result, story, character and theme can be seen quite easily in the source material, and especially whatever is crude or macabre there appears so in the story. Themes particularly, and the author's attitudes, stand out rigid and bony. This indicates, I think, that in such stories Conrad was not concerned to make the imaginative effort required to allow the 'inner truth' to develop, round which he could mould the rest of the work.

The short stories can, therefore, be regarded as an early stage of composition, a stage where themes and character have been determined but where deeper subtleties of interpretation and understanding are missing. The first published version of *The Secret Agent* in *Ridgway's Militant Weekly* would seem to represent a similar stage. All the elements of the final version are there, the characters stand in their final groupings—the anarchists, the police, Verloc, Winnie and Stevie. The basic themes and attitudes are present—the impotent fanaticism of the anarchists, the idea of the 'game', Winnie Verloc's maternal devotion and conviction that certain things won't stand looking into.

We can see particularly at this level that Conrad's use of his source material in anarchist writings, police memoirs and the inane, pointless and macabre anarchist incident was controlled by his strong attitude to revolutionaries: 'The revolutionary spirit is mighty convenient in this, that it frees one from all scruples as regards ideas. Its hard, absolute optimism is repulsive to my mind by the menace of fanaticism and intolerance it contains. No doubt one should smile at these things; but...all claim to special righteousness awakens in me that scorn and anger from which a philosophical mind should be free...'[26] The 'inner truth' that Conrad sought in the anarchist material was only part of the truth, and a part chosen because it suited his preconceived ideas. The use of Liebknecht's classification of anarchists as a basis for the characterisation of the anarchists is an indication of prejudgement. The irony inherent in the figure of Michaelis is obtained through that very complexity of method which created him, in that Conrad is not giving, in the case of any one source, the full moral impact that the source implied. The *suffering* Davitt underwent in prison does not become the motivating force for Michaelis, whose prison experiences are rather smoothed over and civilised by such comment as 'He had come out of a highly hygienic prison round like a tub...as though for fifteen years the servants of an outraged society had made a point of stuffing him with fattening foods in a damp and lightless cellar' (p. 41); the 'saintliness' of Davitt, the uniqueness of his experiences and character, is counteracted by the addition of Bakunin's grotesque, physical appearance; the solitary confinement of Davitt results in the conception of a man no longer able to communicate with others: 'He was no good in discussion...the mere fact of hearing another voice disconcerted him painfully, confusing ...these thoughts that for so many years...no living voice had ever combatted' (p. 45).

The method is interesting, not only because of its complexity, but because of its paradox. Although Conrad did not move far from revolutionary records, it is in his use of such records that 'distortion' of his account of anarchy begins. We must nevertheless concede that Conrad is reflecting with a certain amount of accuracy aspects of the world of anarchy of that time. The final distortion, of course, lies in bringing together so many 'extreme' examples at one time and making each one a posturing, but impotent, egoist.

Ridgway's had, perhaps, some justification for calling the early version of the novel 'A Tale of Diplomatic Intrigue and Anarchist Treachery'. But even in this early version, the significant addition to Conrad's source material is present in the figures of Stevie and Winnie Verloc, for which characters there were only hints in his sources. The only reference to the reaction of Samuels's wife to the death of her brother that I have been able to find is in the letter by Mrs Bevington. Mrs Bevington describes how, after the death of Bourdin, when Samuels had visited her and proceeded to give instructions for making and charging bombs, she 'asked Mrs. Samuels what she thought of all this!! "Oh, it is all right", she said; "I should have objected only a little while ago; but not now I understand the question better."'[27] Had this been Winnie Verloc's reaction, *The Secret Agent* would have been contained within the bounds of the anarchist world, with all that it implied, at least in Conrad's view, of actions and ideas unrelated to anything but their own futility.

Conrad claimed that it was 'the dawning conviction of Mrs. Verloc's maternal passion' that finally put into correct perspective the story of the bomb outrage, of the anarchists and police: 'The figures grouped about Mrs. Verloc and related directly or indirectly to her tragic suspicion that "life doesn't stand much looking into", are the outcome of that very necessity' of telling her story.[28] The further development of what Conrad obviously came to understand as the 'inner truth' of his source material transforms the early version into the completed novel. And it is the 'inner truth' of Winnie's maternal devotion that gives the world of anarchists and police their right proportion within the moral framework of the novel. Conrad denied the novel's social, political or philosophical intentions, but conceded that 'It may even have some moral significance.'[29] The moral significance lies in the recognition that within the world of intrigue and violence of a political and secret kind there could be a private passion as great as Winnie Verloc's, held in greater secrecy than any other in the novel, inspirer of the greatest of all intrigues, and instigator ultimately of the greatest violence. The anarchists are set against, and the bomb explosion takes its significance from, the silently held, totally natural and instinctive but potentially disruptive, maternal passion of Winnie Verloc. The true secret agent in the world of the anarchists is not Verloc but Winnie, whose tool he is: 'This woman, capable of a bargain the mere suspicion of which would have been infinitely shocking to Mr. Verloc's idea of love' (p. 259).

But Conrad also claimed that the novel is '*purely a work of imagination*',[30] and since this, in his mind, debars the possibility of 'invention' one wonders where he discovered the source for Winnie's maternal passion and silence. Conrad wrote, 'Personally I have never had any doubt of the reality of Mrs. Verloc's story',[31] which would imply that he saw her reaction as the 'true' reaction to the tragedy, and also that he had grounds in reality for this view.

Although I believe the Kriegers' marital situation was the basis of the Verlocs', the strength of Winnie's character would seem to suggest the imposition of a nearer and more fully comprehended model. It seems to me possible that there existed the suggestion for Winnie's character in Conrad's life at the time of writing *The Secret Agent*, that it concerned him acutely, at least at that time, and that he saw its relevance to the book he was writing.

There is, to begin with, a small incident in the novel which seems to lead back to an incident in Conrad's personal life which is connected with his wife and his son, Borys. In

Conclusion

January of 1904, when the Conrads were in London, Jessie 'slipped the cartilage of both knees', an accident which was ultimately to make her a permanent cripple. In one of the previously unknown letters to Krieger dated 15 March 1904, parts of which I have quoted already, Conrad writes:

On top of all that [his nerves all to pieces, his worry over the loss of £250 after the Watson bank failure] my wife had a nasty fall in the street and wrenched both her knee-caps. There was an awful business with doctors, nurses, massage, surgical implements and all that. She just can crawl about now, and is gone back to the Pent [Farm]; but I am afraid that for all practical purposes she will remain a cripple.[32]

While they were in London and living at 99b Addison Road, it was arranged for Jessie to go into a nursing home for an operation on her knee. Jessie herself gives an account of the operation and the effect of the event on her 'supersensitive husband':

Next November we went again to London and an operation was decided upon. That Nursing Home was a nightmare and I have only horror of the first time I had faced a surgeon's knife.

Then after a few hours spent in the vain effort to rest, I departed for the Nursing Home with my husband and small son. It was practically my first parting with the boy and I had hard matter to keep a straight face. But the child with a wisdom beyond his years stayed only a few moments after they had seen me in bed, before he assumed control of the business with a mature 'Come along, Dadda', and marched his parent out of the house.

I have a hazy notion that the Nursing Home was at the end of a cul-de-sac, at any rate, Joseph Conrad's restless walk up and down seemed restricted by the end of the road. He told me when it was all over and he was allowed to see me, that he must have acted subconsciously part of the time he waited, and when he found himself he was standing in front of an old dray-horse with his arms literally round the animal's neck. The carter stood by all the time apparently divided in his mind as to whether the swell was hopelessly mad or merely intoxicated. He shook his head ominously, but accepted the half-crown which was offered him with injunctions to give the old horse an extra feed of corn. He pocketed the money with a wink and grumbled discontentedly. 'He's

364

broken-winded, that's what he is, an' he can't eat 'ay. I'll 'av ter get rid of 'im, too 'spensive'. He took up the reins and clambered into the cart, touching his cap and muttering: 'Extra feed indeed, I'll watch it.'[33]

From her earlier account of this incident we learn that Conrad waited outside in the street for three hours while the operation took place and eventually found himself 'brought up close against the nose of an old dray horse'.[34] I think we have here, in Conrad's own experience of taking his wife and her son to the nursing home, the source of that incident in *The Secret Agent* when the mother of Winnie Verloc leaves Verloc's home for the last time, accompanied by Winnie and Stevie and on her way to the Charity Home. During the ride, as it is described in Chapter 8, they are driven off 'on what might well be supposed the last cab drive of Mrs. Verloc's mother's life'. The horse, as in the case of the one Conrad found his arms around during his wife's operation, is 'infirm', 'with the harness hung over his sharp backbone flapping very loose about his thighs' (p. 156). Stevie tried to stop the driver from whipping his horse: 'Don't whip', 'Mustn't whip', and the driver considers the possibility of 'Stevie being a drunken young nipper' and this is what, according to Jessie, the driver thought was the matter with Conrad. When they arrive, Winnie pays the cabman 'four one-shilling pieces' while in Conrad's case, the cabman 'accepted the half-crown', 'pocketed the money with a wink and grumbled discontentedly'. Conrad's strange attention to the old horse which is broken-winded appears to be developed by him into the attention which Stevie bestows on the horse in the story:

'Oh! 'Ere you are, young fellow,' he [the cabman] whispered. 'You'll know him again—won't you?'

Stevie was staring at the horse, whose hind quarters appeared unduly elevated by the effect of emaciation. The little stiff tail seemed to have been fitted in for a heartless joke; and at the other end the thin, flat neck, like a plank covered with old horse-hide, drooped to the ground under the weight of an enormous bony head. The ears hung at different angles, negligently; and the macabre figure of that mute dweller on the earth steamed straight up from ribs and backbone in the muggy stillness of the air.

The cabman struck lightly Stevie's breast with the iron hook protruding from a ragged, greasy sleeve.

'Look 'ere, young feller. 'Ow'd *you* like to sit behind this 'oss up to two o'clock in the morning p'raps?'

Stevie looked vacantly into the fierce little eyes with red-edged lids.

'He ain't lame', pursued the other, whispering with energy. 'He ain't got no sore places on 'im. 'Ere he is. 'Ow would *you* like—'

His strained, extinct voice invested his utterance with a character of vehement secrecy. Stevie's vacant gaze was changing slowly into dread.

'You may well look! Till three and four o'clock in the morning. Cold and 'ungry. Looking for fares...' A silence reigned, during which the flanks of the old horse, the steed of apocalyptic misery, smoked upwards in the light of the charitable gas-lamp.

The cabman grunted, then added in his mysterious whisper:

'This ain't an easy world.'

Stevie's face had been twitching for some time and at last his feelings burst out in their usual concise form.

'Bad! Bad!' (pp. 165–7).

It is, perhaps, significant that Mrs Verloc's mother is a cripple: 'her swollen legs rendered her inactive' and that at the time Conrad was writing the novel Jessie Conrad was also virtually a cripple. In the original incident, there would be Conrad and his wife and Borys their child who, at the time of the journey to the nursing home, would have been almost seven years of age. Stevie's language, although he is an adult, is unusually juvenile and Conrad may have been recalling Borys's talk with the cabman.

Apart from this personal experience of Conrad, there is a certain similarity between the character of Jessie Conrad as it is revealed in her books on her husband and that of Winnie Verloc. Winnie has an 'air of unfathomable indifference', an 'unfathomable reserve'. After Stevie's death, Verloc suddenly exclaims:

Conclusion

I know your deaf-and-dumb trick. I've seen you at it before today...
There's no saying how much of what's going on you have got hold of
on the sly with your infernal don't-care-a-damn way of looking nowhere
in particular, and saying nothing at all...You have a devilish way of
holding your tongue sometimes...Enough to make some men go mad.
It's lucky for you that I am not so easily put out as some of them would
be by your deaf-and-dumb sulks. I am fond of you (pp. 256–8).

Now Jessie Conrad's self-confessed method of dealing with
the difficulties that arose in living with a man of Conrad's
genius was that of holding her tongue, and this method rested
upon a quality of mind which, she says, contributed to
'future understanding': 'Indeed I owe much to my calm
placid temperament, that was in the end such a sound
foundation for our future understanding.'[35] After two years
of marriage, when his son Borys was seven months old,
Conrad still hoped to return to the sea. Clearly Jessie feared
the consequences of such an act but her method of dealing
with the situation is Winnie Verloc's: 'I would never have
raised a dissenting voice...I carefully refrained from the
least show of satisfaction when he finally relinquished the
idea of going to sea and settled down to his writing table.'[36]
Jessie's habit was not to react to any provocation (except
where her children were concerned), not to explain, but to
remain silent. Chased with her child by 'three sinister
figures', and only saved by the arrival of the policeman of
the village, she was delayed in joining her husband who was
staying at the home of Edward Garnett, but she remarks:
'I said nothing on my telegram as to the cause.'[37] In the
ramshackle trap which carried Jessie to their apartments for
a fortnight (Conrad remained apart from her in the Garnett's
home) the journey is passed in silence: 'I forbore to make
any remark because I distrusted my powers of speaking in
a natural voice.'[38] On Conrad grumbling that she had brought
too much luggage for a fortnight's stay, Jessie 'held' her
'peace'.[39] 'I discovered', she confesses, 'that my complacency

was the very best weapon of defence.'[40] Going out into the garden one night to collect a cauliflower in order to make Conrad a meal, Jessie came into terrified contact with a tramp stealing from the garden. Having recorded this event, she goes on to remark: 'I said no word of my unpleasant adventure when I took my little dish upstairs. Not even when I was reproached for the "unconscionable time I had taken over such a trifle".'[41] Learning that a mad man was loose and wanted to attack Conrad because of a slight he felt he recognised in Conrad's story 'Falk', Jessie decides 'to keep everything' to herself.[42] On the occasion in Lyons when Conrad thought his wallet had been stolen, only to have it found by his wife under the bolster, she records: 'All was peace once more, but he insisted that we should get along to Geneva as quickly as possible. "Out of this infernal place, where one gets robbed in the night." I forbore to correct him, and left the room.'[43]

In terms of physical appearances, there are also some similarities between Winnie and Jessie Conrad. When she meets Verloc initially, 'Winnie Verloc was a young woman with a full bust, in a tight bodice, and with broad hips. Her hair was very tidy. Steady-eyed...she preserved an air of unfathomable indifference' (p. 5). Verloc is attracted by 'her youth; her full, rounded form; her clear complexion; the provocation of her unfathomable reserve' (p. 6).* In bed her 'ample form [is] defined vaguely under the counterpane' (p. 177): 'Looking out of the corners of his eyes, he saw her ample shoulders draped in white, the back of her head, with the hair done for the night in three plaits tied up with black tapes at the ends...She moved not, massive and shapeless like a recumbent statue in the rough' (p. 179).

---

* Borys Conrad, Conrad's eldest son, writes of his mother: 'Complete imperturbability and apparent lack of emotion under any circumstances...remained with her throughout her life. This unassailable placidity was almost frightening at times' (*My Father: Joseph Conrad*, London, 1970, p. 18).

Conclusion

Jessie Conrad was also plump (and steady-eyed) as a young woman and put on weight over the years. The photographs taken in 1889 and 1908 (see Jessie Conrad, *Joseph Conrad and his Circle*, pp. 88–9) show this. Indeed, Jessie Conrad herself recalls Conrad's comments on her size: 'Alas! I am not and never was a fairy. Joseph Conrad used to tease me by saying that "he knew when he got married that he had quality, but he had been specially favoured because in a few years he had quantity as well".'[44] Now it is important to remember that, already well-endowed, during pregnancy Jessie Conrad must have been enormous, and we know that Conrad was writing *The Secret Agent* during his wife's second pregnancy. Physical size, obesity, corpulence are endemic in *The Secret Agent*. Guerard was the first to notice that 'whether we look to the left or to the counterrevolutionary right, [poor humanity] is overcome by fatness as by a plague'.[45]

It is possible that this aspect of the novel was connected with his wife's pregnancy and her general tendency to largeness which, at least at that time, was related to deeper emotions in Conrad's relationship with his wife. Certainly Jessie Conrad appears to have had a strongly developed maternal instinct, one which was capable of including not only her children but Conrad as well:

And I may say that already on my part there was, even then [she means at the beginning of her marriage when Mrs Conrad was twenty-three and Conrad was fifteen years her senior], a great deal of maternal feeling for that lonely man who had hardly known anything of a mother's care.[46]

In a very short time all my maternal instincts were centred upon the man I was to marry, he became to me as much a son as a husband.[47]

I realised that here was my chance to prove my worth as wife and mother of this author. His dependence upon me touched my maternal instincts, and to the end of his life I remained a willing buffer between him and the outside world.[48]

We had two very small beds, side by side, but that night he wanted mothering and thought my shoulder the best resting place for his poor head.[49]

Jessie Conrad's reminiscences about Conrad constantly stress her 'double position of mother as well as wife'. The great difference in age between them might have led to a certain suggestion of a father/daughter relationship, but it did not. Conrad often signed himself 'Your boy' in writing to his wife.

Conrad, when he married, was determined that there would be no children, and this led to Jessie's mother's puzzlement as to why he wanted to marry her daughter: 'No family. Then why want to get married?'[50] But Jessie records:

The next event that loomed large upon our horizon was the prospect that I was to become a mother...I had a very clear notion that my husband was not exactly pleased...It seemed to me that I had played him false as it were...I wondered what would happen afterwards. Could I continue to fill this post of general guardian of my husband's peace and do my duty to my child. I saw quite plainly that my allegiance must be somewhat divided.[51]

And it is certainly difficult not to arrive at the conclusion that Conrad saw his own son as usurping some of the mother love which he felt rightly his. Conrad's attitude towards the new arrival expresses itself in a particularly nonchalant manner. In a long letter to Cunninghame Graham a reference to the birth of his first child, Borys, appears in the postscript and then only to explain why his letter missed the morning post: 'This letter missed this morning's post because an infant of male persuasion arrived and made such a row that I could not hear the Postman's whistle.'[52]

Conrad's second child, John, was born on 2 August 1906, while Conrad was working on *The Secret Agent*, that novel being completed early in November. Jessie Conrad recalls: 'While we were awaiting his [John's] arrival there, Conrad was finishing the first and shorter version of *The Secret Agent*. As I did not know in the least what the book was about, I could not account to myself for the grimly ironic expression I used to catch on his face, whenever he came to give me a look-in. Could it have reference to the expected baby? No! it was only a reflection of the tone of the book's'.[53] But Conrad's 'grimly ironic expression' may well have had reference to the expected baby. Conrad's full awareness of the force of that maternal instinct that had first attracted him to Jessie and then outwitted him by producing two children, occurring at a time when he was writing the novel, extended the range of his source material by the addition of very necessary personal and intimate perceptions. And if something of Jessie went into the creation of Winnie, it is likely that a little of Conrad also went into the creation of Verloc.[54] He must have appreciated to the full the irony of the situation in which he found himself, and have derived from it the 'inner truth' that in the macabre and amoral world of *The Secret Agent* a 'maternal passion' was likely to be a more potent force than police or anarchists or secret agents. Thus, once again, Conrad was able to go deeper than the contemporary political concern with which he was dealing, seeing that beneath it, stronger and much silenter, lay the potential of natural human instincts.

We can conclude, I think, that the creative process in the case of each of these major works was the same, whether the source material was personal experience or found in books. It began with a necessary immersion by Conrad in an imaginative sense in order to bring out the 'inner truth' of the material and was followed by the fleshing-out of the 'features and character' with the appropriate facets of the source material. It was clearly, for Conrad, an exhausting and difficult method of creation. His sense of artistic duty is more than a little awe-inspiring but it stems from his conception of the high nature of his calling as a writer. And his intellectual grasp of what he was attempting to achieve is exactly stated by him at the end of the first chapter of *A Personal Record*:[55] 'An imaginative and exact rendering of authentic memories may serve worthily that spirit of piety towards all things human which sanctions the conceptions of a writer of tales.'

APPENDICES

NOTES

INDEX

APPENDIX A

JOHANNES FREIESLEBEN'S DEATH CERTIFICATE*

L'an mil huit cent *quatre vingt dix*, le *trente et unième jour* du mois de *Mai*, devant nous *De Chièvre Fr. X.* Officier de l'Etat-Civil, à *Léopoldville*, ont comparu les nommés *Jules Vanden Boyaude* [?] âgé de — ans *Comd^re de district* et *Keyaert Alphonse* âgé de *38* ans —, lesquels nous ont déclaré que le nommé *Freiesleben Johannes* âgé de *vingt neuf* ans *Capitaine de Steamer* domicilié à *Kinchassa* est décédé à *Tchumbiri* [?] le *29me* jour du mois de *Janvier* mil huit cent *quatre vingt dix*.

Le défunct était *célibataire*; il était né à *Oltesboka* [?] (*Danemark*) [?]; ses père et mère sont *Christian et Elise* [indecipherable].

Les pièces suivantes ont été présentées par les comparants:

....

En foi de quoi le présent procès-verbal a été signé par nous et les témoins après que connaissance leur en a été donné.

Signature des témoins   L'Officier de l'Etat-Civil
(s) *J. Vanden Boyaude*   (s) *F. De Chièvre*
(s) *A. Keyaerts*

* This death certificate is transcribed from the original document; italic is used to show hand-written script.

375

APPENDIX B

MOVEMENT OF SHIPPING THROUGH BANGALA*

MOUVEMENT DU PORT DE BANGALA

Du 1ᵉʳ janvier au 10 juin 1890

M. Hodister, chef du district commercial de Bangala, pour la *Société du Haut-Congo*, nous envoie un intéressant tableau. C'est le mouvement du port de Bangala depuis le commencement de l'année jusqu'au 10 juin, c'est-à-dire jusqu'au moment du départ du dernier courrier. Comme on le voit, le va et vient des steamers est déjà important sur cette partie du haut fleuve, où le premier bateau à vapeur n'a fait son apparition que depuis l'année 1884.

Sous le rapport des pavillons, les entrées se décomposent comme suit: 11 belges (*Société du Haut-Congo*), 8 congolais (État) 6 hollandais, 3 français (Daumas et Cⁱᵉ) et 1 anglais (mission).

Dates d'arrivée	Noms des steamers	Nationalité	Venant de	Chargement
Janvier				
6	Holland	Hollandais	Falls	
11	Florida	Belge	—	Ivoire
12	Général Sanford	—	—	—
13	Stanley	Congolais	Léopoldville	Articles d'Europe
25	Ville de Gand	—	Bangala	
29	Général Sanford	Belge	Equateur	Articles d'Europe
Février				
6	Peace	Anglais	Bolobo	—
10	Holland	Hollandais	Kinchassa	—
10	Ville de Liége	Congolais	Léopoldville	—
15	France	Français	Brazzaville	—
16	Général Sanford	Belge	Mongala	Ivoire
19	Florida	—	Kinchassa	Articles d'Europe
25	Ville de Gand	Congolais	Malinga	
Mars				
6	France	Français	Oupoto	
19	Stanley	Congolais	Falls	
19	Ville de Bruxelles	—	Léopoldville	Articles d'Europe
20	Florida	Belge	Falls	Ivoire
Avril				
5	Général Sanford	—	Mobéka	
7	Frédérick	Hollandais	Kinchassa	Articles d'Europe
20	Holland	—	—	
21	Ville de Gand	Congolais	Malinga	—

* Published in the *Mouvement! Géographique*: spelling as in original.

Movement of shipping through Bangala

Dates d'arrivée	Noms des steamers	Nationalité	Venant de	Chargement
Mai				
7	Frédérick	Hollandais	Falls	Ivoire
11	Roi des Belges	Belge	Kinchassa	Articles d'Europe
15	Florida	—	—	—
20	Holland	Hollandais	Falls	Ivoire
30	Ville de Gand	Congolais	Malinga	
Juin				
5	Roi des Belges	Belge	Falls	Ivoire
6	France	Français	Brazzaville	Articles d'Europe
10	Général Sanford	Belge	Mongala	Ivoire

LE PORT DE BANGALA
Mouvement du 11 juillet au 13 octobre 1890

Dates d'arrivée	Noms des steamers	Nationalités	Venant de	Dates de départ	Allant à
Juillet				Juillet	
11	Ville de Bruxelles	État ind. du Congo	Léopoldville	13	Basoko
	Général Sanford	Belge	Léopoldville	17	Stanley-Falls
24	Holland	Hollandaise	Stanley-Falls	24	Kinchassa
25	Peace	Anglaise	Bolobo	26	Upoto
29	Frédéric	Hollandaise	Kinchassa	29	Mobeka
Août				Août	
2	Frédéric	Hollandaise	Mobeka	4	Kinchassa
7	France	Française	Lulunga	8	Mobeka
11	France	Française	Mobeka	12	Brazzaville
11	Ville de Gand	État ind. du Congo	Léopoldville	13	Itimbiri
14	Peace	Anglaise	Upoto	14	Bolobo
19	Roi des Belges	Belge	Kinchassa	20	Stanley-Falls
22	Henry Reed	Anglaise	Lulunga	22	Kinchassa
25	Ville de Bruxelles	État ind. du Congo	Upoto	26	Léopoldville
27	Holland	Hollandaise	Kinchassa	27	Stanley-Falls
Septembre				Septembre	
5	Frédéric	Hollandaise	Lulunga	5	Mobeka
8	Ville de Gand	État ind. du Congo	Basoko		
8	Frédéric	Hollandaise	Mobeka	10	Kinchassa
8	Ville de Gand	État ind. du Congo		10	Lulunga
12	Ville de Gand	État ind. du Congo	Lulunga		
15	Roi des Belges	Belge	Stanley-Falls	16	Kinchassa
	Ville de Gand	État ind. du Congo		16	Mongala
21	France	Française	Lulunga	22	Mobeka
23	Holland	Hollandaise	Stanley-Falls	23	Kinchassa
24	France	Française	Mobeka	25	Brazzaville
Octobre					
3	Ville de Gand	État ind. du Congo	Mongala		
13	Général Sanford	Belge	Loma		

APPENDIX C

KLEIN'S DEATH CERTIFICATE*

L'an mil huit cent *quatre vingt onze*, le *vingt-huitième jour* du mois de *Juillet*, devant nous *De Chièvre François-Xavier* Officier de l'Etat-Civil, a *Léopoldville*, ont comparu les nommés *Koch Ludwig* âgé de — ans *capitaine steamer* et *Dryepondt Gustave* âgé de — ans *Docteur de l'Etat*, lesquels nous ont déclaré que le nommé *Klein Georges* âgé de — ans *agent de la Société Anonyme Belge* domicilié à *Paris* est décédé à *bord Steamer Roi des Belges* (*Tchumbiri*) le *21ᵐᵉ* jour du mois de *Septembre* mil huit cent *quatre vingt dix*.

Le défunct était *célibataire*; il était né à —; ses père et mère sont —.
Les pièces suivantes ont été présentées par les comparants:

En foi de quoi le présent procès-verbal a été signé par nous et les témoins après que connaissance leur en a été donné.

Signature des témoins	L'Officier de l'Etat-Civil
(s) *Dr. G. Dryepondt*	(s) *F. De Chièvre*
(s) *Ludwig Koch*	

* This death certificate is transcribed from the original document; italic is used to show hand-written script.

APPENDIX D

THE GREENWICH MYSTERY!*

It was on Thursday, Feb. 15th, 1894, at twenty to five in the afternoon, that the sound of a terrible explosion was heard in Greenwich Park, close to Royal Observatory. A park-keeper and some school boys rushed to the spot where the smoke rose lazily among the trees, and there they found the body of a young man.

'He could hardly have been more than 22. The hair and moustache were silky and fair, he had no beard, his eyes were blue. The left hand was absolutely blown to pieces, the right hand was small and delicate. A remarkably short man, 5 ft. 1 in., well nourished and proportioned, but inadequately developed.'

This is a description of the body by a correspondent of the 'Times', it scarcely gives one the impression of a desperate character.

The body presented a frightful spectacle. His arm was blown to fragments, pieces of bone and flesh were lying about. He had a ghastly wound in his stomach, the bowels were protruding. 'Take me home' was all he could say to the park-keeper and school boys who found him. He died soon afterwards. In his pockets were found some papers including a ticket of membership of the Autonomie Club, that showed that his name was Martial Bourdin, well known among the Anarchists in London. But he was not a 'dangerous character'. He was universally looked upon as a quiet harmless young fellow, though wonderfully honest and sincere. He was no speaker, but he could sing, and he would often mount the platform at a dance or concert and sing 'The Camagnole'. He was a clever tailor, and earned three or four pound a week in the busy season. In fact, so strong was the opinion among those who knew him as to Bourdin's harmlessness, that there was a general outcry among them that he had been '*Murdered by the Police*'.

This event spread a panic in London, especially when it was announced that Bourdin was carrying 'a fairly well made bomb', the explosion of which had killed him.

It was the time of the explosions in France, and the world was ringing with the names of Valliant and Henry. It was believed that Bourdin was the agent of a serious conspiracy, and yet, strange to say, the police did

* Written and published by David Nicoll, Sheffield, 1897; spelling as in the original. Copy obtained from the trustees of the British Museum.

not lay hands on his accomplices. In fact, they acted in a very leisurely fashion, quite different to their usual prompt proceedings, in matters of this kind.

The body was found at twenty to five. The police authorities at Greenwich, doubtless, telegraphed at once a full description of the body to Mr. Robert Anderson or Inspector Melville of the Political Department, Scotland Yard. One of them might have been down at Greenwich and have identified the body by eight at the latest, and the houses of all known to be on intimate terms with Bourdin could have been raided in the dead of night and remarkable discoveries made. As to warrants. In a case of evident public peril, the political police can dispense with warrants as they did in the Walsall Case, when the capture of Deakin with a bottle of choloform, was followed by a raid on the Socialist club at Walsall, and the arrest of Charles and Cailes. But this was not done.

The police took their time. Although the morning papers on Friday contained an account of how an unknown young man had been found blown to pieces in Greenwich Park, yet the police took no action till nine on Friday night!

It is curious that after giving the conspirators *twenty four hours notice*, they then proceeded to raid the very places where they knew very well no conspirators could be found. Bourdin's lodgings and the Autonomie Club.

Why, their trusty agent, Auguste Coulon, could have told them better than that. In a communication sent to the 'Pall Mall Gazette' a few days before the Greenwich explosion, he states that 'The Anarchists feel the London police hold them in the hollow of their hands. *Doubtless those that have their misgivings about being watched are correct in their apprehensions*. There are few whose *dossiers* are not filled at Scotland Yard. Even the Autonomie Club, their chosen temple, is now *comparatively deserted*, as it is believed to be infested with mouchards.'—(Spies in English).

It appears from Coulon's statements to a reporter of the 'Morning Leader', February 20th, 1894, that he had been dogging the steps of Bourdin for some days, but he stated that on the fatal Thursday he was not following him.* It seems then, the police must have known that Bourdin was likely to be entrusted with explosives by someone, and therefore, they clearly had an informer in the ranks of the conspirators. How is it then that the rest of band were not arrested? *Was it because, as in the recent case of Bell, they were all in the pay of the police, with the exception of the victim?*

So the Greenwich Mystery is still a mystery. Let us see if we can

---

* See also 'The Anarchist', May, 1894.

throw a little light on it. Not many facts came out at the inquest, the police took good care of that. According to the evidence of a tram conductor, Bourdin came down to Greenwich by tram, he got there at 4.20 p.m. He evidently did not know the neighbourhood, as he went with the tram to the terminus, instead of getting out at the usual stopping place, close to the park gates. It seems, also, according to the statement of his brother, Henri Bourdin, that Bourdin had been out of work for sometime, and that when he called upon him on the morning of the fatal Thursday, his brother who was a small master, had no employment to give him. This was the last he had seen of him. Another gentleman had seen him later. 'In the course of the same afternoon', according to a reporter of the Press Association, 'he was observed in company with another man, in the neighbourhood of Hanover Square, and later on the two parted company in Whitehall, Bourdin then walking over Westminster Bridge and taking the tram to Greenwich.' Who was this unknown individual? And who took the trouble to follow him and Bourdin to Whitehall? A reporter or a detective?

Another gentleman was also interviewed, Mr. H. B. Samuels, then editor of the 'Commonweal'. 'The Central News' states that Samuels 'admitted that he had been in Bourdin's company at two o'clock, and had remained in his company "*a considerable time*". *He was surprised*', he said, '*that a sum of thirteen pounds in gold had been found in Bourdin's possession, and it was a complete mystery to him where he obtained it.* On the previous evening at the Restaurant where he generally supped, he left without paying, and the same thing occurred the day before that.' He continued, 'had not this unfortunate accident occurred, the consequences, I feel certain, would have been terrible. I don't mean that Bourdin intended to commit any outrage on Thursday, but I do think it was *the commencement of an extensive plot*. I have an idea, but I have no proof of its being correct, that the *manufacture of bombs for Continental purposes* has been going on here for some little time.'—'Sheffield D. T.', Feb. 19th.

This remarkable statement, naturally, spread terror among the timid middle class. And Conservative Newspapers, interested in laws, directed against the 'immigration of pauper aliens', raised at once an outcry. 'The Globe', for example, in a leader, declared that 'Society is asking how long the British metropolis will be content to afford a safe asylum for gangs of assassins, who there plot and perfect atrocious schemes for universal murder on the Continent. It is simply a disgrace to London, that Continental ruffianism of the most murderous type should be permitted to use the greatest city in the world as a base of operations.'

Col. Howard Vincent also seized on the occasion to ask a question, in the House of Commons, 'as to whether the Government proposed to place any restriction on foreign immigration.' The enemies of the right of asylum saw at once that the Greenwich explosion, and the statements of Mr. Samuels were a great help to them in the agitation.

Moreover, in the next number of the 'Commonweal', Mr. Samuels informs the public of his great intimacy with Bourdin. According to his account, they had been constant companions for years. Moreover, he is acquainted with the object of the conspiracy. After speaking in high praise of Bourdin, he says, 'Such a comrade was he that, at the age of 26, he undertook the conveyance of dangerous explosive compounds to a secluded spot, where none could have been injured, in order to put to the test, a new weapon of destruction, that could have furnished the revolutionary armoury with another means of terrorizing those who consciously or unconsciously consign so many innocent lives to destruction.'—'Commonweal', March 10th, 1894.

It is evident from this statement, that Bourdin was not only acting in conspiracy with others, but that Mr. Samuels knew all about it. Besides bragging of his intimacy with Bourdin, Mr. Samuels told the 'Central News' 'he was in Bourdin's company at two o'clock, and remained in his company for *a considerable time*. How long is a considerable time? Forty minutes! If so, Bourdin must have left him to start on his journey to Greenwich. As it is known Bourdin travelled by tram, it would have taken him from 2.40 to 4.20 p.m., one hour and forty minutes to reach Greenwich from Hanover Square. We have tested this by actual experiment. He was in Samuels' company at 2 p.m., and arrived at Greenwich at 4.20 according to the evidence of the tram conductor. Samuels was in his company 'a considerable time' after 2 p.m. Did the mysterious stranger, in Hanover Square, and Whitehall, bear any resemblance to Mr. Samuels? How did he escape arrest?

But let us take the statement about the object of Bourdin's visit to Greenwich Park. Did he go there to make experiments with 'a new weapon of destruction'. A man surely does not require £13 in gold for an experiment in Greenwich Park.

As to the new weapon of destruction, the fragments of 'a bottle of sulphuric acid' were found amid the wreck of the bomb. Colonel Majendie, in his evidence at the inquest, made a good deal of mystery about the contents of the bomb, but he stated that it was to be exploded by means of sulphuric acid. Now bombs exploded by sulphuric acid are no new thing. In the 'Manchester Sunday Chronicle' of Jan. 2nd, 1897, appears the following: (it is taken from a description of the bombs, etc., still preserved in Scotland Yard.)

The Greenwich Mystery

'Perhaps the most interesting infernal machine, is the bomb found on Daly. It was a terrible weapon in its time—a *metal* shell, upon which *the ends or lids were screwed.* This was a bomb to be thrown, and exploded on contact. Among its contents was a small piece of lead, which, upon the fall of the bomb, smashed a little *bottle containing sulphuric acid, the acid exploded a substance with which it came in contact.*'

Rather strange that Daly and Bourdin's bombs should resemble one another. According to the statements of Col. Majendie, and a representative of the 'Times', who examined the fragements. The bomb Bourdin carried was of metal, 'one of the fragments *grooved for a screw at one end*, it was not unlike *a piece of water pipe* burst by frost.' The correspondent adds, 'it had evidently been made by a skilled workman.' 'Times', Feb. 17th, 20th and 27th.

Like Daly, Bourdin carried his bomb in a brown paper parcel, and both are exploded by a bottle of sulphuric acid. The resemblance is marvellous. But Mr. Farndale, Chief Constable of Birmingham, stated that Daly's bomb was supplied to him by a police agent. Did Bourdin's bomb come from the same factory? A few passages from Mr. John Redmond's pamphlet 'The Case for Amnesty', will show that these cases resemble each other in more ways than one. 'On the 17th October, 1883, Daly went to Birmingham, and took up his residence under an assumed name in the house of his old friend James Egan, who at that time occupied a respectable position in a business firm in the city. Daly had long being [*sic*] the object of suspicion, on the part of the police, as a supposed Fenian. Inspector Stroud swore at the trial, that from the 11th of October, until the 9th of April, two days before his arrest, the police were never off his track for an hour; they never lost sight of him; and during all that time they "never saw him do anything calculated to arouse suspicion." They had followed Daly about seven months and had never seen him do anything suspicious.' Inspector Black said, 'I got information all the time about what he was doing. We never lost sight of him. On the 9th of April, Daly received a telegram, the contents of which were certainly known to the authorities, asking him, in the name of a man who had been years before associated with him in Fenianism, to go to Liverpool to meet him. Accordingly he went from Birmingham to Liverpool upon that day.' Inspector Black swore 'he was followed by detectives, as usual. In Liverpool, by some strange chance, the detectives "lost him", for the first time for seven months, and according to their evidence they knew nothing of his whereabouts or movements until eight o'clock on the morning of the 11th of April, although he was at the house of the man who sent the telegram, and though the telegram was in the hands of police. At 8 o'clock on the morning of April 11th, Daly appeared at the ticket office of the Birkenhead Railway Station. He was immediately surrounded by a score of plain clothes constables, arrested and searched, and a small parcel which he carried was taken from him and placed in a bag, which one of the constables had ready.'

There are several striking facts in the two cases which resemble each other. Bourdin had also, according to the informer Coulon in his Statement to a reporter of the 'Morning Leader', been watched for some time. Yet, on the fatal Thursday, Coulon did not follow him. Bourdin also carries a brown paper parcel which contains a bomb of a similar construction to that of Daly. In both cases the men who provided the explosives remain unarrested.*

But to quote Mr. Redmond In the year 1887, 'Chief Constable Farndale, the head of the police in Birmingham, who had been in command of the officers who never lost sight of Daly, *solemnly stated that Daly was the victim of a police plot, and the explosives found upon his person had been planted upon him by an agent of the Irish Police.* It seems' said Mr. Redmond 'that the Watch Committee of the Birmingham Corporation had blamed Mr. Farndale for not having arrested the man for whom Daly received the explosives at Liverpool, and that he excused himself by saying that this person was agent in the pay of Irish police.' Did Mr. Samuels owe his freedom from arrest for the same reason as Daly's 'friend'? But perhaps the police did not arrest Mr. Samuels. Because he was a person of such a quiet harmless disposition that he was incapable of conspiracy. Let us look into his previous record in the movement and see. I remember the night I first saw Samuels. It was on a Sunday, in 1886, just after Hyndman, Burns, Williams, and Champion, had been acquitted at the Old Bailey, on a charge of causing a riot in Trafalgar Square. I was present at a meeting held by the S.D.F., at a hall close to Gower street Station, which was addressed by Mr. Hyndman. A large audience had assembled, and the speaker had an enthusiastic reception. At the end of the speech, a pale young man with a dark moustache, and features of the Jewish type rose, and put several questions to the lecturer, supported by a mysterious German, in spectacles. He wanted to know certain things. Among others, what would happen in a city if the reservoirs supplying with water were blown up by dynamite? Hyndman, of course, replied that the inhabitants

---

* The activity of the Birmingham police is worth noticing in this case. Daly was arrested at 8.20 at Birkenhead, on Good Friday morning. Directly the news reached Birmingham, at 9 a.m., Egan's house was raided, and he was arrested, while all those intimate with Daly, had their houses searched by the police for explosives. Why did not Scotland Yard act as promptly after the Greenwich explosion?

1 (a) Conrad before starting for the Congo

1 (b) Hodister

2(*a*) Captain Albert Thys

2(*b*) Camille
Delcommune

3(*a*) Stanley Falls during a Governor-General's inspection

3(*b*) The fortified station at Basoko

4(*a*) Kinchassa station

4(*b*) Klein's grave

5 *Roi des Belges*

6　Alexandre Delcommune

7(*a*)   Cesar Cervoni

7(*b*) Helen Rossetti

7(*c*)   Sir William Harcourt

7(*d*)   Adolf Krieger

8(b) Chief Inspector Melville

8(a) Sir Howard Vincent

8(c) Martial Bourdin

would suffer from lack of water. The young man and the German then demanded why he did not advocate this action. To which Hyndman had no difficulty in replying. The young man worried the lecturer with further questions. And at the end of the heckling, Hyndman inquired the name of his adversary, he replied, 'Samuels'.

When the meeting was over, as the audience was pouring out from the hall, I was attracted by a group evidently in hot discussion. Samuels was in the midst of it, quarrelling with a Social Democrat, and he wound up by taking off his coat and offering to fight his opponent. We have often seen that coat taken off since, but we have never seen a fight yet.

It was a fine day in Hyde Park, during the early days of the Labour agitation in 1889, and some painters at Drury Lane Theatre were holding a meeting to protest against the employment of foreign workmen at the theatre. A crowd of Fair Trade roughs came to the Park; and it happened that the Socialist League were holding a meeting near the Marble Arch. Among the speakers was a German woman, and the roughs surrounded the meeting and broke it up. I remonstrated with one of the gang, and asked him if foreign labour interfered with his branch of industry. 'What is your work' I asked. 'Work, I don't do no work', he replied. 'I am not such a damned fool as that.' A little while after, the roughs formed in a mass near the Reformers Tree, indulging in wild horse play. And suddenly, we heard a still small voice in the midst of them preaching Socialism.

It was Samuels. And these roughs, who had manifested such a strong objection to Socialism, were wildly applauding. We thought little of this at the time, except to marvel at this young man's gallantry and eloquence. For a man who could convert roughs to Socialism, who were hired to bash Socialists, must possess wonderful pluck and genius. Unless, of course, in the orator they recognised a friend, a member of the same party?

Samuels was then in the Socialist League, and was active in the movement, but as his eloquence was highly explosive, he was not looked upon with great favour, by the quieter members of the League. He was at Leeds during the Gas Strike, and sent an account to the 'Commonweal', in which, after describing an attack on the police and troops, by the crowd, he said that 'If the people had the knowledge as they had the pluck, they might have finished off the lot'. It was this sort of language that had a good deal to do with driving William Morris out of the movement.

On another occasion, at a meeting in commemoration of the Chicago Martyrs, held at the Kay Street Radical Club, Samuels, who was fresh from Leeds, narrated how Robert Bingham had been tried, by Justice Grantham, for a speech, but acquitted. He declared that he and others had made up their minds, that if Robert Bingham had been convicted, to arm themselves with revolvers and to shoot the judge. Morris, who was present, and, who evidently regarded both speech and speaker with great dislike, declared that he did not sympathise with these extreme sentiments. I wonder whether Mr Samuels ever proposed this plot in Leeds.

After Morris left the League, Samuels disappeared, and did not return till a little before my arrest. He was very indignant with me for exposing Coulon, and declared that this course of action, would do the movement no good.

The 'Commonweal' died soon after my conviction, but was restarted under Samuels, as editor, in May 1893,* and it was on the point of death when I came out of prison. There was general disatisfaction at its tone and style, save among the 'Commonweal' group, which was not large. Perhaps a few extracts from the paper may give an idea why it was not popular. Here is one: 'Our comrade C. C. Davis, who was tried at Stafford Assizes for smashing a jeweller's shop at Birmingham, last January, has been sentenced to 15 months hard labour...His action proves to us the necessity of similar acts, and also the desirability on such occasions, not merely of throwing valuables into the street, *but of keeping as much as possible for the sustenance of persons and principles.* —'Commonweal', May 1st, 1893.

Though this statement received enthusiastic endorsement from the police organ 'L'International', which was started with money from Auguste Coulon, yet it was not so popular with the mass of the party. It must be clear to all that Mr. Samuels would degrade a bold act of revolt, on the part of a starving man, to the level of an ordinary theft. In reply to an article by Quelch, in 'Justice', he says, 'Smashing windows, robbing misers, coining counterfeit, or smuggling, are not means either to the end; but ends in themselves, and though we do not claim them as means —as Mr. Quelch seemingly does, still we welcome such acts of daring and lawlessness, as they do not strengthen but weaken the present machine of Government and exploitation.'—'Commonweal', Nov. 11th, 1893.

The following article in the 'Torch', of July, 1893, is also illustrative of Mr. Samuels' gospel. He is writing about 'Suicide', very common at that time. And he gives the person contemplating an act of this kind through misery, 'some good advice'. He tells him before he committs the rash act to kill a capitalist, or to 'take some one with him'.

---

* Actually in May 1892 'Arrangements were made to carry on our paper as usual H. Samuels being appointed publisher' (*Commonweal*, 14 May 1892). [N.S.]

The Greenwich Mystery

Hear this gentle philosopher:—'To study and search for the one who has caused the situation, or is responsible in a large or small degree for it, will always be a fruitless task, and will take too much time and energy. When one considers that society can be affected in a greater degree when the 'companion', is *not considered in any way responsible*, the duty of an intending suicide owes to himself and many other miserables is clear, if I must go then, I shall have company, if not a friend, then a stranger shall it be?'

Therefore, not the man, who has caused the mischief, shall the intending suicide strike, but a stranger, guilty of merely being a capitalist, or perhaps of wearing a high hat or frock coat!

And finally, here is the famous 'Bombs' article, published at the time of the Barcelona Outrage. 'A bomb has burst in a theatre at Barcelona, and the English people are trembling even now. Very strange, that an explosion a thousand miles away should arouse such mixed feelings here. Or is it because somebody said it was a good job. Well, I am one of them who welcome the affair as a great and good act—not on the part of those concerned, but *because of the death of thirty rich people* and the injury of eighty others. '*Yes, I am really pleased*; and in spite of the fact, *that comrades and friends have been talking at me over it, I cannot feel sorry there*.'—'Commonweal', Nov. 25th, 1803.

Writing of this description, is calculated to impress the public with the impression that Anarchists are simply a gang of thieves and cut throats, which was exactly the impression that Mr. Robert Anderson, Inspector Melville of Scotland Yard and the lying Scribes of the Capitalist press were endeavouring to produce. And lo they found an 'Anarchist' editor ready to second their laudable exertions. To prove their case they had only to point to the pages of the 'Commonweal'.

When I came out of prison, I was offered the editorship of the paper by a young admirer of Mr. Samuels, on condition that I would read through the files of the 'Commonweal', when edited by that great man, and adopt his principles and his policy. This I thought rather cool. And Mr. Samuels' policy did not please me. At a public meeting, held after my release, he insulted a number of friendly Social Democrats by calling them 'damned cowards'. And afterwards, at South Place, made his famous speech, which soon rendered him notorious in London.

'I claim the man who threw the bomb at the theatre as a comrade. We must have our own some day, they murdered our comrades, and we must murder them. Twenty three killed, how sad?.. An eye for an eye. Ay, twenty eyes for one eye. I claim that unknown comrade has done better work than any philosopher. He has caused such a terror that the rich dare not walk the streets of Barcelona for fear of the bombs. I don't believe in organising bodies of men to meet the Gatling guns. We will fight the bloodsuckers by any means. I don't blame these men, because they are bloodsuckers. I don't blame a dog, but I will kick him damned hard if he bites me. We expect no mercy from these men and we must show them none.'—'Morning Leader', Saturday, Nov. 12th, 1893.

This speech closed South Place Chapel to us, as the 'Bombs' article closed Trafalgar Square, thus we were prevented from explaining what our principles were, while the reptile press of the capitalist libelled and abused us, demanding the expulsion of all Anarchists from England.

I declined to edit the paper on these lines, and expressed my opinion pretty freely regarding Mr. Samuels. I said if he was not a spy, he was being used by one. I was therefore excommunicated by the 'Commonweal Group', though I was on good terms with most Anarchists in London. I can remember well, at a conference, held at the Autonomie, at Christmas, 1893, little Bourdin sitting at the feet of Samuels, and looking up into his eyes with loving trust. To the little man he was evidently a hero to be loved and revered. The last time I saw the poor little fellow, was about a fortnight before the fatal explosion. He was in the bar of the Autonomie, talking with Samuels, when he came up to me and asked me to send some copies of my pamphlet 'The Walsall Anarchists', then just published, to a French newsagent. Poor little chap, he little thought he was to be the next victim. I was then leaving London for a lecturing tour in Scotland. I never saw little Bourdin alive again.

But certainly from H. B. Samuels record the police could not have looked upon him as 'harmless'. How did he escape arrest when in Daly's case, the mere fact that Egan was a Fenian, and on terms of close intimacy with Daly, was sufficient to get him a long sentence of penal servitude? But soon an answer was found to this question. For not many months after the death of Bourdin, some new facts to light [*sic*], which can leave no doubt in the mind of any reasonable man as to the truth about the Greenwich Mystery.

It was towards the end of May that Samuels was working in company with another tailor whom we will call R —. This man was not an Anarchist or Socialist, although interested in the movement. Samuels was talking loudly of his knowledge of explosives, and declaring, moreover, that he had stuff of this kind in his possession, with which he could supply any one who desired to study the art of chemistry. This man did not believe Samuels knew as much as he professed about this difficult and dangerous subject and more in jest than earnest he asked him, if he could let him have some. To his great surprise his fellow workman appeared one day with a fairly large bottle containing some liquid, which Samuels stated was sulphuric acid. He poured out a small quantity in a phial, and gave it to this poor tailor, informing him at the same time he was going 'to distribute the rest to various acquaintances.' R — terribly alarmed at finding himself possessed of a liquid, which, under the just laws of England, might entitle him to ten or twenty years penal servitude, although he was quite innocent of intending to commit any serious offence, hastened to get rid of it. But that night, in the street, he met an acquaintance who was evidently in a high state of excitement. 'Have you heard the news', he exclaimed, 'Samuels has been giving explosives to J —, *and two days after J —'s house was raided by the police.* They evidently expected to find something, for *they tore up the boards of the floor.*'

J — was a French Anarchist, one of the leading spirits of the ultra revolutionary school. He was an extremely excitable and hot headed man, but not likely to commit an act of violence. He was a fair speaker, and most of his influence was due to this circumstance. For some time, his house and shop had been raided again and again, by Melville & Co., and they seemed bent on 'having him'. It was thoughtful, to say the least of it, of Mr. Samuel's to supply him with a 'small bottle of sulphuric acid'.

What an interesting item for the press next day. 'Inspector Melville, with a strong force of Scotland Yard detectives, made a raid upon the house of a notorious French Anarchist, yesterday. A startling discovery was made. In a cupboard, concealed beneath a mass of Anarchial literature was found a little bottle of sulphuric acid, similar to that which exploded the bomb that killed Bourdin. It is evident that the police are on the track of a serious conspiracy. This man, J —, is a dangerous desperado, and has been under observation for some time; he is the leader of the most dangerous band in London.'

This man, J —, has been so hunted and watched by the police, since he made this statement regarding Samuels, that his little business was completely destroyed, and he has been forced to emigrate to America. Two others, also, received similar presents.

At the annual meeting at Monsal Dale of the Midland Anarchists, at which Samuels was not present, though the Leeds group had offered to pay his expenses so he might meet me. A youthful admirer, Mr. W. Banham, who has since left the movement, through a trifling indiscretion with the police, attended as his defender. Mr. Banham stated that these men had been informed by Samuels that he possessed some dangerous stuff, but he was watched by the police, and must destroy it. Whereupon they, full of curiosity, said 'Don't destroy it, but let us have it.' He hesitated for some time, but afterwards provided them, not only with the sulphuric acid, but also with some other stuff. He informed them that the combination of two materials would produce a beautiful and interesting experiment. I have no knowledge of chemistry, but it is probable the 'other stuff' was picrate of potassium, the stuff that was used in the Daly and Bourdin bombs. Picrate of potassium bursts into flame when sulphuric acid is poured upon it. So Col. Majendie informs us. I do not vouch for this story, but I have been informed from another source, that Samuels did give one of these men a 'powder', and told him to distribute it. But like a sensible man he destroyed it. All these facts came to light at once, and when it was remembered that Samuels had been boasting for months of his share in the Bourdin affair, it looked very suspicious. So one evening, a young man who once believed in Samuels, arose solemnly at the weekly meeting of the 'Commonweal Group' and denounced him. Samuels was dumbfounded, he could only ejaculate 'They asked me for it'. It was agreed that the question should stand over till next meeting so that his accusers should attend. Mr. Samuels did not turn up and many said he would not be seen there again. The meeting was adjourned till the next Tuesday, and then Samuels appeared. The accusers told their tale, the question too was raised as to his share in the Bourdin conspiracy. Whereupon he made a remarkable statement. He admitted he had given away sulphuric acid, but said it had been done at the request of his accusers. As to the Bourdin affair, he declared he had stolen the explosives out of the house of a comrade D —, who had them for use in his business, and given them to Bourdin, and that since that affair, he supplied sulphuric acid, etc., to J —, and R — etc., from the same place. Further, he admitted that he went with Bourdin on his way to Greenwich, nearly as far as Westminster Bridge. That they were pursued by detectives and parted there. One to go to his death, while the other returned peacefully home, unmolested by the police. Further, that after the death of poor Bourdin, this calm philosopher, Mr. Samuels, wrote that interview for the 'Central News', and received three guineas for his trouble. Mr. Samuels ought to have a career in 'journalism'.

Some one remonstrated with Samuels when they heard this. 'You ought not to have done it', they cried. 'You go and —— yourself', said Samuels. '*I shall make money how I like.*'

This great man had been boasting for weeks of his share in the Bourdin affair to gaping crowds of youthful comrades. He had not only distributed the materials for making explosives, but receipts for compounding them. 'We are not only going to have deeds by foreigners, but English deeds', he cried. Some more facts might have come out, for R —, and others, were about to ask Mr. Samuels some questions, when he suddenly recollected something, 'My wife is down stairs', he said, 'I'll bring her up.' He brought her up, and she immediately begain to assail the group with violent abuse, and threw the whole meeting in turmoil. 'I suppose I must go', said Samuels, and he 'went,' taking his wife with him. This saved him a troublesome cross examination, which might have been awkward. The 'Commonweal Group' resolved to dispense with Samuels' services as editor, and advised him to leave the group, but they decided 'not to publish' the facts of the case.

A young man, M —, who was then at Sheffield, wrote to Samuels for information. He replied on a post card. 'I only gave R —, and J —, *some drops of vinegar*. Mr. Samuels put the names of these men in full on the post card. He was evidently anxious they should be 'known to the police'.

How was it Samuels escaped arrest? There can be but one answer to that question. But how is it that D — also escaped? D — was a middle-class gentleman who had quite recently joined the movement. Unlike his companion, Samuels, he was a man of agreeable manners, liberal with money, and not unpopular. He was naturally an authority on scientific subjects, and understood chemistry. But still, though free with his cash, and living luxuriously, he was in the habit of declaring he was poor. Many are inclined to acquit D — of anything worse than folly in allowing Samuels to help himself freely to explosive materials from his house. But I cannot believe that D — was quite such a fool as this? Nor can I understand if Samuels stole the materials for Bourdin's bomb from his house. How D —, considering the terrible danger, in which he, an innocent man had been placed, had anything more to do with that gentleman. He must have discovered the theft. The quantity stolen was too much not to be noticed. And yet he goes on placidly smiling, while Samuels steals more stuff, including a large bottle of sulphuric acid, knowing all the time that these proceedings were placing the foreign refugees in deadly peril. Lord Salisbury had just introduced his Aliens Bill into the House of Lords, and every new discovery of explosives, was another argument for his Lordship. Besides, who loaded the bomb? Bourdin and Samuels were *utterly ignorant* of chemistry, and would most likely have blown themselves up long before the bomb got to Greenwich Park. To load a bomb is a difficult and dangerous operation, and the work requires a man who knows something of the nature of explosives. It is also worth noting that D — was closely connected with the *Commonweal*, and I believe found part of the funds by which it was kept going. He also provided it with offices.

The whole business reminds one forcibly of some strange events narrated by M. Andrieux, a French prefect of police in his 'Reminiscences', of how similar plots were got up in France. Here is the passage in question, it appeared in one of the early numbers of the 'Commonweal', April 1885.

'To give the Anarchists an organ', writes M. Andrieux, 'was moreover to *place a telephone between the hall of the conspirators* and the room of the prefect of police. *One can have no secrets from the man that finds the money, and I was about to learn, day by day, the most mysterious plans.* Of course, do not imagine I offered the Anarchists the help of the prefect of police. I sent *a well dressed bourgeois* to one of the most active and intelligent of them. He explained how he had made a fortune as *a druggist*, and how he desired to consecrate part of this fortune to the Socialist propoganda. This bourgeois inspired the "companions" with no doubts. Through him I gave the State the necessary caution money, and the 'Revolution Sociale' appeared. Every day round the editorial table gathered the most acknowledged representatives of the party of action; the international correspondence was read; the methods that science *places at the service of the Revolution were freely communicated. I was represented in the councils, and even when necessary gave my advice.* My object was to watch more easily the honourable companions, by grouping them round a paper.'

Afterwards, as a result of the work of Andrieux's agents, an attempt was made to blow up the Statue of M. Thiers, and a series of explosions took place in Paris and the provinces. These were made the pretext of arresting some of the most prominent Anarchists, including Krapotkin [*sic*], and Louise Michel, although they had nothing to do with these police plots. If the retired wholesale 'druggist' had provided the '*chemicals*' to blow up the Thiers Statue, the whole business would have been curiously like the Bourdin affair.

But who has gained anything by these bogus conspiracies? The same game that has been played in France, has been played by the International police with the object of handing over some of the greatest and best revolutionists to the tyrants of the Continent. But though the International police has had a hand in the work, there can be no question that a section of *a great English political party* has not been above profiting by this detestable business. Lord Salisbury asked years ago, when outrage was common in Ireland, Who profited by these outrages? He replied 'Mr Parnell and the Land League', but who has profited by the Greenwich explosion? Lord Salisbury and the Tory party, for it enabled him to

The Greenwich Mystery

introduce the 'Aliens Bill', and thereby secured, at the next General Election, a good many votes from the frightened middle classes.

It is worth remembering that Sir Howard Vincent, the leader of the Fair Trade agitation, was once Chief of the Criminal Investigation Department, Scotland Yard, and naturally is on good terms with Melville and his gang. It is worth remembering also, that when Samuels' credit was failing with his 'comrades', he received mysteriously through the post a 'certificate' which made him a 'Fellow of the Balloon Society', with whom Salisbury's old friends 'Dear Peters and Kelly' once had some connection. Sham learned degrees, like sham titles, have always been a method by which police agents have imposed on their dupes. The case of Edwards, the spy in the Cato street Conspiracy, who was a 'German Baron', and the more recent case of the notorious 'Baron' Sternberg, who got up conspiracies in Belgium, a few years ago, are cases in point.

What was the object of Bourdin in going to Greenwich Park? My opinion is, that he was asked by Samuels to take the money and the 'brown paper parcel' to some mysterious 'comrade', whom he was to meet in that neighbourhood. He was too weak to refuse; but showed some reluctance, so the tempter was forced to go with him part of the way 'to give him courage'. The £13, like the explosives, doubtless came from D —. Where he got it from I don't know, but doubtless the police were quite justified when at the inquest, they claimed it as their property. But why should Bourdin ascend the zigzag path to the Observatory? Did he intend to blow it up? I never believed Col. Majendie's stupid lie. And, now I have visited the scene, I know there is less reason still to believe it. The Observatory, which stands on a high hill facing the park gates, was doubtless suggested to Bourdin, who did not know his way, as a land mark. When you ascend the zigzag path and reach the top, it suddenly opens into a broad walk, which leads to the gates that open on Blackheath. Blackheath, a wide open space, was a capital place for a rendez-vous. But Bourdin could not have got there. I suspect the police were in ambush not far from the Observatory, and he would not have escaped them. The police were on his track. He was hunted down.

What caused the explosion, perhaps a fall, shattering the glass bottle which contained the sulphuric acid. Perhaps an accidental leakage. Who can tell? That he was the dupe of a gang of scoundrels hired by the police I am convinced. The lack of energy, Scotland Yard showed, in following up the trail, proves that clearly. The case of Bourdin was the case of Daly over again. Only this bit of police business had a terrible termination. Not that those who got the affair up meant to kill him, they only intended to hand him over to the *living death of penal servitude.*

393

Appendix D

But it is time that this hellish work was stopped, but while we have a 'political police', it is bound to continue. All legal bodies make work for themselves, to justify their existence, and a political police is no exception. Especially when a successful piece of 'dynamite business' leads to golden rewards, at the hands of reaction.

The game that Serreaux and that Coulon played, has been played again. Language of insane ferocity in newspapers and speeches; the distribution of explosives, and the arrest or violent death of the dupes; and the provoking agents retiring from business, with the silver of Judas in their hands. It is a sickening story.

But in future, let workmen, however desperate by want and suffering, beware of wealthy men who delight in dynamite, and ferocious orators who distribute it. Another question may be asked. Is it not time that poor men, whose only crime is that they have been led into conspiracy, by scoundrels like these, were released from prison? Have they not suffered enough?

SOME PERSONAL CORRESPONDENCE

We received the following post card after an article, 'Dangerous Anarchists', which appeared in the 'Anarchist' of July, 1894. Mr. Samuels' name was not mentioned in that article. If the cap fits—you know the proverb.

July 22nd, 1894,

18, Glengall Road, London, N.W.

Nicoll,

You are an envious, cowardly liar, and I shall make you eat your paper the first time I see you. No comrade, in London, places any reliance in anything you do or say, as it is well known here, as elsewhere, you are an imbecile, and not responsible.

H. B. SAMUELS

We have received a few more, here is another—

Aug. 4th, 1895, London, N.W.

Mr. Nicoll. You are really a damned fool. If you have any revelations to make, why wait? Do you want me to come to Sheffield to thrash you. And denounce your paymaster. Or shall I treat you as the dog you are, a mongrel cur, who can only bark and dare not bite, or ever come near enough for one to kick.

H. B. SAMUELS

Personal abuse, and threats of violence, are not the way in which an 'innocent man' endeavours to silence an accuser, Mr. Samuels.

APPENDIX E

TWO UNPUBLISHED LETTERS FROM
CONRAD TO KRIEGER

28th of June

Dear Sir,

I am very sorry to hear from Paris that the enclosed cheque has been kept for nearly three weeks by the fault of one of my clerks. I thought it had reached you long ago.

I hope you will excuse the mistake.

Yours very sincerely,
F. ORTINARI

Dear Boy. This is Ortinari's sweet note. Wish he would write every day —or at least every month. Send me a cheque for £7 so that I may pay my rent. No sooner one gets something pretty than one must break into it. This is a brutal world—my masters!

How *are* you? And how's Johnny?

We exist with difficulty here. Jess wants to be remembered to you and your wife. The *Sat. Review* notices my story in the *Cosmo* with great discrimination.

Ever yours,
JPH CONRAD

1904
15th March
17 Gordon Place,
Kensington W.

My dear Krieger,

Pardon the delay, but now you may take this bill as absolutely safe. In fact I shall take it up before it matures. It is made payable at Pinker's office because I've no banker after Watson's failure. Two fifty gone in one fell swoop. I am nearly out of my mind with worry and overwork. My nerves are all to pieces. On top of all that my wife had a nasty fall in the street and wrenched both her knee-caps. There was an awful business with doctors, nurses, massage, surgical implements and all that. She just can crawl about now, and is gone back to the Pent; but I am afraid that for all practical purposes she will remain a cripple.

Yours affectionately,
JPH CONRAD

NOTES

Page references to the works of Conrad are to the 1947 Dent Collected Edition unless otherwise stated.

1. INTRODUCTION (pp. 1–5)

1 'A Familiar Preface' to *A Personal Record*, p. xv.
2 *Joseph Conrad's Letters to Cunninghame Graham*, ed. C. T. Watts (London, 1969), p. 170.
3 Letter of 20 June 1912, *Letters of Joseph Conrad to Marguerite Poradowska, 1890–1920*, ed. John A. Gee and Paul J. Sturm (New Haven, 1940), p. 116.
4 Letter of 29 March 1898, G. Jean-Aubry, *Joseph Conrad, Life & Letters* (London, 1927), I, 231.

2. THE FASCINATION OF AFRICA (pp. 9–14)

1 Author's Note to *Youth*, p. vii.
2 G. Jean-Aubry, *Joseph Conrad in the Congo* (London, 1926), p. 19.
3 *Ibid.* p. 66.
4 Author's Note to *Youth*, p. vii.
5 *Ibid.* p. vii.
6 *Conrad's Polish Background, letters to and from Polish friends*, ed. Zdzislaw Nadjer, trans. Halina Carroll (London, 1964), p. 211.
7 Letter of 22 May 1890, Nadjer, p. 211.
8 'Geography and Some Explorers', *Last Essays* (London, 1926), p. 17.

3. THE DEATH OF FREIESLEBEN (pp. 15–22)

1 *Life & Letters*, I, 124.
2 *Joseph Conrad in the Congo*, p. 40.
3 *Ibid.* p. 41.
4 I was assisted in this matter by A. van Marle.
5 H. Jenssen-Tusch, *Skandinaver i Congo: Svenske, Norske og Danske Maends og Kvinders Virksomhed i den uafhaengige Congostat* (Copenhagen, 1902–5), p. 194. This account differs slightly from Grenfell's, in particular giving different reasons for the original quarrel—this time, it seems, it was not Freiesleben's fault at all:

Notes

'Freiesleben had been employed in the North American navy for four years in the frigate *Essex*, had later done compulsory military service at home (Denmark) and become lieutenant in the naval reserve. Only three months after his arrival in the Congo he arrived at Tschumbiri as master of one of the S.A.B. steamers on 24 January. He and the engineer, Scharffenberg, sent the whole crew ashore to collect firewood and began to eat breakfast. Meanwhile a quarrel developed between the crew and the natives, the captain and the engineer hurried ashore in order to reestablish order and there Freiesleben died, pierced by two bullets, while the engineer was wounded and fled on board, and giving up all hope to rescue the master went up the river to Bangala with the steamer' (p. 194).

6 Otto Lütken, 'Joseph Conrad in the Congo', *London Mercury*, May 1930, p. 43.

4. BORDEAUX TO BOMA (pp. 23–28)

1 Conrad's Congo diary begins 'Arrived at Matadi on the 13th of June, 1890'. The journey from Boma to Matadi was about thirty miles distance and could not have taken more than a day. Moreover, Conrad says in the manuscript of *Heart of Darkness* that he ate one dinner at Boma. He must have arrived there on 12 June.

2 Letter of 15 May 1890, *Letters to Marguerite Poradowska*, p. 10.

3 Letter of 10–12 June 1890, *ibid.* p. 12.

4 Letter of 22 May 1890, Nadjer, p. 211.

5 *Joseph Conrad in the Congo*, p. 53.

6 He was two years older than Conrad, and had been in the Congo with the 'Force Publique', arriving at Boma on 19 June 1889. Within six months ill health had forced him to return to Belgium, and this journey with Conrad was his second to the Congo.

7 Cf. Jonah Raskin, '*Heart of Darkness*: the manuscript revisions', *RES*, new ser., XVIII, no. 69 (1967), pp. 30–9.

8 Jenssen-Tusch, p. 193. Jenssen-Tusch says that Captain Duhst arrived at Boma the day that Coquilhat died. This is an error as Coquilhat died on 24 March 1891. The *Biographie Coloniale Belge* records that Duhst arrived Boma on 15 May 1889 and Leopoldville on 24 June 1889.

It was not by accident that it was a Scandinavian who took Conrad up to the terminal point of the river to Matadi before the overland journey commenced. Almost entirely, the freshwater seamen who attended to the quite large flotilla that sailed that great river were

Notes

Scandinavian, some Swedish but mostly Danish, seamen. A careful check of the records available (I was assisted by A. van Marle)—notices of arrivals and departures in the *Mouvement Géographique*, *Skandinaver i Congo*, and *Biographie Coloniale Belge* (5 vols.)—shows that only three captains served on the lower Congo, taking ships from Boma to Matadi, and between June and December 1890 two of these were Danish, and one Swedish. The Swedish master was Captain Axel Tjulin, born 28 March 1855, who arrived in the Congo in 1889 and stayed three years. Like the master in *Heart of Darkness*, Axel Tjulin was fair.

5. THE COMPANY STATION—MATADI (pp. 29–35)

1 *Joseph Conrad in the Congo*, pp. 47 and 48.
2 See Sir Harry Johnston, G.C.M.G., K.C.B., *George Grenfell and the Congo* (London, 1908), 1, 487–8.
3 *Last Essays*, pp. 161–2.   4 Watts, p. 149.
5 'Geography and Some Explorers', *Last Essays*.

6. MATADI TO KINCHASSA—THE CENTRAL STATION (pp. 36–47)

1 G. W. Brourke, *Suggestions for Surmounting the Congo Transport Difficulty*, 22 June 1888. This memorandum is housed in the Baptist Missionary Society Headquarters, London.
2 *Last Essays*, pp. 162 and 171.   3 *Ibid.* pp. 162, 167, 169.
4 *Ibid.* pp. 169–70.   5 *Ibid.* p. 163.
6 *Ibid.* p. 165.   7 *Ibid.* pp. 163, 164, 166, 167.
8 *Ibid.* pp. 165 and 171.
9 Marlow was greeted with the news of the loss of his command when he reached the Central Station, but Conrad knew of the loss of the *Florida* before he reached Kinchassa. His diary records: 'Tuesday, 29th [July]...At 9 met Mr. Louette escorting a sick agent of the compy back to Matadi...bad news from up the river. All the steamers disabled—one wrecked' (*Last Essays*, p. 168). It was not true that all the steamers were disabled—as I shall show later.
10 *Last Essays*, p. 159. A later reference in the *Mouvement Géographique* gives the date as 4 August.
11 Letter of 28 October/9 November 1890, Nadjer, p. 133.
12 Letter of 26 September, *Letters to Marguerite Poradowska*, p. 15.
13 The exploring expedition will be dealt with in a later chapter.

14 Marlow continues: 'He had served three terms of three years out there...Because triumphant health on the general rout of constitutions is a kind of power in itself. When he went home on leave he rioted on a large scale—pompously. Jack ashore—with a difference —in externals only. This one could gather from his casual talk. He originated nothing, he could keep the routine going—that's all. But he was great. He was great by this little thing that it was impossible to tell what could control such a man. He never gave that secret away. Perhaps there was nothing within him. Such a suspicion made one pause—for out there there were no external checks. Once when various tropical diseases had laid low almost every "agent" in the station, he was heard to say, "Men who come out here should have no entrails". He sealed the utterance with that smile of his, as though it had been a door opening into a darkness he had in his keeping. You fancied you had seen things—but the seal was on' (p. 74). But this was not entirely true of Delcommune who died in 1892 (cf. *Congo Illustré*, second year, no. 5, 26 February 1893).

15 *Life & Letters*, I, 133.

16 Letter of 18 June 1890, p. 14.   17 *Last Essays*, p. 161.

7 KINCHASSA TO STANLEY FALLS (pp. 48–61)

1 *Joseph Conrad in the Congo*, p. 62.

2 Cf. *Joseph Conrad in the Congo*, p. 66: 'It appears that the object of the journey by the *Roi des Belges* was, as Marlow says, to relieve Kurtz-Klein of his post.' Jocelyn Baines states more correctly: 'One of its objects was to collect the Company's agent named Georges Antoine Klein who was seriously ill' (*Joseph Conrad*, London, 1960, pp. 116–17).

3 Continuing his notes about the streamers in his diary on 29 July, Grenfell goes on: 'The [indecipherable] news of the *Ville de Bruxelles* having sunk on a snag, deck under water—Simpson came down in canoe from *Ville de Bruxelles* says she is sunk 1 day this side of Upoto.' On 20 July the agent Hodister, in a report of the shipwreck which was published in the *Mouvement Géographique*, October 19, 1890, comments: 'J'examine la situation du bateau. Il est à 10 mètres de la rive: le bandage de l'avant est à quelques centimètres au-dessus du niveau du fleuve et par un fond de 2^m75. Cinq arbres ont été introduits sous le bateau pour le soutenir. Le

snag ou le bout du snag, qui perce le fond, a 7 à 8 centimètres de diamètre; sa position est oblique. Les eaux sont basses; nous sommes au minima. Si la *Ville de Bruxelles* ne peut être tirée de cette position, dans trois mois il y aura 3^{m}50 d'eau en plus, et l'on ne verra plus sa cheminée!'

4 There were rumours at this time of a possible Arab infiltration from the upper Congo into established Belgian territory.

5 *Mouvement Géographique*, 28 December 1890. These tables were drawn up by the agent Hodister.

6 J. Rose Troup in *With Stanley's Rear Column* (London, 1890) writes: 'We arrived at Bangala about 8.30 a.m. of the 27th July, all well. We had now accomplished half the distance (to Stanley Falls area)—that is, 500 miles.'

7 'De Bangala aux Stanley Falls', *Mouvement Géographique*, 21 September 1890; 'Les Explorations du Steamer le *Roi des Belges* dans le district de Tippo-Tip', *Mouvement Géographique*, 25 August 1889.

8 H. M. Stanley, *In Darkest Africa* (London, 1890), I, 111–12.

9 H. von Wissman, *My Second Journey through Equatorial Africa* (London, 1891), pp. 19–20.

10 J. R. Werner, *A Visit to Stanley's Rear-Guard* (London, 1889), pp. 41–2.

11 Captain Koch was born at Ronnowsholm near Hjorring on 24 December 1865. He was employed as a captain on the Congo for six years. I know he kept a diary during this period, but I have not been able to unearth it. He returned to Europe in 1892. During his first period on the Congo he was successively master of the *General Sanford* and the *Roi des Belges* and the *Princess Clementine*. In his second period, he left the employ of the SAB and was employed by the Congo Free State as master first of the *Ville d'Anvers* and finally of the *Ville de Bruges*. During his first period of service he was wounded twice, once by a spear in his arms and then by an arrow in his cheek (Jenssen-Tusch, p. 195). On returning to Denmark he was employed as mate and master by Alfred Christensen and Company, Shipowners, and then from March 1900 to March 1903 as first mate by the famous Danish shipping firm, East Asiatic Company, and from April 1903 to June 1906 as a master, according to Mr Kruger of that firm (letter dated 15 July 1968). He died in Hamburg in June 1906 aged forty-one.

12 I know nothing further of Vander Heyden, but I have a little more

information about Rollin. He was born at Liège on 14 October 1866. The *Biographie Coloniale Belge*, IV, 768 records: 'Rollin (Edouard-François-Léon), Agent commercial [born] Liège 14.10.1866—[died] Liège, 14.11.1907. Rollin accomplit deux termes au Congo, l'un de 1890 (2 mars) à 1893, l'autre du 6 septembre 1893 à avril 1896. Il remonta l'Ikelemba dont il procura un croquis au *Mouvement Géographique*.'

13 Werner, p. 181. Werner goes on: 'On August 10th I again reached Leopoldville after an absence of nine months...at Leopoldville, the frames and plates of the *Roi des Belges*, another stern-wheeler, belonging to the Compagnie du Congo pour le Commerce et l'Industrie, were only awaiting the arrival of the engineers to be put together.'

14 Conrad is drawing upon his knowledge of the navigation of the Congo in describing Marlow's difficulties in the navigation of *his* river. This is particularly true of the navigation below Stanley Falls/ Inner Station. George Grenfell, who first charted the river and whose charts were used by the State, writes: 'If the Congo is markedly less in size above the Aruwimi [river], it is even more markedly reduced beyond the point where it received the Lomami [river], and the islands become very few. At twenty miles beyond the Lomami [that is about 40 miles from Stanley Falls Station] the channel is once more bounded by steep and often rocky banks about three quarters of a mile apart. During the low-water season [at Stanley Falls the low water season is August and September, the months during which Conrad was on the river], the navigation of the last twenty miles below Stanleyville [Stanley Falls Station] becomes somewhat dangerous because of the reefs of rocks that at that time lie so close to the surface. Boats drawing more than three feet of water find this part of the river impracticable during the dead-low water that sometimes obtains at the autumnal equinox' (Johnston, *George Grenfell*, I, 292–3).

John Carrington, a missionary teacher attached to the Université Libre du Congo, wrote to me on 23 December 1967 about Marlow's approach to Stanley Falls: 'But he refers to finding Kurtz at the station to the *left bank* in which case this can't refer to the Falls station because that was on the right bank—Kisanga-ni: "at the island".' I think however we can take it that Conrad is describing the situation of Stanley Falls for though in the text Conrad writes: 'I could go to the right or to the left of this [sandbank 1½ miles from Kurtz's station]. I didn't know either channel, of course. The banks

looked pretty well alike, the depth appeared the same; but as I had
been informed the station was on the west side, I naturally headed
for the western passage' (p. 108); in the manuscript he had originally
written: 'as I was informed the station was on the east side I naturally
headed for the eastern passage' (p. 129).

15 Troup, p. 125.
16 Temporary master of the *Florida* pending Conrad's arrival.
17 *Last Essays*, p. 159.
18 S. P. Verner, *Pioneering in Central Africa* (London, 1903), p. 409:
'The rules of the steamboat forbade any natives sleeping on the
ship.'
19 Troup, p. 124.
20 Verner, pp. 78–9. Later in his book, Verner has this to say of the
crew of the *Roi des Belges*: 'The Bangala crew of the *Roi des Belges*,
as soon as they recognize the familiar features of the local geography,
and know that they are well inside the upper limit of the pool,
although the river current is scarcely abated, break out into an
uproarious demonstration of songs and yells, hurrahing and beating
the drums, jubilant at the near approach of their monthly holiday
at the naval capital of the Congo. Leopoldville is called by them
its ancient native name, Kintamo, and "Kintamo, Oh! Kintamo,
Ah! Kintamo Tama Ve! Ye! Ye! Ki! Yi! Ho! Ho! Ho-o-o-o!"
is the cry' (p. 142).

    H. H. Johnston, in his standard work on the missionary, George
Grenfell, writing on the Bangalas provides us with the reason why
the Belgians employed these cannibals on their vessels: 'The
Bangala people were popular from the first with all Europeans in
spite of occasional outbreaks of hostility. They were a splendid-
looking race, sometimes with really handsome faces, and almost
always with bodies that are ideals of manly beauty, the women also
being attractive and well shaped. In the 'eighties of the last century
their labour was cheaper than that of any other race on the Congo,
the wages asked being not more than £2 a year!' (Johnston,
George Grenfell, I, 115, n. 1).

21 W. Holman Bentley, *Pioneering on the Congo* (London, 1900), I, 210.
22 *Ibid.* I, 213.
23 Johnston, *George Grenfell*, II, 605.
24 Troup, pp. 103–4. H. M. Stanley, in a letter to Troup, laid it down
that each native would receive on the journey from Bolobo to
Bangala 1 mitako per man per day. After Bangala this amount was

to be reduced to ¾ mitako per man per day (*ibid.* p. 115). It will be seen that the commercial trading company's payment of wages to the crew of 'three pieces of brass wire, each about nine inches long' per week is a great deal less than Stanley's payment. But by the time Conrad arrived in the Congo, the length, at least, of the brass wire had been shortened. Even so, it had not been reduced to nine inches. In 1894, four years after Conrad's visit to the Congo, the length had come down from two feet to ten inches (Bentley, II, 398).

25 Linked with the theme of the seaman's duty is Marlow's discovery of a book in an abandoned hut: 'by the door I picked up a book. It had lost its covers, and the pages had been thumbed into a state of extremely dirty softness; but the back had been lovingly stitched afresh with white cotton thread, which looked clean yet. It was an extraordinary find. Its title was, *An Inquiry into some Points of Seamanship*, by a man Tower, Towson—some such name—Master in his Majesty's Navy' (p. 99). For Marlow, Towson's book is 'something unmistakably real' in the jungle world of insanity, and it has naturally been supposed that Conrad had a particular book in mind. Mrs Eloise Knapp Hay in *The Political Novels of Joseph Conrad* (Chicago, 1963, p. 144, n. 78) has suggested that it could be the work of Alfred Henry Alston, but it has to be taken into account that there was a well-known (in his day and in sailing quarters) writer on sailing matters called John Thomas Towson who lived at the Sailor's Home, Liverpool. On 28 November 1853 he read a paper to the Literary and Philosophical Society, Liverpool on 'Great Circle Sailing'. The British Museum catalogue refers also to his 'Practical Information on the Deviation of the Compass'; 'Icebergs on the Southern Ocean'; 'Lecture to the officers, seamen and apprentices of the Mercantile marine, 1854'.

The manuscript, with its extra detail, does seem to indicate that, at one time or another, a discovery at least of a book in just such a hut was made. The manuscript was heavily scored out at this point but so far as I could judge it read: 'Inside the dwelling was found dismantled. The occupant had left [two words indecipherable]. There was some litter [next word indecipherable] the door I picked up, dry leaves, a milk tin, but near the door I picked up a book' (MS, p. 111).

Notes

8. STANLEY FALLS—THE HEART OF DARKNESS (pp. 62–71)

1 *Joseph Conrad in the Congo*, p. 63.
2 *Last Essays*, p. 17.
3 Albert Chapaux, *Le Congo historique, diplomatique, physique, politique, économique, humanitaire et colonial* (Brussels, 1894), pp. 446–7.
4 *Ibid.* p. 185.
5 For accounts of this see Herbert Ward, *Five Years with the Congo Cannibals* (London, 1890), pp. 196–214, and Werner, pp. 88–122.
6 The expedition was first reported in the *Mouvement Géographique*, 2 June 1889:

'L'expédition Becker est arrivée aux Stanley-Falls le 16 février. Elle avait quitté Léopoldville le 23 janvier. Le voyage a donc été fait en vingt-cinq jours. C'est la première fois qu'il a été accompli avec une telle rapidité. C'est la *Ville de Bruxelles* qui a réalisé ce progrès.

La recontre de Becker et de son ancien ami Tippo-Tip a été très intéressante. Le chef arabe a montré très vivement toute sa satisfaction de revoir l'officier belge avec lequel il avait entretenu jadis, à Tabora, d'excellentes relations. M. Haneuse, le résident de la station des Falls, était remis de son indisposition et sa station avait pris un grand développement.'

On the departure of the resident, M. Haneuse, relations between the Belgians and Arabs were reported as being good: 'M. Haneuse, le résident des Falls, actuellement en route pour rentrer en Europe, annonce que lors de son départ des Falls la situation politique était des plus favorables et que tout était calme. Tippo-Tip, a prié M. Haneuse d'être son interprète auprès du gouvernement de l'Etat pour l'assurer de tout son concours' (*Mouvement Géographique*, 28 July 1889). Becker's mission is dealt with in R. P. P. Ceulemans' *La Question Arabe et le Congo (1883–1892)* (Brussels, 1959).
7 Ceulemans, p. 188, n. 1.   8 *Ibid.* p. 199.   9 *Ibid.*
10 Alexandre Delcommune, *Vingt Années de Vie Africaine* (Brussels, 1922), II, 15–16.

9. KLEIN (pp. 72–78)

1 *Joseph Conrad in the Congo*, p. 65.
2 *Ibid.* p. 66.
3 I am indebted to Mr Donald Wilson of the Department of French, University of Liverpool, for looking up the following information about Klein for me in Paris. According to official records, Klein

was born on 9 April 1863 at 62 rue de Saintonge, Paris IIIe. His father was Antony Klein, born in Paris on 13 November 1832 in the 10th arrondissement, and his mother was Gérardine Elénore Amélie Leveau, apparently not born in Paris. Interesting in view of Marlow's comment on Kurtz: 'His mother was half-English, his father was half-French' (p. 117), is the fact that Klein's paternal grandfather, Antony Klein, apparently married an English lady, Elizabeth Ashe.

4 *Last Essays*, pp. 161 and 167.

5 A reference in a letter written by Grenfell, eleven days after Conrad's arrival in the Congo, did at first seem to bring us nearer to the Kurtz who had such a reputation for collecting ivory: 'he had collected, bartered, swindled or stolen more ivory than all the other agents together'. Grenfell is writing of a journey he made up-river in May/June 1890: 'Mr. Klein seems to have had a very successful trip up the Lulongo [river] in his new boat. He is very [the next word is indecipherable but presumably it could be 'friendly'] ...When the *Peace* returns from the [Stanley] Pool this time, she will bring Mr. Weeks [a missionary] & that he will go for[ward?] to Lulanga—the more I see of that place the more [run off the page —'I like it?']. Perhaps it is greatly due to the splendid A.H.V. there,* for certainly Mr. Klein has a wonderful faculty [of] making things look well. I have not seen a neater or br[ighter?] establishment anywhere.' However, given the fact that this letter was written to Greshoff, manager of the Dutch trading house, while he was on leave, together with the connecting of Klein with the Dutch house at Lulanga, this cannot be a reference to the Klein who was Belgian agent at the Falls. And correspondence with the firm of Lindeteves-Jacoberg in Amsterdam, successors to the Nieuwe Afrikaansche Handels-Vennootschap, and assistance from A. van Marle, revealed that during 1890 there were two agents called Klein working for the AHV. Of the three Kleins on the river at that time, therefore, only one, and that one working for the Dutch house, seems to have had any reputation that might have been talked about—'a wonderful faculty of making things look well'. But this does not help us where the source for Kurtz is concerned.

* The Dutch trading company was first known as the Afrikaansche Handels-Vereeniging but in 1879 it was reconstituted as the Nieuwe Afrikaansche Handels-Vennootschap. Missionary George Grenfell always referred to the Dutch company by the initials of the original Dutch firm.

6 Jenssen-Tusch, p. 599.   7 Werner, pp. 207–8.

8 *Joseph Conrad in the Congo*, p. 66.

9 This is the founder and pioneer missionary at Tchumbiri. On 13 December 1967 Roland Metzger of the American Baptists in Pennsylvania sent me a rough plot plan of the Tchumbiri mission made by Billington himself and a copy of which I sent to Angus MacNeil to help him in his search for Klein's grave.

10. THE JOURNEY DOWN-RIVER (pp. 79–91)

1 *Letters to Marguerite Poradowska*, pp. 16–17.

2 Edward Garnett, introduction to *Letters from Conrad 1895–1924* (London, 1928).

3 Cf. similar experience attributed to Mungo Park in 'Geography and Some Explorers', *Last Essays*, p. 15. See the comments of Eloise Knapp Hay, p. 121, n. 28.

4 *Joseph Conrad in the Congo*, p. 67.

5 Otto Lütken, pp. 41–2.

6 *Letters to Marguerite Poradowska*, pp. 16–17.

7 Najder, p. 213.

8 Letter of 26 September 1890, *Letters to Marguerite Poradowska*, p. 16.

9 *Ibid.*

10 *Ibid.* pp. 15–16.

11 *Joseph Conrad in the Congo*, p. 71.

12 Najder, p. 134.

13 *Letters to Marguerite Poradowska*, p. 17.

14 Najder, p. 133.

15 *Letters to Marguerite Poradowska*, p. 17.

16 *Biographie Coloniale Belge*, II, 550.

17 At the time Conrad passed down this stretch of the river there was only one man who had drowned at this stretch and his name was Kallina, now immortalised in the maps of the river as Kallina Point. But Conrad is wrong to ascribe Belgian nationality to him. He was Austrian and he was not in fact returning home as Conrad suggests. Nor did the sad event take place only some months before but some years before. There are many accounts but I shall keep to one. Stanley in *The Congo: Founding of its Free State* (London, 1885, I, 485–7) gives the most detailed account of the 'young Austrian cavalry lieutenant named Kallina, of aristocratic connections in Vienna' but Werner is short and less moralising in tone: 'right opposite the rocky promontory, now called Kallina Point, after an

Austrian lieutenant who, in 1883, lost his life while attempting to round it in a canoe. This point juts boldly out into the stream, its cliffs rising perpendicularly out of deep water, and diverts the strong current which dashes itself against its upper side, towards the centre of the river, thus forming, under the lee of the cliffs, a return current of almost equal strength. A newcomer ascending the river in a canoe, and keeping, as is always done, close inshore, would not see the broken water beyond the point till his craft was well under the influence of the return current, and being carried, at a speed of three or four miles per hour, right into an opposing current, running at the rate of six or seven. The sudden shock and lurch which follow are almost certain to upset the canoe; and then the best swimmer would need more than human strength to keep his head above the chaos of cross-currents and whirlpools which sweeps him away towards Ntamo falls' (p. 53).

18 *Joseph Conrad in the Congo*, p. 72.
19 Lütken, p. 41.   20 *Ibid.*
21 Jessie Conrad, *Joseph Conrad and his Circle* (New York, 1964), p. 13.
22 *Letters to Marguerite Poradowska*, p. 136.
23 *Ibid.* p. 19.
24 G. F. W. Hope, *My Life at Sea and Yachting* (typescript), p. 269.
25 *Life & Letters*, I, 144.

II. KURTZ (pp. 92–118)

1 *Biographie Coloniale Belge*, I, 516.
2 *Mouvement Géographique*, 17 August 1890.
3 For the movements of the *General Sanford* at this time see Appendix B, the table of arrivals and departures of shipping at Bangala taken from the *Mouvement Géographique*, 17 August 1890.
4 Baert explored the area in 1886.
5 'Chop' is a local term for food.
6 'Exploration de la Mongalla.—M. Hodister, l'actif agent de la Société du haut Congo à Bangala, vient de faire, à bord du steamer *Général Sanford*, une nouvelle exploration de la Mongalla et de son principal affluent l'Eloba. Parti de Bangala le 8 avril dernier, il a poussé jusqu'aux dernières limites de la navigation sur la branche principale de la rivière, le Doua, puis il a remonté l'Eloba. Il nous envoie des cartes intéressantes de son excursion ainsi qu'un rapport dont nous publierons des extraits dans notre prochain numéro. Il est rentré à Bangala le 10 juin.'

Notes

7 Chapaux, p. 189.

8 *Ibid.* pp. 190–1.

9 *Ibid.* p. 190.

10 *Ibid.* p. 190.

11 Ward, *The Congo Cannibals*, p. 293.

12 Hodister's extraordinary influence with the natives was mentioned, in passing, by the Belgian missionary M. Van Ronslé, whose account of a journey from Bangala to Stanley Falls I have quoted from. On arriving at Mobeka on the *Florida*, on which vessel Hodister was travelling, he records: 'Une foule de noirs encombrent le débarcadère et saluent M. Hodister sous le nom de Mpunga' (*Mouvement Géographique*, 21 September 1890). Although there seems to be some doubt as to how the word 'Mpunga' should be translated,* the incident does suggest that Hodister was well known to the natives and popular with them.

   Indeed, Hodister's attitude of friendship and peaceful exploration seems to have been both a matter of principle and a method of trading. Of his later Lomami explorations, the *Mouvement Géographique*, 1890, recorded that Hodister carried them out 'sans avoir perdu un seul de ses hommes, sans avoir tiré un seul coup de fusil, sans avoir eu à entamer une seule palabre pour pouvoir franchir la région' (p. 119). Hodister 'n'avait guère d'autres armes avec lui que des fusils de chasse' (*Mouvement Antiesclavagiste*, August 1892, p. 238). 'Toujours pacifique, il se faisait bien voir des indigènes comme des Arabes, et s'il arrivait dans un village où l'accueil paraissait hostile, il descendait seul à terre, sans armes, agitant de grandes brassées d'étoffe en signe de paix' (*Biographie Coloniale Belge*, I, 515). And during the exploration of the Lualaba area which was in the hands of the Arabs, the *Congo Illustré* (Brussels, 1892), I, 129, reported: 'Il y a deux ans, Hodister, préparant les voies à l'affaire intéressante, tant au point de vue du commerce qu'à celui de la civilisation, dont il a la direction en Afrique, fit une exploration qui, de Bena-Kamba, le conduisit jusque Nyangwe et Kassongo. Il y a rencontra les principaux trafiquants arabes de la région, et se lia d'amitié avec eux. En même temps, aux Stanley-Falls, il traitait

---

* 'Mpunga' is the Swahili term for 'rice' but it seems unlikely that such a sobriquet would be applied to Hodister. A possible meaning of the term in a religious sense is 'Father'—'Mpungu, or Nzambi-Mpungu, i.e. "Father" or "Father of the first born" is regarded...as the overlord' (James Hastings, ed., *Encyclopedia of Religion and Ethics* (Edinburgh, 1917), IX, 280). In a letter of 20 August 1968, John Carrington suggested another meaning: 'An explication which seems to me far more likely, if it was a sobriquet used by the Mobeka people alone, is that they were noticing that Hodister was a talkative person and called him *mpunga*—a type of small monkey that chatters quite a lot.'

Notes

d'importantes affaires avec Tippo-Tib, pour le compte de la Société du Haut-Congo.'

13   *Biographie Coloniale Belge*, I, 515.

14   *Biographie Coloniale Belge*, I, 514.

15   And there is further evidence of Hodister's eloquence. Herbert Ward, who met him at Bangala two years prior to Conrad's arrival in the Congo, recalls in his book *Five Years with the Congo Cannibals* spending an evening with him: 'About midnight I reached the camp of Monsieur Hodister, an agent of the Belgian Trading Company. He was most hospitable, and entertained me until the early hours of the morning by relating incidents that had occurred during his residence among the Mobeka people' (p. 293).

   I think this passage in Ward is the source for Conrad's account of the Harlequin meeting Kurtz and for the conversation they had together, though Ward does not have the same simple nature as the Harlequin: 'They had come together unavoidably...I suppose Kurtz wanted an audience, because on a certain occasion, when encamped in the forest, they had talked all night..."We talked of everything", he said, quite transported at the recollection. "...The night did not seem to last an hour. Everything! Everything!...Of love too"' (p. 127).

16   *Mouvement Géographique*, 2 November 1890, p. 119. A quite impressive list of Hodister's publications appears in *Biographie Coloniale Belge*, I, 518.

17   *Biographie Coloniale Belge*, I, 518.

18   Letter of 10 June 1890, *Letters to Marguerite Poradowska*, p. 13.

19   *Biographie Coloniale Belge*, I, 515.

20   Demetrius C. Boulger, *The Congo State or the Growth of Civilisation in Central Africa* (London, 1898), p. 162.

21   Letters of 23 March, 6 April 1892 published in *Mouvement Géographique*, 21 August 1892.

22   *Mouvement Antiesclavagiste*, August 1892, p. 232.

23   *Mouvement Géographique*, 31 July 1892.

24   The Van der Kerckhoven expedition, which was in the area then, had obviously stirred up trouble to begin with. The *Daily Graphic* commented on 18 October 1892: 'there is no longer room to doubt that the object of the Van der Kerckhoven expedition is to found a station at Wadelai and secure the ivory which Emin Pasha is reported to have left in that neighbourhood'. And Mohara, the Arab in charge of Nyangwe and suspected of organising the massacre,

Notes

'par suite des confiscations faites par Van Kerckhoven, avait perdu de grandes quantitiés d'ivoire pour une valeur d'un million et demi de francs' (Ceulemans, p. 339). And the *Daily Graphic* (18 October 1892) also reported that M. Tobback, resident of the Falls, had 'been at Riba Riba some time previously and threatened to return with a 1,000 guns to drive the Arabs out of the country.' As a result, Michiels had warned the agents of Hodister's expedition that the Arabs were 'mauvais' (Ceulemans, p. 342). An account in *The Times* confirms that this general hostility was turned against Hodister:

'A young official of the Congo Free State visited the village, and stated that the State intended to make it a trading station. The district is really governed by a nephew of Tippoo Tib, who was absent from the town. The Arab leader told the officer that they would not allow him to take the place, but the officer replied that he would come back with 2,000 men and take it. He did return, but with only 15 blacks, and on the Arab asking where the 2,000 men were, the officer said they were coming. The Arabs fell upon the little band, and killed them, and after cutting off their heads, threw the corpses to the blacks to eat. The Arabs had hitherto been friendly, but they were strenuously opposed to the whites dealing directly with the natives. Major Hodister, who was moving up with a numerous following, was well known to the natives, and they regarded him with special favour. His expedition included 12 whites and a great number of natives, with women and children. When they appeared, the Arabs, thinking they were the 2,000 men spoken of, fired into them. Major Hodister was on foot leading his horse, and when the Arabs fired, his followers were about to reply, but he placed himself in front of them, throwing up his arms, and ordering them not to fire. He then advanced towards the Arabs on foot, with his horse still following. The major intended to reason with the Arabs, and thought his presence would prevent bloodshed. He had not advanced far, however, when the Arabs again opened fire. Unfortunately Major Hodister and several others were shot down, and those who did not escape were either shot or otherwise killed, the Arabs making a terrible onslaught on the band' (3 October 1892).

It does seem, therefore, that Hodister's previous good relations with the Arabs were cancelled by the interference of the Van der Kerckhoven expedition and of officials of the State in the area.

25 Chapaux, p. 259.

26 *Biographie Coloniale Belge*, I, 518. The *Mouvement Géographique*, 1892, p. 120, reports that Hodister 'a décliné l'hospitalité de M. Camille Delcommune pour pouvoir partager le sort de ses subordonnés' which may indicate that there was no love lost between Delcommune and Hodister.

27 *Biographie Coloniale Belge*, I, 518. See also 'L'opinion de M. Doré sur Hodister', pp. 114–16, below.

28 Ceulemans, p. 310.

29 Chapaux, p. 253.

30 *Mouvement Antiesclavagiste*, September 1892, p. 304.

12. HENRY MORTON STANLEY—THE YAWL 'NELLIE'
(pp. 119–124)

1 Conrad wrote to his aunt in the year of his return from the Congo: 'Last Thursday I went aboard my friend Hope's yacht, and I have returned to London just this moment' (letter of 22 June 1891, *Letters to Marguerite Poradowska*, p. 29).

2 The name of Captain Loutit, master of the *Duke of Sutherland* during the time Hope sailed in her and well loved by him, appears as the name of the hero in the manuscript of 'End of the Tether' and is subsequently changed to Whalley. This suggests that Hope had some influence upon 'End of the Tether', since Conrad must have heard of Loutit from him.

3 G. F. W. Hope was director of many companies during his lifetime though only one is listed in the *Stock Exchange Year Book* and the *Directory of Directors*. For example, the following entry appears in the *Directory of Directors*, 1885: 'Mr. George Fountaine Weare Hope is joint managing director of John Vernon Hope & Co. Ltd., 104, Hatton-garden, E.C.'

Keen was a channel pilot at the time of the trip on the *Nellie*, but there is no reference to Mears's occupation.

4 Hope sailed in the *Duke of Sutherland* as an apprentice and then as mate between 1873 and 1875. Conrad sailed in her between 1878 and 1879. Hope comments: 'Curiously enough a Mr. Bastard was second mate when Conrad was in her, and also when Mears was in her about eight years later. Mr. B. afterwards got a job at the Sailor's Home in London, and Conrad often used to see him' (p. 212).

5 This was a favourite tavern of Hope.

Notes

13. 'AN OUTPOST OF PROGRESS' (pp. 125–133)

1 'Few men realise that their life, the very essence of their character, their capabilities and their audacities, are only the expression of their belief in the safety of their surroundings...the contact with pure unmitigated savagery, with primitive nature and primitive man, brings sudden and profound trouble into the heart' ('An Outpost of Progress', *Tales of Unrest*, p. 89).

2 Cf. also the delay over Hodister's supply steamer and of the steamer in *Heart of Darkness*. Also, the damage to the *Florida* must be in Conrad's mind here.

3 *Life and Letters*, I, 128, n. 2.

4 Cf. *Heart of Darkness*: 'he sent his assistant down the river with a note to me in these terms: "Clear this poor devil out of the country, and don't bother sending more of that sort"' (p. 89).

5 Stanley, *The Congo*, II, 244.

6 *Ibid.* II, 244–5.   7 *Ibid.* I, 484–5.

8 *Ibid.* II, 268–9.   9 *Ibid.* II, 269.

10 Jenssen-Tusch, pp. 589–90.   11 Stanley, *The Congo*, I, 507–10.

12 *Ibid.* I, 409.   13 Bentley, II, 51.

14 H. H. Johnston, *The River Congo from its mouth to Bolobo* (London, 1884), pp. 247–8.

15 Herbert Ward, *My Life with Stanley's Rear Guard* (London, 1891), pp. 73–4.   16 Bentley, I, 336.

14. 'GASPAR RUIZ' (pp. 137–146)

1 Letter to Sir Algernon Methuen, 26 January 1908, *Life & Letters*, II, 66.

2 *Ibid.*

3 Conrad derived the name 'Erminia' from Edward Eastwick's *Venezuela: or Sketches of Life in a South American Republic* (London, 1868), p. 180.

4 Author's Note to *A Set of Six*, p. vi.

5 Letter to Cunninghame Graham, 30 March 1923, Watts, p. 196.

6 Captain Basil Hall, *Extracts from a Journal written on the coasts of Chili, Peru, and Mexico in the years 1820, 1821, 1822* (Edinburgh, 1824), I, 322.

7 *Ibid.* I, 322–3.   8 *Ibid.* I, 323–4.

9 John Miller, *Memoirs of General Miller in the Service of the Republic of Peru* (London, 1829), I, 261.

10 Captain Basil Hall, I, 368–9.   11 *Ibid.* I, 325–8.

12 *Ibid.* I, 369–70.   13 *Ibid.* I, 360–1.

14 Charles Darwin, *Journal of Researches into the Natural History and Geology of the Countries visited during the Voyage of H.M.S. 'Beagle' round the World* (London, 1882), p. 64.

15 Author's Note to *A Set of Six*, pp. vi–vii.

15. THE GARIBALDINO (pp. 147–161)

1 Galsworthy's account of *Nostromo* in G. T. Keating, *A Conrad Memorial Library* (New York, 1929), p. 138.

2 Letter to Cunninghame Graham, 8 July 1903, Watts, p. 145.

3 John Halverston and Ian Watt, 'The Original Nostromo: Conrad's Source', *RES*, new ser., X, no. 37 (1959), 45–52.

4 Ivo Vidan, 'One Source of Conrad's *Nostromo*', *RES*, new ser., VII, no. 27 (1956), 287–93. Also Edgar Wright, *Joseph Conrad: his expressed views about technique and the principles underlying them, with a study of their relevance to certain novels*, M.A. thesis, University of London, March 1955.

5 Baines, p. 295; also Edgar Wright.

6 Author's Note to *Nostromo*, p. xxi.   7 *Ibid.*

8 *Life & Letters*, I, 308.   9 *Ibid.* I, 315.

10 Watts, p. 143.   11 *Ibid.* p. 145.

12 R. B. Cunninghame Graham, 'Cruz Alta', *Thirteen Stories* (London, 1900), pp. 60–1. Edgar Wright was the first to refer to this source.

13 R. B. Cunninghame Graham, 'The Captive', *Hope* (London, 1910), p. 123.

14 Paul Frischauer, *Garibaldi: The Man and the Nation* (London, 1935).

15 John Parris, *The Lion of Caprera* (London, 1962), pp. 108–9.

16 Frischauer, p. 185.   17 Parris, p. 109.

18 Frischauer, p. 187.

19 The fact that old Giorgio feels contempt for the indigenous population and admiration for the English suggests a further source, for there was in Uruguay another Italian who in vocation and character approximates to Giorgio. The details of Giorgio's inn and his contempt for the natives may have derived from the following passage in R. A. Seymour's *Pioneering in the Pampas* (London, 1869):

'Beside the railway station there was now a fonda or small inn, a great improvement on the old post-house, kept by an Italian,

Notes

named Don Pépé, supposed to be a count in his own country—
I believe he was a man of good family obliged to leave Italy for
some political reasons. He was very popular with the English settlers,
being always ready to oblige and help them in every way; but he
maintained a stern and imposing demeanour towards the natives,
whom he detested, declaring them to be "muy picaros", and possessing
various other amiable qualities.

The Fonda contained three rooms, one of which was used for
the bar...The next apartment was the dining-room, turned at
night into a bed-room; when the mingled odour of garlic, oil, cana,
and tobacco smoke rendered the air *not* of the most balmy description
...The other room was a sleeping-room, reserved for the superior
guests, including, of course, all the English settlers. Don Pépé never
allowed the Gauchos to penetrate beyond the bar' (p. 77).

In Viola's fonda, the café is at one end and 'the other was reserved
for the English engineers' (p. 32). And as in Don Pépé's fonda:
"the noisy frizzling of fat had stopped, the fumes floated upwards
in sunshine, a strong smell of burnt onions hung in the drowsy
heat, enveloping the house" (p. 24). Don Pépé in *Nostromo* is the
ex-officer of Paez 'in charge of the whole population in the territory
of the mine' and called El Señor Gobernador.

20 Rear-Admiral H. F. Winnington-Ingram, *Hearts of Oak* (London,
1889), p. 97.

21 *Garibaldi: An Autobiography*, ed. Alexandre Dumas, trans. William
Robson (London, 1860), p. 197. A further account of Samuel
appears in William Latham's *The States of the River Plate* (London,
1868): 'Meanwhile no effective diversion being practicable by land,
the siege of Monte Video continued, and many gallant feats were
performed by Garibaldi, Tajes, and other chiefs. Some of the most
desperate were performed by "Cockney Sam's" little volunteer band.
"Sam"—history, or rather tradition, does not preserve his family
name—had been a London "bargeman" or "coal heaver", a lithe,
fair-haired, mild, and civil fellow, who occupied himself in the
harbour of Monte Video as a lighterman and trader in bones for
dunnage purposes. When the war interfered with his pacific occupations, he collected all the "daredevils" who were willing to
follow him; and follow him they did, by day or by night, where
few would care to go. Cool as a cucumber, he performed extraordinary
feats under the most desperate circumstances, odds being no odds for
him and his band, which was many a night reduced to a fraction of the

Notes

number that sailed forth. "Sam" would come round to his old patrons and others for small subscriptions for the maintenance of his band, mildly soliciting as for an order for bones. Poor Sam! he returned at length to his peaceful occupation and was subsequently drowned, his little craft capsizing on a voyage to Patagonia' (pp. 266–7).

22 David Larg, *Giuseppe Garibaldi* (London, 1934), p. 40.

23 *Ibid.* p. 56.

24 Garibaldi writes of him: '...when I took service under the republic of Montevideo, and was charged with the organization of the Italian legion, my first care was to write to Anzani to come and share that labour with me. He came, and we never parted till the day when, touching the shores of Italy, he died in my arms.' (*Garibaldi*, p. 144) There is little relationship here with the shop-keeper of the same name who appears as a minor character in *Nostromo*. It is in the great Plaza where Decoud has printed his liberal newspaper, *Porvenir*, that Anzani has his shop:

'It was next to Anzani's great emporium of boots, silks, ironware, muslins, wooden toys, tiny silver arms, legs, heads, hearts (for ex-voto offerings), rosaries, champagne, women's hats, patent medicines, even a few dusty books in paper covers and mostly in the French language. The big black letters formed the words, 'Offices of the Porvenir'. From these offices a single folded sheet of Martin's journalism issued three times a week; and the sleek yellow Anzani prowling in a suit of ample black and carpet slippers, before the many doors of his establishment, greeted by a deep, side-long inclination of his body the Journalist of Sulaco going to and fro on the business of his august calling' (p. 159).

And later, during the revolution, Anzani is 'murdered by the National Guards in front of his safe' (p. 476). Though Conrad has not borrowed from the actual Anzani's character or revolutionary activities, he has borrowed the notion of Anzani as storekeeper: 'On arriving in America, Anzani had presented himself' to 'Messrs. — merchants at St. Gabriel...These gentlemen soon constituted him their factotum. Anzani was at once cashier, book-keeper, and man of confidence' (*Garibaldi*, p. 138).

25 An incident in the life of the actual Anzani has given Conrad suggestions for the character of the bandit, Hernandez. Anzani once beat up an Indian chief who terrorised the city in which he lived, but it is the reputation and method of pillage of this Indian chief which Conrad has made use of:

Notes

'One of the chiefs of these Indians had made himself the terror of this little city, into which, twice a year, he made a descent with his tribe, and which he taxed at his pleasure, without its being able to make any resistance. Coming down at first with two or three hundred men, then with a hundred, then with fifty, in proportion as he saw the increasing terror of his name establish his power, he had ended by feeling himself so much master as to come alone, and, alone as he was, to issue his orders, and declare his wants, as if he had the whole of his tribe at his back, to plunge the city in fire and blood.

Anzani had heard a great deal said about this bravado, and had listened to all that had been told him, without offering any opinion upon the audacity...[he] inspired. This terror was so great, that when the cry, "The chief di Mattes!" was heard, all windows were closed, and all doors were bolted, as at the cry of "a mad dog!"

The Indian was accustomed to these signs of terror, which flattered his pride. He selected the door which it pleased him to have opened, knocked, and the door being opened—which was done with the celerity of terror—he might plunder the whole house without either masters, neighbours, or inhabitants, however numerous they might be, thinking of interrupting his retreat' (*Garibaldi*, p. 139).

This is paralleled in *Nostromo* by Hernandez: 'He [Hernandez] used to ride, single-handed, into the villages and the little towns on the Campo driving a pack mule before him, with two revolvers in his belt, go straight to the shop or store, select what he wanted, and ride away unopposed because of the terror his exploits and his audacity inspired' (p. 108).

Having taken so much of his robber chief from the history of Garibaldi's follower, Conrad completed the picture with certain characteristics of a robber called Cisneros.

Hernandez was a sergeant in the civil war who killed his superior officer. Then 'with a band of deserters who chose him for their chief, he had taken refuge beyond the wild and waterless Bolson de Tonoro' (pp. 107–8). 'His followers, mounted on stolen horses, laughed at the pursuit of the regular cavalry sent to hunt them down... Expeditions had been fitted out; a price had been put upon his head; even attempts had been made, treacherously of course, to open negotiations with him, without in the slightest way affecting the even tenor of his career' (p. 108). Much later in the novel, this

416

fearsome bandit is brought back into the fold (helping in fact to quell the revolutionaries in Sulaco). Nostromo is the intrepid intermediary who brings Hernandez the robber into the service of the loyalist government: '"Yes", murmured Charles Gould; "Captain Mitchell's Capataz was the only man in the town who had seen Hernandez eye to eye...He opened the communications first"' (p. 381).

Like Hernandez, Cisneros was a sergeant who on becoming a bandit made his hideout in impossible wilds. R. B. Cunninghame Graham, who very likely talked to Conrad about Cisneros, writes of him as follows:

'A certain José Dionisio Cisneros, secure in the deep valleys and the mountains of the Tuy district still held out. This rascal who had been a sergeant in the Spanish army, had gathered to himself a band of cut-throats, deserters from both armies, escaped slaves, and all the flotsam and the jetsam that civil warfare brings to the top like scum' (*José Antonio Paez*, London, 1929, p. 210).

'Various discontented ex-officers led bands of brigands, who masquerading under the style of royalists pillaged and plundered the country districts and made the roads unsafe. The most considerable of these, Juan Dionisio Cisneros, defied all the attempts to capture him, safe in the rugged fastnesses of the mountains at the head of the river Tuy' (p. 230).

In *Nostromo*, the influential Father Corbelàn 'had taken into his head to advocate an unconditional pardon for Hernandez the Robber' and it is Nostromo who seeks Hernandez out: 'Padre Corbelàn had got hold of that reckless Italian, the Capataz de Cargadores, the only man fit for such an errand' (p. 196). In Cisernos's case, it was President Paez himself who offered a pardon and who went alone and unarmed in search of the bandit (*Paez*, pp. 256–61).

26 *Garibaldi*, pp. 67–8.

16. NOSTROMO AND DECOUD (pp. 162–170)

1 Author's Note to *Nostromo*, pp. xvii–xviii.

2 For a detailed and scholarly account of Conrad's use of this book see Halverson and Watt, pp. 45–52.

3 Author's Note to *Nostromo*, p. xviii.

4 *Ibid.* p. xix.   5 *Ibid.* p. xxii.

6 Letter of 19 April 1969.

7 Joseph Conrad, *The Mirror of the Sea* (London, 1946), p. 163.

Notes

8 *Ibid.* p. 164.

9 But Nostromo has adventures which clearly cannot be founded upon the experiences of Cervoni. Captain Mitchell, for example, speaks of Nostromo's famous ride, which brings Barrios's relieving forces to Sulaco: 'In the Construction Camp at the rail-head, he obtained a horse, arms, some clothing, and started alone on that marvellous ride—four hundred miles in six days, through a disturbed country, ending by the feat of passing through the Monterist lines outside Cayta. The history of that ride, sir, would make a most exciting book' (p. 482).

Conrad probably derived this event from the famous ride which Clements R. Markham writes of in his *The War between Peru and Chile*: 'Hilarion Daza was of low origin, born at Sucre...General Nicanor Flores...rose against the tyranny of Melgarejo in 1865, but they were defeated...When another revolt broke out against Melgarejo at Sucre, Daza carried the news to La Paz by galloping at the rate of fifty leagues a day, without rest, for 500 miles' (pp. 177–8).

10 Vidan, p. 289.

11 Captain Richard F. Burton, *Letters from the Battle-fields of Paraguay* (London, 1870), p. 285.

12 For reference to the original *Porvenir* see Enrique Santos Montejo, 'El Periodismo en Bogota y en Colombia', *Vinculo Shell*, xviii, 128, 1966, p. 5.

13 G. F. Masterman, *Seven Eventful Years in Paraguay* (London, 1869), p. 301.

14 Charles A. Washburn, *The History of Paraguay with notes of personal observations and reminiscences of diplomacy under difficulties* (Boston, 1871), ii, 519.

15 But Conrad deliberately links this love story with his own first love: 'If anything could induce me to revisit Sulaco (I should hate to see all these changes) it would be Antonia. And the true reason for that—why not be frank about it?—the true reason is that I have modelled her on my first love. How we, a band of tallish schoolboys, the chums of her two brothers, how we used to look up to that girl just out of the schoolroom herself, as the standard-bearer of a faith to which we all were born but which she alone knew how to hold aloft with an unflinching hope! She had perhaps more glow and less serenity in her soul than Antonia, but she was an uncompromising Puritan of patriotism with no taint of the

Notes

slightest worldliness in her thoughts. I was not the only one in love with her; but it was I who had to hear oftenest her scathing criticism of my levities—very much like poor Decoud—or stand the brunt of her austere, unanswerable invective. She did not quite understand—but never mind. That afternoon when I came in, a shrinking yet defiant sinner, to say the final good-bye I received a hand-squeeze that made my heart leap and saw a tear that took my breath away. She was softened at the last as though she had suddenly perceived (we were such children still!) that I was really going away for good, going very far away—even as far as Sulaco, lying unknown, hidden from our eyes in the darkness of the Placid Gulf' (Author's Note, pp. xxiii–xxiv).

The girl here, in her character and treatment of Conrad, is similar to Antonia, and Zdzisław Najder refers to the possibility of two early love affairs of Conrad: 'It has been frequently assumed that he (Conrad) was in love with one of the Taube sisters, Janina, later Baroness de Brunnow, but there is no evidence to support this hypothesis. Apparently he had some flirtation with Antoni Syroczyński's daughter Tekla in Lvov and was severely reprimanded by her father' (p. 13). It may be, however, that Conrad is referring to another unhappy relationship which is represented fictionally in *Arrow of Gold*, the cancelled opening chapters of which refer in a similar fashion to the torments inflicted upon him by a woman he loved: 'I imagine that at first he amused her, then he bored her, (perhaps was in the way of some more serious flirtation) and then discovering that she could make him suffer she let herself go to her heart's content. She amused herself again and again by tormenting him privately and publicly with great zest and method and finally "executed" him in circumstances of peculiar atrocity... Perhaps he was unduly sensitive. At any rate he came out of it seamed, scarred, almost flayed and with a complete mistrust of himself, an abiding fear' (see Baines, p. 29).

To my mind there is insufficient information about Conrad's early life, and particularly about such love affairs, so that the exact personal source of such identification with Decoud must remain speculation.

16 Edward B. Eastwick, *Venezuela: or Sketches of Life in a South American Republic; with the History of the Loan of 1864* (London, 1868). See Baines, p. 295.

17 Ermina's devotion to her father is particularly marked: 'Meantime, I could not help being struck with the love and devotion with which

Señor L. was nursed by his family. His daughters, who, when I first came, had every day been seated, radiant with smiles and beautifully dressed, at the windows, now never left the sick-room. I had the pleasure of seeing, in this instance, that the Creole ladies, who to a superficial observer might appear bent only on coquetry, are in reality not to be surpassed in that affection which binds families together. I had before admired Erminia for her beauty: I now esteemed and respected her for her devotion to her father' (Eastwick, p. 191).

18 Letter of 19 April 1969.

19 Letter written by Tadeusz Bobrowski to Stefan Buszczyński, 12 March 1879, Najder, pp. 176–7. Another aspect of the Cervoni source appears to have a connection with Decoud. In *The Mirror of the Sea*, Conrad describes the relationship between Dominic Cervoni and his nephew Cesar. Dominic is constantly knocking Cesar down, in order to make him a man, and finally, learning that he had stolen Conrad's money belt, he knocks him overboard and he 'went down like a stone—with the gold' (p. 181). This parallels to some extent Decoud's going overboard from the lighter weighted with four ingots of silver. Cesar Cervoni's letter to me makes it clear that Cesar was not even related to Dominic and that he was not killed by him—indeed their attitude to each other is quite a different one to that suggested by Conrad. The weighting of a body with stolen silver or gold presumably does not come from this source, therefore.

20 Najder, p. 13.   21 Watts, p. 65.

17. SIR JOHN AND 'MATERIAL INTERESTS' (pp. 171–181)

1 See Baines, pp. 295–7; also Edgar Wright.

2 Conrad made use of Guzman Blanco's name, changing it to Guzman Bento and giving it to the earlier and tyrannical dictator in his novel.

3 Eastwick, pp. 124 and 203.

4 Maurice H. Hervey, *Dark Days in Chile* (London, 1891–2). See photograph of Moraga opposite page 160 in Hervey's book. Captain Mitchell, the garrulous old seaman, in pointing out Hernandez, comments: 'This is the famous Hernandez, Minister of War. *The Times*' special correspondent, who wrote that striking series of letters calling the Occidental Republic the "Treasure House of the

World" gave a whole article to him and the force he has organized' (p. 480). Hervey was, in fact, a special correspondent for *The Times*, and his book is an account of the journey he made to Chile as the *Times* correspondent. On his return home, his landlady says to him, 'They did print a few letters, which I knew must be from you...because they were from their "Special Correspondent"' (p. 269).

5 Eastwick, pp. 75–6.
6 *Ibid.* p. 76.
7 *Ibid.*
8 *Ibid.* p. 195.
9 *Ibid.* p. 141.
10 *Ibid.* p. 196.
11 *Ibid.* p. 230.
12 Charles Dance, *Recollections of Four Years in Venezuela* (London, 1876), pp. 133–4.
13 *Ibid.* pp. 152–3.

18. DR MONYGHAM AND DON JOSÉ AVELLANOS (pp. 182–189)

1 See Edgar Wright, Ivo Vidan and Jocelyn Baines.
2 Baines, p. 295.
3 Masterman also says of a prisoner called Baltazar: 'and now the sounds of heavy blows, each followed by a shriek from him, proved how much more they were prepared to inflict on us: they were smashing his fingers with a mallet' (p. 258).
4 Masterman, pp. 277–8.
5 *Ibid.* pp. 258–9.
6 *Ibid.* p. 305.
7 *Ibid.* pp. 170–1.
8 'The large door was wide open; but as it looked only into a long arched passage connecting the two courtyards of the Colegio, (for I was within the old Jesuit college), all the light I could get would be that reflected from the wall' (Masterman, p. 149).

'There was no other way left now to enjoy his power but by seeing his crushed adversaries crawl impotently into the light of day out of the dark, noisome cells of the Collegio' (*Nostromo*, p. 139).
9 Masterman, p. 164.
10 *Ibid.*
11 *Ibid.* pp. 308–9.
12 *Ibid.* pp. 268–70.
13 *Ibid.* p. 291.

19. COSTAGUANA AND SULACO (pp. 190–201)

1 'Costaguana is meant for a S. Am^can state in general', letter to Cunninghame Graham, 31 October 1904, Watts, p. 157.

Notes

2 Gustav Morf, *The Polish Heritage of Joseph Conrad* (London, 1930), p. 14.

3 Baines, p. 296.

4 William Eleroy Curtis, *Venezuela; a Land where it's always Summer* (London, 1896), p. 216.

5 Masterman, p. 73.

6 E. M. W. Tillyard, *The Epic Strain in the English Novel* (London, 1958), p. 199.

7 Eastwick, p. 167.   8 Masterman, p. 74.

9 Eastwick, pp. 52–3.   10 *Ibid.* p. 144, cf. Wright, p. 304.

11 Baines writes: 'for some of the topography of the town of Sulaco Conrad draws on Eastwick's description of the inland town of Valencia' (p. 296).

12 Masterman, p. 122.   13 Eastwick, p. 65.

14 Curtis, p. 63.   15 Masterman, p. 296.

16 Washburn, II, 245.   17 Masterman, p. 229.

18 And Captain Mitchell himself recalls how the miners came down from the mine to retake the town from Pedro Montero: 'The miners, sir, had marched upon the town, Don Pépé leading on his black horse, and their very wives in the rear on burros, screaming encouragement sir, and beating tambourines. I remember one of these women had a green parrot seated on her shoulder, as calm as a bird of stone' (p. 477).

19 Masterman, pp. 173–4.   20 *Ibid.* p. 16.

21 Curtis, p. 56.   22 Eastwick, p. 178.

23 *Ibid.* p. 155.   24 *Ibid.*

25 *Ibid.* p. 179.   26 *Ibid.* p. 183.

20. 'THE INFORMER (pp. 205–218)

1 Author's Note to *The Secret Agent*, p. xiv.

2 *Ibid.* p. ix.   3 *Ibid.* p. x.

4 Ford Madox Ford, *Joseph Conrad: A Personal Remembrance* (London, 1924), p. 231.

5 Eloise Knapp Hay, p. 227.

6 David Garnett, *The Golden Echo* (London, 1953), p. 38.

7 Helen Rossetti Angeli, *Pre-Raphaelite Twilight* (London, 1954), p. 144.

8 *Life & Letters*, II, 29.   9 Baines, p. 322, n.

10 Letter to Pinker, 21 February 1906, *ibid.* p. 327.

Notes

11 *Life & Letters*, II, 25.

12 'The mysterious Number One' was a term applied in fact not to an anarchist, but to the Irish Invincibles. The supposed leader of the Invincibles was P. J. P. Tynan known as No. I, a title he was proud enough of to use as an alias in his book.

13 Author's Note to *The Secret Agent*, p. x.

14 Ford Madox Ford, *Ancient Lights and Certain New Reflections* (London, 1911), p. 121.

15 Ford Madox Ford, *Return to Yesterday* (London, 1931), p. 108.

16 Juliet Soskice, *Chapters from Childhood* (London, 1921), p. 4.

17 Emma Goldman, *Living my Life* (London, 1931), p. 164. And George Woodcock, in his study of anarchism, records: 'In loyalty to their foreign ancestry, the Rossetti sisters specialized in introducing the writings of Continental anarchists, and Louise Michel, Malato, Malatesta, Zhukovsky, and Faure all contributed to *The Torch*... while one of the younger contributors was the youth who became Ford Madox Ford' (*Anarchism*, London, 1963, p. 423).

18 Helen was the leading light, the instigator and enthusiast who converted her elder brother and sister. It all began with reading Prince Kropotkin's *An Appeal to the Young*: 'You are just entering on life. Your mind, I believe, is free of the superstitions some have tried to impose on you: you do not fear hell and you do not go to hear parsons and ministers rant.'

19 Letter of 14 March 1967

20 William Michael Rossetti, *Some Reminiscences* (London, 1906), II, 454.

21 18 December 1895. Two further examples will show that Conrad was not being extravagant when he has his narrator exclaim: 'One of them [the anarchist publications] preached the dissolution of all social and domestic ties; the other advocated systematic murder' (p. 89). In the publication *Anarchy of Love* appears the following sentence: 'The courtesan is sexually free; the wife is a slave. The superior moral condition of the former consists in the fact that she can refuse to co-habit or associate with whom she loves not, at any time. The emancipation of woman from her domestic slavery is to be found in the abolition of the marriage laws. Her complete economic independence in the abolition of all other laws.' And as to systematic murder—'Colonna was an honest worker...he was sacked. The outlook was now dreadful, and he resolved to chastize those who stood in his way. He flew at the throat of the boss, was arrested, and in the police-station he stabbed a bobby and ran out in the street.

Another man in blue attempted to arrest him and got stabbed in the heart. Well done! A third bobby and one civilian got the same lesson' (*Commonweal*, 24 October 1891).

22 Isabel Meredith, *A Girl among the Anarchists* (London, 1903), pp. 1–2.

23 Rossetti, II, 454.   24 Juliet Soskice, p. 23.

25 *A Girl among the Anarchists*, p. 35.

21. 'AN ANARCHIST' (pp. 219–227)

1 'Rapport du commandant Bouchet sur la revolte du 21 October 1894 (Ile St. Joseph)', Archives Nationales, Section outre-mer.

2 Liard-Courtois, *Souvenirs du Bagne* (Paris, 1903).

3 Michael Bourdet-Pléville, *Justice in Chains: from the Galleys to Devil's Island*, translated from the French by Anthony Rippon (London, 1960), p. 195.

4 Liard-Courtois, p. 186.   5 Bourdet-Pléville, p. 198.

6 *Ibid.*   7 Bouchet, p. 7.

8 *Ibid.* p. 8.   9 *Ibid.* pp. 8–9.

10 *Ibid.* p. 10.   11 Liard-Courtois, p. 191.

12 Bouchet, p. 13   13 Liard-Courtois, p. 192.

14 The suggestion that conversion to anarchy is a matter of propaganda working on weak minds—Paul has 'a warm heart and a weak head' —might have come from the journal that first published *Lord Jim*— *Blackwood's Magazine*. Referring to the attack on the Prince of Wales made by the anarchist Sipido, *Blackwood's* commented: 'in attempting to shoot a prince he [Sipido] did but obey the lying voice of journalists and orators, and thus he proved once more that it is words not thoughts, that move the unstable mind of the born Anarchist' ('Musings without Method', *Blackwood's Magazine*, May 1900, p. 693).

Paul is first imprisoned for getting drunk in a tavern and shouting 'Vive l'anarchie!' On 18 December 1894 there appeared in *The Torch* the following extract in a section dealing with news from France: 'Poverty is killing off the poor, but as yet they do not revolt. Still signs are not wanting that things will last forever. Here we see a workman abusing the government in a public-house midst the general applause...another has a year's imprisonment for shouting out "Vive l'Anarchie".'

To the central anarchist incident Conrad has added a reflection of his eastern novels as well as suggestions from the worlds of *Nostromo* and *Heart of Darkness*. The narrator, with his scientific and enthusiastic search after butterflies takes us back to Stein of *Lord Jim* and his source in Wallace's book, *The Malay Archipelago*. The lepidopterist meets Paul on the island of Horta which he has visited because it is 'the only known habitat of an extremely rare and gorgeous butterfly...As a matter of fact, I am...a desperate butterfly-slayer' (p. 137). In *Lord Jim*, Stein's greatest passion is also butterflies: 'his cabinet of butterflies, beautiful and hovering under the glass of cases of lifeless wings, had spread his fame far over the earth'. The cattle ranches and Don Enrique, the estuary of the 'great South American river' and the importance of the company reflect the material concerns of *Nostromo*.

22. THE BOMB OUTRAGE (pp. 228–247)

1 Author's Note to *The Secret Agent*, pp. ix–xii.
2 *Life & Letters*, II, 38.   3 *Ibid.* p. 322.
4 Baines, p. 133 and Eloise Knapp Hay, p. 228.
5 A serial version of the novel appeared in *Ridgway's Militant Weekly*, from 6 October to 15 December 1906.
6 According to Jean-Aubry, the pamphlet Conrad received was about the attempt to blow up the Greenwich Observatory and it quoted *The Times* description of the perpetrator of the crime (*Life & Letters*, II, 322, n. 2).
7 Emile Henry was a French anarchist who, three days before the explosion at Greenwich, had thrown a bomb into a restaurant which killed one person and injured twenty others. Conrad probably had this incident in mind when he has Vladimir lecture Verloc on the uselessness of such attacks: 'A murderous attempt on a restaurant ...would suffer...from the suggestion of non-political passion' (p. 32).
8 H. L. Adams records in *C.I.D.: Behind the Scenes at Scotland Yard* (London, 1931): 'The fellow was buried by an undertaker in Tottenham Court Road, who had the face of the corpse photographed as the body lay in the coffin. This photograph, which he has framed, he put in his window, so that any passer-by could see it. It was a very grim picture. The face was punctured here and there with the missiles flung out of the bomb by the explosion' (p. 166). Samuels wrote in the same issue of the *Commonweal* which printed the editorial on his brother-in-law's death: 'The undertaker, Mr. Enefer, 6 Chapel Street, Marylebone Road, W., has cabinet

photos of Martial Bourdin on sale at a shilling each, taken in two positions.'

9 Bourdin was connected in the newspaper reports with the anarchists from the beginning. In its first report of the incident, the *Morning Leader* quoted the Central News Agency's account of the events before Bourdin blew himself to pieces: 'But these facts among others are beyond dispute, that the inquiries of the detectives, although cautiously made, frightened the [anarchist] plotters, that the gang hurriedly scattered, and that its chief met with a horrible death last evening when endeavouring in a panic of fear to carry away to some place the deadly explosives' (16 February 1894).

On 19 February the newspaper put forward a different theory, one which accounted for the fact that Bourdin had travelled unnecessarily far—from Tottenham Court Road to Greenwich—with his infernal machine: 'Beyond all question, Bourdin was well aware of the fact that he was being watched...and the theory has been set up that, instead of taking the train straight to Dover, he, with a view to eluding the observations of the detectives and of a police spy who was supposed to be on his track, got out at New-cross, his intention being to baffle his pursuers and catch a later train for the South Coast. It is thought that while thus waiting, he, in order to kill time, went for a ramble in the neighbourhood and found himself in Greenwich-park, where he was so soon destined to meet his terrible fate.' This was a pretty tall story and was not repeated by the newspaper.

Anarchist friends of Bourdin held a different view: 'Their idea is that he went to the park with a new combination of explosives of his own invention with the intention of trying how it would work. They believe that he intended going to some remote part of the park and there making the experiment. They do not for a moment conceive that he had any design against the Royal Observatory, as he had, they say quaintly, "no spite against that building"' (*Morning Leader*, 17 February 1894).

Another view put forward was that Bourdin had a rendezvous at Greenwich Park with other anarchists in order to hand over chemicals to them. Yet another was that the anarchists had to move the explosives away from one hiding place which might be raided to an out-of-the-way park like Greenwich: 'a comparatively unfrequented park like that of Greenwich, which abounds in solitary spots, where a man might even dig with a reasonable prospect of not being observed, offered a desirable resort. But against this theory, it is pointed out, may be placed the fact that there are parks which are much easier of access—to say nothing of the river—to a man living off the Tottenham Court Rd. than Greenwich could have been' (*Morning Leader*, 17 February 1894). Then it was declared that 'possession of explosives had become very risky [and he] resolved to get rid of his share of the "stuff" by using it against some Government building' (*Morning Leader*, 17 February 1894).

10 Author's Note to *The Secret Agent*, p. x.

11 *The Greenwich Mystery*, p. 6: see p. 382, below.

12 *Ibid.* p. 5: see p. 381, below.   13 *Ibid.* p. 15: see p. 393, below.

14 *Ibid.* p. 13: see p. 390, below.   15 *Ibid.* p. 12: see p. 389, below.

16 David Nicoll, *Letters from the Dead* (Sheffield, 1898), p. 3.

17 *Anarchist*, 18 March 1894.   18 *Ibid.* 13 May 1894.

19 'The funeral of the Anarchist Bourdin...took place on Friday, Feb. 23, in Finchley Cemetery...an Anarchist who attempted to deliver a speech at the grave was promptly suppressed by the police, who had afterwards to protect him from the violence of the crowd. The windows of the Autonomie Club [a well-known anarchist meeting place] were broken, and a mob in Fitzroy Square indulged in anti-Anarchist manifestations' (*Illustrated London News*, 3 March 1894).

23. THE ANARCHISTS (pp. 248–252)

1 Irving Howe, *Politics and the Novel* (London, 1961), p. 96.

2 Author's Note to *The Secret Agent*, p. xiv.

3 Letter of 8 February 1899, Watts, p. 116.

4 Author's Note to *The Secret Agent*, p. xiii.

5 Letter of 9 February 1899, *Joseph Conrad: Letters to William Blackwood and David S. Meldrum*, ed. William Blackburn (North Carolina, 1958), p. 48.

6 *Life & Letters*, I, 277.

7 W. C. Hart, *Confessions of an Anarchist* (London, 1906).

8 *A Girl among the Anarchists*, p. 272.

9 *Confessions of an Anarchist*, p. 7.

10 *A Girl among the Anarchists*, pp. 272–4.

11 *Confessions of an Anarchist*, p. 8.

12 Albert J. Guerard, *Conrad the Novelist* (Massachusetts, 1966), p. 221.

1 Woodcock, p. 436.
2 Quoted by Henry David, *The History of the Haymarket Affair* (New York, 1958), p. 88.
3 *Beast of Property* was reprinted in the *Commonweal*, 30 May 1891.
4 *Ibid.*
5 Author's Note to *The Secret Agent*, p. ix.
6 Emma Goldman, I, 380.
7 Max Nomad, *Apostles of Revolution* (London, 1939), p. 300.
8 *A Girl among the Anarchists*, p. 285.
9 Quoted by Woodcock, p. 143.
10 E. H. Carr, *Michael Bakunin* (New York, 1961), p. 395.
11 James Joll, *The Anarchists* (London, 1964), p. 108.
12 *Commonweal*, 15 November 1890.
13 *Ibid.* 29 November 1890. 14 *Ibid.* 28 November 1891.
15 Yundt's confessed inability to find even three men for his purpose is Conrad's ironic comment on the movement.
16 Of the Professor, Irving Howe writes: 'It is difficult to regard this grimy lunatic as anything but a cartoon' (*Politics and the Novel*, p. 97).

1 *Annual Register*, 1867, Part II, 'Chronicle of Remarkable Occurrences'.
2 None of the ringleaders was, like Michaelis, a locksmith by trade. Allen was a carpenter, Gould a draper and a soldier of fortune, Larkin and Condon were both tailors.
3 'The Convict Condon, alias Shore—One Sunday morning, the Governor of the New Bailey Prison received an intimation that the sentence of death upon Condon for the murder of Sergeant Brett had been commuted to penal servitude for life' (*The Times*, 27 November 1867).
4 The true reason for the reprieve is suggested, however, in a letter from Gathorne Hardy to Queen Victoria: 'Though he [Shore] might justly be made amenable to the extreme penalty of the law, it has been thought more politic and expedient to recognize a slight distinction between him and the other three convicts whose execution will suffice for example. Penal servitude for life will be his punishment' (*Letters of Queen Victoria*, 3rd ser., ed. G. E. Buckle, London, 1926, I, 468). Both Condon and Gould [O'Brien] were Irish Americans and it

Notes

seems that the American minister in Britain, Adams, was persuaded to intercede on their behalf. He was successful in Condon's case. See William d'Arcy, *The Fenian Movement in the United States: 1858–1886* (Washington, 1947), p. 270.

5 'The Royal free pardon of the Fenian convicts Patrick Melody and Edward O'Meara Condon, the "ardent Irishman" for whose release the U.S. Government have so persistently applied, passed under the Great Seal yesterday, so that in a few hours the men will be liberated on the condition of the pardon that they shall not reside within the Queen's dominions (*The Times*, 11 September 1878).

6 'The whole proceedings from the time of leaving Portland [prison] till their departure from Southampton were conducted with the greatest secrecy' (*The Times*, 18 September 1878).

7 F. Sheehy-Skeffington, *Michael Davitt: Revolutionary, Agitator, and Labour Leader* (London, 1908), p. 46.

8 M. M. O'Hara, *Chief and Tribune: Parnell and Davitt* (Dublin and London, 1919), pp. 167–8.

9 D. B. Cashman, *The Life of Michael Davitt, Founder of the National Land League* (Glasgow, n.d.), p. 146.

10 Sheehy-Skeffington, p. 57.   11 *Ibid.* p. 37.

12 *Ibid.* p. 266.   13 O'Hara, pp. 32–3.

14 Sheehy-Skeffington, pp. 63–4.

15 P. Kropotkin, *Mutual Aid, a Factor of Evolution* (London, 1902).

16 *Nineteenth Century*, February 1888, p. 165.

17 Kropotkin, pp. 222–3.

18 Edward Bellamy, *Looking Backward: 2000–1887* (Boston and New York, 1926).   19 *Ibid.* p. 133.

20 Benjamin Tucker, the famous American 'individualist' anarchist, the disciple of Stirner, argues that Marx 'concluded that the only way to abolish the class monopolies was to centralize and consolidate all industrial and commercial interests, all productive and distributive agencies, in one vast monopoly in the hands of the State...the remedy for *monopolies* is MONOPOLY.' Referring to the nationalists, he argues that they 'follow Karl Marx filtered through Edward Bellamy'. Quoted by Irving L. Horowitz, *The Anarchists* (New York, 1964), p. 174.

21 Bellamy, pp. 52–6.

22 Richard Michaelis, *A Sequel to Looking Backward* (London, n.d.).

23 E. H. Carr, *The Romantic Exiles* (London, 1949), pp. 252–3.

24 Carr, *Michael Bakunin*, p. 251.

Notes

1 Letter of 7 October 1907, Watts, p. 170.
2 *Criminal Man: According to the Classification of Cesare Lombroso* (London), p. 14. This was not translated into English until 1911, though his views were well-known long before then. See also his pamphlet on anarchists (*Gli Anarchici*) summarized in Appendix IX of *Criminal Man*.
3 *Ibid.* p. 15.   4 *Ibid.* p. 16.
5 *Ibid.* p. 18.
6 Max Nordau, *Degeneration* (London, 1898). Conrad sees the Professor as an 'unwholesome-looking little moral agent of destruction' who exults silently when he meets in a side-street the representative of law and order, Chief Inspector Heat: 'The unwholesome-looking little moral agent of destruction exulted silently in the possession of personal prestige, keeping in check this man armed with the defensive mandate of a menaced society. *More fortunate than Caligula, who wished that the Roman Senate had only one head for the better satisfaction of his cruel lust*, he beheld in that one man all the forces he had set at defiance' (p. 83) [my italics]. Conrad most probably had this image suggested to him while reading *Degeneration*: 'Finally, in its extreme degree of development, ego-mania leads to that *folly of Caligula in which the unbalanced mind* boasts of being "a laughing lion", believes himself above all restraints of morality or law, and *wishes the whole of humanity had one single head that he might cut it off*' (p. 265) [my italics]. What Caligula is actually reported to have said was: 'Utinam populus Romanus unam cervicem haberet—I wish the Roman people had only one neck.'
7 Nordau, pp. 263-5.
8 First Secretary Vladimir, for his own purposes, tries to persuade Verloc that more forceful measures are necessary: 'You anarchists should make it clear that you are perfectly determined to make a clean sweep of the whole social creation' (p. 32).
9 Felix Dubois, *The Anarchist Peril*, trans. Ralph Derechef (London, 1894), p. 31.
10 The term which stands out in the Professor's expression of the idea of destroying the masses is 'Exterminate, exterminate!' It looks as if Conrad is merely returning here to an earlier phrase, one which has often caught the eye of readers of *Heart of Darkness*.

Kurtz in a 17-page report for the guidance of the 'International Society for the Suppression of Savage Customs' ended with the postscriptum: '*Exterminate all the brutes.*' Now it may well be that Conrad heard this remark from some Belgian agent while he was serving in the Congo, but my view is that it had an anarchist origin, a similar phrase being used by the anarchist, Johann Most. Most was obsessed by the desire for revolutionary violence, and his cry was 'Extirpate the miserable brood', by which he meant all class exploiters of the masses. He had urged, as early as 18 December 1880, in his anarchist paper *Die Freiheit*, 'Exterminate the contemptible breed'.

11 Quoted by E. V. Zenker in *Anarchism: A Criticism and History of the Anarchist Theory* (London, 1898), p. 236. And in *Freedom*, December 1892, we find this: 'The false assumption that what is legal is synonymous with what is right had caused people to confound many acts which would not be anti-social, were the universal interests considered, with such as really are so. Thus it comes about that society...revenges itself upon the victims who rebel against its own cruel and unjust laws...immoral law makes criminals of those who otherwise would not be criminal.'

12 Dr Creaghe, a medical practitioner in Sheffield in the 1890s, was an anarchist of an extreme kind—he had earlier been involved in a South American revolution—and Conrad's Professor could well be based on some aspects of Creaghe's history and character. Referring to an argument he had had, he wrote in the *Commonweal*: 'he called me a firebrand and alluded contemptuously to my inches' (4 June 1892), thus recalling Conrad's professor who 'walked along, with his head carried rigidly erect, in a crowd whose every individual almost overtopped his stunted stature' (p. 72). There is yet a third place where Conrad could have found the motto. In the *Commonweal*, 30 August 1890, the famous apostle of anarchism Kropotkin writes of Blanqui: 'The man who more than anyone else was the incarnation of this system of conspiracy, the man who paid for his devotion to this system by a life in prison, threw out just before his death these words, which are a programme in themselves, "Neither God nor master".'

13 'Little Known English Anarchists', *War Commentary*, 14 July 1945. It would appear that even Cunninghame Graham made his contribution to the Professor in a conception which, though it appears briefly, is vivid, and in the Professor's system, significant. 'Madness

and despair! Give me that for a lever and I'll move the world', the perfect anarchist claims. Conrad went so far as to quote this in a letter to Cunninghame Graham, as I have shown, and one wonders whether Cunninghame Graham felt any sense of recognition, for an account of a speech of his which appeared in the *Commonweal*, 18 October 1890, stated: 'The only crime that is never pardoned or forgiven is poverty. Well, *fear, is a good lever, too*, you know. Having your lever, though you want a fulcrum...Archimedes could have *moved the world* could he have found a fulcrum. Where is your fulcrum?' [my italics]. Archimedes is reputed to have said: 'Give me a lever long enough, and a fulcrum strong enough, and single-handed I can move the world.' This is variously quoted as 'Give me where to stand and I will move the world', 'Give me a base and I will move the world', 'Give me a firm place to stand, and I will move the earth. On the lever.' Conrad's modification of this anecdote is similar to Cunninghame Graham's, the one introducing the notion of 'fear', the other of 'madness and despair' as a lever. In his 'A Familiar Preface' to *A Personal Record*, Conrad again returned to Archimedes: 'Don't talk to me of your Archimedes' lever...Give me the right word and the right accent and I will move the world' (pp. xi-xii).

14 Quoted from Louis Adamic, *Dynamite: The Story of Class Violence in America* (New York, 1934), p. 47.

15 *Contemporary Review*, May 1894, p. 679.

16 *The Greenwich Mystery*, p. 13: see p. 390, below. And another anarchist, Mrs Bevington, stated: 'Samuels came to my house at the end of May (long after he had taken to writing as a politician and aspired after ballooning), and, without more ado, sat down, and proceeded to give minute instructions for making and charging bombs...and, after an elaborate lession, he said, "I am telling this to everybody; there are soon going to be English acts, too; it is high time there should be"' (*Letters from the Dead*, p. 3).

17 'In 1883 Luke Dillon and Jimmy Cunningham left Philadelphia for London. They brought with them the one argument to which no tyrant can remain deaf. It was the morning after the Derby, and the elite of England's aristocratic robbers were sleeping off the effects of their carouse in the ultra-select Carlton Club. Single-handed, Luke advanced to the attack, and the startled Lords, M.P.s and aristocrats woke up to find the edifice crumbling about their ears. On the same morning Jimmy Cunningham, in an attempt to

blow up the Army and Navy Club, demolished a wing of Sir Watkyn Wynne's town house. Cunningham was arrested, and the ill-treatment he received during his six years' torture in a British jail seriously affected his mind.

1884 saw Luke Dillon in London once more, with Roger O'Neill. They had decided to enter the enemy parliament:—in the only way likely to achieve anything save dishonour for Ireland. Luke was being conducted with a party of tourists to various places of interest. "This", said the guide, "is where the Irish members are creating so much trouble." "I'd have them all hanging at the end of a rope!" commented an Englishman. With that the crash of O'Neill's bomb echoed through the hall and the party fled in panic—all save Luke. He ascended the gallery, calmly placed his bomb in position—and in a few minutes another explosion rang out.

Two wounded police lay on stretchers, and four police barred the door. Luke ordered an officer who told him he could not leave to stand aside, and walked through them. The sensation caused in England—and throughout Europe—by this attack on the nerve-centre of British power was tremendous. In America its effect was to stimulate recruiting for the Clan-na-Gael.'

The Times, 5 April 1892, provides a list of the outstanding dynamite outrages which took place in Britain from 1881 to 1891, and a vast list it is. But the two we are concerned with are listed as follows: 'May 30, 1884—An explosion of dynamite at the Junior Carlton Club, St. James's square. About 14 persons were injured.' 'January 24, 1885—An explosion in the House of Commons (probably caused by a similar amount of the same explosive' [similar to the explosive used against the Tower of London on the same date. This was 5 to 8 lbs of Atlas powder of American make]. And a note follows that in connection with the three last-named outrages (at the Tower of London, Westminster Hall and House of Commons) two men (Burton and Cunningham) were afterwards convicted and sentenced to penal servitude for life. In an earlier issue of *The Times*, 1 June 1887, in an article entitled 'The Dynamite Party, Past and Present', is the following reference: 'The third group commissioned by the Clan-na-Gael, included Cunningham and Burton, sentenced for the double attempt upon the House of Commons and the Tower, but also known to have been concerned in the cloak-room explosions, as well as those on the Metropolitan Railway.'

What ultimately broke the dynamite faction of the Clan-na-Gael was the fact that the British police seemed to be able to keep such an accurate watch over the Fenian terrorists, seemed to know for what purpose they arrived in England from America before they were able to carry out that purpose.

Dillon was born in 1848 in Leeds of Irish parents and the family emigrated to America when he was six, living first in New Jersey and afterwards settling in Philadelphia. He saw active service in the frontier campaigns against the Red Indians, regarded them with friendship and learnt their language. Luke Dillon's background in no way agrees with that of the Professor until, on being discharged from the United States Army, he was recruited into the Clan-na-Gael, no. 448, in Philadelphia.

18 Desmond Ryan, *The Phoenix Flame* (London, 1937), p. 225.

19 Louis Le Roux, *Tom Clarke and the Irish Freedom Movement* (Dublin, 1936), pp. 21–2.

20 Letter of 26 December 1903, Watts, p. 149.

21 *Joseph Conrad and his Circle* (New York, 1964), p. 103.

22 Letter to W. H. Nevinson, 27 November 1928, quoted by A. F. Tschiffely, *Don Roberto* (London, 1937), p. 392.

27. LAW AND ORDER: SIR ETHELRED
THE HOME SECRETARY (pp. 286–295)

1 'Scotland Yard: Its Mysteries and Methods', *Reynolds News*, 14 April 1895.

2 Author's Note to *The Secret Agent*, p. xi.

3 Sir Robert Anderson, *Sidelights on the Home Rule Movement* (London, 1906). Cf. also A. Fleishman, *Conrad's Politics* (Baltimore, 1967), p. 213.

4 *Dictionary of National Biography*, Second Supplement, January 1901–December 1911 (London, 1912), LXVIII, 203.

5 S. H. Jeyes and F. D. How, *Life of Sir Howard Vincent* (London, 1912), p. 106.

6 Author's Note to *The Secret Agent*, p. xi.

7 Conrad's Sir Ethelred does use phraseology which is undoubtedly derived from Sir William Harcourt's remarks on Anderson. To the Assistant Commissioner on the occasion of their first meeting he says: 'But your idea of assurances over there seems to consist mainly in making the Secretary of State look a fool' (p. 136).

8 The Parnell Commission, which opened on 22 October 1888 and

sat for 128 days, sought to inquire into allegations made principally against Parnell, the Irish leader, by *The Times* newspaper. The Commission received world-wide publicity and especially sensational were the revelations of Sir Robert Anderson's 'private' informer, Le Caron, and the discovery that incriminating letters, published by *The Times*, as having been written by Parnell, were forgeries produced by Richard Pigott for money.

9 Anderson, *Sidelights*, p. 21.

10 *Dictionary of National Biography*, LXVIII, 203.

11 A. G. Gardiner, *The Life of Sir William Harcourt* (London, 1923).

12 From the Radio Times Hulton Picture Library.

13 E. T. Raymond, *Portraits of the Nineties* (London, 1921), p. 150.

14 *Ibid.* p. 151.

15 *Dictionary of National Biography*, LXVIII, 211.

16 *Ibid.* LXVIII, 198.   17 Raymond, p. 150.

18 Gardiner, II, 551.   19 *Ibid.* II, 581.

20 Author's Note to *The Secret Agent*, p. xiv.

21 Letter of 7 October 1907, Watts, p. 170.

28. THE ASSISTANT COMMISSIONER (pp. 296–301)

1 Jeyes and How, p. 104.

2 Leonard Gribble, *Stories of Famous Detectives* (London, 1963), p. 61.

3 Jeyes and How, p. 103.   4 *Ibid.*

5 George Dilnot, *The Story of Scotland Yard* (London, 1926), p. 251. Jeyes and How echo this point of view: 'It was, no doubt, a weakness in Vincent's method of work that, like most young administrators, he wished to do everything himself, and did not easily reconcile himself to the necessity of delegation' (p. 63).

6 Jeyes and How, p. 69.

7 The lady patroness attracts to her drawing-room all manner of men: it 'was probably the only place in the wide world where an Assistant Commissioner of Police could meet a convict liberated on ticket-of-leave'. She is very old—'three generations had admired her infinitely'. Baroness Burdett Coutts held her drawing-room parties and social gatherings in her famous Stratton Street home, at the corner of Stratton Street and Piccadilly, and during sixty years she made welcome at her house 'anyone and everyone with a claim to distinction' (Clara Burdett Patterson, *Angela Burdett-Coutts and the Victorians*, London, 1952, p. 42). 'Clergy, soldiers, authors, artists and actors were in due course to be found at Stratton

Street as well as political celebrities...there was no great or celebrated person then who was not entertained there at one time or other' (*ibid*. p. 44). This famous lady patroness had a wide variety of friends including Dickens, Rajah Brooke and the Duke of Wellington. Her long life (1814–1906) and her wealth and philanthropy made her a special figure in the Victorian era. The fact that she died (as did the anarchist Most) while Conrad was writing *The Secret Agent* might have led Conrad to introduce a similar figure into his novel. The title, lady patroness, was never applied to my knowledge to Burdett-Coutts, but we find Isabel Meredith (pseudonym for the Rossetti sisters) using it in her answer to the anarchist Kosinski's charge that she is a bourgeois socialist merely offering the help of her property: 'I think it a little unfair to assume me to be a mere bourgeois, attempting to play the part of lady patroness to the revolution' (*A Girl among the Anarchists*, p. 35).

8 Major A. G. F. Griffiths, *Mysteries of Police and Crime* (London, 1904), p. 133.   9 *Ibid.*

10 Eloise Knapp Hay, p. 248, n. 73.   11 Jeyes and How, p. 82.

29. CHIEF INSPECTOR HEAT (pp. 302–313)

1 Charles Kingston, *A Gallery of Rogues* (London, 1924), p. 219.

2 Griffiths, p. 131.

3 Melville L. McNaughton, *Days of My Years* (London, 1914), p. 83.

4 Sir Robert Anderson, *The Lighter Side of my Official Life* (London, 1910), p. 176.

5 To Vladimir, ambassador of a foreign power and employer of the double agent Verloc, the Assistant Commissioner repeats his view: 'All that's wanted now is to do away with the agent provocateur to make everything safe' (p. 228).

6 Speaking before the Commission, Sir Henry James, the barrister, distinguished between Le Caron and the typical *agent provocateur* who manufactured evidence: 'Well, I will admit that there is one class of informer that represents a very objectionable man. That is the man who, not content with devoting himself to the detection of crime so as to defeat it, will use his association with criminals to induce them to commit crime which they would not otherwise commit, and then hands them over to justice. We had, as your Lordship knows, at least it was floating matter, in the history of one informer in Dublin such allegation made, and I confess we can feel no sympathy, but feel the reverse, with men who cause crime

Notes

to be committed in order that they may obtain the advantage of saying that they detected it. But where is the suggestion that Le Caron ever acted any such part?' (Sir Henry James, *The Work of the Irish Leagues*, London, 1890, p. 494).

7 Anderson, *Sidelights*, p. 128.
8 'Crime and Punishment', *Contemporary Review*, December 1896, pp. 96–7.
9 Le Caron became famous in England when he appeared before the Parnell Commission in 1889 to speak on behalf of *The Times* newspaper. The mystery and drama surrounding this figure, which is reflected in the following report, was enhanced as he was part of the scandal of the Parnell affair:

'FORTY-FOURTH DAY
February 5 [1889]

To-day the Attorney-General entered upon the American part of his case. An interesting personage is Honoré Le Caron, private and subsequently major in the Northern army during the great war, and afterwards, and now—according to his own account—a high and responsible officer in the Fenian organization which still dreams of overthrowing the power of Great Britain. His name is French; but the man himself, the "Senior Guardian" of Fenian Camp No. 463 (now altered to 421), is an Englishman, whose birthplace is Colchester. My baptismal name is Thomas Miller Beach, said the major. He paused at each of his three names, pronouncing them with slow, distinct emphasis, and nodding his head as if to punctuate them. Major Le Caron is short and slightish in build; erect—like a soldier—and imperturbably cool; he has a lofty forehead, and smallish, alert eyes, which look straight. The major's is one of the boniest faces in or out of the New World,—a death's-head with a tight skin of yellow parchment. With his arms folded over his chest—like another short man, the great Napoleon—he raps out his answers, short, sharp. "Yes, yes", he says, snappishly sometimes, pronouncing it "yus"' (John Macdonald, *The Daily News Diary of the Parnell Commission*, London, 1890, p. 120).

10 Anderson, *Sidelights*, p. 130. 11 *Ibid.* p. 90. 12 *Ibid.* p. 83.
13 Moore-Anderson, *Sir Robert Anderson and Lady Agnes Anderson* (London, 1947), pp. 46–7.
14 Henri Le Caron, *Twenty-five Years in the Secret Service* (London, 1893), p. 272.

30. VERLOC (pp. 314–324)

1 *The Greenwich Mystery*, pp. 11–12: see p. 388, below.
2 *A Girl among the Anarchists*, p. 53.
3 *The Greenwich Mystery*, p. 8: see p. 385, below.
4 *Ibid.* p. 11: see p. 387, below.
5 *A Girl among the Anarchists*, p. 45. Nicoll describes Samuels when he first met him in 1886 as 'a pale young man with a dark moustache, and features of the Jewish type' (*The Greenwich Mystery*, p. 8).
6 Prominent characteristics of Samuels, according to Nicoll, would appear to have been his belligerence and energy. He distributed explosives and gave instruction on making bombs. Accused of making money from his press interviews on the Bourdin affair, he retorted: 'You go and — yourself...I shall make money how I like' (*The Greenwich Mystery*, pp. 13–14).
7 *Morning Leader*, 20 February 1894.
8 *Anarchist*, 1 May 1894. Nicoll in his pamphlet *The Walsall Anarchists* (London, 1893) printed a report of part of the trial, demonstrating how Coulon's involvement in the incident was covered up:
   'In cross-examination by Mr. Thompson, witness said that... among the foreigners he had inquired about there was not one named Coulon. He knew a man of that name who was a well-known Anarchist. He had often been in Coulon's company, but not at Scotland Yard. To his knowledge Coulon had never been there. He would not swear that he had never given Coulon anything to do for him, but he did not remember having done so. He would not swear that he had not paid Coulon money, for he had paid lots of anarchists money.
   Mr. Thompson: Have you paid him any money?
   Witness asked the Bench if he were to answer such a question, and Mr. Young said that if these questions were designed merely to get the name of the informer they could not be put.
   Mr. Thompson: My theory is this, that any suspicious element in this case is the work of this man Coulon, who is an agent of the police.—(loud applause)
   The Mayor: If there is any of that we shall clear the Court. We decide that on the ground of public duty the question should not be put' (pp. 13–14).
9 *Reynolds News*, 14 April 1895.   10 *Ibid.*
11 *The Walsall Anarchists*.

Notes

12 J. Bruce Glasier, *William Morris* (London, 1921), p. 130.
13 *Anarchist*, 15 April 1894.   14   James, pp. 820–1.
15 Le Caron, pp. 219–20.

31. A. P. KRIEGER—A SPECULATION (pp. 325–333)

1   Letter to Cunninghame Graham, 7 October 1907, Watts, p. 169.
2   Baines, p. 331.   3   *Ibid*. p. 482, n. 71.
4   *Ibid*. p. 331.   5   Nadjer, p. 113.
6   *Ibid*. p. 114.
7   According to Nadjer, literally 'Sir Brother', a mode of address by one nobleman to another (p. 40, n. 1).
8   Letter of 22 May 1888, Nadjer, p. 124.
9   Nadjer, p. 126.   10   *Ibid*. p. 127.
11   *Life and Letters*, I, 117.   12   *Life and Letters*, I, 88.
13   The descendants of Adolf Krieger proved very difficult to trace— it took me two years—primarily because after the first world war and following on Krieger's death, his wife changed her name to Reynolds, her maiden name. Ultimately, through the assistance of a bank manager at Poole, in Dorset, I was able to contact a Mr Mann there who was one hundred years old and who had known the Kriegers. He thought that a son of theirs had gone to South America with the English and Jamaican Bank. I was then able to discover that Mr Krieger's son, Mr Reynolds, had worked for the Bank of London and South America, and I was able to trace the grand-children, some still in South America, others who had returned to England.
14   *Letters from Conrad, 1895 to 1924*, ed. E. Garnett (London, 1928), pp. 107–8.
15   *Letters to William Blackwood and David S. Meldrum*, pp. xxi–xxiii.
16   Letter of 9 February 1889, *Letters to William Blackwood and David S. Meldrum*, p. 48.
17   Letter of 10 February 1899, *ibid*. p. 49.
18   *Ibid*. p. 53.   19   *Ibid*. p. xxii.
20   *Ibid*. pp. xii–xxiii.
21   Letter to Mr Blackwood, 14 December 1900, *ibid*. p. 119.
22   *Ibid*. p. xxii.
23   Conrad had his problems as a writer and it is difficult to see how else he could keep above the level of subsistence. Five years later (17 January 1909) we find him writing to Mrs Galsworthy in the following vein: 'Excuse this discordant strain; but the fact is that

I have just received the accounts of all my publishers, from whic
I perceive that all my immortal works (13 in all) have brought me
last year something under five pounds in royalties' (*Life & Letters*,
II, 94).

24 Copy in the possession of Mrs Ogilvie.

32. CONCLUSION (pp. 337–372)

1 *A Personal Record*, p. 25.

2 *Ibid.* p. 99.

3 'A Familiar Preface' to *A Personal Record*, p. xvii.

4 *Ibid.*   5 *Ibid.* p. xviii.

6 *Ibid.*   7 *Ibid.* p. xix.

8 *Ibid.*

9 'Geography and Some Explorers', *Last Essays*, p. 17.

10 *Last Essays*, p. 16.   11 *Ibid.* p. 17.

12 Apart from his dislike of Boma and the short time he stayed there,
Conrad has good artistic reasons for treating the seat of government
as he did. Marlow's journey has been increasingly into the nightmare
of the primitive and pointless, and the introduction at this point of
the facts of civilisation at Boma would have been an unwarrantable
break in the movement of the story. Boma is therefore reduced to
a 'primitive little wharf' and a reference to the 'government
chaps'.

13 Giving some support to this belief is the letter attributed to Conrad
and quoted by E. D. Morel in *King Leopold's Rule in Africa* (London,
1904), p. 117: 'During my sojourn in the interior, keeping my eyes
and ears well open too, I've never heard of the alleged custom of
cutting off hands among the natives' (see 'A Conrad Letter' by
John L. Winter, *Notes and Queries*, new ser., XIII, no. 3 (March,
1966), 94.

14 Except in the case of Kurtz and Marlow.

15 Cf. for example, Thomas Woodbine Hinchliff, M.A., F.R.G.S.,
South American Sketches (London, 1863); John Hawkshaw, F.G.S.,
Reminiscences of South America (London, 1838); Robert Crawford,
M.A., *Across the Pampas and the Andes* (London, 1884). There are
accounts of a similar journey by at least two ladies and one of these
by Mrs Howard Vincent, wife of Colonel Howard Vincent (cf. *The
Secret Agent* section) would appear to have been used by Conrad,
since we can find a specific parallel between it and *Nostromo*. Mrs
Gould, we are told, during her journey through the province, wore

Notes

as 'a further protection...during the heat of the day' 'a small silk mask' (p. 86). Mrs Vincent also protected her face from the heat: 'I had saved my face...by means of a linen mask and a paste of cold cream and vaseline' (*China to Peru over the Andes: A journey through South America*, London, 1894, p. 116).

16   Author's Note to *Nostromo*, p. xix.

17   Michael G. Mulhall, *The English in South America* (Buenos Ayres and London, 1878).

18   *South American Sketches*, p. vi.

19   Ed. Dr Norton Shaw, IV, no. 2 (1859–60), 47.

20   Wilfred Latham, *States of the River Plate* (London, 1868, second ed.).

21   *Ibid.* pp. 317–18.   22   *Ibid.* p. 319.

23   *Ibid.* pp. 330–1.

24   Thomas J. Hutchinson, *The Parana: with Incidents of the Paraguayan War, and South American Recollections, from 1861–1868* (London, 1868), pp. viii-ix.

25   *Garibaldi: An Autobiography*, ed. Alexandre Dumas, p. 148.

26   'A Familiar Preface' to *A Personal Record*, pp. xix–xx.

27   *Letters from the Dead*, p. 3. This pamphlet, the second on the Greenwich mystery, is made up of letters by Nicoll and others.

28   Author's Note to *The Secret Agent*, pp. xiix–iii.

29   *Life & Letters*, II, 38.   30   *Ibid.*

31   Author's Note to *The Secret Agent*, p. xiii.

32   See Appendix E for a copy of Conrad's letter to A. P. Krieger.

33   *Joseph Conrad and his Circle*, pp. 89–90.

34   *Joseph Conrad as I knew him* (London, 1926), p. 121.

35   *Joseph Conrad and his Circle*, p. 9.

36   *Ibid.* p. 60.   37   *Ibid.* p. 62.

38   *Ibid.*   39   *Ibid.* p. 63.

40   *Ibid.* p. 70.   41   *Ibid.* p. 79.

42   *Ibid.* p. 83.   43   *Ibid.* p. 125.

44   *Ibid.* p. 92.   45   Guerard, p. 225.

46   *Joseph Conrad as I knew him*, p. 25.

47   *Joseph Conrad and his Circle*, p. 16.

48   *Ibid.* p. 50.   49   *Ibid.* p. 100.

50   *Ibid.* p. 15.   51   *Ibid.* p. 51.

52   Letter of 14 January 1898, Watts, p. 65.

53   *Joseph Conrad as I knew him*, pp. 53–4.

54   That there was something suggesting the secret agent in Conrad is revealed in the following incident described by Jessie Conrad which

took place during their journey to France for their honeymoon: 'One incident disturbed me greatly during that run to Southampton. We were passing through a long tunnel, there was no light in the carriage and we were sitting opposite each other in the most decorous fashion. Without the least warning there was a terrific detonation somewhere very close at hand and the carriage was momentarily filled by a blinding flash. I was startled and for a second a sickening fear held me dumb. It was then that I realised how great an adventure it was on which I had so lightheartedly embarked, and how little I really knew of the man I had married. Suppose he turned out to be a member of some secret society? The flash and explosion had seemed to be in the very compartment, and he had made no sound since...I was ashamed to tell him the reason of my sudden fright' (*Joseph Conrad and his Circle*, p. 20).

55 *A Personal Record*, p. 25.

INDEX

NOTE: The names of fictional persons, places, ships and journals are followed by initials (in brackets) indicating the works in which they occur, as follows:

NOVELS

HD *Heart of Darkness* SA *The Secret Agent*
N *Nostromo*

SHORT STORIES

'OP' 'An Outpost of Progress' 'I' 'The Informer'
'GR' 'Gaspar Ruiz' 'A' 'An Anarchist'

443 29-2

Index

Index

Index

crews (Congo), 59–61
crime, current views on, 309–11
Criminal Investigation Department, 236, 246, 282, 297–8, 305
Criminal Man (Lombroso), 430; quoted, 275, 276
Cunninghame Graham, R. B. (friend of Conrad), 2, 149, 249, 285, 295, 431–2; influence on *Nostromo*, 150, 417; quoted, 417
Curtis, W. E., quoted, 191, 199

Daily Graphic, 325; quoted, 111, 113, 294, 303; letter quoted, 112, 409, 410
Dakar (W. Africa), 23
Dance, Charles, 180; quoted, 180, 181
Dard (n.c.o.), 224, 225
Darwin, Charles, quoted, 145
Davitt, Michael, 265–9, 285, 361; pamphlet quoted, 265–6
Daza, H., ride of, 418
Decoud, Juan (newspaper editor), 165–6; brothers of, 165–6
Decoud, Martin (*N*), 154, 158, 176, 338, 356, 359, 420; originals of, 165–70
Degeneration (Nordau), 275; quoted, 430
Delcommune, Alexandre (explorer), 12, 70, 82, 83, 103; journal of, 51–2; quoted, 70; expedition of, 84–5; in relation to Conrad, 86, 339
Delcommune, Camille (company manager), 41, 49, 50, 56, 103, 115, 399, 411; in relation to Conrad, 44n., 45–7, 82–3, 104, 339; letter quoted, 80
Deligne (brick-maker), 43
Dennis, Mrs (daughter of Helen Rossetti), 213
Deptford, 317
diary, Conrad's Congo, 9, 34, 36, 48, 74, 88; quoted, 33, 37, 38–9
Dictionary of National Biography, 287; quoted, 288, 291, 292
Dillon, Luke (terrorist), 283–5, 432–4
Dilnot, George, quoted, 298–9
Djamba Louis (pastor), 77–8
Doña Delinquente, La (Lombroso), 310
Doré, Jacques, defence of Hodister, 114–16
Dreyfus affair, 307
Dubois, Felix, quoted, 279
Duhst, Captain (of *Ville de Gand*), 20, 21–2, 28, 81, 88, 397; diary quoted, 88

Duke of Sutherland (sailing ship), 122, 123, 411
Dumas, Alexandre, 156, 158n.
Duteil, Captain, 168
dynamite, 254, 258, 280–4

Eastwick, Edward B., 167, 171, 177, 193, 199, 351, 354; in Venezuela, 172–3; quoted, 173–4, 176, 177, 179, 180, 192, 193, 194, 195, 200–1, 419–20
Ecuador, 191
'ego-mania', 276–8, 430
Eldorado Exploring Expedition (*HD*), 83–4, 103
Eloba (river, Congo), 97
Emin Pasha, 14
'End of the Tether, The', 152n.; manuscript of, 411
English in South America, The (Mulhall), 355
Entreprises Agricoles et Industrielles (trading company), 17
Epping Forest, 242
Erminia, 167, 419–20
Erminia, Doña (wife of Ruiz, 'GR'), 137–8, 140, 143
Esmeralda (*N*), 190
'Ethics of Dynamite, The' (Herbert), quoted, 281
Etoile (journal), 114

Falcon, General, 172, 180
'Falk', 368
Faust, 342, 350
Fenian movement, 249, 269, 283, 287, 308, 323, 437; Manchester outrage of, 261–4; London dynamite campaign, 288, 297, 432–4
Firebrand (journal, 'I'), 211
Florida (river-steamship), 18, 20, 85; wrecking of, 40–2, 47, 50, 398; ivory cargo of, 68
Ford, Ford Madox (friend of Conrad), 2, 206–10, 218, 248, 285, 321–3, 423; quoted, 206, 211; cousins of, 211
Freedom, quoted, 431
Freeman, Rosemary, article of, 152n.
Freetown (W. Africa), 23
Freiesleben, Capt. Johannes (of *Florida*), 56n.; death of, 16–22, 41, 343, 347, 397; death-certificate of, 375
Freiheit, Die (journal), 255, quoted, 281, 431

446

Index

Index

Index

449

Index

Lopez, Francisco Solano, 147, 165, 197
Lord Jim, 148, 337, 425
Lothaire, Lieutenant, 20
Loutit, Captain (of *Duke of Sutherland*), 122, 411
Lualaba (river, Congo), 103, 107, 109
Lualaba (ship), 43, 88–9
Lukolela (Congo), 76
Lukunga (Congo), 37
Lulu Bohlen (steamer), 56n.
Lütken, Capt. Otto, 80–1, 88; account of Conrad in Congo, 21; quoted, 22
Lyons, 368

Macdonald, John, quoted, 437
McIntyre, Detective-Sergeant P., 286; quoted, 286–7, 307, 320, 321
McNaughton, M. L., quoted, 304–5
MacNeil, Angus (missionary), 77; letters quoted, 77–8
Madsen, Captain (of *Stanley*), 20, 40n.; diary of, 130
Mafile (anarchist, 'A'), 226
Mahute (officer), quoted, 68
Maiz, Father, 183, 184
Majendie, Colonel (Home Office expert), 233–5, 237
Malatesta (anarchist), 279
Manchester Martyrs, 261
Manyanga (Congo), 37, 39, 41, 46, 74, 88
Margate, 124
Marlow, Captain (*HD*), 9; Congo journey of, 10–13, 23–61 passim, 401, 440; account of predecessor's death, 15–16; differences of journey, 39, 48, 71, 81; account of Central Station, 46n.; in attacked steamer, 52–4; in relation to Kurtz, 75–6, 93–5, 100; sickness of, 88–90; on dangers of wilderness, 116–17; significance of, 343–9; finds seamen's book, 403
Marseilles, 163, 167
Marx, Karl, 271, 273, 429
'Massacre of the Island' ('GR'), 141
Masterman, G. F., 147, 165, 166, 182–9, 193, 353; tortured, 182–4; quoted, 183, 184, 185, 186, 187–8, 188–9, 191, 193, 194, 196, 197, 198, 421
Matadi (Congo), 11, 13, 14, 21, 27, 46, 74, 88, 95, 115, 345; account of, 29–35; railway, 30–2, 345; social life in, 33

Maturin (Venezuela), 180
Mears (friend of Hope), 122, 124, 411
Meldrum, D. S., letters quoted, 250, 330–1
Melville, Inspector, 286, 302–5, 311, 313, 320, 321
Memoirs of General Miller, quoted, 140–1
Mendoza, republic of ('GR'), 138, 143
'Meredith, Isabel' (pseudonym of Rossetti sisters), 215, 216, 315; quoted, 250, 257, 316, 436
Michaelis (*SA*), 251, 253, 256, 257, 259, 260–73, 278, 296; parallels with Davitt, 264–9, 361; political philosophy of, 269–72
Michaelis, Richard (pamphleteer), 272
Mikils, Lieutenant, 110
Milan, Conference in (*SA*), 230, 246
Milan, Don Leonardo, 160–1
Mirror of the Sea, The, 163, 208, 420; quoted, 168
Mitchell, Captain (*N*), 161, 196, 353, 357, 420, 422; conducted tour of, 199–200
Mobeka (Congo), 96
Modern Fiction Studies (periodical), 152n.
Moharra (chieftain), 114, 118
Monai (river, Congo), 98
Mongala (river, Congo), 74, 96, 97–8
Montero, General (*N*), 166, 174–6
Montero, Pedro (*N*), 177–9, 191
Montevideo (Uruguay), 154; siege of, 155–6, 157
Monygham, Dr (*N*), 147, 158, 164, 192, 197, 353; torture of, 182–6; on 'material interests', 357, 359
Moraga (agent, *N*), 173, 176
Moraga (sea-captain), 173
Morf, Gustav (author), 190
Morning Leader, 230, 233; quoted, 231, 232, 234, 235, 236, 237, 238, 245, 282, 302, 304, 317–18, 426–7
Morning Post, 31
Morris, William, 258, 321; quoted, 272
Morrison (company agent), 73, 74
Mosca (warder), 223
Moscow, 257
Most, Johann (anarchist), 254–6, 259, 285, 299, 431; obituary quoted, 256; glorifies dynamite, 281
Mouvement Antiesclavagiste (periodical), quoted, 100, 408
Mouvement Géographique (review), 10, 21, 32n., 42, 55, 81, 96, 102, 104, 130, 348, 376; quoted, 13, 27, 31, 31–2,

450

Index

Index

Index

Index

technique, Conrad's, 337-9, 371-2; in *Heart of Darkness*, 17, 24, 28, 35, 39, 42, 47, 71, 78, 87, 118, 121, 339-50; in 'An Outpost of Progress', 125, 129, 130-1, 133; in 'Gaspar Ruiz', 138, 141, 143; in *Nostromo*, 148, 154, 161, 162-3, 175, 181, 185, 187, 190, 192, 194-6, 350-9; in 'An Informer', 217; in 'An Anarchist', 219, 220-1, 224, 226-7; in *The Secret Agent*, 234, 236, 239, 243, 245-6, 247, 249, 252, 269, 273, 274-5, 285, 295, 296-7, 302, 314, 315, 360-71

Temps, Le (newspaper), 110, 111, 112

Teneriffe, 23

Teresa, Señora (*N*), 151, 154

Thames, River, 119, 121

Thirteen Stories (Cunninghame Graham), 150; quoted, 150-1

Thys, Capt. Albert (director of SAB), 12-13, 17, 103

Tierra Firme, 162

Times, The, 31, 267, 307, 325, 421, 435, 437; on Hodister's expedition, 110, 112, 114, 117, 410; a speech of Stanley's, 120-1; on the Greenwich Park explosion, 230, 233, 237, 425; a reply of Asquith's, 247; on the Manchester outrage, 263, 428, 429; on a Fisheries Bill, 294; on dynamite outrages, 433

Tippo Tib (Arab chieftain), 67, 68, 70, 107, 404

Tjulin, Axel (ship's captain), 398

Tobback, Lieut. Nicholas (resident at Falls), 64, 68, 410

Toodles (secretary to Home Secretary, *SA*), 290, 294

Torch, The (anarchist journal), 211-12, 213, 220, 259, 278, 279, 423; quoted, 424

Towson, J. T. (writer), 403

T.P.'s Weekly, 293; quoted, 293

Tremolino (ship), 163, 164, 168

Triangle, the, 323

Trias, General, 173-5, 351, 354

Troup, J. R., quoted, 58, 58-9, 61

Tucker, Benjamin, quoted, 429

Twenty-five Years in the Secret Service (Le Caron), quoted, 312, 323

Tyabo (tribal king, Congo), 100-1

Tynan, P. J. P., 423

Tyskowa, Maria (cousin of Conrad), 82

Underwood (factory manager), 33

Up-river Book (Congo), Conrad's, 40, 48, 58

Uruguay, 187

Valencia (Venezuela), 177, 192, 195, 199; tour of, 200-1

Vander Heyden (commercial agent), 56, 56 n., 400

Van der Kerchoven, expedition of, 409-10

Van de Velde (Belgian minister), 299

van Eetvelde (Secretary of State), letter quoted, 112

Van Gèle, Captain, 64

Vanity Fair (periodical), 301

Venezuela, 167, 171; finances of, 172

Venezuela (Curtis), quoted, 199

Venezuela (Eastwick), 171, 178, 192, 359; quoted, 173-4, 177, 179, 180, 192, 193, 194, 195, 200-1

Venezuela, Recollections of Four Years in (Dance), quoted, 180, 181

Verloc, 229

Verloc, Adolf (secret agent, *SA*), 228, 231, 237, 240, 251, 276, 286, 296, 311, 313, 314-24, 363, 368; compared with Samuels, 314-16; other partial sources, 317-21, 327-9, 371; portrayed with humour, 323; visit to embassy, 325

Verloc, Winnie (*SA*), 229, 247, 314-15, 328, 338, 362-71; maternal devotion of, 360, 362-3; mother of, 365, 366

Verner, S. P., quoted, 59, 402

Vidan, Ivo, 147, 165, 182-3

Ville de Bruxelles (troop-carrier), 40 n., 67, 69, 85, 404; wrecking of, 50-1, 102, 106, 399-400

Ville de Gand (river-steamship), 20, 21

Ville de Maceio (steamship), 13, 23, 25, 31, 56 n.

Vincent, Sir Howard, 246-7, 288, 297-9, 306, 435; cartoon of, 301; wife of, 440-1

Viola, Giorgio (*N*), 149-58, 355; sources of, 150-4, 157-8

Vivi (trading-post, Congo), 25, 88, 106, 128

Vladimir (diplomat, *SA*), 228, 231, 243, 244, 246, 296, 315, 323, 430; source of, 325-7

Walpole, Hugh, 318 n.

Walsall affair, the, 313, 320

454

Index

Kent Farm
Possingworth
near ...
Kent

1904
17 15th March
Gordon Place
Kensington W.

My dear Kroeger:

Pardon the delay;
but now you may
take this bill as
absolutely safe. In
fact I shall take
it up before it
matures.